A Prescription for Change

THE LUTHER H. HODGES JR. AND LUTHER H. HODGES
SR. SERIES ON BUSINESS, ENTREPRENEURSHIP, AND
PUBLIC POLICY

Maryann Feldman, *editor*

This series provides a forum for social scientists, public policy scholars, historians, and others investigating the economic, political, societal, and geographic contexts and conditions that foster entrepreneurship, innovation, and economic development in the United States and around the world. As place-based inquiry has gained currency, scholarship in the areas of business, entrepreneurship, and public policy increasingly consider spatial and cultural issues. A basic aim of the series is to challenge analyses that privilege globalization with the view that place—and human attachment to place—influence the expression of creativity and innovation.

MICHAEL KINCH

A Prescription for Change
The Looming Crisis in Drug Development

The University of North Carolina Press *Chapel Hill*

This book is published with the assistance of the Luther H. Hodges Jr. and Luther H. Hodges Sr. Fund of the University of North Carolina Press.

The University of North Carolina Press has been a member of the Green Press Initiative since 2003.

Library of Congress Cataloging-in-Publication Data
Names: Kinch, Michael, author.
Title: A prescription for change : the looming crisis in drug development / Michael Kinch.
Other titles: Luther H. Hodges Jr. and Luther H. Hodges Sr. series on business, entrepreneurship, and public policy.
Description: Chapel Hill : University of North Carolina Press, [2016] | Series: The Luther H. Hodges Jr. and Luther H. Hodges Sr. series on business, entrepreneurship, and public policy | Includes bibliographical references and index.
Identifiers: LCCN 2016018224 | ISBN 978-1-4696-3062-5 (cloth : alk. paper) | ISBN 978-1-4696-4757-9 (pbk. : alk. paper) ISBN 978-1-4696-3063-2 (ebook)
Subjects: LCSH: Drug development. | Drugs—Research—Economic aspects. | Pharmaceutical industry.
Classification: LCC RM301.25 .K55 2016 | DDC 615.1/9—dc23
LC record available at https://lccn.loc.gov/2016018224

For Kelly, Sarah, and Grant . . . my continuing inspirations

Contents

Acknowledgments

This book is the result of the intellectual contributions and passions of a series of close colleagues, friends, and family.

The author's passion for applying science to address the medical needs of human health was kindled in the laboratory of Dr. Keith Burridge at the University of North Carolina at Chapel Hill and made possible by the belief conveyed by Dr. Gordon Coppoc of Purdue University to recruit a young and naïve post-doctoral fellow as a professor and thus to initiate this lifelong pursuit. Thanks also go to Dr. Wayne Hockmeyer and David Mott of Med-Immune, who recruited a thoroughly inexperienced academic to create and lead an oncology group at a rising biotechnology powerhouse. At Med-Immune, Dr. Peter Kiener took this still-naïve scientist under his wing and instilled enough experience and confidence that he could take another leap and lead research and development at Functional Genetics, a small biotechnology company founded by the legendary researcher Dr. Stanley Cohen of Stanford and led by a former head of the Defense Advanced Research Projects Agency (DARPA), Dr. Michael Goldblatt.

This particular project to evaluate the past, present, and future of new medicines began as an offshoot of activities at the Yale Center for Molecular Discovery (YCMD), where the author was recruited by the visionary scientist–entrepreneur, Dr. Craig Crews, in 2010. Having cofounded one successful biotechnology company and in the process of developing a second, Craig realized early on the pitfalls and opportunities of the expanding Valley of Death in drug development and cajoled the administration at Yale to create a center to carry out this valuable work that was being abandoned by others.

As the newly-hired director of a center that blended very different scientific teams into a new entity, I sought to unify the team using an approach promoted by Jim Collins and Jerry Porras in their 1994 book *Built to Last*, which assessed the key properties of "visionary" companies. Using an approach known as a Big Hairy Audacious Goal (BHAG), I challenged the YCMD team to create a novel collection of all active ingredients in medicines that had been approved by the U.S. Food and Drug Administration (FDA). This assemblage was intended to provide the basis for a screening collection to be used to support drug "repurposing," which is an approach to ask if existing medicines, approved for one indication, might be used to treat other, unrelated diseases.

This challenge was met by the team with the obvious question: "What medicines have been approved by FDA?" No one knew the answer to that question—including the FDA.

Working with the Director of Chemistry, Dr. Denton Hoyer, and his gifted team of experienced computational and synthetic chemists, including Dr. Mark Plummer, Eric Patridge, and William Hungerford, we aggregated a list of all active chemical ingredients in approved medicines. This professional accomplishment was accompanied by a personal curiosity to identify the individuals and organizations that had contributed to the discovery of each of these medicines.

The project might have remained a footnote in my career but, as the information coalesced and trends emerged, I turned to colleagues at Yale, Drs. John Soderstrom, Jane Merkel, and Richard N. Foster (a former leader of McKinsey & Co.), who encouraged me to write first a series of more than twenty peer-reviewed scientific manuscripts and then this book. These inspirations were put into place in parts, one of which was the co-creation of the nonprofit Institute for Life Sciences Collaboration (ILSC), headed by the out-of-the-box thinker Rick Flath. Working with Rick, we explored opportunities for combining the expertise of various nonprofit organizations to address medical needs that were under-served by the private sector.

Just as this outsized project was beginning, I received an extraordinary opportunity to help lead innovation and entrepreneurship activities at Washington University in St Louis. This move proved to be instrumental in the decision to write this book for two reasons. First, my new boss was Dr. Holden Thorp, who quite literally wrote the book (*Engines of Innovation*) on how universities can translate fundamental knowledge into innovative new products. The team Holden has assembled, including Emre Toker (a serial entrepreneur, inventor, and educator) and Dr. Dedric Carter (an expert in private–public sector partnerships), is second to none as far as both identifying and implementing progressive change. Second, Holden saw the potential in this work and helped create a new organization at Washington University, the Center for Research Innovation in Biotechnology, to broaden and deepen our work on FDA-approved products and their innovators.

This enormous task would not have been possible without the active support and understanding of my family, who accommodated my work/

hobby for more than a year. Specifically, I would like to thank my wife, Kelly Carles-Kinch, who is a gifted pharmaceutical scientist. Throughout my career as well as personal life, Kelly has remained my closest confidant and greatest source of grounded advice. She can see and inspire practical guidance in a way that complements perfectly the actions of her undeserving other half. This project has literally been a family affair, inspired first by the medical crisis of our son Grant, and our daughter, Sarah, who spent a summer in high school working with me to help research the origins of many of the FDA-approved medicines. Likewise, I would like to thank my parents, Sue and Frank Kinch, who instilled the importance of education and curiosity. The inspiration of my entire family, their encouragement and sense of humor, have enriched this work and all aspects of the author's life.

Introduction

How Did We Reach This Point?

The Ride Home

The traffic was unusually heavy for a Monday afternoon. I left my office at the Yale University Center for Molecular Discovery, just four miles from the intended destination, and encountered a backup on I-95 North that was usually reserved for later in the week. Being a beautiful summer day, it seemed a few too many fellow commuters in New York City and western Connecticut had decided to call it an early day. Leaving the highway for the back roads, I pulled into the parking lot five minutes late.

Patiently waiting were my twelve-year-old son, Grant, and his teenage sister, Sarah. They had finished the first day of a two-week kayaking camp on the Long Island Sound. As my wife and I had been raised in the Midwest, a thousand miles from the closest ocean, we lived vicariously through our children in a desire to embrace a coastal lifestyle. The kids looked well tanned but exhausted, Grant particularly so. This was to be expected, since Grant was the essence of perpetual motion, requiring very little sleep and always full of energy. Once settled in the car, we initiated the obligatory small talk of how the day had gone, which I learned was spent cruising around the Sound. When not kayaking, the camp provided many snacks, and Grant proudly indicated he had disposed of at least three cupcakes. The stories of paddling, new friends, and junk food filled most of the drive home as we returned to the cavalcade heading north on I-95.

During the ride home, Grant complained of an upset stomach but ate most of his dinner that night, protesting as usual about the mandatory vegetables. He looked exhausted and announced an hour or so after dinner that he was headed to bed early. My wife, Kelly, and I guessed that he likely had gotten a bit too much sun and sea and may have been the victim of a touch of seasickness. After all, this was one of the first times he had ever been on the water, much less boating for an entire day. The three cupcakes probably didn't help.

A few minutes past midnight, we were awakened by the sound of Grant becoming violently ill. He had always been a trooper when sick, which was rare, and he didn't want to wake us. The vomiting and dry heaves persisted through most of the night as my wife and I took turns with him (with her doing the bulk of the work). He had a minor fever (less than 100° F) but otherwise felt as well as one can given the circumstances. By dawn, his stomach seemed to have settled down but there was no way he was going to kayak that day. As it turns out, the first day of summer camp was also to be his last.

I went to work and my wife stayed home that day, leaving Grant at home with his older sister, who apparently had also had her fill of nautical adventures. I called home a few times that day to check on Grant, who seemed to feel about the same and was able to hold down some water and a bit of Popsicle. That night, he complained his stomach was sore and we attributed this to the extreme workout to which his abdominal muscles had been subjected the night before. His low-grade fever persisted but responded nicely to ibuprofen. The rest of the night was uneventful and Grant again retired early for the evening. As the evening wore down, my wife and I decided we would take him to the doctor the next day if he weren't feeling better. Bounded by a high density of people on three sides, the Long Island Sound isn't known as the cleanest body of water. My wife and I had both earned doctorates in microbiology and immunology at Duke University and we reasoned that Grant might have ingested some unwanted organisms, perhaps a common water parasite. My wife had an early morning meeting and, since she had taken off the previous day, I volunteered to take him to the doctor.

On Wednesday morning, Grant was still in bed after the rest of us had dressed and eaten breakfast. This was unusual, indeed, and we checked in, finding him weak with a higher elevated temperature, now reading 101° F. Most troubling were the sunken eyes, which lacked the spark that has always characterized his ever-present bounciness. Likewise, his pasty complexion contrasted with the well-tanned boy of just two days before. Rather than wait for the doctor's office to open, my gut instinct was to take him to the local hospital, a satellite of the Yale–New Haven Hospital (YNHH) system, one town over. Barely able to walk, Grant leaned heavily on me as we approached the automatic double doors to the emergency room. This particular hospital is in a quiet part of a quaint New England coastal town in Connecticut. The receptionist saw us coming and met us at the door with a wheelchair. Grant was wheeled into the emergency room and helped into a gurney.

Fortunately for us, it was a slow day in the emergency room and the young doctor was able to focus on Grant. His pallor was an obvious sign of dehydration and two intravenous lines were masterfully snaked into his small, collapsed veins. Within the next hour, more than three liters of fluid were fast-dripped into him. Rehydration works wonders. Grant started to look and act a bit more like the boy we had known for the past twelve years, playfully scolding me in front of the doctor for my not believing he was actually sick. While the improved spirits were encouraging, his eyes remained dull. With the intravenous line established, the doctor also began a course of treatment with two antibiotics to address potential causes of Grant's fever. One of the antibiotics selected was Flagyl, whose generic name is metronidazole; it is an older drug, first approved in 1963.

After a thorough history was obtained and an examination performed, the young doctor recommended that Grant have an ultrasound to assess the integrity of his abdomen. A key question was whether his appendix might be inflamed. The gurney was wheeled into the ultrasound room and the technician performed a general assessment. Everything seemed in place. Whereas the doctor and technician anticipated an inflamed appendix, this wasn't seen. In fact, the appendix seemed to be hiding. The technician excused himself and returned a minute or two later with the head of the imaging unit. Neither was able to find the appendix, which, I learned, was not necessarily unusual, as a non-inflamed appendix can be quite small. He was then wheeled back to his room. Having reviewed the results, the doctor suggested we might want to move Grant to the parent YNHH hospital in New Haven. She had already inquired as to the availability of a bed at the hospital. She informed us that he would be number 812, which meant that there were 811 patients with priority over him.

The doctor also recommended one last test, a CAT scan, to peer inside his abdomen. Grant was rolled into the CAT scan room and shimmied onto the cold stage. I left the room while the radiologist did his job and immediately thereafter, things began to accelerate wildly. What had been anticipated to be a laid-back morning in a doctor's office transformed into an hours-long blur of surgeons and confusion, and a roller coaster of emotions. I walked with the gurney as it was being wheeled back to his room and the doctor pulled me aside and said that Grant was now number one in the queue for YNHH. Moreover, they had already summoned an ambulance, which was now waiting to expedite his transfer.

Grant's appendix was not observed in the ultrasound because the organ no longer existed. The inflamed appendix had disgorged its contents, as well as a healthy dose of Grant's internal gut bacteria, which had distributed themselves all throughout his peritoneal cavity. In other words, the beneficial bacteria that lived in his gut and helped him to digest his food were now strewn throughout his insides, with multiple sites of peritonitis perforating his abdomen. The magnitude of infection suggested that the appendix must have burst many days before, which was remarkable because the child was completely asymptomatic just two days before.

Just as I was taking all this in, my wife, Kelly, arrived at the hospital. Her instincts told her to leave work immediately after her early meeting and come directly to the urgent care. She arrived and was updated on all that had happened, the three liters of intravenous fluids, the tests, and the Flagyl. Remarking on the latter, she pointed out, "Hey, that is one of ours." This reference was to the fact that her employer, Pfizer, had acquired Flagyl as a result of its acquisition of Pharmacia Corporation in 2003.

A company with European roots, Pharmacia had, itself, acquired Monsanto, a St. Louis, Missouri, company in 2000. The name Pharmacia is a derivation of the Italian word, "farmacia," which reflects, in part, the Milanese origins of the company founded by pharmacist Carlo Erba in 1853. The company merged with another Italian drug company, Farmitalia, in 1978, and then with a Swedish company, also named Pharmacia, in 1993. The Nordic Pharmacia was an agglomeration with its origins in an early twentieth-century pharmacy, Elgen Pharmacy in Stockholm. Over the years, the company acquired multiple pharmaceutical interests, including the Swedish firm, Kabi Vitrum, as well as the American pharmaceutical giant, Upjohn. Likewise, prior to being purchased by Pharmacia, Monsanto, in turn, had merged with GD Searle & Co. in 1980, which itself had licensed the drug from a French company, Rhone Poulenc, in the early 1960s and had received FDA approval for its sale in 1963. Thus, by the time this particular drug had been injected into our son, a milieu of multi-national pharmaceutical companies had played a role in developing or overseeing this life-saving medicine.

While Kelly rode in the ambulance with Grant for the fifteen-mile ride to New Haven, I followed in our car, trying to reason what was happening. For the first time that day, I thought to myself, "How did we reach this point?" Grant was fine just a couple of days before and now he has full-blown peritonitis?

Upon arriving at YNHH, we were immediately escorted to the 11th floor of Pediatric Specialty Center, where a group of three surgeons were waiting for us. The urgency of the situation crystallized when I realized the surgeons were waiting for us and not the other way around. They reviewed his charts, noting with obvious scorn to one another that the urgent care doctor had prescribed an outdated drug like Flagyl. They then placed him on two more recent and cutting edge antibiotics. We were then told the procedure would likely take thirty to forty-five minutes. As soon as an operating room was available, Grant was anesthetized and rushed into surgery. Thirty minutes passed, then an hour, then two. One of the surgeons finally emerged to inform us the situation was worse than anticipated and that it would take an additional half hour or so "to clean up his gut."

During his recovery from anesthesia, we were confronted with another bit of bad news. The tests from the urgent care revealed that Grant was septic, meaning that the infection in his gut had progressed into his blood. Thus, bacteria were invading all throughout his body. A third and fourth antibiotic, including Cipro (ciprofloxacin), was added to the cocktail.

Whereas Flagyl was my wife's antibiotic, Cipro was mine. Well, kind of. My indirect claim of ownership was the fact that my job at the university was to lead the Yale Center for Molecular Discovery. The Center was tasked with the discovery of new medicines and was located on the former North American research and development (R&D) headquarters for a multi-national company. This was not just any company or any R&D site, but the Bayer Pharmaceuticals site, where ciprofloxacin had been discovered and manufactured for many years. Indeed, Cipro was discovered just one building over from where my office was located. Cipro had gained international notoriety for a time in 2002, as it proved to be an effective treatment for anthrax exposure following the letter attacks of 2002. At that time, the West Haven site was the only one in the world capable of manufacturing clinical-grade Cipro. This fact created a potential target for any terrorist organization that might intend to launch an anthrax attack. Recognizing this vulnerability, the West Haven manufacturing plant was, for a time, guarded by armored vehicles while efforts were made to disperse Cipro manufacturing across multiple sites around the world. A few years later, Bayer decided to downsize its R&D efforts and shuttered the West Haven location, selling the site to Yale for pennies on the dollar.

Including the two antibiotics administered in the urgent care center, our son had been treated with a total of six different antibiotics. He had survived surgery and we were now in a wait-and-see mode to determine if he would be strong enough to fight the infections raging throughout his body. The next bit of news was potentially catastrophic. Of the six antibiotics he was given, the bacteria in his gut were resistant to four of them. The only antibiotics that worked were Flagyl and Cipro. It is not a stretch to say that the young doctor, who was mocked by the elite surgeons for her naiveté in prescribing an antiquated drug like Flagyl, had made the key decision determining whether our son would survive (as this was the first drug administered that morning).

For the second time in twenty-four hours, I again asked, "How did we reach this point?" Specifically, a burst appendix simply releases the bacteria that are always present in one's gut into a place where it ought not to be.

These bacteria are normally resident in our intestines, where they provide beneficial effects necessary for our survival. Yet, the bacteria in Grant's belly were inherently resistant to antibiotics. Other than an occasional earache as an infant, Grant had not been given antibiotics. Why, then, were two-thirds of the antibiotics given to him ineffective?

Fortunately, this particular story ends well, for us at least. Grant recovered and was soon back to his old self. The sparkle in his eyes returned and we moved on, though not entirely. This episode left a lasting impact on all of us, but particularly our daughter Sarah and me. Sarah's initial response to Grant's burst appendix had been the typical response of a teenager: "Whatever." After all, burst appendices happen all the time. As the magnitude of Grant's situation became clear, she recognized that she had almost lost her best friend and confidant.

Doing Drugs with Your Family

Determined to make a difference, Sarah and I began working with a small group of investigators at Yale University on a "weekend and evening" (that is, volunteer) project to analyze all drugs approved by the FDA. Sarah and I were particularly interested to learn more about antibiotics. The first and most obvious question was, "What are all the drugs that have been FDA-approved?" Unfortunately, the answer was not obvious. It was true that the FDA has a comprehensive list of all medicines that can be prescribed at this time, a resource known as the *Orange Book*. However, the *Orange Book* was incomplete since there are many medicines no longer marketed, either because they weren't profitable or perhaps have been withdrawn due to toxicities. So, the first task was one of compiling a list of all medicines that have ever received approval from the FDA.

Once this list was complete, we began to ask questions about who developed these medicines and what happened to them. Thus began a yearlong odyssey, again performed largely during spare time in the weekends or evenings, to catalog the history of an entire industry; two industries, actually, when you factor in pharmaceuticals and biotechnology. The family joke became, "Dad is doing drugs again" as we settled into a nightly routine of working on the project. The fruits of our labors were finalized at midnight on 31 December 2013, at which point we had compiled a list of all drugs approved by the FDA from the very beginnings through that very moment. We saw that the first drug was actually discovered more than 10,000 years before the FDA and was characterized and distributed 100 years before the founding of the agency. In compiling our list, we unearthed fascinating stories about the inventors of these medicines, the organizations they worked for, and what happened to these people and organizations over time.

A Personal Journey

Unexpectedly, this story was one that hit home, as it paralleled my own journey over the past few decades. I started professional life as a professor at Purdue University. My own research focused on innovative ways to target breast and prostate cancer with a new class of drugs known as monoclonal antibodies. As it turns out, the health of our son Grant again factors into the story. Although Grant has been vibrant for most of his life, a recurring theme is that his illnesses seem somehow to direct my career. Grant was born six weeks premature and, like many preemies, he was given a special medicine meant to prevent infections by a virus commonly called RSV. To you, me, and most people, an RSV infection causes a cold-like illness and we carry on with our lives. Preemies like Grant are often born with immature lungs and, if infected in their first year of life, RSV infection can be devastating, often leading to death. Even if the infant survives, the repercussions can include life-long ailments such as severe asthma. Fortunately, a biotechnology company by the name of MedImmune had discovered a way to prevent RSV infection in preemies using monoclonal antibodies a few years before Grant was born. My wife and I, who were both working on monoclonal antibody research, thought it was kind of neat that our son was on Synagis, one of a handful of monoclonal antibodies approved by the FDA at that time.

The drug did its job and, a short time later, I intended to make a brief stop in my office after returning home on a redeye flight from Los Angeles. The goal was to check in with my students and my mail, but the phone rang just as I was gathering my papers to leave for home. The president of the university was calling (for a young assistant professor, this was a first) and informed me that a prominent alumnus was in town and might want to talk later that morning. The president thought he might be interested in discussing my work on monoclonal antibodies. Being exhausted, I tried to beg off, and asked for the name of the alumnus. The response, "Wayne Hockmeyer," was a name that sounded vaguely familiar (though I've always been awful with names). So I asked what company he had founded. The second response, "MedImmune," didn't ring a bell until he volunteered that MedImmune had recently received approval for a drug called Synagis. That pretty much sealed the fact I was not destined to get a nap that morning, since this was, indeed, not just the founder of the company that made Grant's medicine, but the actual inventor himself. While at Walter Reed Hospital, Dr. Hockmeyer had been the key driver of this innovative new drug.

I agreed to meet him, and a lively half-hour conversation about our shared interests blossomed into a follow-up visit to Maryland a few months later. I found myself agreeing to found and lead an oncology department at this relatively obscure biotechnology company. To the amazement of my colleagues, I gave up my tenured position, earned the year before, and "turned to the dark side," selling my scientific soul to the private sector. Over the following five years, the company expanded from a hundred or so employees to many thousands. My own department alone expanded from one (me) to over sixty scientists. It was an extraordinary time, for the biotechnology industry, for MedImmune, and for a naïve young scientist embarking on a career for which he was totally unprepared and unqualified.

In late 2006, I left MedImmune to seize an opportunity to lead research and development at a struggling startup company founded by the legendary Stanford professor, Dr. Stanley Cohen (more on him later). The company was a mile down the road from MedImmune and I figured it would make for a slightly shorter commute and another great learning experience. The company was developing new medicines for a viral disease few had heard of or cared about at the time, called Ebola virus infection. The next few years were a sleepless blur as we discovered and advanced new approaches for combating Ebola and other viruses.

In mid-2010, a conversation began with Yale University regarding "The Valley of Death" in drug development, a concept that will capture the rest of this introduction and the second half of this book. I returned to academia by leading a center at Yale devoted to determining how universities can help discovery and advance new medicines. The Yale Center for Molecular Discovery was located on the West Campus, a fitting tribute to the Center's mission as, just a few years before, Yale had purchased the campus from Bayer Pharmaceuticals, who had shuttered their North American R&D operations. The decision to abandon West Haven and North America was one example of a larger trend in which major pharmaceutical companies were abandoning many activities in early stage drug discovery and development.

While we were exploring ideas of how universities could compensate for the steady erosion of private sector activities in drug development at Yale, I found myself talking with the man who, literally, wrote the book on how universities can and must serve at the "engines of innovation" to address unmet needs in drug discovery and beyond. Dr. Holden Thorp had just transitioned from being the chancellor at the University of North Carolina in Chapel Hill to Washington University in St. Louis and, rather than talking about how to do it, he was intent on actually making it happen. Once again, I took the plunge and began my transition to St Louis.

End of an Era (and an Industry)

Returning to the compilation of information about FDA-approved drugs, our hobby revealed objective information that verified suspicions and rumors that pharmaceutical, biotechnology, and academic enterprises are all at a crossroads. Many companies and entire industries will not survive this transition. The tumultuous years to come will also impact public health, as the source and ability to make new medicines is fundamentally at risk.

The conventional approach to discovering new drugs had been primarily led by the pharmaceutical and then biotechnology industries. Companies such as Pfizer, Merck, and others had grown into behemoths over the decades based on a continuous outflow of innovative research and development. In recent years, these organizations had refined their organizational strategies and many elected to severely curtail or abandon altogether early stage drug research activities. The collective outcomes of these decisions were raising important questions about how or, indeed, if these activities might be performed in the future.

As we will see, the decisions by many large pharmaceutical companies to de-emphasize (and sometimes eliminate) early stage discovery and research activities were highly rationale and occurred over a long time frame, starting in the 1970s. Despite the fact this is hardly a new trend, virtually no one noticed the slow-motion dismantlement of the pharmaceutical industry within the context of the parallel rise of biotechnology industry. Aggressive new companies quickly filled and, indeed, encouraged any gaps left by the pharmaceutical industry's decisions to progressively withdraw from early-stage research. The problem was that, as of the beginning of the new millennium, the biotechnology sector was itself suffering from two conspiring trends: many successful companies had been acquired and fewer new companies were created to replace them. Thus, we began experiencing a lack of private sector organizations to address gaps in early-stage discovery activities. The question that led me to Yale—and then later to Washington University in St Louis—was whether and how academia might address the vacuum created by the withdrawal of the private sector. Many research institutions were, themselves, questioning their own futures in the context of declining federal research budgets, which have been staunching the life-blood of academia.

This selfish foray into my own personal odyssey leads back to the present day and the realization that key decisions are to be made over the next few years will fundamentally alter not just how but, indeed, if we will be able to develop new medicines. This has practical implications in terms of public health but also implications for industries that are worth trillions of dollars. In realizing the gravity of the situation, I, yet again, found myself asking, "How did we reach this point?"

TO ANSWER THIS QUESTION, we looked to the database of FDA-approved drugs, this time with the idea of asking if understanding of the past might help guide us in the future. This was going to be a monumental task and, as motivation, I looked to the primary currency of academia: publications. In a moment of audacity that was utterly inconsistent with my humble Midwestern roots, I cold-called the managing editor of one of the world's preeminent scientific journals, *Drug Discovery Today* and told him about our database, offering to write a series of articles documenting the history of pharmaceutical research. From his London office, he was intrigued and asked how many articles this would entail (journal space is always limited and even more so in a journal like *Drug Discovery Today*, which only publishes articles that are actively invited and peer-reviewed).

In an out-of-body experience, I heard myself responding, "How about twenty?" To my utter amazement, he agreed, and as I tried to replace the receiver back on its cradle, my hand began shaking uncontrollably. The little voice in my head began screaming, "You just agreed to write twenty articles for peer review, within a year, and best of all—before you even looked at the data." Thus began a ride even more intense than the headiest days at Med-Immune and, in some ways, on par with the adrenalin-provoking events of that summer day in the emergency room with Grant. We did, indeed, complete twenty articles and, to my astonishment, initiated each without any pre-conceived notions, led by the simple and naïve scientific notion that "the data will lead us to the truth."

Those peer-reviewed articles are their own independent set of information, and I would refer interested readers to the series at *Drug Discovery Today*. This book was inspired by these articles but takes a very different approach. Rather than a recapitulation of twenty academic studies, this book is an amalgamation of the real-life decisions, and the people who made them, which have shaped the evolution of the pharmaceutical industry from its very beginnings to the present time. Some of the people and the decisions are good, some bad, but all are very real and very human. These are the people who, collectively, built industries that have literally saved or fundamentally improved billions of lives and have generated trillions of dollars in revenues. An unexpected outcome of our research was a question of whether the modern drug discovery enterprise can be sustained. This book is intended not to advocate a particular position on the subject but to allow the reader to assess the health of a multi-trillion dollar industry that is essential for conveying future life-saving medicines and to ask if this valuable enterprise may now be teetering on the edge of collapse.

This book, at its heart, is a story of how the ever-accelerating pace of change in the communities of science, business, and government have evolved and regressed in ways that threaten our fundamental abilities to make new medicines. These changes also created opportunities, both in terms of new medical breakthroughs and entrepreneurial creation of a new industry from the ashes of its well-established predecessors. We are now in the midst of a crossroads and the decisions to be made in the coming months and years will dramatically impact the lives of billions of people in the future, both in terms of their future health and wealth.

Antibiotics as the Canary in the Coalmine

In recent years, the world has begun to awaken to the antibiotics crisis, a debacle that has arisen as a result of complacency and hubris, buttressed by sound fiscal decisions. These actions have been mutually reinforced by a combination of private and public sector entities, including pharmaceutical companies, corporate and individual investors, as well as the federal government. Without exception, the individual choices that led to the current situation were well-reasoned and taken with good intentions, and each individual decision was highly defensible. Yet each contributed to a calamity that threatens the sustainability not just of discovering new antibiotics but whether we will be able to salvage the drug development enterprise as a whole. As a result, we already live in a post-antibiotic world, a situation not familiar to any generation of Americans since before the Second World War. The actions leading to this point are not unique to antibiotics. Rather, antibiotics are the prototypical canary in the coalmine, portending the future of drug discovery and development.

A central theme of this book is that the collective outcome of rational decision-making over the past four decades has fundamentally threatened our ability to discover and develop new medicines. In the mid-twentieth century, the Harvard economist Joseph Schumpeter coined the term "creative destruction" to describe an innovation cycle characterized by long, stable periods punctuated with catastrophes. Biological scientists have long been familiar with this concept, which characterizes periods of massive and rapid change, commonly known as punctuated evolution. Unlike these pillars of the economic and biological sciences, the ongoing dismantling of drug discovery is not the result of evolution but devolution, as activities are abandoned, not in favor of a better way but simply based on the desire to no longer perform them. Traditional models that underpinned the creation of a medical research enterprise with a market cap well in excess of a trillion dollars are no longer practiced. Industries that had led the financial markets do not seem sustainable absent a major correction or the creation of an entirely new species of business. To those unfamiliar with the drug discovery business, the idea of Schumpeterian or Darwinian destruction of the pharmaceutical and biotechnology industries may come as a surprise, but the potential is quite real and already upon us.

The early impact of these changes is beginning to be felt in some of the less visible parts of the health infrastructure. For example, dwindling federal support for basic research risks the shuttering of private and public sector research centers and a dearth of early-stage drug discovery projects. More obvious are the waves of industry consolidation that have wracked the pharmaceutical and biotechnology industries. As we will see, these activities have fundamentally threatened the ability to discover and develop new medicines in ways that are unprecedented and potentially irreversible.

These changes come at a time of increasing pressures on the public health infrastructure. New threats are emerging from a changing climate, as reflected by recent headlines about Ebola virus infection. Ebola is merely the tip of the infectious disease iceberg and even greater threats are looming, with exotic names such as, Chikungunya, Dengue, VEE, EEE, and MERS. A significant part of my professional life has been spent trying to find treatments for many of these deadly pathogens, most of which had been of interest to the United States and its allies only based on their potential use as agents of bioterrorism. Now, the threat is real and coming from the environment. As stated by Dr. Michael Goldblatt, a former head of the Defense Sciences Office at DARPA (and CEO of my last company), "Nature is the worst terrorist of them all." As evidence, seasonal influenza virus infection continues to routinely kill 30,000 to 40,000 Americans each year.

As we will see, pandemic influenza can cut down a hundred million people, yet is an inevitable and quite normal part of nature. As a history buff, I was shocked when I first learned of the idea that the First World War was not ended by any particular battle but because the 1918 pandemic swine influenza outbreak depleted the number of troops available to fight. In a scene reminiscent of movie depictions of the Dark Ages, carts and wagons were driven down the streets of Philadelphia, Baltimore, and many other towns as a means of collecting the dead. All of this happened less than 100 years ago and will happen again (again, as part of a natural and inevitable process). As of the time of this writing, there are multiple strains of pandemic influenza circulating, any one of which could comparably impact the world. Despite the gains in technology and sophistication, these circulating viruses are insensitive to modern antiviral treatments and hold the potential to wreak havoc in a way not seen for almost a century.

In newly emerging economies, lifestyle changes have ushered in diseases that have been commonplace in the West, such as metabolic (for example, obesity and diabetes) and cardiovascular diseases, but on a scale never before seen. An aging population in the developed world is increasingly confronting diseases such as Alzheimer's and Parkinson's at rates that are unmanageable. Yet, as we will see, the development of new medicines for these diseases has, paradoxically, slowed at this critical juncture. In the same way, we are letting down our guard against other enemies, old and new. For example, drug-resistant HIV/AIDS viruses are emerging at a time when new drug development for the disease has all but evaporated. Likewise, the promise conveyed by sophisticated mosquito nets designed to prevent the scourge of malaria has run up against evolution as the mosquitoes themselves have begun to change in ways that render these barriers obsolete.

This book is a story of extraordinary success that changed the world and benefited countless people, both in terms of increasing the quantity and quality of life. The history of drug discovery is a combination of increasing knowledge and serendipitous collisions of people, some of whom are heroes and others who are less than perfect. It is also a story of how short-term thinking has undone decades of progress. Most of all, it is a story about people, of patients suffering diseases and volunteering to help test new medicines, of the doctors fighting these disease and the basic researchers who devote their lives to developing deep knowledge of subjects, often seemingly esoteric, that ultimately end up changing the world.

It is also a story about money, government regulation, entrepreneurship, and decision-making. We will explore the history of how entire industries were built from the ground up within a single lifetime. These same industries are being disassembled even more quickly. This is not a story of good versus evil, nor is it a story of Schumpeterian creative destruction. Rather, we will explore certain unique features of the pharmaceutical and biotechnology industries that seem to defy explanation, including:

- Why did the fifth statin drug, which was comparably effective to the innovative first statin, make 100 times more money?
- Why has the consistently most innovative pharmaceutical company, the "Apple" of the latter half of the twentieth century, fallen through the league tables while the fasting growing pharmaceutical companies ignore R&D altogether?
- Why is one of the most prestigious research institutions facing imminent bankruptcy?

Our exploration of these subjects will also be filled with stories of serendipity, unintended consequences, and fortuitous collisions, such as:

- Franklin Delano Roosevelt and the cousin of the Red Baron unknowingly teamed up to help cure cancer.
- The author of *Jurassic Park* almost prevented the biotechnology revolution.
- A swarm of flies pointed the way to reviving a ward full of children in comas and nearing death.

This work is based on research conducted by a valued set of colleagues at the Yale Center for Molecular Discovery, including my daughter Sarah, who was motivated by what happened to her younger brother that fateful summer. Twelve chapters will address the following subjects:

Chapter 1, "Why Regulate Medicines," examines the evolution of medicines from the earliest days of drug discovery (often by individuals and passed down through word of mouth) through the 1938 Food, Drug, and Cosmetic Act. Along the way, we will link real-life snake oil salesmen with Coca-Cola and learn how a federal official who routinely made his staff eat poison became obsessed with the fizzy drink. After a discussion of the birth of antibiotics, we will close with the tragedy of how another flavored drink killed scores of children and impelled Congress to create the modern pharmaceutical industry.

Chapter 2, "Trials and Tribulations," provides an overview of how drugs are tested and why this has changed over the past century. We will tell the story of James Lind, a navy doctor, who helped Britain become a hyper-power and how the Nuremburg war crime trials modernized the science of drug development. In a discussion of clinical trials, we will learn how a tragic mistake in London caused one patient's head to swell to the size of a watermelon and created a backlash that still resonates with the FDA. We will also see how one of the first world's most popular drugs caused a horrific tragedy that was halted on U.S. shores by a new junior employee at FDA, who saved thousand of lives through her righteous stubbornness.

Having established the activities required for identifying and launching a new drug, chapter 3, "Dreams of Greatness" will detail the birth of the modern pharmaceutical industry. Our story will start with the discovery of opium and how the recipe for making morphine was almost lost to the ages before being rediscovered by a bombastic Renaissance man. Opium later triggered a trade imbalance that hobbled the world's oldest civilization and triggered a literal trade war that still influences foreign policy today. The legacy of opium also transformed a one-person apothecary with its roots in the seventeenth century into an international pharmaceutical powerhouse. We will explore how bad housekeeping at a London hospital and a rotting cantaloupe in Iowa saved millions of lives. We will also evaluate the origins of modern cancer chemotherapy and diabetes therapy.

Chapter 4, "Triumph and Tragedy," provides an overview of the golden age of pharmaceuticals, its transformation from a cottage industry into a major sector of the world's economy, and how it bent but did not break when confronted with the world's deadliest plague. The roots of the National Institutes of Health (NIH) will also be traced as a background to understand its extraordinary role in combating disease. In a potential example of the changing tides of regulatory oversight and over-correction, we will see how the controversial discovery of a compound found in tree bark indirectly spawned a tragedy that killed thousands, with sustained repercussions for the future of drug development.

Chapter 5, "Ivory Tower of Power," details the birth of the modern research university from its roots in the Kaiser's Germany to its early adoption in the United States. We will then detail the extraordinary disaster of the blue death, which claimed tens of millions of people and forever changed medical research and development. We will also witness how academic, governmental, and the private sectors came together to discover wonder drugs that have saved millions from heart disease.

Chapter 6, "The DNA of Biotechnology," will describe the founding of the biotechnology industry, from the discovery of DNA through the industry's origins in the San Francisco Bay Area. In doing so, we will uncover how popular culture almost killed the industry during its infancy and explore how an age of miracle drugs and magic bullets gave way to a bureaucracy built around patents. We will end the chapter by showing how a critical piece of Congressional legislation gave rise to a multi-billion dollar industry.

Chapter 7, "Blockbuster and Bombs," will convey some of the pressures faced by the pharmaceutical industry in the waning decades of the twentieth century. We will see how knowledge gave way to hubris and how a combination of the generics industry, blockbuster products, me-too drugs, and high-profile failures formed a lethal combination that threatens the continued viability of the pharmaceutical industry.

Chapter 8, "Sea Monsters, Immunauts, and Death Panels," will continue our discussion of biotechnology, defining its key features and conveying the challenges that made and broke biotechnology companies and now threaten the entire industry. As one example, we will track the spectacular rise and downfall of the first biotechnology company. We will also document the dangers of success, the importance of execution, and why medical breakthroughs do not necessarily translate into successful products.

Chapter 9, "Drama on the I-270 Tech Corridor," focuses on a local geographic area in suburban Maryland as a microcosm for the dramatic growth, opportunities, risks, and challenges facing biotechnology companies. We will review the genesis of the human genome project and how strong personalities created a watershed program that created and destroyed extraordinary riches. The region also shows the challenges confronting companies seeking to expand beyond being a "one-hit wonder."

Chapter 10, "Autophagy," details the waves of corporate consolidation that allowed a series of middling companies to transform the entire pharmaceutical and biotechnology industries. We will detail the rise of "big pharma," including the growth of a new movement that threatens the sustainability of future drug discovery.

Chapter 11, "Three Views of a Train Wreck," conveys how a convergence of activities from the private and public sectors raises key questions about how and if we will be able to maintain the momentum that has given rise to fundamental improvements in the quality and quantity of life. These changes have created an impending state of crisis, forewarned by a "valley of death" that threatens to halt and even reverse these benefits.

Chapter 12, "Bridging the Valley," describes opportunities to overcome the ever-widening "valley of death," which could lead to unprecedented opportunities for entrepreneurial growth and public health improvements, but requires quick action and a sense for urgency from both the private and public sectors to do so. We will explore ongoing experiments meant to develop new medicines in unconventional ways and suggest bureaucratic and regulatory changes that could incentivize and reinvigorate new drug discovery.

Our goal is to provide a new perspective on an issue with massive ramifications for individual as well as overall public health. A failure to develop new medicines could have catastrophic consequences, particularly in light of new threats such as Ebola virus, ever-increasing rates of Alzheimer's and other neurodegenerative diseases, and old adversaries including antibiotic-resistant bacteria and drug-resistant HIV/AIDS. The economic implications of the impending crisis should also interest anyone with a 401K plan, since pharmaceutical and biotechnology companies are among the most robust, lucrative, and common investments in the retirement portfolios and mutual funds of virtually all Americans who hold such vehicles. As an eternal optimist, I believe the ongoing uncertainties provide unprecedented opportunities to create new structures and models with massive implications for health and finance. But, the change needs to begin now.

CHAPTER ONE

Why Regulate Medicines?

The quest to discover new medicines is as old as civilization. Our earliest ancestors were hunters and gatherers, whose quarry extended beyond simple nutrition to identifying and, ultimately, cultivating animals or plants with beneficial properties. The sources of some of the most common medicines of today literally have their roots in discoveries of herbal and folk remedies dating back to Paleolithic times (more than 10,000 years ago).

The story of discovery is at its heart a story of people, their needs and motivations. While it is healthy to remember that the majority of people are inherently noble and well intentioned, a small number of less virtuous individuals often stand out as more interesting. In the field of medicine, as we will see, a bad seed can be deadly. Thus it has been necessary to put into place regulations that protect the many from the few. In this chapter, we will detail how the United States came to see the need for regulating medicines and how the laws have evolved over time. The causation for major changes will be emphasized, using stories of real people who motivated the formation and evolution of organizations that became the underpinnings of the modern United States Food and Drug Administration (FDA).

Snake Oil

The phrase "snake oil salesman" entered the modern lexicon to denote the lowest form of huckster or politician. The actual meaning of the term itself is controversial. One school of thought maintains that the term "snake oil" refers to a traditional remedy for joint pains as practiced by Chinese laborers who collected fat from the Chinese water snake (*Enhydris chinensis*, or sheyou).[1] Ancient cultures from Egypt to the Far East had similarly found some snake oils conveyed analgesic (pain-relieving) or restorative properties.[2] There is a scientific rationale, as some snake oils, like those from the Chinese water snake, are enriched with eicosapentaenoic acid (EPA), an omega-3 fatty acid with verified anti-inflammatory properties.[3]

Snake oil acquired less positive connotations in nineteenth-century western United States.[4] The story goes that Chinese laborers' familiarity with traditional medicine spread the concept of snake oil from West to East, following the path of the transcontinental railroad. Given the lack of Chinese water snakes in Arizona and Texas, the local specialty, rattlesnakes, provided a substitute. Though rattlesnakes have low levels of EPA concentrations, reports of their curative properties spread like wildfire. Over time, the juicing of any snake would suffice. As fame and demand spread, a ready supply of snakes dwindled. Yet, the name stuck.

The most famous snake oil salesman is Clark Stanley, "the Rattlesnake King," who captured the limelight in the 1893 Chicago World's Exposition.[5] Stanley mesmerized crowds by dramatically grabbing a live snake from a bag (we must assume not a rattlesnake), cutting it open, and scraping its guts into a boiling pot of water. Like any fat-laden stew, the fat rose to the top and the Rattlesnake King spooned the oil into a vessel that was sold on the spot to a lucky buyer. Clifford was sympathetic to the needs of the crowd, who were able to buy samples from crates of snake oil, which happened to be just behind the curtain (and which actually consisted of mineral oil, beef fat, red pepper, turpentine, and camphor).

Like competing salesmen hocking different products, this definition of snake oil has been questioned. An alternate story is that the term arose in the eastern United States and traveled west. This version maintains that "snake oil" is an etymological variation of "Seneca oil."[6] The alternative maintains that "Seneca oil" morphed over time into "snake oil" and was sold to the masses based on its reputed analgesic and restorative properties. The Seneca Nation of Indians, the largest of the Six Nations of the Iroquois Confederacy, spanned a large area that included the western counties of modern-day New York and Pennsylvania. This region was, indeed, known for a black, oily substance that seeped from the ground, and the nearby Drake well, near Oil Creek in Titusville, Pennsylvania, was the first source of American petroleum. Like many aspects of snake oil, it isn't clear which story to trust.

Parasitizing upon America's Obsession with Diets

Anyone who has found themselves digging out a credit card at three o'clock in the morning in a sleep-addled response to an infomercial for a new diet fad can take comfort in knowing they are participating in a great American tradition[7]. America's obsession with weight loss has a long history, as exemplified by a late nineteenth-century advertisement: "Fat [is] the ENEMY that is shortening your life" announced an advertisement from WT Bridge, a New York chemist.[8] Rather than relying upon other ways to shed fat, such as "diets, baths, or exercise," the advertisement maintains the solution is "easy-to-swallow, jar-packed tape worms." Before recoiling in horror, recognize these were not just any tapeworms, but "sanitized" tape worms. The poster states unequivocally that there are "no ill effects" and "no danger." The ad features a lovely women standing behind piles of food, with the rejoinder to "Eat! Eat! Eat! & Always Stay Thin."

The truth is that a tapeworm diet works. Worm aficionados know the head of the tape worm is a scolex, a word whose pleasant sound nicely captures the beauty of its structure.[9] The scolex is composed of a double crown of about two dozen beak-like hooks surrounded by a series of suckers. The scolex tears into the intestine of its host, generally preferring muscle tissue, as this makes for a nice anchor to hold the worm in place while its feeds on your insides. You share your dinners with the tapeworm, which grows over time until, in humans, it reaches a length of ten meters (almost thirty-three feet). The tapeworms are not relegated to simply growing in size, but also in number. Tapeworms are hermaphrodites, meaning that a single parasite possesses both male and female reproductive organs and, therefore, releases and fertilizes up to a million eggs per day.

The weight loss in tapeworm-infested people is, indeed, real and results from nutrient deprivation.[10] While this may sound appealing, the symptoms of diphyllobothriasis (the scientific terminology for this weight loss strategy) include diarrhea, abdominal pain, vomiting, fatigue, constipation, and general discomfort. Before rushing out to start this plan, the unfortunate symptoms of tapeworm infection include a chronically-swollen abdomen, which generally counteracts the beneficial cosmetic improvements of the dramatic weight loss. The parasite growing inside you also has the rather rude habit of monopolizing vitamin B12 and, thereby, blocks the production of red blood cells and ultimately destroys your spinal cord, causing a condition much like cystic fibrosis.[11] Thus, the melting of fat may cause you to look great in that new swimsuit (at least until abdominal swelling commences) but comes at the cost of premature death.

We can dismissively reflect on snake oil and tapeworms as nineteenth century examples of quacks preying upon our unsophisticated ancestors. However, modern society still has a snake oil salesman or two.

Laetrile

A modern example of hucksterism can be seen in the story of laetrile. Laetrile and its various forms, such as amygdalin (aka vitamin B27 or Prussic acid), is a natural product isolated from peach or apricot pits as well as a type of nut known as a "bitter almond."[12] Not to be confused with the everyday sweet almond, the bitter version is shorter, fatter, and deadly.[13]

The toxicity of laetrile has been recorded as far back as ancient Egypt. "The Penalty of the Peach" was a drink distilled from whole peaches (including the pit) and was the preferred form of capital punishment for apostates who revealed the divine secrets of the Egyptian gods.[14] Similarly, the Roman general and politician Publius Quinctilius Varus used this drink as the vehicle to execute Antipater, who was convicted of trying to kill his father, Herod the Great (Herod the Great is cited in the gospel of Matthew in the New Testament as the Judean king who ordered the Massacre of the Innocents in an effort to kill the infant Jesus).[15]

First isolated in 1830, the toxic component of peach pits, amygdalin, periodically gains notoriety as a means of treating cancer.[16] Based on desperation and wishful thinking, many patients have travelled around the world in the hope that amygdalin might help themselves or a loved one.[17] A prominent example was the Oasis of Hope Hospital in Tijuana, Mexico.[18] For three decades, patients claimed to have been cured by a treatment with a form of amygdalin known as laetrile or vitamin B17. Like snake oils of the past, these claims were unfounded and laetrile was, in fact, a chemical version of a serial killer.

The toxicity of laetrile lies in the fact that, once in the body, the molecule is metabolized into cyanide.[19] Cyanide kills the energy-producing part of the cell and is particularly dangerous because the body largely lacks the ability to eliminate the toxin. Consequently, cyanide kills one cell, recycles, and then kills again until the entire organism (in this case, the person) is dead. The infamy of cyanide came to the American public's attention in the closing days of the Second World War, as it was the active agent in the Zyklon-B showers of concentration camps and the chemical inserted into the false teeth that facilitated the suicides of prominent Nazis such as SS Reichsfuhrer Heinrich Himmler and Hermann Goring.[20]

Precursors to the FDA

The refusal to approve laetrile is but one example of the critical role of the United States Food and Drug Administration (FDA). Tasked with the difficult job of deciding which medicines can be marketed, the FDA is a magnet for criticism. The agency is frequently accused of being too lax or too vigilant, often both at the same time. With this in mind, it is important to convey a brief history of how the FDA came into being and how its mission has changed over the decades. This is essential to understand the ongoing predicament that fundamentally threatens our ability to discover new medicines in the future.

In 1820, the federal government asked each state to send a representative to create a comprehensive list of all medicines used in the United States.[21] A pharmacopeia was needed since each state had its own unique set of drugs and there was little standardization or assurance of quality. Of the twenty-one states extant at the time, just over half (a total of eleven) sent a representative. Each monograph (a Greek term referring to a writing on a single subject) captured the means and standards of making each elixir, pill, or ointment in a document known as the United States Pharmacopeia (USP).

The first leader of the USP was Dr. Jacob Bigelow.[22] Bigelow discovered a passion for medicine while a student at Harvard but, as Harvard did not offer a medical degree at the time, he moved to Philadelphia to study with Dr. Benjamin Rush. Rush was a Forrest Gump-like character who played a key role in many historical activities, including working with Thomas Paine on the pro-independence pamphlet, *Common Sense*, signing the Declaration of Independence, serving as the Surgeon General of the Continental Army, training Meriwether Lewis in preparation for his exploration of the new Louisiana Purchase, and restoring the friendship of John Adams and Thomas Jefferson after the mud-slinging election of 1800.[23]

Under Rush, Jacob Bigelow trained as a physician and gained a second love, this time for botany, which was fueled by the fact that most medicinal treatments of the day were derived from plants. As a companion document to the USP, Bigelow published a multi-volume work on native medicinal plants and devised a novel method of printing pictures of these plants in color.[24] A man before his time, Bigelow also advocated what today is known as science-based medicine and conveyed his ideas by cofounding a new educational organization later known as the Massachusetts Institute of Technology (MIT).

The USP established standards to ensure the proper use and quality of medicines. Quality and application were cornerstones of the Age of Reason, and a contemporaneous example is the establishment of the United States Patent and Trade Office in 1790. One of the first acts of the U.S. Congress (House Resolution 41) was to establish an organization with the authority to grant or refuse a patent after deciding whether it was "sufficiently useful and important."[25] A patent is a simple exchange. The patent holder is granted a period of exclusivity in which they alone can "practice the invention." In return, the inventor must disclose in writing the background and application of the novel concept for all to see. Thus, while ensuring a period of exclusivity, the patent teaches the competition and, in doing so, allows competitors to develop an even more innovative product. A well-managed patenting process can ensure a continual flow of innovation, with obvious economic advantages for those countries adopting such a system.

An early leader in the United States Patent Office was Lewis Caleb Beck.[26] Beck was an expert in medicines, and his 1846 book, *Adulterations of Various Substances Used in Medicine and the Arts*, decried the inclusion of artificial contaminants in natural medicinal products and argued for their outlaw. Inspired by this manifesto, the U.S. Congress passed the Drug Importation Act of 1848, which required U.S. Customs to intercept the entry of adulterated drugs from other nations. Dr. Beck thereafter led an office, known as the Bureau of Chemistry, meant to evaluate medicines for safety and adherence to the USP. The Bureau of Chemistry later evolved into the modern Food and Drug Administration (FDA).

In summary, we can see a chain of custody starting with the founding of the United States Pharmacopeia and U.S. Patent Office that later inspired the formation of the precursor to the Food and Drug Administration. The early mission of the Bureau of Chemistry (continued by the FDA) was to eliminate adulterated foods and medicines. Adulteration is a rather general term, and as we will now see, the meaning of the word has changed considerably over time.

Patent Medicines and Muckraking

The half-century following the Civil War was one of rapid and sometimes reckless growth and change. From the perspective of public health, the period was typified by the emergence of a quasi-industry focused around patent medicines. Snake oils are one type of patent medicine; these were joined by various salves, elixir, liniments, and oils.[27] The term "patent medicine" itself is ironic because these medicines were generally shams and not patentable. Indeed, this misnomer becomes all the more outrageous when considering that one of the requirements for being granted a patent is a demonstration that the invention is "sufficiently useful and important." Patent medicines were neither.

The most famous patent medicine was a direct consequence of the Civil War. John Stith Pemberton, born in 1831, was a pharmacist living in Columbus, Georgia, until the secession of Southern states.[28] John and his uncle, John Clifford Pemberton, both sided with the Confederacy and joined the army. The uncle is best remembered as the general in charge of the defense of Vicksburg, Mississippi, which ultimately surrendered to Union General Grant after a prolonged siege.

The younger nephew was not at Vicksburg but instead participated in the very last battle of the Civil War, the Battle of Columbus (Georgia). John Pemberton's 12th Cavalry Regiment was outnumbered four to one by two full Union cavalry divisions.[29] The battle was a rout and the younger John Pemberton was slashed in the chest by an enemy sabre and nearly killed. Like many wounded men from the Civil War, Pemberton was treated with morphine and quickly became addicted to the painkiller. As a trained pharmacist, he began a quest to overcome morphine addiction.

Pemberton's preferred concoction to avoid addiction was a mixture of alcohol, coca leaves, kola nuts, and damiana. The irony of this elixir is that its anti-addictive properties are based on a combination of alcohol, caffeine, and cocaine. Coca leaves had been chewed as a stimulant by various Eastern Andean societies as far back as 8,000 years ago but the active component, cocaine, was first reported by the German chemist, Albert Niemann in 1859.[30] Developed in Columbus, Georgia, in 1866, "Pemberton's French Wine Coca" was largely marketed to urban intellectuals in Atlanta. The rationale for targeting Atlanta was that city life was thought to be the cause of many diseases, including anxiety and impotence, which were brought on by the stress and the fast-paced lifestyle. Pemberton's French Wine Coca was a hit but was doomed by a temperance movement that swept Atlanta in the mid-1880s.

To preserve the nascent business, a non-alcoholic version was developed in 1885 that retained the coca leaf and kola nut but excluded alcohol and damiana.[31] While much has been made of the fact that the beverage contained cocaine, the absence of alcohol also meant the syrup could not extract the cocaine, a largely insoluble alkaloid. The new Coca-Cola (named for the sources of cocaine and caffeine, respectively) was first served in Atlanta, Georgia, in May 1886.[32] Although the product was intended to be a syrup-based patent medicine for treating headaches (and addictions), an accidental but fortuitous mixture of the base syrup with carbonated water was a commercial success. As a consequence, Coca-Cola was, instead, marketed as a fountain drink to be served in pharmacies, which had ample supplies of carbonated water.

Patent medicines were also key drivers of the modern advertising and media industries.[33] An emphasis on branding a medicine gave rise to a generation of advertisers, many of whom located their business on Madison Avenue in Manhattan. Patent medicines also fundamentally altered the newspaper business, as many periodicals were established with the sole goal of promoting a particular patent medicine. Some of these papers tried to embarrass the competition by reporting on the frauds and quackeries of competing patent medicines. Competitive reporting quickly gave way to legitimate investigative journalism. A prominent example is that of Samuel Hopkins Adams, a New York reporter who penned a series of eleven articles for *Colliers Magazine* in 1905 that exposed patent medicines as "The Great American Fraud."[34] Adams declared patent medicines were "founded mainly on fraud and poison." The opening paragraph of the first article captures the essence of his reporting:

> Gullible America will spend this year some seventy-five millions of dollars in the purchase of patent medicines. In consideration of this sum it will swallow huge quantities of alcohol, an appalling amount of opiates and narcotics, a wide assortment of varied drugs ranging from powerful and dangerous heart depressants to insidious liver stimulants; and, far in excess of all other ingredients, undiluted fraud. For fraud, exploited by the skillfulest of advertising bunco men, is the basis of the trade. Should the newspapers, the magazines and the medical journals refuse their pages to this class of advertisements, the patent-medicine business in five years would be as scandalously historic as the South Sea Bubble, and the nation would be the richer not only in lives and money, but in drunkards and drug-fiends saved.

At the same time readers were captivated and enraged by Adams' articles in *Colliers*, they were digesting an intriguing series of news reports about the "The Poison Squads."[35]

The Poison Squads

Harvey Washington Wiley was a medical doctor and chemist, born in an Indiana log cabin in 1844.[36] He progressed through a series of academic appointments before landing at the newly founded Purdue University in Lafayette, Indiana, in 1874 with an appointment as the official state chemist of Indiana. Among the assigned responsibilities were tasks to assess the purity of sugars and syrups sold within the state. His mission to detect any adulterations would become a *cause celebre*, bordering on obsession, for the rest of Wiley's life.

Wiley accepted the post of Chief Chemist for the United States Department of Agriculture in 1882, where he became further concerned about the additives and preservatives used in food and drug products.[37] Wiley lobbied Congress relentlessly for years until they allocated $5,000 in 1902 to assess the safety of these chemicals.[38] To do so, Wiley assembled a team of "twelve young clerks, vigorous and voracious," whose qualifications included passing the Civil Service examination, pledging only to eat food prepared for them, and not to sue the federal government for any harm done. Rather than receiving extra pay or a bonus, the free meals were considered adequate compensation, particularly since the meals were served on fine china and prepared by the former "head chef for the Queen of Bavaria."[39]

Consistent with the adage about no free lunches, each meal was laced with a popular preservative of the day, such as borax, copper sulfate, formaldehyde, salicylic acid, saltpeter, sodium benzoate, or sulfuric acid. The studies were performed with the highest scientific quality of the day, with the exception that the guinea pigs were on the federal roll. Beyond ingesting daily poisons, the men were subjected daily to intrusive analysis to assess change in weight, pulse, temperature, bladder, bowel, and other physiological functions.

While the employees knew they were hired to eat potential toxins, they were at first hidden within certain foods. As taste often betrayed the tainted foodstuffs, the men naturally avoided foods they knew to be poisoned. Therefore, Wiley abandoned the guessing and required each participant to swallow a gelatin capsule containing the toxin while he watched. A typical study was conducted for six months (unless blatant poisoning was detected beforehand) and new rounds of experiments persisted over a five-year period. Amazingly, none of the volunteers died or suffered long-lasting effects.

While Wiley referred to the experiments as the "Hygienic Table Trials," the participants were better known as "The Poison Squad."[40] The press gave them that name and the studies were reported in real time to a public who clamored to learn of the outcomes. Wiley was forced to cast a veil of secrecy after learning that the "head chef for the Queen of Bavaria" was leaking news of the outcomes to reporters through an open basement window.[41] Over time, Wiley's measured scientific studies became more of a crusade and he became as much a showman as a public advocate.

The 1906 Pure Food and Drugs Act

Wiley's closely-watched "Poison Squad" studies fueled outrage already ignited by the *Colliers* articles and the growing public anger spilled over in the passing of the 1906 Pure Food and Drug Act. Signed by President Theodore

Roosevelt, The Wiley Act was the first major consumer protection law to address adulteration of medicines.[42] Since the federal government has limited authority within a particular state, the act governed interstate transport of medicines and empowered the U.S. Bureau of Chemistry to "prevent the manufacture, sale, or transportation of adulterated or misbranded or poisonous or deleterious foods, drugs, medicines, and liquors." To do so, the Bureau of Chemistry was authorized to inspect products to ensure their purity would conform to standards established by the USP. The new laws required that the active ingredients for each drug product be clearly placed on the label. A truth-in-labeling clause also defined the terms "misbranding" and "adulteration" to end inappropriate advertising and promotion that characterized patent medicines. Notably, the new laws did not require the manufacturer to demonstrate the drugs were safe and effective—an omission that would come back to haunt many times in the decades to follow, not to be fully corrected until the early 1960s.

To enforce the provisions of the act, Congress named Harvey Washington Wiley as head of the Bureau of Chemistry and thereby set into action a collision of two powerful forces. Wiley, as you may remember, had a particular sensitivity for assuring the purity of sugary syrups.[43] An increasingly popular sugary syrup served in pharmacies was, therefore, an obvious target for Wiley's enforcement of the 1906 Pure Food and Drug Act.

The United States versus Forty Barrels and Twenty Kegs of Coca-Cola

Harvey Washington Wiley's concern with Coca-Cola centered upon high levels of the stimulant caffeine. Caffeine is a bitter alkaloid compound found in the seeds, leaves, nuts, and berries of certain plants, where it functions as a natural pesticide.[44] The ingestion of caffeine short-circuits the insect's nervous systems, paralyzing and usually killing them.[45] Harvey Washington Wiley, therefore, initiated a crusade, convinced that a similar fate would fell people drinking Coca-Cola.

The history of caffeine intake largely parallels that of human civilization. As early as 3,000 B.C.E., an apocryphal Chinese legend suggests that a supernatural figure named Emperor Shennong noted that the falling of certain leaves into boiling water created an aromatic drink with restorative properties (Emperor Shennong is also credited with introducing agriculture to the Chinese civilization).[46] This legend is widely interpreted as discovery of tea and the effects of its caffeine. The actual origins of tea are nonetheless controversial, with dates ranging from 10,000 years B.C.E. to some time during the Zhou Dynasty (1046–256 B.C.E.).

Regardless of its stimulating history, caffeine became a target of Harvey Washington Wiley, particularly upon learning that young children particularly enjoyed Coca-Cola.[47] By this time, John Pemberton had long-since sold his stake in the Coca-Cola Corporation to Asa Candler and died at the age of 57, still addicted to morphine.[48] As a former pharmacist and purveyor of patent medicines, Asa Candler utilized the marketing expertise characteristic of patent medicines and Madison Avenue to turn Coca-Cola into the icon it remains today.[49] Among other innovations, Candler issued coupons for a complementary glass of Coca-Cola at pharmacies and distributed novelties such as calendars, clocks, and lamps, all adorned with the Coca-Cola trademark.[50] By 1895, Coca-Cola could be purchased in every state and territory in the United States. Moreover, advances in bottling technology near the turn of the century meant that the drink was no longer restricted to pharmacies but could be enjoyed at home or in restaurants.

All of this was too much for Wiley and it came to a head in 1909, when he ordered the Bureau of Chemistry into action. Bureau agents were lying in wait in a stakeout on the evening of 20 October, 1909 at the Georgia–Tennessee state line and seized forty barrels and twenty kegs of Coca-Cola syrup that were being shipped from Atlanta to its Chattanooga, Tennessee, bottling plant.[51] These actions were taken in the name of protecting interstate commerce from product adulteration with caffeine. Wiley later declared caffeine to be a poison "injurious to health" with deleterious effects on motor skills and mental performance.

COCA-COLA FOUGHT BACK. As part of its defense, it already had data from animal research of caffeine but lacked comparable information in people. To correct this, a team from the Coca-Cola Corporation went to New York and asked a leading psychologist at Columbia University to conduct a study of the effects of Coca-Cola on people. At that time, accepting money from a company was considered, at best, gauche, and, at worst, beyond the integrity of "respectable" academics. In response, the team crossed Broadway Avenue to Barnard College and approached Harry Hollingworth, a newly-minted student of the very same Columbia professor.[52] Hollingworth had recently accepted a position at Barnard and, needing the money, accepted the offer, as he was young and "had as yet no sanctity to preserve."

The trial would start within days and the heat was on. Despite extreme time pressures, Hollingworth designed a double-blinded trial that is still cited as a paragon of integrity and sophistication.[53] Three independent studies, each evaluating a battery of twenty different cognitive and dexterity tests, were conducted over a six-week period. Working with his wife (who also needed the money to pay for her own doctorate in psychology from Columbia), Hollingworth compiled the results of each day's trial that evening; Hollingworth found no negative impact of caffeine itself or of the Coca-Cola syrup.

On 13 March 1911, the federal government initiated a case alleging that Coca-Cola was adulterated and misbranded.[54] An interesting side note is that the defendant was the actual objects (the kegs and barrels) and not the Coca-Cola Company. Quite literally, Coca-Cola was on trial. The alleged adulteration was the inclusion of a harmful source of additional caffeine, beyond the natural levels supplied by the kola nut. The allegation of misbranding was also based on the idea that Coca-Cola had no coca (that is, no cocaine) and was therefore an "imitation."

As the trial was already under way, Hollingworth was rushed by train to Chattanooga to testify that neither caffeine nor the Coca-Cola syrup had any deleterious effects on motor skill or mental performance. Hearing this, the judge dismissed the case. Wiley appealed the case and again lost.[55] Again Wiley appealed, this time to the Supreme Court, which heard the case on Leap Day (29 February) 1916. Three months later, Justice Charles E. Hughes wrote the majority decision, which stated, "whether a specific ingredient is harmful is a jury matter," which had the effect of throwing the decision back to the lower courts. The Court also ruled that "an ingredient may be considered added regardless of whether a product's formula called for it." This was a pyrrhic victory for Wiley, who had argued that the caffeine was an adulteration.

Hollingworth's results all but discredited Wiley's campaign against caffeine and, in exasperation, Wiley resigned from the Bureau of Chemistry. Coca-Cola likewise sought resolution and instead of engaging in a second round of trials, it reached a settlement with the government in which it voluntarily reduced the amount of caffeine and repaid all trial costs, thus ending the legal fight.

Although beaten, Wiley wasn't quite done with Coca-Cola. He had left the bureau to lead the Good Housekeeping Research Institute, the accreditor of the much sought after "Good Housekeeping Seal of Approval."[56] In his new capacity, it was clear that Coca-Cola would never gain such approval and Wiley utilized this prominent position, which he held until his death in 1930, to continue his assault on "drugged products" in general and Coca-Cola in particular.

Wiley's use of the 1906 law to prosecute Coca-Cola was a misguided, albeit important, moment in the pre-history of the Food and Drug Administration. A much more meaningful application of the law would arise with the development of new medicines to combat the largest mass killer of people throughout the ages.

Salvarsan and Protonsil

Infectious diseases have been the scourge of civilization from time immemorial. For most of recorded history, the transmission of epidemic diseases was believed to occur via a noxious form of bad-smelling air, known as miasma.[57] In the latter half of the seventeenth century, a Dutch drapery maker, Anton van Leeuwenhoek, took up a hobby of lens making. A length of common soda lime glass could be heated in a flame and formed into small spheres. Van Leeuwenhoek found that particularly small spheres could serve as lenses (like modern-day magnifying glasses).[58] By perfecting his technique with diligent practice, his magnifying glasses revealed worlds never before seen. Considering himself a businessman and not a scientist, he never published his observations but did send letters to the Royal Society in London noting his findings about "the little animals" existing at microscopic levels.[59] We now refer to these "little animals" by their more popular name: bacteria.

Based on van Leeuwenhoek findings, mid-nineteenth-century innovators such as John Snow, Louis Pasteur, Paul Ehrlich, and Robert Koch established the germ theory of disease. In one oft-cited example, John Snow gathered data in the midst of an 1854 cholera epidemic in the Soho district of London.[60] The miasma theory of bad air still reigned supreme, and most assumed the "bad air" of London caused cholera.[61] However, Snow assembled a map of where each afflicted patient lived and noted a water well at the center. He deduced this one well, a public pump on Broad Street, was causing the cholera outbreak. As it turns out, this particular well was, indeed, located immediately next to a cesspit. After failing to convince the local town council, he simply went to the well and broke the handle off the pump, thereby rendering it inoperable. He later treated the well with chlorine and showed this was sufficient to prevent further spread of the disease. These actions halted the outbreak and Snow is now recognized as the "Father of Epidemiology," the science of understanding the patterns of health and disease.

Paul Ehrlich was another pioneer of this renaissance in the understanding of infectious diseases and immunity.[62] Ehrlich made extraordinary contributions to many fields, including cancer research and infectious diseases, and he discovered the immune system (for which he won the 1908 Nobel Prize). He was particularly gifted at utilizing chemical dyes to help identify novel tissues and cells. The German chemical industry far outshone any other country, and Ehrlich's access to novel chemical dyes allowed him to discover different cells in the blood, including many previously unknown components of the body's immune system. He also identified certain dyes that could selectively identify bacteria or protozoan microbes and conjectured that such dyes might provide the means to seek out and kill these pathogens. Indeed, his work on dyes ultimately led to the creation of a "magic bullet" to kill bacteria. The chemical, known as arsphenamine or Salvarsan, provided a novel way of killing *Treponema pallidum*, the bacteria that causes syphilis.[63]

Salvarsan was marketed by a little-known chemical company that became an early pharmaceutical pioneer, Meister, Lucius & Bruning AG (later re-named Hoechst AG).[64] Salvarsan allowed Hoechst to become the purveyors of the first "blockbuster" medicine, a drug used widely and around the world. Despite the beneficial impact of Salvarsan, Ehrlich himself was criticized within certain circles; particular emphasis was placed on his identity as a Jew, being used to suggest that he had excessively enriched himself at the expense of the sick and infirm.[65]

The utter dominance of the German chemical industry placed the relatively new central European country at the epicenter of the nascent pharmaceutical industry. As a young and insecure country, Germany was a hotbed of extremism and anti-Semitism. Among the most vehement anti-Semites was Walter Gross.[66] 1925 was a pivotal year for Gross, who had just left an appointment at the University of Greisswald to accept a position at the University of Munster. As part of the offer, Gross was also offered a job at Bayer laboratories at Wuppertal. 1925 was also pivotal for Bayer, as it was incorporated into IG Farbenindustrie (IG Farben), the dominant industrial conglomerate of its day.[67] In this same year of 1925, and just two years after the failed Munich Beer Hall Putsch, Walter Gross joined the National Socialist German Workers Party (whose shortened name, Nazis, is more familiar to most people).[68] As an early adopter, Gross maintained a senior position throughout the life of party, rising to lead the National Socialist Office for Enlightenment on Population Policy and Racial Welfare.[69] In this capacity, Walter Gross authored and implemented indoctrination policies meant to favor "ethnic improvement" by sterilizing "undesirables" and forbidding Germans to inter-marry with Jews.[70]

Joining Gross as he transitioned from Greisswald to IG Farben was another new faculty member at the University of Munster, Gerhard Domagk. Domagk was working on a degree in bacteriology from the University of Kiel and was wounded in the early months of the Great War.[71] After his recovery, he was assigned to the Sanitary Service, where he was dismayed with the inability of hospitals and doctors to control cholera, typhus, and other infectious diseases that often killed more German soldiers than enemy bullets and shells. Upon conclusion of the Great War, Domagk completed to his studies at Kiel and then accepted a position at the University of Greisswald, where he met Walter Gross.

There is no evidence that Domagk shared Gross' repugnant political or racist views, but he did take a job under his senior colleague in 1925. While Gross' raging anti-Semitism put him into the camp of those complaining of Ehrlich's supposed profiteering, Gross was enamored with Ehrlich's brilliant knowledge and techniques. Therefore, he encouraged Domagk to continue with the groundbreaking work of Ehrlich to identify chemical dyes that could kill bacteria. Domagk's work flourished and he was granted a leave of absence from the university in 1927 to pursue his research on antibacterial dyes at Bayer/IG Farben.[72] During his productive tenure at IG Farben, Domagk identified a burgundy-red dye, known later as Protonsil, which killed streptococcal bacteria. In December 1931, Domagk demonstrated that Protonsil could kill bacteria in mice, and clinical trials in humans began almost immediately thereafter. Among the experimental subjects was Domagk's daughter, who came down with a life-threatening infection. In in desperation Domagk gave her a dose of the experimental medicine, though Domagk did not mention this ethically questionable action in his seminal report of 1935.[73]

Protonsil and related drugs were known as sulfanilamides, and their welcoming by the medical community was thunderous.[74] By 1939, Domagk had been awarded the Nobel Prize. This recognition turned out to be a mixed blessing, since Germans had been forbidden by this time to receive the award (because a vehement anti-Nazi pacifist had won the 1935 Peace Prize).[75] Rather than accepting the most illustrious prize in science, Domagk was, instead, awarded with a visit from the Gestapo, who held him in detention for a week. Within a few short years, the impact of sulfanilamide had extended around the globe. In a well-publicized example, President Franklin Delano Roosevelt's son was cured of a life-threatening streptococcal throat infection in 1936, which instantaneously spread word of its promise all throughout the United States.[76]

Raspberry-Flavored Massacre

The much-needed promise of sulfanilamide created a public frenzy. Most major American pharmaceutical companies of the time, including Eli Lilly, Merck, and Squibb, released their own versions. Triumph quickly turned to tragedy. Most sulfanilamide medicines sold throughout the world took the form of a pill or tablet. A regional company, S.E. Massengill of Bristol, Tennessee, developed a different approach.[77] Their salespeople were convinced that Southerners didn't like to swallow pills and would prefer a syrup; better yet, they decided to call it an elixir, which connoted visions of a magical potion. Therefore, Massengill tasked their chief pharmacist, Harold Watkins, to develop a good-tasting syrup. Watkins came back with a sweet solution, which was enhanced by flavoring with raspberry extract and further sweetened with saccharin and caramel. A smooth texture and underlying sweet taste was provided by diethylene glycol. The problem was that diethylene glycol, a major component of antifreeze, is a potent toxin that decimates the kidneys, particularly in children.

In September 1937, 240 gallons of Massengill's Elixir Sulfanilamide was dispersed across the country.[78] The unique feature of a sweet-flavored syrup was particularly attractive to the parents of young children. By October, eight children and an adult patient in Tulsa, Oklahoma, had died of renal failure. The Food and Drug Administration (or FDA, the new name given to the Bureau of Chemistry in 1927) was dispatched to determine what had happened. They mobilized their entire internal staff and reached out to academic laboratories to assess the causes of death. Among the academic researchers was a young Frances Oldham Kelsey, who was working on her doctorate at the University of Chicago.[79] As we will see, Kelsey was destined to make an even greater contribution to the FDA in the years to come.

Ultimately, the FDA realized that diethylene glycol was the cause of poisoning but found that there was no violation of the law since Massengill had transparently listed the ingredients in the elixir, as required by the 1906 federal law. In fact, the only violation was designating the concoction as "an elixir," since this word technically was set aside for liquids containing alcohol.[80] The deaths continued. Massengill sent telegrams to its salesmen and pharmacists suggesting they return unsold bottles, but did not explain why at first. The FDA mobilized its entire staff and, in a Herculean effort, tracked down all Massengill salesmen and learned the location of all bottles, sold and otherwise, in an effort to stop the deaths.

In total, at least 106 people in fifteen states died. Most were children. Worse still, the means of death was particularly agonizing. The president, Franklin Delano Roosevelt, relayed a letter received from a desperate parent:

> The first time I ever had occasion to call in a doctor for [Joan] and she was given Elixir of Sulfanilamide. All that is left to us is the caring for her little grave. Even the memory of her is mixed with sorrow for we can see her little body tossing to and fro and hear that little voice screaming with pain and it seems as though it would drive me insane. . . . It is my plea that you will take steps to prevent such sales of drugs that will take little lives and leave such suffering behind and such a bleak outlook on the future as I have tonight.[81]

The president and the public were incensed. In response, the federal Food, Drug, and Cosmetic Act sailed through Congress and was signed by the president on 25 June, 1938.[82] This act of legislation essentially replaced the 1906 Pure Food and Drug Act, overhauling its statutes in ways that would preclude future recurrences of tragedies like Elixir Sulfanilamide. Among the corrective procedures, companies were now required not simply to list the ingredients, as required by the 1906 law, but also to prove that each ingredient was safe in animals and humans. The 1938 act also stated that before a drug could be marketed, the FDA must approve standards that ensured the identity, quality, and fill of container, including controls at every step of a drug's manufacturing. In doing so, the Food and Drug Administration gained regulatory powers to control the approval, production, distribution, marketing, and interstate transport of all medicines in the United States.

As we will see in the next chapter, these requirements have changed somewhat over time, but essentially remain as written in 1938. Based on the lessons learned from the Elixir Sulfanilamide tragedy, stringent FDA enforcement of the 1938 Federal Food, Drug, and Cosmetic Act has allowed the United States to avoid other tragic disasters.

CHAPTER TWO

Trials and Tribulations

The 1938 Food, Drug, and Cosmetic Act created a framework, enforced by the FDA, to regulate the safety of medicines. Within a decade, these regulations had given birth to the modern pharmaceutical industry, an enterprise that flourished by translating new scientific knowledge into lucrative products. Building upon the regulations presented in the last chapter, we will summarize how clinical trials are conducted and why they are time-consuming, expensive, and absolutely necessary. This information will provide a foundation to understand why the pharmaceutical industry began to flourish within just a few years after the Elixir Sulfanilamide tragedy and why its continuation is in jeopardy today.

The Pre-History of Clinical Trials

A well-designed clinical trial is a modern phenomenon. History is replete with examples of fortuitous accidents and bold actions. For example, John Snow's breaking of the pump handle at the Broad Street well makes for a sanitized story of how the 1854 London cholera outbreak was contained.[1] Upon closer inspection, the story grows murkier, and as Snow himself admitted, the epidemic was already declining at the time of his dramatic action:

> There is no doubt that the mortality was much diminished, as I said before, by the flight of the population, which commenced soon after the outbreak; but the attacks had so far diminished before the use of the water was stopped, that it is impossible to decide whether the well still contained the cholera poison in an active state, or whether, from some cause, the water had become free from it.[2]

Dr. James Lind, a Scottish physician in the Royal Navy, is often credited with performing the first successful clinical trial.[3] Scurvy is an age-old disease, described by Hippocrates in the fourth century BCE and characterized by malaise and lethargy that is followed by spotting of the skin and unexplained bleeding and a loss of integrity in the cheeks and gums.[4] With time, the disease progresses to include pus-filled wounds, a characteristic loss of teeth (as the gums fail to hold them in place), jaundice (a sign of liver failure), and death.

In the mid-eighteenth century, Britannia ruled the waves and the Royal Navy was the pointy edge of Britain's economic, political, and military spear. As such, the health of the sailors in the Royal Navy was a crucial factor defining military readiness and thus was of paramount concern to the British government. At the time, scurvy was unavoidable for crews serving on long deployments and this fact led Lind to try an experiment. He believed scurvy was the result of tissue putrefaction (rotting) and could be ameliorated by treating with acids. Such ideas were buttressed by rumors that certain acidic citrus fruits seemed to alleviate the symptoms of scurvy.

To test the idea that acids could block scurvy, Lind devised a study in 1753 in which twelve scurvy sailors on the HMS *Salisbury* were randomly divided into groups of two each.[5] The six groups were given either: seawater (a control since it was not expected to have any effect), cider (a source of acetic acid), vitriol (sulfuric acid), vinegar (acetic acid), two oranges and a lemon (ascorbic acid), or a spicy paste made with barley water. The experiment had to be suspended before the week was out because the sailors ran out of fruit, yet the results were nonetheless remarkable. The two men provided with fruit had recovered, whereas the scurvy in other sailors worsened. Lind's subsequent paper on these dramatic outcomes was largely ignored, perhaps because he could not overcome his own bias that scurvy must be so complicated that it couldn't possibly be treated just with citrus fruits. We now know that the citrus fruits were a prominent source of vitamin C (ascorbic acid). Not believing his own data, Lind did not recommend citrus fruits but instead advocated a more complex strategy in which sailors should grow watercress salad leaves (which also happen to contain vitamin C) on web blankets that had been strewn on the decks of sailing ships. It must have made quite a sight to pull alongside a mighty Royal Navy ship-of-the-line and see its decks covered in lettuce.

Rather than festooning their decks with greenery, naval officers individually and then collectively began to supply their crews with concentrated lime or lemon juice. This was formally put to the test in 1794, when the HMS *Suffolk*, a seventy-four-gun ship of the line, endeavored on a twenty-three-week voyage to India.[6] Each sailor was issued a small amount of lime juice each day and the ship arrived at port without a single sailor suffering from scurvy. This conclusive outcome convinced the British Admiralty to issue lemon or lime juice to all sailors and, in short order, the sailors of the Royal Navy became widely known as "limeys."

Lind's finding had powerful geopolitical implications in allowing the Royal Navy to increase the number and length of its deployments. Time would show the use of a controlled clinical trial set an equally important precedent. Other advances would arise from the increased adoption of randomization of volunteers to ensure that no unintended bias, conscious or unconscious, be introduced into trials.

The subject of volunteering for a clinical trial seems obvious to us today but this is a recent phenomenon spurred, in part, by tragedies inflicted as a result of the extremist views of Dr. Walter Gross and others. The myriad crimes against humanity by the Nazi party horrified the world in the closing days of the Second World War but one legacy bears repeating here. In the months after victory in Europe, the Nazi surgeon Dr. Karl Brandt and twenty-two others were convicted of war crimes resulting from the forced sterilizations of more than 3.5 million German citizens, which you may recall was the brainchild of the Nazi leader and pharmaceutical scientist, Gross.[7] In a case known as "the Doctors' Trial," the Nuremburg war trials court found Brandt and others guilty and Brandt was sentenced to death by hanging in 1947.

These criminal trials encouraged the adoption of the Nuremburg Code.[8] The 1947 agreement codifies an ethical framework for the proper conduct of clinical trials and, among other actions, requires informed consent for volunteers and bars the use of coercion. While not directly adopted into law by the federal government of the United States, some individual states have done so. Other key provisions of the Nuremburg Code mandate animal experimentation and proper justification as prerequisites before initiating any clinical investigation in humans. The Nuremberg Code also requires that unnecessary suffering must be avoided and that subjects are at liberty to end an experiment at any time.

With the Nuremburg Code in mind, we will provide a brief overview of clinical trials, what they are, and how they are used to guide the development of new medicines.

The Mazes and Phases of Clinical Trials

As specified by the Nuremburg Code, clinical investigation in humans cannot begin until proper tested has been completed in animals. In the United States, the investigational new drug (IND) program regulates whether a particular drug candidate can be tested in people. Because of limitations on the extent of power held by the U.S. federal government (as compared with individual states), technically, the IND is a means to control the transport of an investigational new medicine across states lines before that medicine has received marketing approval from the FDA. An IND application must be submitted, even for an already-approved drug, if there is an intended change in how the drug is administered, the amounts to be given (if higher than an existing approval), or if a different disease or population of patients is to be investigated. The sponsor of the IND application is required to convey information about three critical areas.

First, an IND must provide information from animal-based pharmacology and toxicology studies. Specifically, the FDA generally requires that the drug be tested in at least two different types of animals to establish the safety of the experimental drug at multiple doses and to identify potential toxicities. To address both issues, these studies are performed at both macroscopic and microscopic levels. In other words, the results must consider both gross manifestations of toxicity, such as measurable symptoms, as well as microscopic damage, using a technique known as microscopic histopathology. Histopathology can identify traces of toxicity that are missed by a simple analysis of how a subject looks or acts. Additional batteries of tests, collectively known as safety pharmacology, assess any impact of the experimental drug on vital organs such as the lung, heart, central nervous system, and other organs. Importantly, these studies are performed at many different doses to identify the levels of drug exposure that cause damage versus those that do not. This is important because any substance, including everyday chemicals including water or oxygen, will eventually become toxic when administered at a high enough dose. The key is both to identify the toxicity and the dose level that causes the toxicity so that this information can be used to guide the intended future examination of an experimental drug in human clinical trials.

Production Value

A successful IND application also requires a comprehensive analysis of the manufacturing processes used to produce the material to be used in clinical trials. This may seem rather esoteric but sufficient assurances must be conveyed to demonstrate that the sponsoring organization can produce, store, and transport material in a safe and reproducible manner. A comprehensive assessment of compound stability is also performed, because many drugs can become unstable while sitting on a shelf or may degrade as a result of temperature, humidity, light, or other environmental changes. While a particular drug itself may be safe, the degraded products may not be and, thus, it is important to provide assurances that the drug administered in clinical trials is exactly what is intended.

A much-hyped cancer drug candidate from the 1990s named angiostatin conveys a prominent example of how manufacturing and stability issues can scuttle a potential medical breakthrough. As a brief background, Judah Folkman was a Harvard Medical School professor, who published a ground-breaking 1971 paper in the *New England Journal of Medicine* in which he proposed an idea that cancer might be treated by destroying its blood supply.[9] By the time the paper appeared, oncologists were frustrated by the fact that cancer cells generally have a high rate of intrinsic mutation and this allows them to escape from chemotherapy. Dr. Folkman realized that a tumor, like every other part of the body, requires a stable blood supply to provide oxygen and nutrients for its continued survival. He further recognized that the tumor secretes certain factors that attract and encourage the growth of new blood vessels into and throughout the tumor through a process known as angiogenesis. By targeting the angiogenesis of these blood vessels, rather than the tumor itself, Folkman reasoned that one might be able to starve a tumor of much-needed oxygen and nutrients and, thereby, kill the tumor. Over the following years, Folkman put his theory to the test and identified a set of promising molecules with these capabilities. One of the most prominent was a protein known as angiostatin.[10]

Folkman worked with EntreMed, a biotechnology company based out of Rockville, Maryland, to develop angiostatin as an experimental cancer drug.[11] The early results of human clinical trials at Harvard and other Boston hospitals gained considerable notoriety in the press as a potential breakthrough medicine. James Watson, who along with Francis Crick, had discovered the structure of DNA, was famously quoted in 1997 as saying, "Judah will cure cancer within two years," and the columnist and *60 Minutes* correspondent Andy Rooney called for an annual "Judah Folkman Day" to recognize his extraordinary medical contributions.[12] The excitement also triggered a lucrative partnership between EntreMed and Bristol-Myers Squibb.

However, the manufacturing of angiostatin proved to be complex and inefficient. The results from material produced by the Boston researchers, who worked with Folkman and EntreMed, were promising but the material used in other studies, including a high-profile clinical trial at the National Cancer Institute (NCI) in Bethesda, Maryland, yielded no beneficial effects. Making things worse, the scientists at Bristol-Myers Squibb encountered difficulties producing any material at all. Such outcomes created murmurs that there must be something "special" about the Boston materials, which implied sloppy techniques or worse. In the end, the NCI was finally able to reproduce Folkman's findings with angiostatin but this was

announced on the day after Bristol-Myers Squibb elected to end its partnership with EntreMed.[13] The drug itself was doomed because low yields and
poor reproducibility confounded its ability to be utilized on a broad scale.
Angiostatin was unable to meet the unrealistic expectations emerging from
the early days of its testing. Folkman was later vindicated by the approval of
Avastin and other drugs that target angiogenesis and were more amenable
to large-scale manufacturing and stability.

INDs and Shutdowns

The sponsoring institution is also required to provide detailed clinical proto-
cols and the credentials of the investigators who will perform the studies. This
information assures that appropriately trained and experienced personnel will
oversee safe and proper procedures. Among the information provided is a detailed assessment of how the informed consent process will be conducted. As
you may recall, informed consent is a process, mandated by the Nuremburg
Code, that prevents any form of coercion to assure that volunteers have enrolled in a trial of their own free will and that they retain the ability, at any
time, to withdraw from the trial if they feel their wellbeing may be in jeopardy.

The information required for an IND is compiled into an application,
which is submitted to the FDA via an electronic file. If the information were
to be printed on paper, this would entail tens of thousands of pages of data
as well as detailed summaries from the preclinical studies in cells and animals. The FDA then has thirty days to review this expansive information
and, absent any communication to the contrary, a trial can commence immediately after this time period expires. Quite frequently, the FDA will
place a trial on hold until the applicant has adequately addressed particular
questions or concerns. This back-and-forth exchange of information is necessary to assure the safety of clinical investigation in humans.

The fact that, unless notified otherwise, a clinical trial can commence
thirty days after the submission of an IND has created occasional uncom-
fortable and unintended circumstances. One such example was triggered by
a squabble between Congress and the White House in 2013, which caused
the U.S. government to abruptly shut down from October first until the seventeenth of that month. The furlough of 800,000 federal employees included most staff at the Food and Drug Administration.[14] Companies that
had submitted IND applications that reached the thirty-day release within
the first half of October 2013 were left in a quandary. Technically, the FDA
had not instructed them not to proceed, but that was because the FDA was

closed (and phone calls to the agency went unanswered for weeks). Many companies were left scratching their heads, as a double negative does not necessarily translate into a positive. Compounding this, a backlog of new drug applications submitted to the FDA during the shutdown (since the private sector kept advancing) meant the agency faced an unprecedented logjam that, likewise, added to the already-considerable confusion. Fortunately, history does not record that anyone was harmed by this episode, but the impact identified issues that linger to this day.

It is important to note that the IND application does not require a demonstration of efficacy. Rather, the IND is solely meant to assure the safety of an experimental drug that will be tested in people. An organization would be truly foolish with its resources to invest the extensive resources needed to support an IND submission, which can cost millions of dollars, if there is no evidence of efficacy. Nonetheless, the FDA does not formally require a demonstration of effectiveness until the applicant seeks to conduct pivotal Phase III human clinical trials.

Phase I Trials

The Phase I clinical trial is the most common way in which clinical investigation of a new medicine normally begins. Also known as a first-in-human trial, the goal of a Phase I is to utilize a small number of patients, usually from a few to as many as fifty people, to ask at what dose levels the drug is well-tolerated with little or no side-effects. In parallel, Phase I studies assess how the drug behaves in people in terms of how much drug can be detected in the blood (or other relevant body fluid or tissues) and how long it remains in the body.

A unique feature of a Phase I trial is that a small number of patients (known as a cohort) are given a very low dose of the drug, usually one-tenth of the lowest dose that might be expected to have any effect on the body. The group is assessed for toxicities based on extensive monitoring and the results are reviewed by a board of dispassionate physicians (that is, not directly involved in the study or financially-linked to the sponsor) to assure that unwanted toxicities are evaluated. If this group concludes that there are no adverse effects, then the dose can be increased by a particular increment that they recommend. The process is repeated again and again until either an adverse event, known as a dose-limiting toxicity or DLT, is observed or until the study reaches the intended maximum dose. As strange as it may sound, the detection of a toxic response is the more highly desired outcome, as it also clarifies the potential signs of a dangerous dose level, which can be useful information when the experimental drug is tested in a larger population during Phase II and III trials.

The conduct of a Phase I clinical trial, like all clinical investigation, is closely monitored to maintain the highest standards of patient protection and scientific conduct. During the entire course of treatment, many analyses are performed to ensure that the volunteers remain happy and healthy. Blood samples are collected at multiple times after drug administration to measure the amount of drug in the body and where it goes over time, using the science of pharmacokinetics, which literally means drug movement over time. Using complicated formulas, this information can be used to predict whether enough of the drug candidate can be given to have the desired efficacy in future studies.

There are different types of Phase I trials. Almost invariably, the first trial in humans is known as a single ascending dose (SAD or Phase Ia) trial. As the name suggests a SAD trial is characterized by each volunteer receiving a single dose of drug. This type of trial may be sufficient if a single dose of drug is anticipated to be needed for treatment, but this is usually not the case. When multiple doses are needed, a multiple ascending dose (MAD or Phase Ib) trial is conducted. The doses selected for the MAD depend on the outcomes of the SAD, but the idea is the same. Patients are given a low dose of drug at a pre-determined interval and the toxicities and pharmacokinetics are measured at multiple time points.

Phase I clinical trials are relatively inexpensive, costing single-digit millions of dollars, and are often performed by contract research organizations (CROs), who provide clinical support to pharmaceutical companies at reasonable rates. The CROs in turn recruit volunteers who are paid for their services. Thus, the average Phase I clinical trial subject tends to be aged eighteen to twenty-five, male, and enrolled in a major university. Until recently, women have largely been excluded from early-stage clinical trials out of concerns about potential hormonal variations, but increasing evidence of gender similarities and differences is finally changing this view. This has raised important and ongoing questions about whether the outcomes of a trial with a young and hungry college student are applicable to a well-fed octogenarian.

The exception to the rule of using healthy, normal adults arises when compassionate use dictates that a Phase I clinical trial be conducted with a special population. For example, a subset of patients with a terminal illness will gladly volunteer to test a new drug if there is even a small chance that it can extend their quality or quantity of life. These brave volunteers are the inspiration for many of us in drug research and development, and have immeasurably advanced the development of new medicines. Nonetheless, the use of volunteers with terminal, generally late-stage, disease itself raises unresolved ethical and practical questions. Specifically, testing with an unhealthy patient population, where all conventional attempts at treatment have failed, presents a very high hurdle for a new medicine and, as important, the results with such a population may not reflect what will be observed in healthier patients.

Paradoxically, a demonstration that a drug works to ameliorate or cure disease is not an endpoint of a Phase I trial. Rather, the goals are, first and foremost, to establish that the drug is safe and that the amount of drug can be measured over time in the volunteers. While there is always hope that a volunteer's tumor will magically disappear, or a comparable outcome with other diseases, this is rarely the case. Indeed, by looking too hard for signs of efficacy, ignoring random chance, or discounting the very real impact of the placebo effect, doctors and researchers can fool themselves into investing more time and energy into less promising opportunities.

Horror in London

The potential perils of a Phase I clinical trial were vividly brought to the world's attention on 13 March 2006. On this date, investigators from Parexel, an established and respected CRO, were initiating a new Phase I project at their site on the premises of Northwick Park and St. Mark's Hospital in London.[15] The subject of investigation was TGN1412, an experimental medicine developed by TeGenero ImmunoTherapeutics of Wurzburg, Germany. The company was developing a type of leukemia drug known as a monoclonal antibody. The idea behind TGN1412 was that the antibody drug would essentially short-circuit cancer cells and thereby halt the disease. In general, antibody drugs had a reputation for being safe and effective and TeGenero had performed the required investigation in animals to verify the safety of the drug. Certain differences in how TGN1412 functioned in animals versus people meant that the results in animals were not necessarily applicable to humans but this was not unusual, as the issue often arises with monoclonal antibody therapeutics.

The intended study utilized a 3:1 model with eight volunteers, which meant that six volunteers would receive the drug and two would receive a placebo.[16] This was the first cohort of a dose escalation study, which meant that the lowest level of drug would be tested and the safety was assumed, since levels 500 times higher than this initial dose had shown no deleterious effects in monkeys. Notably, the study was conducted in a double blind manner, which means that neither the staff nor the patients knew who had received the drug and who had received the placebo. The volunteers, ranging in age from nineteen to thirty-four, were all healthy males with no known medical concerns. Their motivations for volunteering for the clinical trial varied. One volunteer planned to send the money to his brother in Egypt to help him set up a new business, but all were lured with the promise of a £2,000 honorarium, which was considerably higher than the "few hundred quid" for comparable studies elsewhere in London.[17]

By eight A.M. all of the necessary paperwork and preparations had been completed and the study commenced. As an additional safety feature, all volunteers received TGN1412 as an infusion over three to six minutes, rather than a bolus. A bolus injection is comparable to a typical flu or tetanus shot, in which the drug is injected as quickly as the doctor can push in the plunger. As a means of minimizing potential untoward effects of a sudden increase in medicine, known as a bolus effect, TGN1412 was slowly introduced into the blood stream over a few minutes. The infusion also meant that it took ten minutes to go from patient to patient and, therefore, the last patient finished their treatment by nine thirty A.M. At about the same time that the final drips were administered to the last patient, the first patient treated began to complain of a headache, followed shortly thereafter by muscle pain, nausea, diarrhea, redness, and a profound drop in blood pressure. Like clockwork, the remaining five patients who had received the drug developed comparable symptoms over the following hour. Worse still, the constellation of symptoms accelerated and expanded and over the following five hours, progressed to high fever, a rapid drop in blood cells, and a rapid heartbeat. At approximately eight P.M. that evening, one of the patients was diagnosed with multi-organ failure, a name that captures the fact that the heart, lungs, kidneys, and other vital organs stopped functioning without external assistance. A second patient followed around two in the morning, and within the next three hours, all six volunteers were experiencing multi-organ failure and required external ventilation. The severity and types of reactions varied from volunteer to volunteer, but a few stand out, including one whose fingers and toes had to be amputated and an Egyptian man, whose head swelled to many time its normal size such that he became known as "The Elephant Man."[18] As a gentle reminder, all of this was done for a £2,000 stipend.

The volunteers were the victims of a host defense response known as a cytokine storm.[19] This condition arises when the body believes it is under attack from a foreign pathogen and responds with everything it has. Such a condition is a well known cause of death for a wide array of maladies such as an allergic bee sting and is the primary way that some of the planet's most deadly pathogens kill, including Ebola virus or pandemic influenza infection.[20] Remarkably, all of the volunteers survived, which, in part, represents the quick and heroic efforts of the staff in the nearby intensive care facility at the Northwick Park and St. Mark's Hospital. The fact that the trial was conducted with young and healthy subjects may also have played a role in their survival. Unfortunately, the prognosis for these volunteers is unknown but not promising, as all are believed to be at risk for the development of serious autoimmune diseases and cancers.[21] The repercussions of the TGN1412 debacle also continue to be felt around the world, particularly by regulatory agencies such as the FDA.[22] While new breakthroughs in research promise new types of medicines, this incident reminds us of the need to remain vigilant. As we will see in a later chapter, the TGN1412 example also contributed to the rising costs of drug development, as many regulatory agencies later required clinical trials to include an ever-wider array of tests for safety to avoid a repetition of the experiences seen in London.

Phase II Trials

Once the results of a Phase I clinical trial have been compiled, a project team analyzes the data to decide whether the findings warrant continuation of the program. If the results are obvious, either because the drug was toxic at low doses or because there was no toxicity (and perhaps even a hint of efficacy), then the decision is a relatively simple one. More often, the decision-making is agonizing and must weigh the millions of dollars and thousands of hours invested into the product already against the millions of dollars and thousands of hours that will be invested should the project continue.

As clinical investigation continues, the stakes constantly rise. For example, the larger size and more extensive monitoring of patient outcomes may mean that a Phase II trial costs ten to 100 times more money. Whereas a typical Phase I trial may cost a few million dollars and take a few months to perform, a Phase II campaign frequently costs tens of millions of dollars and requires years to complete. To assist the decision-making as to whether and how to proceed, the project team will generally summarize their findings to the FDA and seek guidance as to the design, should they move forward, of the Phase II investigation.

If a decision is made by the sponsor to continue clinical investigation, then Phase II trials still emphasize the evaluation of safety and pharmacokinetics, but in a larger number of subjects. However, Phase II trials tend to differ from their Phase I predecessors in two ways. First, the Phase II trial seeks to assess if there is any sign of efficacy. Thus, rather than focusing on random college students, the Phase II is generally focused on the intended patient population. In this way, the aforementioned questions about whether a college student is representative of the situation in the intended populated can start to be resolved. The second major difference distinguishing a Phase II from its predecessor is that the trial tends to be focused on a small number of doses, generally two. The doses selected must be safe, as guided by the review of Phase I data and with consent from the FDA.

The overall goal is to see if clinical improvement can be achieved and, if so, whether the magnitude of effect relates to the dose administered. In addition, most well designed Phase II clinical trials involve an additional set of patients that are treated with the generally accepted standard of care. The inclusion of this arm of the trial helps determine how the new drug compares with the conventional way of treating the disease.

In the course of developing new medicines, a few counter-intuitive issues have arisen that are relatively unique to Phase II clinical trials. First, the results of a Phase II trial are not always indicative of what will occur in later studies. Whereas the results with anti-infective agents (aka antibiotics) tend to behave the same in a Phase II trial as what will be observed in Phase III and beyond, the situation with oncology trials is particularly problematic. A series of consistent studies has shown that a positive result with a Phase II clinical will be reproduced in a Phase III trial only 28 percent of the time.[23] To put this in perspective, that is roughly the same as correctly calling heads or tails twice in a row. Such findings are not easily explained or understood, but one explanation it that such findings may represent unconscious bias by oncologists when they decide which patients should enroll in a particular trial. From the standpoint of a pharmaceutical executive (or an investor) about to invest hundreds of millions of dollars into a particular trial, such findings are unsettling.

The second issue unique to Phase II trials relates to reimbursement. Any doctor has the ability to write a prescription for any drug. Therefore, the most powerful oncology drugs can be prescribed, in a process known as "off-label use," by a physician who lacks direct experience or even knowledge of that drug. However, an off-label prescription is not likely be covered by insurance. An exception to the rule has been made for oncology drugs.[24] Many oncology drugs address properties shared by cancers such as killing fast- or inappropriately-growing tumor cells, regardless of the type of cancer. Therefore, the oncology community has adopted an approach known as a "compendium expansion." As a brief summary, if objective data from independent Phase II studies support the concept that an approved oncology drug works for another cancer, then the insurance company will generally reimburse the patient for the drug. This practice has shortened the time and expense needed to "repurpose" drugs approved for one indication to another.

Phase III Trials

Phase III trials can be summarized in two words: large and expensive. The reason trials are large is that they are required to demonstrate the new drug is at least as good, and generally better, than the current standard of care. Before the trial can begin, the FDA and the sponsoring organization must reach an understanding of the magnitude of efficacy, relative to a standard of care, which will be required for the FDA to judge a particular trial successful. Often, the FDA will also require that a successful outcome in one trial be repeated in an independent second study. Rare exceptions can, however, occur if the Phase III trial scores a "home run," in which the results are so obviously definitive that repeat investigation is not warranted.

Because the outcome must be statistically significant and at least as good as the existing standard of care, the trial generally requires a large sample size, which can range from hundreds to thousands of patients and cost many hundreds of millions of dollars. Further upping the cost is the fact that the company sponsoring the trial is required to pay for the costs of both their own arm as well as that of their comparator (known as a control). If the comparator is an already approved drug (which is normally the case), this places some organizations in the almost ironic situation of being a major contributor to the success of their competitor's product.

Once all the requirements of a campaign of clinical investigation have been completed, the information is compiled into a package known as either a New Drug Application (NDA; generally for small molecule therapeutics) or a Biologics License Application (BLA; generally for a class of drugs known as biologics). The purpose of the NDA/BLA is to address three questions: 1) Is the drug safe and effective, particularly in comparison with the current standard of care and do the benefits outweigh the risks? 2) Is the label, which defines who should be prescribed the drug and how it will be advertised, appropriate? 3) Is the process used to manufacture the drug sufficiently robust to assure quality, identity, potency, and purity?

The NDA or BLA is submitted electronically and, if printed out and stacked, can exceed the height of the Empire State Building.[25] The NDA also assesses the ability of the sponsoring organization to reproducibly manufacture, supply, store, and distribute the new drug following approval. As such, the review of the NDA can take months and even years. The review often includes back-and-forth communications, generally in the form of written documentation, which is often communicated to the public (and investors) to assure the transparency of the process. Different committees of FDA-appointed investigators also hold advisory panels, which are generally open to the public, to discuss the findings and allow the different committees to make recommendations to the FDA. The ultimate decision of whether to approve a particular drug for commercialization is made by the FDA itself and can be particularly tricky if different advisory panels disagree on whether to support approval.

The success or failure of a Phase III clinical trial can make or break companies. In the case of small companies, the costs of the trials and BLA/NDA submission may completely exhaust their funding. For larger companies, a highly publicized and expensive failure could trigger, at minimum, a change in management or force the company into a merger. For these reasons and others, the period in which a company's product is being evaluated in Phase III clinical trials can fill the organization with anxiety, which is particularly problematic when the trial itself lasts for years. Another consideration is that the "standard of care" itself can change. For example, an expensive Phase III trial can be rendered useless if a competitor gains approval for a product that is at least as good for the indication as your drug. Such risks explain why established pharmaceutical companies often devote considerable resources to competitive intelligence to be sure that the millions of dollars and years of R&D invested into a drug are not wiped away by a competing product that was not anticipated.

Kevadon

An example of the pressures on companies and regulatory officials pertaining to the outcomes of clinical trials is exemplified by the drug application to the FDA for a drug named Kevadon. The story is filled with tragedy, risk, politics, and, ultimately, success.

The story of Kevadon begins in April 1954, when the German company Chemie Grunenthal identified a molecule with the complicated chemical nomenclature of (RS)-2-(2,6-dioxopiperidin-3-yl)-1H-isoindole-1,3(2H)-dione.[26] This complicated name was shortened to a more easily pronounced name, thalidomide. Chemie Grunenthal chemists and biologists found that thalidomide showed promise for the treatment of respiratory infections and initiated clinical trials in November 1956, and gained approval for marketing in West Germany for this indication the following year under the name Grippex (*grippe* is the German and French word for flu).[27]

In the course of their studies, Chemie Grunenthal investigators noted that thalidomide decreased vomiting and was particularly useful in ameliorating many of the symptoms of not just influenza, but other indications, including morning sickness in pregnant women.[28] Thus, the company expanded its use for this indication and began marketing an over-the-counter version (that did not require a prescription) under the name Contergan. Hailed as a panacea for many different types of malaise (colds, flu, allergies, cough), Contergan was a blockbuster and was successfully marketed in more than thirty different countries.

Buoyed by this international success, Chemie Grunenthal licensed its rights for sales in North America to a small pharmaceutical company, Richardson-Merrell Pharmaceuticals of Cincinnati, Ohio.[29] Chemie Grunenthal had originally intended to license the product to one of the largest American pharmaceutical companies of the time, Smith, Kline & French, but was rebuffed. An FDA document that had been lost in its archives for more than five decades later revealed that Smith, Kline & French had performed its own animal and human clinical trials but was unimpressed with the findings and elected not to take a license from Chemie Grunenthal, despite its blockbuster status in Europe.[30]

Richardson-Merrell applied for FDA approval in 1960. At that point, the FDA allowed a company to begin selling a product sixty days after the submission of its application to the FDA unless the agency raised concerns in the meantime. Based on a long track record of sales throughout the world, Richardson-Merrell was confident that Kevadon would sail through FDA approval. Richardson-Merrell was so assured of its success that it had already produced tens of thousands of samples "for research purposes" and had distributed these to their network of doctors while they waited through the sixty-day review period.

FDA management seemed equally confident Kevadon would sail through the FDA regulatory process based on an established track record in Europe. Therefore, the agency assigned the task of reviewing the Kevadon application to a newly hired employee, Francis Oldham Kelsey, who had started just a month before.[31] You may recall that Kelsey was a graduate student at the University of Chicago, where she had helped the FDA investigate the Elixir Sulfanilamide tragedy in 1938. In the intervening twenty years, she had earned both and M.D. and Ph.D. and had worked as an editorial associate for the American Medical Association as well as a lecturer in pharmacology at the University of South Dakota. By 1960, Kelsey found herself living in Washington, D.C., and she applied for a job at the FDA.

In evaluating the application from Richardson-Merrell, Dr. Kelsey noted the company had not provided any data from its own testing and requested this data. The company refused. Kelsey then asked for the names of the doctors and patients to whom the Kevadon samples had been sent. Richardson-Merrell again refused. Kelsey was particularly concerned about an English study, which suggested Kevadon caused unwanted nervous system side effects, including drowsiness, dizziness, and confusion. Despite repeated requests, Richardson-Merrell refused to actively address the questions raised by Dr. Kelsey and, following each rejection, simply re-submitted the application. This cycle was repeated six times, with the company hoping each time to pass the sixty-day limit. Moreover, Richardson-Merrell increased the pressure with each new submission, going over Kelsey's head to her supervisor and accusing her of being a bureaucrat or worse. They also challenged Kelsey and the FDA with a lawsuit. According to a 15 July 1962 article by *Washington Post* investigative reporter, Morton Mintz, who broke the story: "She saw her duty in sternly simple terms, and she carried it out, living the while with insinuations that she was a bureaucratic nitpicker, unreasonable—even, she said, stupid . . . What she did was refuse to be hurried into approving an application for marketing a new drug."[32]

Almost two years after the original Kevadon application had been submitted to the FDA, it had become widely known that the miracle drug thalidomide had a much darker side. The aforementioned side effects on the nervous system paled in comparison with catastrophic birth defects.[33] From its approval in 1957 through its withdrawal in 1962, more than 10,000 children in forty-six countries were born with severe congenital deformities. The afflicted included fifty children born in America to mothers had been given the "research samples" from Richardson-Merrell. These children were born with deformities that included congenital malformations of the face and/or limbs and, at times, the complete absence of arms and legs in a condition known as phocomelia. More than half of these children died within months after their birth.

In recognition of her role in preventing the approval of a bad drug and potential birth defects arising from its use, Kelsey was awarded the President's Award for Distinguished Federal Civilian Service by President John F. Kennedy in 1962, and continued a long career at FDA, retiring in 2005 at the age of ninety.[34]

Kefauver-Harris Drug Act

Estes Kefauver is hardly a common name today but he was a lion of his own era.[35] A long-standing senator and vice-presidential candidate under Adlai Stevenson in 1956, Kefauver chaired the powerful Senate Antitrust and Monopoly Subcommittee from 1957 to 1963. In this capacity, he was particularly troubled by what he viewed as excessive profits made by the pharmaceutical industry, compounded by concerns that the pharmaceutical industry was too intimately involved with the American Medical Association. The thalidomide scandal drove him into action.

In 1962, a bill sponsored by Estes Kefauver and Oren Harris of Arkansas amended the 1938 Federal Food, Drug, and Cosmetic Act by requiring "proof of efficacy." Whereas the previous legislation was focused on drug safety, the Kefauver-Harris amendment required that companies provide conclusive evidence that new drugs were at least as effective as the current standard of care.[36] To address concerns raised by thalidomide, the amendment also required drug advertising to disclose information about side effects, an outcome that is now well-known to all Americans who own a television set.

The Kefauver-Harris amendment also implemented all of these rules in a retroactive manner. To verify that even well-established medicines were effective, a Drug Efficacy Study Implement (DESI) program was initiated by the FDA to require studies of all drugs approved before 1962 to assess whether they were effective, ineffective, or required additional investigation. By 1984, the DESI program had found that about one-third, or 1,051 of the 3,443 drugs approved by FDA lacked efficacy and were withdrawn from the market.[37]

Despite these changes, and indeed because of them, the story about thalidomide was not quite complete. Through a combination of serendipity and astute observation, Jacob Sheskin of Hadassah University in Jerusalem noted that thalidomide was useful in the treatment of *erythema modosum leprosum* (ENL), a painful complication of leprosy.[38] The use of thalidomide for leprosy was first allowed in Brazil, where patients were strictly counseled about the risk of birth defects.[39] Nonetheless, at least 100 cases of birth defects were reported in Brazil between 2005 and 2010.[40]

Thalidomide finally gained approval in the United States in 1998 for the treatment of ENL, but its use has been very strictly controlled. Specifically, a thorough system, known as STEPS, was implemented to ensure education and handling. This STEPS program includes both the patients themselves and anyone else who might come into contact with thalidomide (for example, roommates, spouses, or children) and includes limitations on who can prescribe and dispense thalidomide as well as registries to monitor patients.[41]

The final chapter in the thalidomide story began in 1994, when Harvard University Professor Robert D'Amato found thalidomide to be a promising inhibitor of tumor angiogenesis.[42] D'Amato was following up on pioneering work by Dr. Judah Folkman, also of Harvard, who, as we have seen, postulated in 1971 that all cancers must obtain a newly made blood supply and that targeting newly formed blood vessels with compounds known as anti-angiogenic agents could provide a new means to treat cancer. Thalidomide demonstrated a potential ability to block angiogenesis and was utilized off-label for certain cancers until 2006, when the FDA approved thalidomide for the treatment of newly diagnosed multiple myeloma, again utilizing strict controls to minimize the risk that pregnant women might come in contact with the drug. Thus, while the United States had held the distinction of refusing approval for thalidomide four decades before, the demonstration of efficacy, as required by the Kefauver-Harris Drug Act, facilitated its ultimate approval for leprosy and then cancer.

CHAPTER THREE

Dreams of Greatness
The Birth of the Pharmaceutical Industry

In the previous chapter, we established the activities required for identifying and launching a new drug. Here, we will show the birth of the modern pharmaceutical industry. The industry grew quickly, particularly after the Second World War, with the number of approved drugs rising from three at the beginning of 1930 to 1,453 by the end of 2013.[1] These approvals were awarded to just over 200 different companies. The earliest drug introduced into continuous use was morphine from Merck, and this milestone will serve as the initial anchor in our story. Rather than telling the stories of more than a thousand drugs and hundreds of companies, a few representatives will show how the modern pharmaceutical industry developed.

This chapter will start with the opium trade, which formed the foundation for the discovery of morphine and ultimately transformed a one-person apothecary with roots in the seventeenth century into the powerhouse known today as Merck & Co.[2] Science, serendipity, and myth often go hand-in-hand and we will see examples of how Franklin Delano Roosevelt and the cousin of the Red Baron unknowingly worked together to expedite the birth of modern cancer chemotherapy. We will also debunk some of the myths associated with the discovery of penicillin and learn how a well-timed swarm of flies pointed the way to a miraculous cure that restored a roomful of children who were within hours of death. In parallel with these human dramas, we will profile the emergence of major pharmaceutical companies, with an emphasis on two, Merck and Eli Lilly, who rank among the dominant innovators in the twentieth century, comparable in many ways to Google and Apple of today.

The God of Dreams

Opium is one of the oldest drugs known to man. Depictions of opium poppies adorn ancient Sumerian artifacts, dating back to at least 4000 B.C.E., when it was known as *Hul Gil*, "the plant of joy."[3] This name reflects the psychoactive properties of opium-derived narcotics, which alter the fundamental chemistry of the brain to cause bouts of euphoria and to decrease sensations of pain. The demand for opium grew with increasing trade and the magical poppy spread in all directions from the Fertile Crescent to civilizations in Egypt, Minoa, mainland Greece, Rome, India, and all throughout the Persian Empire. Trade along the Silk Road eventually brought opium to China, where, as we shall see, it played a key role in transforming Chinese society, with repercussions that are still felt to this day.

The drug itself arises from *Papaver somniferum*, an ornamental plant that also gives rise to the seeds commonly found on bagels and poppy seed oil, which is highly prized for its high content of vitamin E.[4] The oil contains virtually no narcotic and the seeds don't convey enough drug to trigger any psychoactive properties. However, the urban legend that a poppy seed bagel can cause a positive drug test is true because, while low, the levels of morphine in seeds can trigger some particularly sensitive drug-monitoring tests.[5]

The real source of psychoactive compounds in *Papaver somniferum* is derived from the latex harvested from the seedpod. When small, perfectly timed slits are cut into an immature seed pod, a viscous white fluid, known as latex, exudes from the pod and dries into a yellow residue.[6] The residue is further dried, which can then be consumed either by smoking it or infusing it into tea. The use of the term "smoke" in this case is a misnomer because opium is quite heat-labile. Specifically, heating opium to greater than 70° C (158° F) will degrade its psychoactive properties. Instead, opium is vaporized in specialized implements known as "opium pipes." Likewise, opium teas must be kept cool to avoid degrading the narcotic. Though opium teas can be found around the world, these are generally very dangerous because the levels of opium within the teas can vary widely and particularly strong batches can be deadly.

Opium has also entered our modern lexicon in another interesting way. The Greek term *mekonion* literally means "poppy juice" and refers to a thick, viscous, dark green latex from seed pods whose slits were not as well timed (or from other parts of the poppy plant).[7] The dark green color of *mekonion* contrasts with the yellow hue of the ideal material. Over time, the word *mekonion* has morphed into "meconium," which describes the thick, dark green material excreted from otherwise adorable newborn infants (which as all new parents are well-aware, also can trigger a different but equally powerful psychoactive response).[8]

References to opium-based elixirs can be found in ancient texts.[9] The Rig Veda scripture of the Hindu religion refers to a secret potion from the Soma plant, which is regarded by many to be a reference to opium. Likewise, allusions to opium-based elixirs proliferate all throughout the Middle

East and Mediterranean basin. Although popular in the eastern Roman Empire, the formula for these opium elixirs disappeared following the Ottoman sack of Constantinople in 1453 but was rediscovered by a fifteenth-century Swiss polymath with a mouthful of a name: Phillippus Aureolus Threophrastus Bombastus von Hohenheim.[10] Also known as Paracelsus, von Hohenheim was a physician who traveled throughout Europe and the Middle East seeking knowledge from as many different sources as he could find. In doing so, he helped found the science of toxicology, named a metallic element now known as zinc, and was the first to propose the concept of unconscious thought.[11] As a friend of Johann Wolfgang von Goethe, von Hohenheim is believed to be the inspiration for the fictional character of Dr. Faustus, who was willing to sell his soul to the devil in exchange for gaining unlimited knowledge.[12] According to contemporaries, von Hohenheim's knowledge apparently increased proportional to an already over-inflated ego and outspokenness. One of his middle names is mistakenly attributed as the original source of the word, "bombastic," but that attribution is itself a bit inflated.

Von Hohenheim was traveling in Constantinople in 1522 when he stumbled upon a formula to make an opium-based elixir that he called "laudanum" from the Greek word meaning "to praise," suggesting that he was quite a fan.[13] He described the psychoactive properties of laudanum, including its ability to cause euphoria, promote sedation, and halt the sensation of pain (and one wonders if or how laudanum also played a role in his revelation of the subconscious brain). With the rediscovery of the opium elixir in hand, Paracelsus returned to Europe, where the recipe quickly became popular among physicians and recreational users across Europe and North America. Beyond the ability to ease pain, laudanum-based patent medicines gained popularity for their abilities to halt coughing and induce constipation, both useful for the treatment of periodic outbreaks of cholera and dysentery. Unfortunately, these therapeutic benefits of laudanum were often offset by the addicting properties, which sustained sales but, otherwise, were bad for public health.

A Real Trade War

In the twelfth century, the writings of Marco Polo paved the way for European trade with Central and East Asia.[14] Catalyzed in part by interactions with invading Mongol armies, interactions between Europe and East Asia increased each generation, creating trade imbalances that favored the Chinese. Europe remained relatively poor, which limited the outflow of resources, but all this changed with Columbus' discovery of the New World, or, more specifically, South American silver. Over the next three centuries, the imbalance continued, with silver essentially migrating from South America through Europe and then on to Asia to pay for lopsided trade.[15] The Europeans became increasingly desperate to identify ways to balance trade more in their favor

By the eighteenth century, the British were particularly concerned about the Chinese trade imbalance, largely because of their adoption of tea as a national pastime, and thus were particularly motivated to implement a plan. By this time, the Empire included modern-day South Asia (India, Pakistan, and Afghanistan). *Papaver somniferum* grew well in many parts of this region and opium was a favorite of Chinese peasants, though the land in the population-dense coastal regions of the Forbidden Kingdom was not ideal for growing the poppy. The British East India Company saw their opportunity and began shipping opium to China.[16] As of 1686, the Qing Dynasty had limited international trade to the southern port of Canton (now Guangzhou).[17] The British merchants traded with their Chinese counterparts in Canton, who, in turn, distributed the product to the masses. By the 1830s, the highly addicting opium had rebalanced trade with China and, unsurprisingly, the Chinese government became increasingly alarmed at both the economic and societal concerns associated with illicit drugs.

In 1838, the emperor of the Qing Dynasty appointed Lin Zexu, a highly respected and ethical scholar, to develop an approach to address the rampant drug problem.[18] Lin enacted a plan to clear Canton of opium, its dealers, and all drug paraphernalia. Within months, Lin had arrested more than 1,700 dealers, confiscated more than two and half million pounds of opium, and destroyed more than 70,000 opium pipes. In parallel, he appealed directly to Queen Victoria with an open letter to request help in ending the opium trade based on moral grounds:

> We find that your country is sixty or seventy thousand li [a li is roughly a half kilometer] from China. Yet there are barbarian ships that strive to come here for trade for the purpose of making a great profit. The wealth of China is used to profit the barbarians. That is to say, the great profit made by barbarians is all taken from the rightful share of China. By what right do they then in return use the poisonous drug to injure the Chinese people? Even though the barbarians may not necessarily intend to do us harm, yet in coveting profit to an extreme, they have no regard for injuring others. Let us ask, where is your conscience?[19]

In addition to the confiscation and destruction of British property (including some chests of opium still on the decks of British ships in Canton harbor), the Chinese closed the sea route to Canton to prevent additional shipments of opium into the trading port.[20]

From the British perspective, this action not only destroyed British property (and wealth) but also trapped British traders as hostages in the city and led the Royal Navy to blockade the port of Canton. Amid an incident in which a British merchant ship (not carrying opium) attempted to run the blockade, a skirmish broke out between Chinese and British naval vessels.[21] This precipitated a lopsided war in 1839, in which British technology outgunned their Chinese counterparts on land and sea. The British occupied Canton, Shanghai, and other coastal cities. This First Opium War was followed almost two decades later by a second war, which again resulted in a humiliating Chinese defeat. The defeat of the millennia-old Chinese civilizations in the Opium Wars left a legacy of western imperialism in China that arguably still fixates contemporary governmental policy at a time when trade imbalances once again favor China.

From Morphine to Merck

Going back as far as six millennia, the poppy has been the source of a pain-relieving substance. A frequent problem historically involved the quality and quantity of material needed for the desired effect. As discussed, the most potent forms of opium were obtained by labor-intensive means, by making narrow slits in immature poppy pods. The quality of the meconium varies based on its age, where it grows, as well as who and how the opium is harvested, and these many variables negatively impact quality and reproducibility. The inevitable inconsistencies caused rather than ameliorated headaches for early pharmacists (apothecaries), at whom the ire of frustrated doctors and patients was frequently directed.

In 1804, Friedrich Serturner was a twenty-one-year-old apprentice for a local apothecary in the Prussian city of Schloss Neuhaus (now Paderborn).[22] The apothecary of that era was a cross between a modern pharmacist and a shaman, tasked with mixing herbal and chemical ingredients into concoctions with presumed medicinal powers. Though he lacked a formal education, Serturner was a product of the Enlightenment and sought, during his off-hours, to isolate the substance in opium that was responsible for its analgesic effects. To do so, he dissolved raw opium in various solvents and found that by first dissolving opium in acid and then neutralizing the concoction with ammonia, an insoluble substance could be isolated.[23] This substance reproduced the sedative and pain-relieving properties of opium and, more important, the purified material could be dispensed in a way that overcame the batch-to-batch variations that created headaches for apothecaries preparing opium.

Excited by his finding, Serturner sought to publish his work but was rebuffed. In a fit of anger, he gave up on his project until a toothache caused him to reconsider.[24] Having cured the pain with his new substance, which he named morphine in honor of Morpheus, the Greek god of dreams, Serturner continued to test morphine on local children (a fact most historians would prefer to forget) and ultimately decided to sell morphine from his own pharmacy, which he had started in Hamelin (home to the legendary Pied Piper). A few years later, Sertuner convinced an ambitious fellow apothecary, Heinrich Emmanuel Merck, of the advantages of purified morphine over inconsistent batches of opium.[25]

Heinrich Emmanuel Merck was a 6th-generation purveyor of an apothecary shop in Darmstadt, the capital of the independent country of Hesse.[26] A distant great uncle of Heinrich's had bought the Engel-Apotheke (Angel Pharmacy) in 1668 and passed this to his nephew upon his death. After a series of father-to-son transitions, the apothecary ended up in Heinrich's hands in 1816. Up to this time, the Engel-Apotheke, like virtually all the others, had a single pharmacist, and Heinrich was determined to make some changes. First, he changed the name of the business to E. Merck, and then in 1827, he sought to transition from the conventional one-person approach to an industrial-scale pharmaceutical supplier. Rather than using a mortar and pestle to make small batches one at a time, his goal was to scale up production and then sell his higher quality materials to other pharmacists. Upon his death, he was employing dozens of chemists and apothecaries.

Merck's goal was to focus his business around a set of chemicals known as plant alkaloids. This decision was based on his knowledge that the alkaloids were the components of plants responsible for the efficacy of many traditional herbal remedies.[27] He, therefore, made it his business to identify useful alkaloids and, in doing so, purchased the process for making morphine from Serturner. Thereafter, Merck combined business strategy with an inherent sense of understanding medicinal products to create the world's first continuously run pharmaceutical company.

Although an iconoclast in many ways, Heinrich did adhere to the tradition of passing down the business to his sons. The sons, in turn, shared their father's drive to expand the business and did so throughout the world. In 1889, E. Merck published an index of chemicals that served as the definitive chemical resource for scientists and professionals for generations.[28] The

Index was followed ten years later by the Merck *Manual of Diagnosis and Therapy* for physicians. *The Merck Index* and *Merck Manual* also provided extraordinarily successful advertising tools, with the latter quickly labeled as the "Physicians' Bible."

In 1891, Georg Merck emigrated from Darmstadt to New York City and founded an American branch of E. Merck (known as Merck & Co.). Beyond its role as a pharmaceutical manufacturer and distributor, Georg Merck turned Merck & Co. into a posh place to be seen. Their Manhattan store sold drugs, candy, and various knick-knacks in a way that was both innovative and scandalous relative to the times.

Business thrived for Merck & Co. until the United States joined the First World War. Federal Judge A. Mitchell Palmer had been an outspoken critic of foreign influence on America and was tasked by President Wilson with seizing companies owned the German government or German nationals.[29] By the end of the Great War, Palmer was managing more than 30,000 trusts with assets exceeding a half billion U.S. dollars while another 9,000 trusts worth a third of a billion dollars awaited evaluation. The trusts under Palmer's control included German-owned Merck & Co. By then Georg's son, George, had taken the helm at Merck & Co. and George maintained that American Mercks, like himself and his father, would still run the business. Palmer ultimately disagreed and sold the German-held Merck stock at auction to repay the post-war German war debts.

Consequently, the irreparable break that occurred has created confusion ever since. There exist two distinct Merck pharmaceutical companies, one in Europe and the other in the United States. Merck Serono (known as EMD Serono in North America) is the parent company, founded in 1668 and still headquartered in Darmstadt, Germany. As a direct result of the split managed by Palmer upon the American entry into the First World War, the American Merck & Co., headquartered in White Station, New Jersey, is a distinct company, and has eclipsed its European predecessor in terms of sales and market capitalization. From here forward, we will refer to "Merck" as the New Jersey-based company, Merck & Co., unless otherwise stated.

We will return to George Merck's amazing career momentarily, but will end this section with a brief postscript about Judge Palmer. After the war, A. Mitchell Palmer became Attorney General under President Wilson, where his suspicions of foreign intrigue continued. Moving on from Germans, he became particularly concerned with perceived threats from foreign anarchists and communists.[30] A failed assassination attempt involving a package bomb mailed to his house was interpreted by Palmer as much as a personal affront as a political one, and he launched a series of high-profile and controversial "Palmer raids" to arrest and/or deport potential plotters.[31] To lead these operations, he created a new division of the Justice Department, the Bureau of Investigation, and hired a twenty-four-year old J. Edgar Hoover from his Enemy Alien Bureau to lead this nascent organization, thus giving roots to the modern FBI.[32]

The creation of Merck and the commercialization of morphine convey an example of the first pharmaceutical company and product that still exists. While morphine remains an important component of the pharmacopeia, the greatest killer over time has consistently been infectious diseases, and this provided an early target for the pharmaceutical industry in its formative years.

"The Admirable M&B"

In the days following the tragedy of the Elixir Sulfanilamide, the need for a means to combat bacterial infections outstripped this tragic setback. Indeed, one of the first drugs approved by the FDA following the passage of the 1938 Food, Drug, and Cosmetic Act was sulfapyridine (trade name Dagenan), for which FDA approval was granted in the United States to Eli Lilly and Co. in early 1939.

Sulfapyridine was discovered by Lionel Whitby, a British veteran of the Great War, who participated in some of the most dangerous battles of the Great War, surviving the Serbian Campaign and Gallipoli, as well as the Macedonian and Western fronts.[33] He was serving as a captain of the Machine Gun Corps at the bloody Battle of Passchendaele, earning a Military Cross for gallantry, when his luck ran out. Whitby's unit was targeted by intensive artillery fire and his leg was utterly shattered and had to be amputated. Inspired by his wound, he earned his medical degree and become a world-renowned clinical pathologist and surgeon at Middlesex Hospital in London. In his rare spare time, Whitby was a passionate researcher and, in 1937, discovered a new class of sulphonamides (also known as sulfa drugs), including sulfapyridine, and worked with the British pharmaceutical company, May & Baker, to expedite its use in the clinic.

The new drug, widely known as M&B (named after its supplier, May & Baker) was highly successful, and this is where the character of British Prime Minister Winston Churchill enters our story. Churchill was a prototypical workaholic, and though sixty-nine years old, he undertook an arduous journey in 1943 through the Middle East, including the Tehran

Conference. Having run himself into the ground, Churchill acquired a raging case of bacterial pneumonia that nearly ended his life.[34] He reluctantly submitted to a forced convalescence in Carthage, Tunisia. Although inaccurate rumors attributed his recovery to penicillin, Churchill himself verifies it was M&B in his 1943 Christmas radio broadcast: "This admirable M&B from which I did not suffer any inconvenience, was used at the earliest moment and, after a week's fever, the intruders were repulsed."[35] As always, Churchill was full of wit and charm and thereafter referred to his doctors, Lord Moran and Dr. Bedford, by their initials, M&B. While M&B was gaining extraordinary free advertising in the United Kingdom, it was distributed in the United States via a license with Eli Lilly and Company.

Sulfa drugs were the first shot in the war against bacterial infections but their firepower was quite limited. While the efficacy of sulfa drugs was an improvement upon dye-based drugs, the safety margins needed were not high enough and side effects were common. Many people became allergic to the dugs and if dosed improperly, brain damage was a prominent side effect. A much better solution was needed and found in the form of penicillin.

A Wonder Drug

The discovery of penicillin seems to have aggregated its own mythology, much of which is inaccurate. One mistaken belief, as just mentioned, is that a timely injection saved Winston Churchill's life in a critical period of the Second World War. This inaccuracy is eclipsed by one of the most re-told stories in all of science, the serendipitous story of its discovery. In the words of Alexander Fleming himself: "When I woke up just after dawn on September 3, 1928, I certainly didn't plan to revolutionise [*sic*] all medicine by discovering the world's first antibiotic, or bacteria killer. But I suppose that was exactly what I did."[36]

Alexander Fleming, a Scottish bacteriologist working at St. Mary's Hospital in Paddington, London, had spent much of his summer growing Staphylococcal bacteria (the source of Staph infections) for scientific experiments. Normally, these cultures are grown in sanitary conditions (to keep other contaminating organisms from growing on the plates). Fleming was not known for his neatness and he must have really needed a vacation, as he left a stack of plates sitting in a sink while he went on an extended holiday in August 1928.[37] Normally, in that time, the bacteria would have completely filled the plate. Returning to the lab on 3 September, he was intrigued by one particular plate, where there was a cleared area devoid of bacteria, which caused him to say quite simply, "That's funny." Upon closer inspection, Fleming noticed a small bit of blue-green mold growing in the middle of this cleared area and realized the fungus must have produced a substance that was deadly to bacteria. He then grew a sample of the mold and found that the "mould juice," as described by Fleming, reproduced the ability to kill bacteria. As a bacteriologist rather than chemist, Fleming was not able to identify the particular substance responsible for the anti-bacterial effect from his mold, which he named *Penicillium notatum* (meaning "notable *Penicillium*," the type of mold Fleming had identified).

This makes for a great story but isn't quite fair to the memories of those upon whose shoulders Fleming was standing. Going back millennia, an-cient cultures, from Egypt to India, had used mold as a means to produce antibiotic substances to treat infection.[38] For example, in ancient Egypt, an-cient papyri indicate that moldy bread was crumbled onto open wounds to accelerate their healing.[39] The tradition was extended by mixing wet bread (a known delicacy for mold) with spiderwebs (which contained mold spores) to create a substance for treating wounds.[40] Within St. Mary's Hos-pital itself (Fleming's place of employment in 1928), Sir John Scott Burdon-Sanderson had demonstrated more than fifty years before, in 1870, that certain molds could prevent the growth of bacterial cultures.[41] (This also leads one to the obvious question of why no one had fired the cleaning staff of St. Mary's Hospital in the intervening half century.)

Following upon Burdon-Sanderson's findings, Joseph Lister, the father of antiseptics, described a fungus in 1871, which he called *Penicillium glaucum*, which produced a substance he called "Penicillium" that was successfully used to treat an otherwise incurable wound from a patient at King's College Hospital in Lambeth, London.[42] Likewise, Louis Pasteur found a *Penicillium* mold in 1877, which was able to inhibit *Bacillus anthracis* (the deadly cause of anthrax). Other overlooked researchers with similar findings include Vin-cenzo Tiberio, a University of Naples physician who discovered a mold in a water well that killed bacteria in 1895, and Ernest Duchesne, a physician at l'Ecole du Service de Sante Militaire de Lyon, who published an 1897 doc-toral dissertation on the identification of a mold that cured guinea pigs of typhoid.[43] These are just a few of the many stories of investigators, whose work preceded Fleming's. While Fleming's quote was likely not intended as a slight against his predecessors, it is important that the record demonstrate their many contributions and to remind us that great discoveries are almost invariably the result of collaborations among many generations of investiga-tors, most of whom are destined to be forgotten by history.

Fleming himself did not identify the substance responsible for the antibacterial actions of the "mould juice." That discovery would occur a decade later and be led by Howard Walter Flory, an Australian pharmacologist working at Oxford University.[44] Ten years after the discovery of *Penicillium notatum*, Flory had been impressed by Fleming's papers and sought to identify the chemical source of anti-microbial action. The next year, Flory hired Ernst Boris Chain and a more junior team member, Norman Heatley, who isolated and characterized the substance responsible for the antibiotic activity.[45] Fleming, Flory, and Chain went on to share the 1945 Nobel Prize.

The more junior Heatley is a particularly attractive character, whose contributions have been largely overlooked. Heatley performed the majority of the actual labor and provided much of the technical expertise required to isolate, identify, characterize, and produce penicillin. Legend states he was working so hard that he reportedly put his underwear on backward one day out of exhaustion after a long experiment the night before.[46] Heatley was known to be good-natured and, sadly, his absence in receiving the Nobel Prize was not the only time he was overlooked for his contributions to the field. In 1941, Heatley worked with an investigator at the U.S. Department of Agriculture in Peoria, Illinois, to help devise a way to scale-up penicillin production. While the two worked closely to address this problem, his "collaborator" remained mum and later submitted both a paper and patent on the process, conveniently leaving out Heatley's contributions so he would not have to share the credit or patent royalties.[47] In an effort to help even the score, we will quote a 1998 remark from Henry Harris, an Oxford professor: "Without Fleming, no Chain or Florey; without Florey, no Heatley; without Heatley, no penicillin."[48]

Returning to our story, in the same year Fleming, Flory, and Chain shared the Nobel, Dorothy Crowfoot Hodgkin utilized X-ray crystallography to solve the structure of penicillin. This information was critical both for understanding how the medicine worked and to create next-generation versions of antibiotics that were more effective and easier to produce and to administer.[49] For example, the first penicillin had to be delivered intravenously, but Hodgkin's work allowed for later versions that could be orally administered. Hodgkin later won the 1964 Nobel Prize for her work on deciphering the structure of vitamin B12 and was only the second woman (behind Florence Nightingale) ever to receive the Order of Merit.[50]

In the midst of the Second World War, the need for penicillin increased in proportion to the number of battlefield wounds, and much effort was invested into scaling up production. In the beginning, cultures of *Penicillium notatum* were grown up in hospital bedpans.[51] An early improvement was achieved by feeding the fungi a nutrient mixture consisting of corn steep liquor, a byprod-uct of the cornstarch production process. By March 1942, Merck & Co. had produced enough material to treat one patient, and by June, there was enough only for ten patients.[52] Penicillin was so scarce that, upon learning that 80 percent of the original penicillin passed through the body, the urine of early patients was collected in an effort to re-use this material.[53]

Heatley again made a pivotal contribution. During his visit to Peoria in 1941, Heatley was walking through a street market and noticed a particularly over-ripe and moldy cantaloupe. On instinct, he purchased the melon, cul-tivated the mold, and found it was a particularly prolific strain, producing twenty times more penicillin than any other strain. This made the differ-ence and more than twenty billion units were produced in 1943. By war's end, more than 650 billion units were distributed each month. Whereas the costs of producing penicillin were prohibitive in 1941, the cost of penicillin by the end of the war "was scarcely more than the cost of material and labor to put it into an ampoule."[54]

The development of penicillin was a remarkable joint effort by an in-ternational consortium of private and public sector organizations, which, according to Charles Grossman, "included five American and four British universities as well as five British and ten American commercial firms, one British and four American government organizations and two British and two American research foundations."[55] From a commercial standpoint, the early-adopting agencies included Merck & Co., E. R. Squibb & Sons, Lederle Laboratories, and Charles E. Pfizer & Co. As such, these companies ulti-mately benefited by leading the sales and distribution for widespread civilian use of penicillin in the days following the end of the Second World War.

War, of course, is not defined by remedies such as penicillin, but by the agents of death. Entering the Second World War, the memories of the Gen-eral Staffs were occupied by recollections of the poison gases that caused such gruesome carnage in the First World War. On the American side, a full campaign was launched to understand these noxious chemicals, with the idea of developing ways to prevent or treat battlefield injuries.

What they found instead was a cure for cancer.

FDR's Other Secret

Sulfur mustards are a class of chemical agents named for their odor, which often smells like mustard, garlic, or horseradish. Although the initial discov-ery of so-called mustard compounds remains somewhat unclear, an early report from 1860 attributes it to British scientist Frederick Guthrie. Shortly after joining Edinburgh University in Scotland, Guthrie combined two chemicals, ethylene and sulfur dioxide, and noted the irritating taste of the newly-made substance (chemists often sampled the products of their labors): "Its smell is pungent and not unpleasant, resembling that of oil of mustard; its taste is astringent and similar to that of horse-radish. The small quantities of vapour, which it diffuses, attack the thin parts of the skin as between the fingers and around the eyes, destroying the epidermis."[56]

German chemist Alfred Niemann, who had just discovered cocaine in 1860, somehow still had the energy to confirm Guthrie's research on mustard compounds later that year.[57] Sporadic work with mustard compounds continued over the following fifty years, primarily focused around academic questions. In 1913, an English chemistry student, Hans Thacher Clarke, was working with the legendary chemist Emil Fischer in a University of Berlin laboratory, experimenting with a synthesis reaction to create a new mustard compound when the flask broke on Hans Clarke's leg.[58] The chemical burns were so bad that Clarke remained hospitalized for two months. Fischer's report on the accident to the German Chemical Society reportedly captured the attention of a few key individuals in the Kaiser's army, who contemplated the potential military use of such a weapon. Within the year, Germany was at war and the German Army deployed its first mustard gas weapon against British and Canadian trenches in the 1917 Third Battle of Ypres.

Mustard gas is a blistering agent and, as the name suggests, the immediate effects include widespread chemical burns, much as Hans Clarke experienced, on exposed tissues. In its gaseous form, the tissues exposed include the delicate surfaces of the lung, which literally dissolve almost immediately after exposure. The result is a ghastly death in which the victims drown in their own blood. Mustard gas is also an alkylating agent, which describes a process in which the chemical irreversibly binds to particular types of biological molecules, most notably DNA. The binding of mustard compounds to DNA can alter, or mutate, the genetic code via a process known as alkylation.[59] In autopsies of soldiers killed in gas attacks, Dr. Edward Krumbhaar, a Philadelphia physician recruited into the American Expeditionary Forces, worked with his wife, Helen, to demonstrate that fast-growing cells of the immune system are particularly sensitive to alkylating agents.[60] This led a few select scientists to wonder if these alkylating agents might have utility against cancer, in particular, leukemia or lymphoma.

After the gruesome experiences of the Great War, sixteen of the most powerful countries of the world signed the Protocol for the Prohibition of the Use in War of Asphyxiating, Poisonous, or other Gases, and of Bacteriological Methods of Warfare, also known as the Geneva Protocol of 1925.[61] The stigma assigned to chemical agents largely precluded much work on mustard gas, even for potential non-military uses. The advent of the Second World War changed perceptions as concerns grew that the Axis Powers might be prepared to use chemical weapons. Indeed, Mussolini's troops had used mustard gas during the 1935 invasion of Ethiopia, killing an estimated 150,000 while the Imperial Japanese Army killed countless Chinese soldiers and civilians with chemical weapons from 1937 onward.[62] Given their extensive chemical industry, the Germans were also known to have developed and stockpiled many nerve agents, including tabun, sarin, and soman.

In response to concerns about chemical warfare, the Allies developed and stockpiled chemical munitions and the U.S. Army developed a Chemical Warfare Corps, tasked with developing both offensive and defensive capabilities. In a 1937 announcement, President Franklin Roosevelt discussed the Chemical Warfare Corps:

> I am doing everything in my power to discourage the use of gases and other chemicals in any war between nations. While, unfortunately, the defensive necessities of the United States call for study of the use of chemicals in warfare, I do not want the Government of the United States to do anything to aggrandize or make permanent any special bureau of the Army or the Navy engaged in these studies. I hope the time will come when the Chemical Warfare Service can be entirely abolished.[63]

In 1940, Cornelius P. Rhoads, a pathologist with expertise in anemia and leukemia, was recruited from the Rockefeller Institute to lead Memorial Hospital in New York City.[64] After Pearl Harbor, Rhoads was drafted as a colonel and assigned as the Chief of Medicine in the Chemical Weapons Corps. Also in 1941, President Roosevelt signed an Executive Order to create the Office of Scientific Research and Development (OSRD), and recruited Vannevar Bush, the president of the Carnegie Institution, to act as chairman.[65] Bush was a well-known engineer and scientist who had acted as Roosevelt's unofficial science advisor up to this time. Under Bush, the OSRD developed a series of wartime R&D breakthroughs, including the proximity fuse, the nuclear bomb, and a project to study chemical warfare agents.

To assist the chemical warfare agents project, OSRD contracted with Yale University to follow up on Krumbhaar's reports that nitrogen mustards might have the ability to suppress lymphoid cells.[66] In particular, two Yale scientists, Alfred Gilman and Louis Goodman, worked in tandem and in great secrecy (given the continued sensitivity of any work with chemical weapon agents) to reproduce the effects of nitrogen mustards on the immune cells of mice.[67]

In early December 1942, Goodman and Gilman discussed the possibility of testing the drug in patients and approached Professor Gustav Lindskog, the Chair of Surgery at Yale.[68] One of Lindskog's patients, known only as J. D., was within hours of dying of a massive head and neck tumor. J. D. volunteered to become the first patient for this new treatment, which was simply known as "Substance X" due to the need for secrecy. Within a week, J. D. had not only survived but regained the ability to eat and then to move his head and arms. Within a month, the tumor could not be detected. Unfortunately, the disease was too far along and ultimately killed J. D. three months later. Although the results with J. D. and a small set of five additional patients were promising, it was a small sample and there was a great need to test the drug on a much larger population.

Through a strange coincidence, an unintended large-scale experiment was conducted in December 1943, when German bombers struck the Italian port of Bari on the Adriatic coast.[69] The Italian port served as a major disembarkation point for supplies to support the Allied invasion of Italy, which had commenced in September. By early October, the Italians overthrew Mussolini and capitulated. This was a significant blow to the Germans, depriving Hitler of thirty to forty Italian divisions. While this had the desired effect of decreasing overall Axis strength, reports began circulating in Washington and London that Hitler intended to use chemical weapons to compensate for these losses.[70]

In response to growing anxiety, particularly among his military leaders, Roosevelt took two actions. First, he publically declared a "no first-use" policy.[71] At the same time, the president ordered the shipment of 2,000 M47A1 mustard gas bombs to be shipped immediately to the Italian theater. These bombs were intended to be used as retaliation weapons were the Germans to initiate the use of chemical munitions.[72] A nondescript Liberty ship, the *John Harvey*, was loaded with the deadly cargo and set sail for the port of Bari. The mission was performed in complete secrecy and few outside the General Staff were aware of the deadly cargo in the *John Harvey*.

While the Germans were concerned about the loss of their Italian allies, there is no clear evidence they were prepared to deploy chemical weapons. Rather, Field Marshal Albert Kesselring was looking for more conventional ways of disrupting the British Eighth Army advance up the east coast of the Italian peninsula. The field marshal was particularly intrigued by an idea from the head of his air forces, Field Marshal Wolfram Freiherr von Richtofen.

Wolfram von Richtofen was the latest member of the Prussian military dynasty, and his generation of warriors included two even more famous cousins. Manfred von Richtofen, also known as the Red Baron, was credited with eighty kills before he himself was shot down and killed, and a second cousin, Lothar von Richtofen, was credited with forty kills in the Great War. Wolfram was himself an ace, credited with eight kills, and commanded the notorious Kondor Legion in support of General Franco during the Spanish Civil War.[73] In particular, Wolfram was responsible for the terror bombing of the Spanish town of Guernica, which inspired Picasso's famous painting. Von Richtofen also led Luftwaffe forces in virtually every theater and major battle of the war, including the Polish campaign, the invasion of Western Europe, the Battle of Britain, the Balkans Campaign, and many key battles at the Eastern Front.

The idea von Richtofen conveyed to Kesselring in December 1943 was a lightning raid on the Bari harbor as a means of disrupting the flow of Allied supplies.[74] In support of this idea, von Richtofen had instructed frequent reconnaissance flights over Bari and this intelligence revealed more ships entering the harbor each day than could be unloaded. He reasoned that the accumulation of merchant marine ships would not only provide a rich source of targets but, if enough could be damaged or sunk, the harbor might be rendered unusable until the wrecks were cleared. A high-altitude reconnaissance flight over Bari on 2 December by Lieutenant Werner Hahn revealed a backlog of dozens of Allied cargo ships waiting to be unloaded. The information was rushed to Kesselring, who conferred with von Richtofen and ordered an immediate strike. Most of the remaining German aircraft left in the theater were ordered into this desperate attack. While a loss of these forces would effectively cripple the German defense of the Italian peninsula, the opportunity to strike a decisive blow was deemed worth the risk.

Little known to Kesselring or von Richtofen, the air defenses of the British-controlled port were non-existent. Hubris led the RAF to convince themselves the Germans had already lost the air war in the Italian theater. There were no RAF squadrons to protect the port and ground defenses were inadequate. On the very day the attack was launched, Air Vice Marshal Coningham announced to the press, "I would consider it as a personal insult if the enemy should send so much as one plane over the city."[75] Within hours, just over 100 Luftwaffe Ju-88 medium bombers struck and destroyed twenty-eight ships, damaged a dozen more, and effectively shuttered the harbor for the next two months.[76] The attack was so thorough that it was called "Little Pearl Harbor."

One of the ships destroyed in the raid was the *John Harvey*. A spectacular explosion jettisoned its lethal contents into the air. An ensign on a nearby ship noted the smoke from the *John Harvey* and said, "I smell garlic." Experienced naval officers from the Great War recognized this as mustard gas, and as the signs of chemical weapons proliferated, suspicions grew that the Germans had used chemical weapons. The cargo of the *John Harvey* was still secret and Prime Minister Churchill was particularly adamant that an admission of the presence of mustard gas be expunged from all official British records (as Bari was under British control). The Bari incident remained classified until 1959.

Immediately after the attack, General Dwight Eisenhower sent an envoy, Lieutenant Colonel Stewart F. Alexander, to investigate the situation at Bari.[77] Alexander had spent a year working on mustard gases at the Edgewood Arsenal complex in Maryland, which was part of Cornelius Rhoads' Chemical Weapons Corp. After arriving in Bari, Alexander assisted in the treatment of survivors and oversaw the autopsies of 617 deaths, finding widespread destruction of white blood cells. These responses were noted by military doctors and conveyed to Cornelius Rhoads, chief of medicine for U.S. Army's Chemical Weapons Division. Given his background in leukemia research before and while at Memorial Hospital, Rhoads was particularly intrigued by the findings.

At war's end, Rhoads returned to Memorial Hospital, which had been expanded and endowed in 1945 by Alfred P. Sloan, the head of General Motors, and Charles F. Kettering, the founder of the Dayton Electric Company (later known as DELCO). Thereafter, Memorial Hospital was known as the Memorial Sloan Kettering Institute.[78] Inspired by the Bari incident and early data from Goodman and Gilman at Yale, Rhoads initiated an intensive program to evaluate the potential efficacy of nitrogen mustard compounds as cancer therapeutics. As the veil of secrecy over the Yale investigation lifted, Rhoads' insider information about Bari expedited FDA approval of the first mustard-based cancer chemotherapy, mechlorethamine (trade name Mustargen) in 1949.[79] The new miracle drug was marketed for the treatment of lymphoma and leukemia by Merck & Co. and heralded a virtual explosion of chemotherapy research and drug development that continues to this day.

The concept of industry working with academic (including government) laboratories was not unique to cancer drugs or even Merck, but had its roots in a modest Indianapolis-based company that would grow to become the leading innovator for decades to come.

Enter the Colonel

Eli Lilly was born in Baltimore and raised in Kentucky and Indiana, where he was fascinated by science and medicine.[80] Eli served as an apprentice chemist and pharmacist at the Good Samaritan Drug Store in Lafayette, Indiana, and learned basic business skills before enrolling in the Indiana Asbury University (now DePauw University) to study pharmaceutical sciences. Shortly after opening his own drug store in Greencastle, Indiana, Lilly enlisted in the Union Army. As a fervent opponent of slavery, Lilly underwrote the costs of a series of recruitment posters and enlisted his friends and colleagues into the 150-man, Eighteenth Battery of the Indiana Light Artillery, also known as the Lilly Battery. Unsurprisingly, Lilly was elected to serve as its commanding officer (though his military experience was minimal, he had, after all, paid for the recruiting posters), and the unit saw action in many battles, including the bloody Battle of Chickamauga. Late in the war, the now-Colonel Lilly was captured by the infamous Nathan Bedford Forrest (who was responsible for the Fort Pillow Massacre and was an early leader of the Ku Klux Klan). After his release, Lilly elected to remain in the South for a time, where he managed a cotton plantation before ultimately returning home to Indianapolis in 1877.

Back home again in Indiana, the Colonel (a nickname that would follow him to his death) had a vision of creating a wholesale manufacturing facility (much like Merck had done in Germany). Unlike the dubious patent medicines of the time, Lilly was determined to sell "ethical medicines" that disclosed the composition of each product.[81] He also was responsible for the concept of gelatin-coating (which, as you may recall, enabled Harvey Washington Wiley to ensure that his Poison Squads received their full dose of toxin each day).

Despite the emphasis on ethical medicines, Eli Lilly and Co. did not adopt the research-based approach for which it would become known until the passing of the Colonel and the appointment of his son Josiah as company president. Josiah ushered in an era of science, building a state-of-the art research campus near the old family home in Greenfield, Indiana, and embracing automation. Beyond science, Josiah also expanded the impact and geographical reach of the company by improving manufacturing efficiency to the point it was considered "the most sophisticated production system in the American pharmaceutical industry."[82] By the time of the American entry into the First World War, the company was producing more than two and a half million capsules a day. Lilly also adopted an aggressive approach of licensing products from other companies, including the aforementioned license from May & Baker in the late 1930s for sulfapyridine.

Embracing the relatively new approach of developing science-based medicines, one of Eli Lilly and Co.'s earliest recruits was George Henry Alexander Clowes.[83] Clowes was born in Ipswich, England, where he became interested in the family business of brewing beer. After receiving a Ph.D. in chemistry from the University of Gottingen in 1899, Clowes worked with Paul Ehrlich (Mechnikoff, Buchner, and Ehrlich, later Hoechst) before migrating to the United States. Although his primary interest was in cancer, Clowes gained experience and notoriety in many different areas, including service in the U.S. Chemical Warfare Service in the waning days of the First World War. After the war, Clowes was recruited to join Eli Lilly and quickly moved up the ranks to become Director of Research in 1921, a year that was going to prove critical for Clowes, Eli Lilly and Co., as well as the entire budding pharmaceutical industry.

Islands of Life

To understand the importance of the events of 1921, it is necessary to briefly look back a half century to a Berlin classroom. In 1868, Paul Langerhans was a twenty-one-year-old student studying medicine at the Humboldt University of Berlin.[84] One day in class, while peering through a microscopic at a small piece of pancreas, he noticed little islands of a distinct type of clear tissue that were scattered throughout the pancreas. The young Langerhans asked his instructor about its identity and function, but was informed that no one had actually bothered to notice, or at least to catalog, these structures before. Langerhans wrote up his findings in a scientific manuscript and the structures were thereafter known as the "islets of Langerhans" thereby memorializing the young student who discovered them.[85]

The islets of Langerhans cells were not the only unknown feature of the pancreas, as the six-inch-long, comma-shaped organ nestled behind the stomach was a mystery in the late nineteenth century. Based on its location, it was assumed to play a role in digestion, and in 1889, two professors at the University of Strasbourg, Oskar Minkowski and Joseph von Mering, conducted a study in which the pancreas was removed from a dog.[86] Two unexpected outcomes were reported in the seminal manuscript.[87] First, the dog survived but began to urinate frequently despite the fact it had been house-trained prior to surgery. Second, the urine attracted flies, which were drawn in swarms to the puddles. Minkowski and von Mering realized that both properties (frequent urination and sugar in the urine) were symptoms of diabetes mellitus, a disease described as far back as ancient Egypt.[88] While the causes of diabetes were a total mystery before their study, von Mering and Minkowski concluded the pancreas must produce some unknown substance responsible for preventing diabetes.[89]

Thirty years later, the Canadian physician Frederick Banting was unsuccessfully managing a struggling clinical practice. To make ends meet, Banting agreed to teach a few lectures at the University of Western Ontario in 1920.[90] One lecture focused on the pancreas, and Banting scrambled to learn more about the mysterious organ. In doing so, he read Minkowski and von Bering's experiences with the diabetic dog and became intrigued about the subject. Another interesting paper, from Eugene Lindsay Opie, a distinguished chair of pathology at the Washington University School of Medicine in St. Louis, postulated that the isles of Langerhans might be the source of the substance that blocked diabetes.[91] Likewise, Edward Sharpey-Schafer, a professor from the University of Edinburgh, conjectured a similar idea, naming the mystery substance "insulin" after the Latin term for island, *insula*, to honor Langerhan's identification of these islets.[92]

While the substance had a function and a name, its identity remained unknown. We now know this is because insulin is rapidly degraded by trypsin, an enzyme that chews up proteins and is also secreted by the pancreas. Trypsin has myriad uses, including as a meat tenderizer, and is used in everything from baking goods to beer.[93]

During Banting's preparation for his lectures on the pancreas, he also came across a newly published paper from Moses Barron, a professor at the University of Minnesota, who showed that sewing up the pancreatic duct killed those parts of the pancreas that produce trypsin.[94] This finding set Banting to thinking that Barron's procedure might allow him to harvest the unknown insulin. Lacking his own laboratory, Banting approached John James Rickard Macleod, a Scottish physiologist working for a spell at the University of Toronto.[95] Macleod had a long-standing interest in diabetes but was preparing to summer in his native Scotland. Nonetheless, he generously offered Banting some lab space, as well as the use of a student, Charles Herbert Best, to explore the new means of isolated insulin.[96] The choice of Best was one of those amazing times when luck intervenes, as Macleod had two students and a coin toss determined who would work with Banting.

Over the summer of 1921, Banting and Best used Barron's procedure to isolate a substance from one dog that lowered blood sugar when injected into a diabetic dog.[97] The duo anticipated Macleod's return at the end of the summer but as a more experienced and objective observer, Macleod was cautious of the team's success and wanted to see additional studies.[98] Banting was quite proud and paranoid, and became deeply affronted at Macleod's measured response. The perceived insult precipitated a fierce argument that was resolved when Macleod agreed to pay Banting and Best, who had been volunteering their time, to continue their studies.[99] The tension spilled over again and again as Macleod, the more senior and a better speaker, was invited to present on the team's findings rather than Banting. To ease such tensions, the overly generous Macleod declined serving as an author on the landmark publication, which appeared in early 1922.[100]

To extend their findings from dogs to people, it was necessary to produce larger amounts of insulin. A young biochemistry lecturer from the University of Alberta, James Collip, was on a sabbatical leave with Macleod, who by now was focusing all his efforts on the insulin projects.[101] Collip was uneasy about all the tension in the laboratory but agreed in December 1921 to help Banting and Best isolate insulin from fetal calf pancreas.[102] Banting and Best were dedicated researchers but lacked Collip's biochemistry skills and were too proud to admit their insulin was of insufficient quality to initiate human testing. The pair instead administered the crude insulin preparation to Leonard Thompson, a fourteen-year-old severe Type 1 diabetic patient, who had only weeks to live. Because the insulin was of such poor quality, Thompson suffered a severe allergic reaction.[103]

Immediately after this setback, Collip spent almost two weeks of continuous work in a Herculean effort to improve the isolation and purification of insulin.[104] Still hanging on, the young Leonard Thompson was given a second dose, which dramatically reversed the symptoms of diabetes and eliminated sugar in his urine. At this time in history, sick children with Type 1 diabetes were kept in large wards with dozens of patients in a single room. As the disease progressed, the children developed diabetic ketoacidosis, entered a coma, and, invariably, died. In an extraordinary moment of science, Banting, Best, and Collip went from patient to patient, injecting insulin. An amazing story is told that before they had dosed the last child, the earlier patients had begun to awake from their comas and the crying of exuberant parents rang throughout the ward.[105]

Despite these successes, simmering tensions destroyed the team. In frustration with Banting, Collip left in early 1922, and Banting become increasingly uneasy with the fact that the more senior Macleod was in charge of producing insulin and organizing the large-scale clinical trials.[106] Banting felt that he alone was responsible for the success of insulin and to again ease the tension, Macleod elected to move to a new research topic in 1923. In this same year, Banting and Macleod shared the Nobel Prize. In recognition of the team's contributions, Banting shared half his prize money with Best and Macleod shared half of his money with Collip.[107] Over time, it was determined that Best was inappropriately excluded from the prize and the Nobel committee officially conceded this mistake in 1972, a few years before Best's death in 1978.[108]

Banting and Best, still resentful, began spreading stories that Macleod not only was unhelpful in the discovery of insulin but was actively disruptive to the research and "had made no contribution other than to leave the keys to the laboratory when he went on vacation."[109] The mudslinging continued for years, but in the long run, the true story of the discovery of insulin finally emerged and demonstrated the considerable contributions by Macleod and Collip. Furthermore, it is now Banting and Best that appear to have been given too much credit, as they had not acknowledged the work of Nicolae Paulescu, a Romanian physiologist who had published about the purification of insulin fully a year before Banting and Best.[110]

Regardless of these childish spats, the discovery of insulin had extraordinary implications for the treatment of diabetes. The final part of this story occurred shortly after publication of the pivotal Banting and Best manuscript. George Henry Alexander Clowes, the head of research at Eli Lilly and Co., approached the Toronto team with an offer to assist with the purification and to scale-up production of insulin, vital steps needed for widespread use of this potential wonder drug. Within months, Eli Lilly's chief chemist, George Walden, utilized cutting edge approaches to optimize a manufacturing process that improved the stability and purity of insulin by ten- to 100-fold.[111] As a consequence, Eli Lilly and Co. began sales of Iletin (a name that is yet another tribute to the islets of Langerhans) in 1923. While the British/Canadian government did not grant Eli Lilly and Co. exclusive rights to their patent, the improved processes gave Eli Lilly and Co. a clear competitive advantage over their rivals. As we will see in a future chapter, Eli Lilly and Co. continued to emphasize cutting edge technology, particularly around the insulin franchise, and a half century later were the first company to market recombinant human insulin via a partnership with a small upstart biotechnology company from South San Francisco named Genentech.

A theme that runs throughout these different stories is the active and varied role of the government and academia as partners for the emerging pharmaceutical industry. We will continue this theme of detailing the rapid evolution of the pharmaceutical industry but will note throughout the intimate and varied roles played by academia and the federal government in drug discovery and how these roles have changed over time.

CHAPTER FOUR

Triumph and Tragedy

In the first two chapters, we demonstrated the need to regulate medicines and the creation of the Food and Drug Administration (FDA). We then witnessed the birth and maturation of the modern pharmaceutical industry in chapter 3. In this chapter, we will build upon this framework to convey an intersection between regulation and industry growth, with emphasis on two crises, the HIV/AIDS pandemic of the 1980s and the Vioxx tragedy of the early 2000s. Both events triggered changes in legislation that improved access to medicine and the efficiency and impact of the FDA. As we will see in future chapters, some of these changes unintentionally led many pharmaceutical companies and investors ultimately to change or abandon altogether investments in new drug discovery and development.

Industry Innovation

Paralleling the growth of the high-tech sector, the pharmaceutical industry has witnessed extraordinary change, particularly over the past half century. Since many of these changes are highly technical in nature and not readily discernible to the public, they have gone relatively unnoticed, but a few are worth mentioning. One of the most impactful changes has been the rise of high throughput screening. Historically, experiments were performed using test tubes roughly the size of a finger or plates approximately the size of an adult hand. Such studies required relatively large amounts of material and were cumbersome, expensive, and slow. Studies conducted at this scale were prone to mistakes and not amenable to being performed in duplicate, triplicate, or more, since this would double or triple the amount of time and money required. Thus, from a practical as well as statistical standpoint, it was not always feasible to repeat studies or interrogate large number of samples.

    The name Gyula Takatsy is almost unknown today, even to most within the research community.[1] Yet the impact of this physician–scientist ranks among the highest of any individual who ever contributed to biomedical research. Takatsy was a tinkerer and inventor, and these skills were pressed into use during a devastating 1951 influenza outbreak in his native Hungary. The epidemic overwhelmed his hospital's equipment as hundreds or thousands of samples flooded into the laboratory each day. These pressures led Takatsy to develop what are now known as microwell plates, which divided a single plate into a vessel that could evaluate multiple samples at once.[2] This technology was later married to advances in robotics, and the combination revolutionized the screening of medical samples. In the same amount of time once needed to prepare one experiment, hundreds or even thousands of samples can now be evaluated. The increase in scale was accompanied by a decreased cost per sample. The use of robots increased the exactness of delivering small volumes and introduced a concept known as "robustness." Robustness, in the pharmaceutical industry sense, is a word that describes objective (statistically-defined) means to ensure that a study performed one day can be accurately reproduced days, weeks, or years later. Computerized data analysis has also improved the quality of interpreting the results of large studies.

Imagine the dismay of a scientist from days gone by were we to challenge her to carry out a complex study of 5,000 samples using test tubes or individual plates. Once the experiment was physically set up, which itself would require a Herculean effort, we would then ask our exhausted technician to analyze the results and report back to us as to the best five candidates. Not only would the enormity of the data be overwhelming, but our young scientist would also have to identify and eliminate spurious findings caused by variability, as measured by mathematical models of robustness. With the advent of robotic high-throughput screening and data analysis algorithms, what might have been a month-long campaign in the 1960s can now be performed in an afternoon.

A comparable set of advances allowed the field of chemistry to blossom. Whereas a research chemist from the 1950s could create a few new compounds per year, today's counterparts might synthesize several thousands within weeks. These exponential increases are the result of a process known as combinatorial chemistry.[3] Along with the advent of computational chemistry, some studies can interrogate trillions of compounds using only a computer.[4] Computational chemistry allows scientists to infer information about the shape and structure of complex proteins and other biological molecules to design drugs. Even once-esoteric concepts such as quantum physics now play a pivotal role in helping modern structural biologists and chemists predict and test new drug candidates.

To demonstrate the real-world deployment of these technologies, we turn to a fundamental challenge to modern medicine that first came to the public's eye in the 1980s. The HIV/AIDS pandemic fundamentally threatened public health, and as we shall see, while we won the first round of the fight, we may have lulled ourselves into a premature notion of triumph as new waves of disease threaten to re-emerge in even more devastating forms.

The New and Surprisingly Old History of HIV

The response to the HIV/AIDS pandemic conveyed both the strengths and deficiencies of the public–private sector partnership. The strengths included a remarkable implementation of scientific expertise that, once mobilized, identified the virus and then discovered new medicines to combat the disease. In our research of FDA-approved medicines, we recapitulated the timeline of HIV/AIDS drug discovery.[5] The first medicine to combat HIV/AIDS was approved six years after the first cases were reported, four years after the virus was isolated, and eighteen months after starting clinical trials. This remarkable achievement resulted from focused and intense deployment of federal resources combined with an incentivized private sector, and sprinkled with a bit of luck. The scientific, medical, and regulatory communities joined forces in a way that was unprecedented and expedited the introduction of multiple medicines to combat the lethal plague. The results saved the lives of millions and transformed what had been widely considered a death sentence into a manageable chronic condition.

Hijacking the title of a book highly critical of the federal response in the early years of the pandemic, the band continues to play on as a focused attack on HIV/AIDS has given way to a false sense of complacency. Thus, we conclude our story on HIV with a back-to-the-future scenario where, like the movie, we soon find ourselves back in a situation reminiscent of the 1980s, where we are comparatively unprepared for the emergence of drug-resistant HIV.

Based on extraordinary detective work, a team of scientists from the universities of Oxford and Leuven recently analyzed viral samples from people and apes in Africa to recapitulate a history of HIV in humans.[6] HIV has coexisted within people for much longer than has been generally appreciated by the general public, who first became aware of the virus in the early to mid-1980s. This information can help us understand how the crisis surreptitiously crept its way across the planet and then suddenly burst forward as a profound challenge to the world's public health, research, development, and regulatory infrastructures.

At some point in the first decade of the twentieth century, a virus jumped from monkeys or apes to people.[7] This infectious agent was not just any virus but an exotic type known as a retrovirus. Retroviruses were unknow-ingly first described by two Danish scientists, Villhelm Ellermann and Oluf Bang, in 1908, when they identified an infectious agent that caused a type of leukemia in chickens.[8] Three years later, Peyton Rous, a scientist at Rockefel-ler University, identified the same activity and the virus became known as the Rous sarcoma virus.[9] These tumor-associated viruses displayed the unusual property of having RNA, not DNA, as their genetic material. Even more strangely, these retroviruses used a novel enzyme to turn RNA into DNA and then back again.[10] The word retrovirus reflects the fact that, whereas the con-ventional idea had been that DNA is necessary for the production of RNA, retroviruses worked backward, using RNA to create DNA. This finding is more than esoteric and would become the linchpin that prolonged or saved the lives of millions throughout the world.

At first glance, the fact that retroviruses like HIV depend upon reverse transcriptase to replicate their genetic material seems a terribly bad strategy. Reverse transcriptase is quite sloppy, making a mistake, or mutation, about once for every 30,000 times it does its job.[11] While you or I might think that such a mistake rate sounds comparatively good, an infected patient may pro-duce ten billion virus progeny every day. That means that the virus is con-stantly evolving at an extraordinarily fast rate. That would seem to be good news, since most of these mutations create "dead" viruses. The high muta-tion rate also means that HIV is particularly well suited to adapt to new con-ditions. Sometimes, all it takes is a single mutation to allow a particular virus particle to survive in an otherwise hostile environment. As it turns out, the mutation rate also can serve as a type of biological clock and allow scientists to determine how and when a particular virus has changed.[12] In the past few years, this clock has unveiled a fascinating timeline.

Using mutations as a biological clock, scientists established that HIV evolved from an ancestor in monkeys.[13] Until the past few years, it had been assumed the ancestor, known as the Simian Immunodeficiency Virus (SIV), was itself relatively new to monkeys, perhaps jumping from other animals to infect monkeys a few hundred years ago.[14] However, studies of primates on a remote island off the coast of West Africa reveals SIV jumped to monkeys at least 30,000 to 80,000 years ago.[15] Much more recently, the virus made a fateful leap into humans.

A likely scenario is that around the time the First World War was getting underway, a hunter from the Baka people of Cameroon, thinking he had just gotten lucky in bagging a chimp or sooty mangabey monkey, soon felt rather unlucky for having been bitten by his quarry.[16] Lest we believe such behaviors are restricted to our forefathers, the 2014 Ebola virus outbreak is believed to have begun similarly.[17] Gorilla, chimpanzee, or monkeys, collectively known as bushmeat in the rainforests of southeast Cameroon, remain a staple food source, accounting for 80 percent of protein consumption even today.[18] An estimated average of three gorillas are killed daily for food in Cameroon alone. By comparing the biological clocks of human immunodeficiency virus (HIV) and its simian cousins (SIV), it seems likely that our unlucky hunter's fateful encounter occurred with a sooty mangabey or chimpanzee around the year 1914.[19]

While it is certain the hunter became infected, it is not known whether this event ultimately resulted in any symptoms being felt (beyond the undoubtedly painful bite from a wild monkey). This is because the rapid evolution of HIV could mean that early forms of the virus were comparatively benign. Even if the hunter were fated to die, we can conclude he survived long enough to transmit the virus to at least one other person. In roughly the year 1920, around the same time Frederick Banting agreed to make a few extra dollars by teaching lectures on the pancreas, either the infected hunter or someone to whom he had passed the virus found themselves on a riverboat journey down the Sangha River from the rainforests of Cameroon to the local metropolis of Leopoldville.

The traveler would have known that Leopoldville had grown into one of the most important trading posts in West Africa, and the town was preparing to be upgraded to the capital of the Belgian Congo.[20] Boat travel to Leopoldville was a primary means of supporting the trade in rubber and ivory between the German colony of Cameroon and the Belgian colony of Congo, where interactions likely rebounded quickly in the months following the 1918 Armistice. Trade had been in the ascendant since the 1898 completion of a ninety-three-mile portage railway to the port city of Matadi, Congo.[21] This same railway would catalyze the infection of a lone hunter into a global pandemic, one that has already killed at least thirty-nine million people worldwide and may kill up to 100 million people in Africa alone by 2025.[22]

From Leopoldville, now known as Kinshasa, the virus remained local and had reached only as far out as Brazzaville, a mere four miles away, by 1937.[23] Soon thereafter, HIV rode the rails from Kinshasa to cities throughout the Congo, including Kisangani and Lubumbashi. HIV had claimed its first confirmed victim by 1959, a man in the Congo whose mysterious death caused the doctors to collect tissue samples, which later were found to be infected with HIV.[24] The following year, 1960, was pivotal, both for Congo, which gained its independence, and for HIV. The transition from colonial rule to independence was complicated by the refusal of the Belgian military commander to admit African officers into the ranks of the new army. A resulting mutiny by African troops caused the Belgian government to introduce troops, ostensibly to protect Belgian citizens but also to protect Belgian economic interests in a resource-rich country.

To ensure stability and a peaceful withdrawal of Belgian forces, the young United Nations undertook its first-ever large-scale peacekeeping operation, the United Nations Operation in the Congo (or ONUC).[25] ONUC quickly expanded beyond peacekeeping into a mandate to promote stability and encourage economic development. To do so, the UN drew upon French-speaking professionals throughout the world and many were recruited from the Francophone island of Haiti.[26] Congo provided a combination of civil unrest, infrastructure instability, and a mixing of individuals from around the world in a way that catalyzed HIV into a mass murderer. The virus hopped on ocean liners and airliners, spreading around the world. In or around the year 1966, the virus had arrived on the island of Hispaniola, coincident with the return home of many Haitians serving in the Congo.[27] Even before this time, the virus had entered the United States, likely as a result of a single infected individual.

Although HIV/AIDS was first recognized as a health concern for the United States in the early 1980s, it had already claimed its first American victim more than a decade before (and there are unverified suspicions of even earlier victims). In the closing days of 1968, a fifteen-year-old African-American, Robert Rayford, entered the City Hospital of St. Louis complaining of swollen genitalia and hemorrhoids.[28] Given his unusual symptoms, he was referred to Dr. Marlys Witte at Washington University in St. Louis, who diagnosed him with a rare chlamydial disease. What made this patient's case so unusual was that chlamydia is normally localized to a single site by the body's defenses. However, Robert's chlamydia had spread throughout his body. A related finding was that the patient demonstrated generalized immune suppression, including low levels of T lymphocytes. The patient died in May 1969 and an autopsy revealed anal scarring, suggesting the patient was homosexual or abused. The other major finding of the autopsy was evidence of rare lesions known as Kaposi's sarcoma. This rare tumor is caused by a type of herpes virus that is relatively widespread but, like chlamydia, is normally kept in check by the body's immune system. Otherwise, there were no clear signs of what caused his massive immune depletion. Fortunately, the medical team had the foresight to collect tissue and blood samples, which remained stored in the back of a freezer for the next few decades.

News of the epidemic spread quickly in early 1981, when the Centers for Disease Control (CDC) noted a dramatic uptick in a rare form of pneumocystic pneumonia.[29] The disease was prominent in homosexual males, first localized to San Francisco and then sporadically throughout the nation. One reason why the CDC became aware of this outbreak was that this rare pneumonia is only responsive to one particular drug, pentamadine diisethionate.[30] The CDC tightly controlled the distribution of this medicine and required specific requests before it would be released. Around the same time, the CDC began receiving reports from the same geographic areas about an increased prevalence of Kaposi's sarcoma.[31]

As word spread of a disease in homosexual men associated with immune suppression, Dr. Witte recalled her experience with Robert Rayford and penned a 1984 letter to the *Journal of the American Medical Association*.[32] The letter was published as an article and detailed the similarities of the case with the newly-named Acquired Immune Deficiency Syndrome (AIDS). Laboratory studies confirmed the presence of HIV in Robert's samples. Based on its internal clock, we now know the HIV variant in Robert was slightly different than the one circulating in the early 1980s. The presence of HIV in 1969 suggests the virus made multiple, independent entries into the United States. Bearing in mind the symptoms of AIDS often occurs up to a decade after initial HIV infection, this suggests Robert Rayford could have become infected in St. Louis as early as the late 1950s or early 1960s.

As has been described in great detail in the Randy Shilts's book, *And the Band Played On*, the HIV/AIDS crisis grew in severity, with several missed opportunities for the Centers for Disease Control and the FDA to recognize and adequately address the emerging epidemic.[33] Throughout the early half of the 1980s, the magnitude of the crisis escalated and captured the attention of healthcare providers, federal regulators, and the media as the number of victims and countries reporting AIDS-like symptoms surged. This recognition, albeit belated, triggered an international effort to identify the causative agent, which was presumed to be a new virus. By 1983, a French virologist from the Pasteur Institute, Luc Montagnier, had isolated the virus.[34] An American scientist, Robert Gallo of the National Cancer Institute (NCI), utilized samples provided by Montagnier to independently discover the virus at roughly the same time.[35] Dr. Robert Gallo of the National Cancer Institute also showed the virus, ultimately named Human Immunodeficiency Virus, HIV, was directly responsible for the symptoms characteristic of AIDS. Once the virus had been identified, the question immediately moved to one of how such knowledge could be used to develop a new medicine.

To understand the remarkable discovery and development of medicines to combat HIV/AIDS, we must take a few moments to convey the creation of the National Institutes of Health (NIH).

Instituting a Hygiene Lab

The foundations for the National Institutes of Health were set in 1798 with the creation of the Marine Hospital Fund (MHF).[36] In an act signed by then-President John Adams, the MHF was tasked with the medical care of the merchant marine, Coast Guard, Navy, and Marines. By deducting twenty cents from the monthly pay of each sailor and marine, a series of Marine Hospitals were built near major naval bases and ports, thereby providing the first publically funded health care agency in the United States.

In the years immediately following the Civil War, the MHF was underfunded and in disarray, with frequent, high-profile allegations of scandal and misuse of funds. For example, only eight of twenty-seven hospitals were functional in 1864.[37] In response, an Army surgeon and former medical inspector of William Tecumseh Sherman's army, John Maynard Woodworth, was appointed to reorganize the MHF into a new structure, known thereafter as the Marine Hospital Service (MHS).[38] Dr. Woodworth joined Sherman on his famous March to the Sea and, in doing so, was famed for the fact his ambulance Corps performed this audacious act without the loss of a single wounded or sick soldier. Upon assuming leadership of the MHS, he instilled a sense of discipline, requiring all employees to wear uniforms (usually of the United States Navy in recognition of its roots in the MHF) and to receive military-style ranks.[39] Dr. Woodworth himself became nation's first Surgeon General.

Over time, the MHS itself underwent many changes and was renamed the United States Public Health Service (PHS) Commissioned Corps in 1889. Consistent with its role as a proponent of public health, the PHS gradually became the authority for quarantines, which were frequent in times of cholera and yellow fever. Two years before his death, Woodworth oversaw the creation of a one-room, United States Hygienic Laboratory within the Staten Island-based MHS hospital to track infectious diseases.[40] Despite the widespread prevalence of epidemic diseases, the laboratory was staffed by a single physician, Joseph J. Kinyoun, a St. Louis Medical College (now known as the Washington University School of Medicine) graduate, who trained with Robert Koch. Dr. Koch was the German founder of the new field of bacteriology, which sought to understand these microscopic organisms and how they cause disease. Within months, Kinyoun confirmed John Snow's suspicions about cholera (you may recall the incident with the broken water pump handle) by demonstrating the microbial basis of the disease and identifying the bacterium responsible for cholera transmission. In 1891, the Hygienic Laboratory, or more accurately its sole employee, Kinyoun, moved from Staten Island to Washington D.C. The laboratory maintained its focus on infectious diseases through the First World War, including the Spanish flu epidemic of 1917–1918 and the laboratory's name was changed to the National Institute of Health in 1930.[41] These deep roots in infectious diseases would serve the institute well as it dealt with the HIV/AIDS crisis.

Dr. Broder's Wars

In the spirit that the Public Health Service was a uniformed agency of the federal government, its leading general in the war against HIV was Samuel Broder, who joined the NIH to fight a different war. In December 1971, then-President Richard Nixon signed the National Cancer Act on 1971, formally declaring a "war on cancer."[42] Within months, a newly trained physician from the University of Michigan, Samuel Broder, joined the intramural program of the National Cancer Institute as a foot soldier in this new war. At the NCI, Broder worked under Thomas Waldmann, a pioneering immunologist who, among other things, was a key expert in the discovery and understanding of the HTLV-I retrovirus.[43] Dr. Robert Gallo had discovered this particular retrovirus, a closely related cousin to HIV, and showed that it caused aggressive adult T cell lymphomas.[44] Within a few years, Broder had worked with HTLV-I and rose through the ranks. He was asked to lead the NCI oncology program in 1980.

The place, time, and experiences encountered in his training situated Broder in the front lines of the nascent HIV/AIDS epidemic. He recalls seeing a patient referred to the NCI in 1981 who presented with classic HIV/AIDS symptoms: immunodeficiency combined with rare infections and tumors.[45] Although it quickly became clear that HIV/AIDS was infectious, the fact that Robert Gallo, Sam Broder, and others were at the National Cancer Institute fated that this institute would take the lead in identifying new drugs to combat the disease. Reinforcing this was the fact that the NCI was only institute at the time with a proven track record in pharmaceutical-style testing of drug candidates. In another twist of fate, it was a drug that NCI had funded more than a decade before that would ultimately provide the first effective treatment against HIV/AIDS.

Jerome Horwitz was a chemist working at the Detroit Cancer Institute and his work was supported by a National Cancer Institute extramural grant to develop novel compounds for the treatment of cancer.[46] His expertise included the ability to design and produce compounds known as antimetabolites.[47] These molecules resemble the components of DNA, amino acids or other vital building blocks of the cell. This similarity allows antimetabolites to act as a Trojan horse and poison the machinery needed for cell growth and survival. The rationale for using antimetabolites to treat cancer was the knowledge that the rapid growth of tumor cells tends to put them into a feeding frenzy as compared to more properly behaved benign cells. Stated another way, cancer cells will ingest and become poisoned by these antimetabolites, whereas normal cells, which tend to be more discriminating in their tastes, will tend to ignore the antimetabolites.

As is often the custom in scientific research, Herculean efforts often go unrewarded. Throughout much of the 1960s, Horwitz laboriously identified a suite of anti-metabolites but none demonstrated sufficient ability to poison cancer cells.[48] These were literally put on a shelf. Among the shelved compounds were zidovudine (now known as AZT), stavudine (d4T), and zalcitabine (ddC).[49] AZT looked like an interesting drug early on, especially for the treatment of cancers caused by the murine leukemia virus (MuLV).[50] In hindsight, this is a remarkable finding because MuLV is another retrovirus responsible for tumors in mice. One day, in jest, Horwitz told his colleagues at the Detroit Cancer Institute that his work identified "an interesting set of compounds that were waiting for the right disease."[51] The passage of time would ultimately validate this prediction.

As soon as HIV was confirmed as the causative agent for AIDS, a team of NCI investigators, including Drs. Broder and Gallo, worked with the pharmaceutical company, Burroughs Wellcome, to literally take everything off the shelf and test for their ability to stop HIV.[52] Horwitz's compounds were sitting on a shelf at NCI and some showed promise.[53] Based on positive findings in the laboratory with one of these compounds, AZT, Broder and his NCI colleagues quickly progressed to clinical investigation and found remarkable responses in HIV-infected patients in the early Phase I clinical trials in 1985.[54] Burroughs Wellcome, who by then had patented the use of AZT against HIV/AIDS, expanded the program and funded additional clinical investigation. The FDA approved Burroughs Wellcome's new drug application on 20 March 1987, four years after the virus was first identified and a mere twenty-five months after the first demonstration of AZT efficacy in the laboratory.[55]

There were many lessons learned in the development of AZT. First, the crisis forced the basic and applied research communities to work together to identify the cause of the disease and then to expedite the development of a much-needed treatment. The breakthrough was possible as a result of "drug repurposing," a process whereby compounds made for one particular application (for example, AZT for cancer) were successfully developed for another (HIV treatment). Indeed, not one but three of Horwitz's drugs for cancer (AZT, d4t, and ddC) were ultimately approved by the FDA for the treatment of HIV/AIDS decades after their initial discovery.

Another lesson focused on the financial implications of private–public sector partnerships and drug repurposing. Since the patents for these compounds had already expired, Horwitz did not realize any financial gains for HIV and, unsurprisingly, became embittered for a time by this fact.[56] Burroughs Wellcome, instead, benefited, as it had filed what are known as the "use patents" for HIV/AIDS. This fact angered many in the public, and particularly those in the research and advocate communities. Burroughs Wellcome was accused of profiteering from federally-funded research, first by developing Horwitz's NCI-funding compounds and then benefiting from the NCI-funded investigation.[57] Making matters worse, the company priced the drug at $10,000 per year, which was considered outrageous and unaffordable for most HIV-infected individuals (both in the United States and in sub-Saharan Africa).[58]

The high costs and demand for HIV/AIDS drugs also triggered a confrontational and aggressive form of patient advocacy. In particular, the AIDS Coalition To Unleash Power (ACT UP) was created in March 1987 (the same month AZT was approved) to support legislation to increase the amount of funding for HIV/AIDS research and therapeutic development.[59] The founder of ACT UP was Larry Kramer, an outspoken playwright and gay rights activist. In the late 1980s, ACT UP held a series of high-profile demonstrations, many of which were directed at what it believed to be the Food and Drug Administration's slow action in prioritizing the review of HIV/AIDS drugs. Their primary goals were to shorten the drug approval process by allowing immediate access as soon as Phase I trials demonstrated safety. They also sought to eliminate double-blind placebo trials, to include volunteers from all stages of infection, and to require that all forms of insurance (both public and private sector) pay for experimental drugs. To demonstrate their earnestness, ACT UP supporters held a demonstration and took over the FDA headquarters in Rockville, Maryland, on 11 October 1988. Among the responses to these demands, Congress passed the Health

Omnibus Programs Extension (HOPE) Act of 1988, which mandated the creation of the AIDS Clinical Trials Information System (ACTIS), a database designed to inform interested individuals in what experimental investigation was being conducted as well as to provide the outcomes of these trials.[60]

Over time, the arsenal of new drugs targeting HIV/AIDS swelled to twenty-eight approved molecules by the end of 2014.[61] These drugs can be broadly divided based on their targeting of three different HIV molecules: reverse transcriptase, HIV protease, and HIV integrase. While high throughput screening was used to identify many of the early compounds, high-resolution understanding of the structure of the HIV proteins facilitated the prediction and then confirmation of new drugs based on structure-based design.

A key lesson learned early in the war against HIV was that individual drugs were effective only for a short time. Their usefulness was quickly lost as a result of the frequent mutations that characterize HIV. The high mutation rate, combined with its ability to massively reproduce, meant that viral mutants quickly arose that were unperturbed by the drugs. Much to the consternation of scientists, health care workers, and patients, HIV had the ability to outrun new drugs that had been arduously developed over many years and at great expense. Indeed, reports of a drug-resistant virus were often published even before new drugs had gained FDA approval. Thus, a great need arose to overcome and outpace HIV drug resistance.

A decade after the initial approval of AZT, two landmark studies appeared in the *New England Journal of Medicine* on 11 September 1997.[62] Both papers detailed multi-institutional studies to evaluate the use of a cocktail of multiple HIV drugs to slow the HIV/AIDS disease progression. These studies opened the way to an approach known as HAART (Highly-Active Anti-Retroviral Therapy).[63] This approach takes advantage of the fact that by targeting a virus with many different medicines at once, each of which ideally targets a different part of the virus, these pressures minimize the likelihood that a mutant variant will arise that is simultaneously able to escape this combined assault. HAART revolutionized HIV/AIDS treatment, increasing patient survival and turning a potential death penalty into a chronic disease that can be managed so long as treatment continues.[64] Like diabetes before it, many life insurance companies have modified their criteria so that HIV-positive individuals now qualify for coverage.

A declaration of "mission accomplished" for the war on HIV/AIDS is premature. While combination drug therapy has improved, from HAART to even more complex and effective cocktails, these treatments are effective only if the pressure on HIV remains constant. Such diligence requires that all patients take the proper dose of medicine each day for the rest of their lives. If treatment is discontinued, even for a short time, this provides an opportunity for the virus to mutate and gain the ability to escape the cocktail.

Practical impediments inevitably fate conventional approaches to HIV/AIDS treatment to obsolescence. Despite public outcries, the medicines remain quite expensive. Given the prevalence of HIV infection in low-income populations and nations, some individuals simply lack the resources to continue treatment. Compounding this, the HIV cocktail can cause nagging side effects that include but are not limited to fatigue, diarrhea, nausea, dizziness, insomnia, and pain.[65] It is, therefore, not surprising that some patients discontinue treatment altogether while others observe "drug holidays," in which they interrupt treatment during, for example, a long-anticipated vacation.[66] The risks of lowered compliance accelerate the inevitability that a drug-resistant virus will emerge.[67]

The prevalence of drug-resistant HIV is, indeed, increasing. A 2012 report from the U.S. Centers for Disease Control and Prevention revealed one in five HIV-positive individuals harbors a virus that is resistant to at least one component of the current cocktail.[68] More troubling is the fact that the rate of resistance to all three classes of conventional HIV/AIDS drugs has risen to 0.6 percent, or about one of 150 patients. The problem of drug resistance is increasingly urgent because the introduction of new medicines for HIV/AIDS has evaporated. Whereas the late-1990s witnessed the approval of an average of two new drugs per year, it presently stands at approximately one new drug every other year.[69] At the same time, studies by the author evaluated the number of companies that have successfully developed HIV drugs and has found that seven of ten of the most successful companies have discontinued HIV/AIDS research. The combination of a "mission accomplished" assumption with the high costs and time required to obtain a new drug approval for an HIV/AIDS drug now places us at a higher risk for a resurgence of HIV/AIDS than any time since the early 1980s.

Faster, Better, Badder?

The passions conveyed by ACT UP combined with the perceptions of bureaucracy to trigger President George H. W. Bush to form a presidential advisory panel and evaluate FDA practices. This panel was led by Dr. Louis Lasagna, a pharmacologist at the Tufts Center for the Study of Drug Development, an academic center devoted to the study of the drug approval process. Dr. Lasagna's commission estimated that delays in approving new drugs caused thousands of unnecessary deaths annually.[70] In response, the FDA introduced plans for expedited approval of drugs for life-threatening diseases and expanded compassionate use access to drugs for patients with limited treatment options.

In addition, the Prescription Drug User Fee Act (PDUFA) was signed into law by President George H. W. Bush on 29 October 1992.[71] To expedite the drug approval process, the act allowed the FDA to collect an application fee from drug manufacturers. These funds were designated to increase the staffing and efficiency of reviewing new drug applications. To ensure these funds were effective, the FDA was required to meet performance benchmarks. A major benchmark was a requirement to review new drug applications within ten months. The law also waived the fee from applications submitted by small business and for drugs targeting orphan diseases and other unmet medical needs. The law was designed to be reviewed and considered for reauthorization on a five-year cycle to ensure the scrutiny of FDA would be constant and updated to meet the needs of changing times.

The consequences of PDUFA included the clearance of a logjam of new drug applications (NDAs), resulting in a burst of approvals in the years immediately following its passage.[72] Whereas the number of new drug approvals had generally hovered at an average of roughly thirty per year, this rate temporarily increased to a peak of fifty-seven in 1996, which reflected the clearance of the backlog.

While the FDA has improved its processes, an air of caution still pervades since the penalties to its image from a quick approval of a "bad drug" vastly exceed a slower approval for a "good drug." As described in a 2014 report from the Manhattan Institute for Policy Research: "*When* bad drugs are approved quickly, the FDA is scrutinized and criticized, victims are identified, and their graves are marked. In contrast, when good drugs are approved slowly, the victims are unknown."[73] An exemplar of this experience is conveyed by the situation with Vioxx.

Heart Breaker

Going back to the beginnings of history, humankind has sought ways to alleviate pain. At least as far back as Hippocrates (in the fifth century B.C.E.), our predecessors were advised to chew on willow bark or drink willow tea as a means of easing their pain.[74] Many species of willow tree convey this beneficial effect that we now know is due to the presence of the chemical, salicin, or salicylic acid. Over time, the use of willow for analgesia became entrenched as a folk remedy. In 1763, an English rector, Edward Stone, sent a letter to the Royal Society in London and noted that, while walking in a meadow one day, he was suffering "agues" and decided to nibble on some willow tree bark, which ameliorated the pain.[75] This led him to gather and dry out a pound of willow bark, the powder of which conveyed the desired benefits. Unbeknownst to Reverend Stone, he had rediscovered and popularized salicylic acid. Although beneficial, salicylic acid is quite corrosive. Like caffeine, willow trees produced salicin as an anti-microbial agent that kills pathogenic bacteria and fungi by boring holes through their cell walls and membranes

The discovery of a chemical variant of this natural molecule, acetyl-salicylic acid, or aspirin, is frequently affixed to Felix Hoffman at Bayer. However, this attribution is incorrect. A French chemist, Charles Frederic Gerhardt, was the first to synthesize aspirin, in 1853.[76] Gerhardt was an academic chemist and looking for ways to make new chemicals. He was not terribly interested in exploring the new compound further or its biological properties. Sadly, he died three years later, poisoned by another discovery (explaining perhaps why the age-old practice of chemists tasting their discoveries has fallen out of favor).[77] To make things worse, Gerhardt did not correctly name the compound and, thus, is often overlooked as the initial discoverer of aspirin.

Forty-five years later, chemists working at Bayer AG produced a variant of salicin that was less caustic and, thus, better tolerated in the stomach.[78] Bayer continues to attribute the 10 August 1897 discovery to Felix Hoffmann, the gifted son of an industrialist from Ludwigsburg, Germany.[79] However, this, again, is inaccurate. An objective analysis conduced by the University of Strathclyde in 1999 supports the claim of a rival.[80] Arthur Eichengrun was another gifted chemist, who began working at Bayer in 1896.[81] In 1908, he quit Bayer to form a rival company. Later, as a Jew, he was later arrested by the Nazis and deported to the Theresienstadt concentration camp. Eichengrun survived this ordeal and in 1949 claimed he was responsible for the discovery of aspirin. He further claimed his contributions had been intentionally expunged by the Nazis due to his Jewish identity and the fact that Bayer had been incorporated in 1925 into the notoriously pro-Nazi IG Farben conglomerate. Bayer denied the claim for decades but an assessment by Walter Sneader, published in the *British Medical Journal*, supports Eichengrun's claims.[82] The deciding factor was an obscure footnote in an equally obscure report from Albrecht Schmidt, who had written of Eichengrun's discovery in a 1934 history of chemical engineering at Bayer/IG Farben.

Since its commercialization by Bayer in 1899, aspirin has had an extraordinary run; it is arguably the most widely used and impactful drug in history. Its list of positive attributes include the ability to block pain, reduce fever, combat inflammation, and prevent blood clot formation, heart attacks, and strokes. Aspirin may also play a role in blocking various cancers. However, the drug is not without its side effects, prominent of which are gastrointestinal distress and bleeding. This fact created an opportunity for identifying other drugs to fight inflammation and pain with fewer gastrointestinal side effects.

In the search for ways to minimize the bleeding associated with aspirin, an entire field of investigation sought to identify how aspirin works (there are many ways in which the miracle drug seems to work), with a focus on distinguishing mechanisms associated with blocking inflammation. A prominent target was a family of molecules known as cyclooxygenases.[83] The first cyclooxygenase identified by this research gained the unsurprising name of COX (now known as COX-1) and provided a means for targeted intervention to block inflammation.

As a brief aside, targeted intervention is the idea of selectively impairing (or in some cases, stimulating) the biological activity of a particular molecule by developing highly specific molecules that impact only that target. An analogy is the use of satellite-guided cruise missiles to seek out and destroy a particular building while leaving the rest of the neighborhood intact. The military-inspired vernacular of many pharmaceutical researchers now includes terms such as "collateral damage," "homing," and "off-target impact." This targeted approach differs from the historical approach used to discover aspirin, morphine, and other drugs that were based on knowledge that a drug worked without necessarily knowing why or what other molecules or functions were being modified.

With this in mind, COX-1 served as a target for selective intervention and a variety of COX-1-directed drugs were developed, including well-known names such as ibuprofen (Motrin®) and naproxen (Naprosyn®). However, COX-1 also plays an important role in the stomach to prevent the lining from being eroded by digestive acids. Consequently, while COX-1 inhibitors were effective, their use was often limited by similar gastrointestinal side effects as those experienced with aspirin.[84] Thus, the need remained unfulfilled for a stomach-sparing medicine.

A series of breakthroughs arose with the identification of a closely related but different cellular protein, COX-2. Work published in 1982 by Dr. Phillip Needleman at Washington University in St. Louis reported a second form of COX in brain tissue and then in other cell types.[85] Almost a decade later,

Dr. Daniel Simmons of Brigham Young University, and in an independent study, Dr. Harvey Herschman of UCLA, identified a gene that increased in cells infected with the Rous sarcoma virus.[86] This gene was similar to, but different than, COX-1 and so was named COX-2. Meanwhile, Dr. Needleman was determining how COX-2 worked and, in doing so, determined that COX-2 regulates inflammation but does not have a role in the stomach.

In what was a revolutionary move at that time, Dr. Needleman, a respected academic scientist and member of the National Academy of Sciences, moved from Washington University in St. Louis to lead research and development at nearby Searle Pharmaceuticals. There, he continued his work to develop a medicine that blocked pain and inflammation but without gastrointestinal bleeding. This action served as a starting gun for a race among multiple pharmaceutical companies, most notably Searle and Merck. Searle was the first to obtain an FDA approval for osteoarthritis with its COX-2 inhibitor, celecoxib (Celebrex®), on 31 December 1998. Merck followed soon thereafter with approval for rofecoxib (Vioxx®) on 20 May 1999, and Pharmacia's product, valdecoxib (Bextra®) was approved in November 2001. This new class of drugs was so highly anticipated and valued that Pharmacia purchased Searle (the creator of Celebrex) in 2000, and Pfizer, in turn, acquired Pharmacia three years later.

Even before receiving an approval from the FDA, Merck launched a clinical trial of Vioxx called VIGOR (Vioxx GI Outcomes Research) in January 1999 to compare Vioxx with its commercial rival, Naprosyn. The goal of this 8,000-person trial was to compare the toxicities of Vioxx with Naprosyn and presumably demonstrate improved gastrointestinal safety. Half of the patients were given Vioxx and the remaining were given Naprosyn. By May, Vioxx was approved and, in October, the first results of the VIGOR results were assessed by a safety panel.[87] The initial safety review confirmed Merck's hopes that Vioxx patients did, indeed, have less stomach bleeding and fewer ulcers.

Unexpectedly, at the next VIGOR meeting in November, it was noted that seventy-nine of 4,000 patients on Vioxx had experienced serious heart problems, including some fatal heart attacks. In comparison, forty-one of 4,000 patients on Naprosyn had comparable outcomes. The trend continued in December but Merck scientists concluded that Naprosyn, like aspirin, might be protective rather than Vioxx being detrimental. By March 2000, the VIGOR trial had been completed and the data was prepared for publication in the *New England Journal of Medicine*. The publication appeared in November 2000 and reported seventeen heart attacks in the Vioxx treatment group.[88] Three additional heart attacks as well as other data suggesting cardiovascular complications were curiously omitted from the report.

Nine months later, a large-scale meta-analysis of Vioxx and Naprosyn data was published by Dr. Eric Topol of the Cleveland Clinic.[89] The August 2001 report in the *Journal of the American Medical Association* demonstrated both that Naprosyn does not protect the heart and that Vioxx damages this vital organ. The following month, the FDA issued a warning letter to the CEO of Merck, accusing the company of deceptive promotion, stating:

> You have engaged in a promotional campaign for Vioxx that minimizes the potentially serious cardiovascular findings that were observed in the Vioxx Gastrointestinal Outcomes Research (VIGOR) study (see *March 2000*), and thus, misrepresents the safety profile for Vioxx. Specifically, your promotional campaign discounts the fact that in the VIGOR study, patients on Vioxx were observed to have a four- to five-fold increase in myocardial infarctions (MIs) compared to patients on the comparator non-steroidal anti-inflammatory drug (NSAID), Naprosyn (naproxen). . . . You assert that Vioxx does not increase the risk of MIs and that the VIGOR finding is consistent with naproxen's ability to block platelet aggregation like aspirin. That is a possible explanation, but you fail to disclose that your explanation is hypothetical, has not been demonstrated by substantial evidence, and that there is another reasonable explanation, that Vioxx may have pro-thrombotic properties [that is, cause heart attacks]. . . . Your minimizing these potential risks and misrepresenting the safety profile for Vioxx raise significant public health and safety concerns.[90]

The FDA then commenced a six-month period of negotiations, culminating in an April 2002 agreement in which the Vioxx label was revised to reflect the cardiovascular side effects and a letter was distributed to physicians from John Yates, the vice president for Medical and Scientific Affairs at Merck.[91] The message was substantially watered down from a "Warning" to a "Precaution," and was accompanied by a neutered statement that "the significance of the cardiovascular findings from these three studies (VIGOR and two placebo-controlled studies) is unknown."

Meanwhile, Vioxx sales soared above $2.5 billion dollars in 2003.[92] Over the following two years, the number and magnitude of concerns about Vioxx's cardiovascular damage escalated. By the time Merck ultimately withdrew Vioxx in September 2004, an estimated twenty million people had taken Vioxx.[93] Later research published in the *Lancet* revealed that 88,000 to

160,000 people had heart attacks as a result of Vioxx, with at least 38,000 being fatal.[94] Heart disease is complex and it is impossible to know the final impact of Vioxx, but estimates range upward to hundreds of thousands of premature deaths.

Repercussions

The ramifications of the Vioxx tragedy were abrupt and long lasting. Among the immediate consequences were a flurry of civil court actions against Merck & Co. and a federal multidistrict litigation was established in Louisiana with over 50,000 claimants.[95] Many private claims remain to be litigated as of this writing. These lawsuits contended that Merck deflected concerns about safety, was slow to respond to the clinical findings of cardiovascular damage (for example, from the VIGOR trial), and the company engaged in inappropriate sales and marketing tactics. In response, Merck agreed to a settlement with the federal government to pay $950 million dollars and to plead guilty to misdemeanor charges of illegal marketing. The company also reportedly set aside almost $5 billion for legal claims.

One particularly vocal critic was Senator Charles Grassley, chair of the Senate Committee on Finance, who charged that Merck worked with the FDA to suppress information about Vioxx's heart-related side effects.[96] These critics, combined with public outrage, led the FDA in 2005 to create the Drug Safety Oversight Board (DSB), which advises the FDA on proper handling and communication of drug safety issues.[97] The DSB is composed of senior-level government officials representing a gamut of activities from basic research (for example, NIH and Centers for Disease Control) through distribution (for example, Medicare, Medicaid, Veterans Affairs, and Indian Health Service) and was codified into law in 2007.[98] This law also required the registration and reporting of clinical trials data on an accessible website: www.clinicaltrials.gov. Managed by the National Library of Medicine at NIH, this website had its roots in the ACTIS program, which was created to report clinical trials of experimental HIV/AIDS drugs.

Another outcome of the Vioxx tragedy was a decrease in the number of new drug approvals. Whereas an average of more than thirty drugs had been approved in the years before the withdrawal of Vioxx, if one eliminates the surge following enactment of PDUFA, the average dropped to just over twenty in the years after the withdrawal of Vioxx.[99] It is too early to know if this drop is simply coincidental or sustainable, but this had led to much finger pointing.

Piling On

The Food and Drug Administration, headquartered in Silver Spring, Maryland, is tasked with ensuring the safety of all food, drugs, vaccines, cosmetics, radiation-emitting devices, tobacco, blood (and blood products), veterinary products, vitamins, and dietary supplements sold in the United States. Together, these products account for 25 percent of all consumer purchases, or more than a trillion dollars (a one with twelve zeros) per year.[100] This is a massive task involving 223 field offices and thirteen laboratories in the United States as well as sites in multiple foreign counties that inspect drugs or foodstuffs manufactured outside national borders but sold in the United States.[101]

These activities are performed with a staff of fewer than 12,000 people and an annual budget of $4.4 billion (as of 2012).[102] To put this in perspective, a single drugstore chain, CVS Health, employs 200,000 employees, and a single supermarket chain, Kroger, employs 343,000 people. Excluding its 500,000 volunteers, the American Red Cross, which accounts for two-thirds of the nation's blood supply, employs twice as many people as its regulator, the Food and Drug Administration.

If we limit our analysis to pharmaceuticals, the FDA's Center for Drug Evaluation and Research (CDER) activities are performed by a staff of fewer than 1,500 people, who are responsible for evaluating all new applications for clinical trials (IND applications), for final commercial approval (NDA applications), for expanding the use or existing drugs, and for approving generic equivalents and over-the-counter medications. CDER is also responsible for ensuring that the advertising and promotions for all approved drugs are conducted in a manner that is both ethical and scientifically accurate. A well-known example is the rapid listing of potential side effects that the FDA requires to accompany any beneficial claims on televised advertisements. Recalling the situation where thalidomide was approved for leprosy but primarily sold off-label for oncology (prior to its receiving full FDA approval in later years), the manufacturer was not allowed to advertise this information and the FDA had to ensure that its communications with doctors (including communications by salespeople) did not violate this rule.

Beyond their ability to approve and regulate new drugs, CDER is tasked with safety surveillance for all marketed drugs. As a condition for approving a particular drug, the FDA may require additional follow-on investigation of drug safety or efficacy. These studies, known as Phase IV clinical trials, are monitored to determine if the use of the drug, known as its label, should be modified to include or exclude certain patient populations or doses, or to convey potential safety concerns. In addition, CDER is responsible to ensure that the drug's sponsor (usually the company marketing the drug) complies with reporting any unexpected serious or fatal adverse events associated with a drug within fifteen days and all other adverse events on a quarterly basis.

In the months following the Vioxx withdrawal, the FDA was in the unenviable position of being criticized from all directions at once. When the rate of new drug approvals drops, the FDA is charged with overregulation, as occurred during the early years of the HIV/AIDS crisis. The criticisms of overregulation in the 1980s ultimately escalated to the point where angered advocates occupied FDA headquarters. Yet, the Vioxx crisis raised the opposite complaint, that the FDA was too quick to approve drugs and under-valued safety. During his testimony on 18 October 2004 before the Senate Committee on Finance, Dr. David Graham, the associate director of the FDA Office of Drug Safety, stated: "I would argue that the FDA, as currently configured, is incapable of protecting America against another Vioxx. We are virtually defenseless."[103]

After the FDA distanced itself from such comments, Graham again testified before Congress of his perception that he had been "marginalized by FDA management and not asked to participate in the evaluation of any new drug safety issues. It's a type of ostracism."[104] The attacks were later joined in 2007 when the former head of the *New England Journal of Medicine*, Marcia Angell wrote an article for the *Boston Globe* stating: "It's time to take the Food and Drug Administration back from the drug companies. . . . In effect, the user fee act put the FDA on the payroll of the industry it regulates. Last year, the fees came to about $300 million, which the companies recoup many times over by getting their drugs to market faster."[105] Furthering this claim, a 2006 survey of FDA employees by the Union of Concerned Scientists, a nonprofit scientific advocacy group, indicated one in five FDA scientists "have been asked, for non-scientific reasons, to inappropriately exclude or alter technical information or their conclusions in a FDA scientific document."[106]

Imagine trying to recruit and retain the staff of an organization with such a broad mandate and workload, which also serves as a high-profile pincushion for both the left and the right. In 2007, the FDA Science Board Subcommittee of Science and Technology published a report titled *FDA Science and Mission at Risk*, which emphasized inadequate funding for a mission with an ever increasing pace and complexity.[107] The report further cited high rates of turnover caused by excessive work pressures and low morale, which created large gaps in expertise.

The FDA has actively sought to address the issues identified both by the Vioxx tragedy and the 2007 report. A November 2012 report titled *The State of the FDA Workforce,* by the Pew Charitable Trusts, concluded that while progress had been made in terms of new hiring, recruiting efforts were inefficient and unable to attract the most qualified candidates.[108] On the other hand, the report charged that new employees received insufficient training and mentoring and raised concerns about the use of temporary employees, which constitute at least one-quarter of the agency workforce and threaten the need for consistency and continuity.

As evidenced by the heroics of Dr. Frances Kelsey, the mission of the FDA is vital to both the health and economy of the United States. There remain many unsung heroes comparable in intellect and ability in the agency. When they do their jobs well, which is often, no one appreciates the service. The exceptions are highly visible and tragic. A 2012 quote in honor of the fiftieth anniversary of the Kefauver-Harris amendments from then-Commissioner of the FDA, Dr. Margaret Hamburg, summarizes the need and opportunity:

> Going forward, smart regulation requires regulatory flexibility that responds to changing situations, new information, and new challenges. It also demands that we advance regulatory science: the knowledge and tools necessary for the meaningful and timely review of products for safety, efficacy, quality, and performance. . . . Regulation such as this requires a strong, robust FDA, one endowed with the necessary resources to ensure smart, sound, science-based regulation.[109]

Frances Kelsey would have insisted upon nothing less.

CHAPTER FIVE

Ivory Tower of Power

Innovation has always been at the core of modern drug discovery. The academic community looms prominently in the discovery and development of new medicines. While universities rank among the world's oldest institutions, the concept of a research university is a comparatively new one. Much of the innovation has been performed at research universities, where the published manuscript is the coin of the realm. Recent research has shown that scientific knowledge, as measured by publications, has sustainably grown at a logarithmic rate for almost five centuries. In studies first published in the 1960s, Derek De Solla Price showed the number of scientific publications has grown since the seventeenth century at an average annual rate of almost 5 percent, which translates to a doubling of published knowledge every fifteen years.[1] This information will set the stage for a later discussion of the fact that the entire drug discovery enterprise is presently at risk due largely to dwindling federal support for basic and applied research. As we will see, these ongoing funding trends threaten the sustainability of an enterprise that has conveyed extraordinary benefits in terms of both public health improvements and economic value.

Birth of the Research University

The author recently became excited by the opening line of a seminar in which the speaker stated, "eight of ten of the world's oldest continuously-run institutions are universities." After a few minutes of fact checking, the statement retains its catchiness but, sadly, is inaccurate (though it remains a great way of introducing a chapter). In truth, the distinction of being the oldest continuously-run institution is controversial. Rival claimants include the Japanese Chrysanthemum Throne (the Emperor), which dates to 660 B.C.E. (though indisputable evidence of its existence prior to 270 C.E. is lacking) and the Catholic Church, founded two millennia ago.[2] While there are older religions (Hinduism's Vedas can reportedly be tracked to five millennia ago), these are not necessarily associated with a particular organization. By contrast, the *Guinness Book of World Records* awards the distinction of the first degree-granting institution to the University of Karueein, a mosque and religious school founded in 859 A.D. in Fez, Morocco (a claim that the less influential United Nations Educational and Scientific Organization (UNESCO) supports as well).[3] By this time, there were at least seven private-sector companies in operation, including three Japanese hotels.[4]

For most of its history, the university simply provided a service of regurgitating past knowledge and opinion. The roots for this activity span well into the past and were little changed from earliest civilizations through ancient Greece and up to the nineteenth century. In 1810, the Prussian education minister, Friedrich Wilhelm Christian Karl Ferdinand von Humboldt, convinced the Kaiser to create the University of Berlin, now simply known as the Humboldt.[5] Universities had existed in Europe since the eleventh century, but the University of Berlin took the novel approach of balancing the teaching of established knowledge with the creation of new understanding. Over time, this approach would attract a diverse array of scholars, including Robert Koch (whom you may remember as the father of bacteriology), Karl Marx, Friedrich Engels, Otto von Bismarck, W. E. B. Dubois, Max Planck, and Albert Einstein.[6] This was a revolutionary concept and took a while to take hold, first in Germany and then in the United States.

The United States replicated the "German" educational system of research universities through the Morrill Act, which was signed by then-President Abraham Lincoln in 1862.[7] The act granted federal lands to each state, which could be sold to generate an endowment to be used for the creation of a "land-grant school." Iowa was the first state to embrace the new law and created what is now known as Iowa State University in 1864. More than seventy additional universities followed, including some of the most prominent state and private schools in the United States, such as Cornell University and the Massachusetts Institute of Technology (MIT). Beyond the Morrill Act, one particular university stands out in replicating the model set forth by von Humboldt.

Johns Hopkins was a shrewd Quaker grocer from Baltimore, Maryland.[8] Hopkins and his brothers established a mobile store that sold merchandise from the backs of Conestoga wagons in the early nineteenth century and was, at heart, always a businessman. Hopkins was temporarily expelled from the Society of Friends' meetinghouse for the frowned-up practice of trading groceries for moonshine, which, in turn, was marketed in Baltimore as "Hopkins' Best." Beyond his thriving grocery business, Hopkins had a penchant for investing and made many fortunes by investing in the Baltimore and Ohio (or B&O) railroad. Hopkins was also an inveterate abolitionist and offered free use of the B&O railway to the Union Army, a fact that strained his local reputation and many personal and professional relationships in slave-holding Maryland. After the Civil War, Baltimore was in shambles, in part because Union forces had occupied it and other towns in Maryland to prevent the state from seceding. A crumbling infrastructure rendered the city susceptible to outbreaks of cholera, yellow fever, and other epidemic diseases. Ameliorating these causes and restoring his good name in Baltimore became the focus of Hopkins's final years.

Upon his death, the philanthropic Johns Hopkins endowed many organizations, including a university that would carry his name. This was not meant to be just any university, but one focused on the new German methods. In addition, Hopkins required half of the bequest be directed to create a medical center. The resulting university was founded on 22 February 1876, a date intentionally selected to emphasize both George Washington's birth date (22 February) and the centennial of the United States (1876). The first president, Daniel Coit Gilman, began his tenure by touring German universities and learning more about von Humboldt's new model for combining research and education.[9] Upon his return, Gilman hired researchers and teachers with the goal of blending their expertise. Gilman placed particular emphasis on finding physicians experienced in hands-on learning and research using the German model. This was particularly radical since most contemporary medical students were taught solely from books, with little contact with professors and no interaction with patients. By 1884, Gilman had hired, as the first physician of the Johns Hopkins medical school, a German-trained physician–scientist with expertise in these radical new methods. His name was Dr. William Henry Welch.

William Henry Welch quickly ascended from a relatively unknown first recruit at the equally obscure Johns Hopkins Hospital to become one of the leading minds in the country.[10] In the years after joining Johns Hopkins as a pathologist in 1884, Welch founded a prestigious medical journal and served as president of many national scientific organizations. With America's entry into the First World War, Welch enlisted in the army and was appointed lieutenant colonel in 1918. After a grueling cross-country inspection tour of American military camps to assess hygiene, he began a much-needed vacation in the mountains of North Carolina.[11] On 22 September, Welch received notice to report immediately to Camp Devens in Massachusetts, which was experiencing a particularly pesky off-season outbreak of influenza. What Welch didn't now was that, in the coming days, he was destined both to change the face of American medicine and to go toe-to-toe with the most devastating killer in recent memory and perhaps in all of history.

Blue Death

Influenza virus infection has been known throughout recorded history, described by Hippocrates as early as the fifth century B.C.E.[12] Though returning each year, the causes for the disease were a mystery at the time Welch received the fateful order to Camp Devens. Fundamental understanding of influenza had even eluded the advent of modern bacteriology in the late nineteenth century. Microbiologists had become quite adept at crafting filters that could capture microscopic bacteria while letting other fluids pass through. In 1901, two scientists from the University of Innsbruck, Max von Gruber and A. Lode, used such filters to try to identify the organism responsible for a particularly severe outbreak in chickens.[13] The wattle of infected chickens had turned blue (reflecting cyanosis, or a lack of oxygen) and the birds died soon thereafter. However, all attempts to capture the organism on the filters failed. What the investigators did not know was that the agent responsible for the disease was the influenza virus and that virus particles, much smaller than a bacterium, had passed straight through the filter.

We will diverge for a moment to convey a quick note that may come as a disappointment to the ego. Contrary to what we are often taught in school, humans are not at the top of the food chain. Not even close. This bit of hubris has built up over the millennia as our species had gained the courage first to come down from the trees and then to cultivate the land and dominate the planet with its technologies. Even in our present geological epoch, known by some as the anthropocene, when humans have remodeled significant portions of the Earth's ecosystems and farm the land and sea, we ourselves are being farmed quite efficiently.[14] We are the foodstuffs of viruses. Viruses are consummate parasites and have evolved over billions of years by harvesting their own food, which includes you and me. Viruses are always at least one step ahead and can readily adapt to practically any medicine we throw at them. The only proven way to prevent this constant infestation is by developing a powerful vaccine. As evidenced by the fact that we need to receive a new dose each year, and it often fails to be effective, modern vaccine technology lags far behind the influenza virus.

The name "influenza" nicely captures the mysteries and historical misconceptions of the disease. The name is derived from the Italian word for "influence," which reflects the concept that the disease arose as an "influence of the cold," presumably because the disease is most prevalent in the winter months. Despite modern understanding of the disease, it still is not clear why influenza is most prominent in the winter months at the northern and southern extremes of the planet. Theories to explain these trends include the idea that cold or dry air may allow the virus to live longer. Alternative thoughts are that increased travel (during the holiday season) or indoor confinement might facilitate spread from one person to another. What we do know all too well is that influenza kills an average of 30,000 to 40,000 American each year.[15] The most susceptible populations tend to be the very young and the very old, and if you plot those killed by influenza based on their ages, the graph tends to look like the letter V.

There are many different types of influenza virus and, as we will see, the virus is constantly changing through a complex process known as "shifts and drifts."[16] This explains why a new flu shot is needed each year, as last year's strains often do not return for a comeback tour. Increasing understanding of how the virus spreads now allows scientists to predict, with imperfect accuracy, the strains that are likely to be encountered in any particular area months in advance. Each year, the Centers for Disease Control and Prevention (CDC) and the World Health Organization (WHO) evaluate data coming from 141 national influenza centers in 111 countries, and this surveillance is used to predict what virus strains are likely to occur in each country.[17] The top three are selected for inclusion in a vaccine on a country-by-country basis. In the United States, the CDC generally makes its recommendation for the coming year on the last day of February. This date generally provides time for the laborious process of making enough of that particular vaccine to protect Americans, which will be needed by the following autumn. In the meantime, both public health officials and manufacturers hold their breath since an inaccurate call arising from "shifts and drifts" can cause tens of thousands of additional deaths. The accuracy of their decision will not be known until the casualties begin mounting in the new season, which normally begins in the northern hemisphere in the late autumn and peaks in the weeks following Christmas (as viruses are efficiently shared during annual gathering among friends and families). On average, the educated guesstimates are accurate about two-thirds of the time.[18]

With the billions of dollars and ever-increasing knowledge of influenza, you may ask why we don't have 100 percent accuracy in predicting the strain of influenza that will prevail in your neighborhood. The ability of influenza to remain cagey and evade the otherwise protective influence of vaccination, the "shifts and drifts," is possible by the fact that influenza has seven or eight distinct RNA segments encoded within each viral particle. Unlike HIV, influenza does not solely rely upon the sloppiness of its polymerase to introduce mutations at a high frequency and thereby escape vaccination.

Influenza polymerase is error-prone, but much less than HIV reverse transcriptase. Otherwise, the rapid and easy spread of drug- and vaccine-resistant viruses might quickly conclude its domination of *Homo sapiens*, along with the species' delusion of being at the top of the food chain.

The bad news is that if a person becomes infected with more than one strain of influenza, the seven or eight RNA segments can mix and match, in a process known as re-assortment, in ways that may create unique and sometimes catastrophic progeny. One can think of this ability in terms of a closet full of shirts, pants, shoes, socks, hats, coats, and gloves. A closet with just a few of each type of clothing can allow a different outfit to be worn every day for years.

The worst news is that influenza is particularly well adapted to survive in an aerosol form, which allows it to be readily transmitted from one infected individual to another. A single sneeze can propel a virus across a room and, once there, particularly if it is cold and dry, the virus can wait like a patient hitchhiker for a lift to its next host. The host does not even have to be a person. Influenza virus has the ability to infect a wide range of animals, including dogs, cats, pigs, birds, camels, ferrets, and even whales.[19] Birds are a particular problem because of their mobility. Unlike pigs, which tend to have a limited range, a bird can move quickly, and in the case of migratory fowl, their ranges can extend for thousands of miles. Were an influenza-infected bird to come into contact with a pig, dog, person, or other bird that happens to be infected with another version of the influenza virus, the re-assortment process can introduce a never-before-seen pathogen into a susceptible population.

Occasionally, an influenza virus enters an animal and undergoes a re-assortment to emerge as a very distinct and extremely dangerous variant. The planet experiences this on an uncomfortably frequent basis, on average every few decades, and these events are known as influenza pandemics.[20] These pandemics tend to spread quickly and engulf larges swathes of territory. Over the past hundred years, the world has experienced five pandemics, including the H1N1 flu pandemic (2009–2010), Russian flu (1977–1978), Hong Kong flu (1968–1969) and Asian flu (1957–1958). For the most part, these pandemics were relatively mild (by flu standards) and only claimed the lives of an additional 100,000 to two million people each. While each pandemic influenza outbreak was its own tragedy, they all pale in comparison to the events of 1917–1919.

Almost a century later and despite considerable investigation, the original source of what became known as the Spanish flu remains uncertain.[21]

Much of the world was exhausted by the most devastating conflict experienced up to that time, and morale was near a breaking point for all the European belligerents. Conveniently, Spain was a neutral in the Great War and not subject to wartime censorship. Thus, when the high-profile Spanish king, Alfonso XIII, was himself afflicted with the disease, the pandemic was thereafter labeled "the Spanish flu" (even though the English king was suffering from the same condition at roughly the same time). The moniker is understandably resented on the Iberian Peninsula since the disease was knowingly encountered in many other countries before Spain. However, most of these nations were engaged in a worldwide war and the name persisted due to disinformation and censorship that forbad them from admitting the catastrophe may have started in their own backyard.

There are many competing theories as to the source of Spanish flu.[22] A 2009 book by Andrew Price-Smith of Colorado College suggests the Austrian–Hungarian archives had documented infections in that country as early as the spring of 1917.[23] A different theory espoused by Mark Osborne Humphries of Memorial University of Newfoundland attributes the pandemic to a November 1917 outbreak in China that was spread to Europe by Chinese laborers building trenches in wartime France.[24] A third theory popularized by the best-selling author John M. Barry places the origins in a pig farm in Haskell County, Kansas.[25] It is conceivable that the truth is an amalgamation of all these ideas, as the virus might have captured little bits and pieces of its devastating character as a consequence of multiple encounters and re-assortments on all three continents.

Regardless of its origins, what is known is that the virus started slowly, causing relatively mild symptoms in people infected during the first half of 1918. Early documentation can be found in Haskell County, Kansas, in January 1918, when a local doctor, Loring Miner, contacted the U.S. Public Health Service to warn of an influenza outbreak.[26] He was particularly concerned about a sudden onset of severe symptoms combined with the fact young and otherwise healthy patients were dying of the disease (which is inconsistent with the well-known V shape of influenza mortality charts). In February, the Spanish tourist haven of San Sebastian began to record its first cases of flu. What made it unusual was, again, a propensity to strike healthy adults. By March, a soldier became ill during training at Fort Riley, Kansas, and within a week, 100 soldiers at the camp were bedridden with severe flu. A few days later, more than 500 patients had overwhelmed the base hospital. More than a quarter of the inmates at San Quentin prison became ill, and a thousand workers at the Ford motor plant in Michigan called in sick.

Unbeknownst to these survivors, they were the lucky few who had gained resistance to the more devastating forms of the virus soon to follow. Yet, the band played on and no one seemed particularly perturbed.

In May, just as flu rates should have been declining, the dam burst. More than eight million people became ill in Spain, often with death occurring just hours after the first symptoms.[27] Over one-third of the population of Madrid came down with the disease, including the closely tracked case of Spanish King Alfonso XIII. The British King George V also became quite ill that month, but the censors tamped down any reporting until after his recovery. However, the King's Grand Fleet and army were effectively sidelined, with tens of thousands bedridden. This was offset by illnesses in the army of his cousin, Kaiser Wilhelm III, where Eric von Ludendorff was planning a key offensive. The German offensive, if fully manned, might have won the war for the Germans prior to the arrival in the theater of fresh U.S. troops. The Spanish flu became truly historical at that time because von Ludendorff later complained it was responsible for the failure of his pivotal July offensive. Later that summer, the flu suddenly vanished for two months, even from the most highly affected areas, allowing the world literally to breathe easy for a time.

That was to change with a sudden jolt. In August 1918, Spanish flu returned with a vengeance. Whereas the earlier flu outbreaks had conventional symptoms, albeit more severe than seasonal strains, the new variant cut down entire populations. The more aggressive disease killed by a process known as a cytokine storm.[28] This is the same pathology that causes the gruesome deaths associated with TGN1412 and with Ebola and other hemorrhagic fever viruses.[29] Within the body, the virus triggered a vigorous host defense in which the disease-fighting cells of the body literally dump all their powerful chemicals into the blood within a short span of time. These sudden changes cause the blood vessels to become leaky, and oxygen-carrying red cells escape from the circulation into tissues. Thus, the symptoms can include spontaneous hemorrhaging of blood from the eyes, nose, mouth, lungs, and/or rectum. The lack of oxygen-carrying capacity means the infection can cause massive cyanosis within hours after the first symptoms. There are many cases where patients turned completely blue or black (similar to von Gruber and Lode's chicken wattles) before dying. An infected individual could start their day feeling fine, with a sudden manifestation of symptoms at noon and be dead before dinner. In other cases, a slightly more benign disease arose and the cause of death was an accompanying bacterial pneumonia that conveyed the *coup de grace* to their influenza-scarred lungs.

The second wave of influenza hit the United States at or near major troop embarkation ports of the eastern seaboard.[30] It isn't clear whether the disease was coming from or going to Europe, but in many ways, the war had arrived on U.S. soil. On 28 August 1918, the first sailors at the Boston receiving ship reported respiratory distress, and within the first three days, sixty sailors had been hospitalized.[31] The public health system was quickly overwhelmed, and makeshift hospitals were established throughout Boston and surrounding towns. By mid-September, the disease was spreading in both military and civilian communities and the death toll jumped from 19 to 334 in Boston alone within days.

William Henry Welch, accompanied by his colleague, Victor Vaughan, Dean of the University of Michigan medical school, arrived at Camp Devens in late September.[32] As an expert pathologist, Welch asked to see the autopsies of the dead recruits. According to his long-time assistant Rufus Cole, and documented by Dr. Howard Markel:

> In the autopsy suite, Welch turned pale at the sight of the cadavers' blue, fluid-filled and swollen lungs. It was hardly the gruesome sight of scores of flayed-open bodies that made Dr. Welch so queasy. In his long career, he had presided over tens of thousands of postmortem examinations. Rather, Welch realized that he was on the ground floor of what he could only categorize as a 'new and terrible plague.'[33]

By the time William Henry Welch had received instructions to report to Camp Devens on 22 September, panic was gripping most of the northeastern United States. Schools were closed and this was soon to be followed by the shuttering of all places of public gathering. While the government tried to stem panic, the epidemic gathered momentum, reported in Chicago and San Francisco within hours of Welch's arrival in Boston. In a well-documented case from John Barry's omnibus book, *The Great Influenza*, the city of Philadelphia held a rally to promote the sales of war bonds and this crowd provided an ideal way to disseminate influenza.[34] Within days, the rates of new cases soared. The death rate for Philadelphia rose to 700 times its normal level and there were scenes recalling the Dark Ages with priests pulling wagons down residential streets, calling for people to bring out their dead.

An unintended positive consequence was that the depletion of troops accelerated the end of the Great War. By Armistice Day on 11 November, the nation and the world were cautiously optimistic, and a brave few emerged into the streets to celebrate, many for the first time in public since the outbreak. Like a patient sniper, the unrelenting virus surged in the days that followed and cut down many celebrants. The pandemic would continue until at least March 1919, when the last American cases were reported in Seattle, Washington.

The final death toll will never be known. A 1927 study estimated twenty-two million deaths and this was revised upward to thirty million by 1991.[35] A 2002 estimate puts the death toll at fifty to 100 million worldwide.[36] These estimates rival the Plague of Justinian in the sixth century, which nearly destroyed Western civilization.[37] To put this in perspective, the deaths of 100 million influenza victims within the single year of 1918, combined with the sixteen million killed in the Great War, meant that 6.5 percent (more than one in twenty) of the world's population who had been alive in 1913 was dead by the start of 1919. A chart of average life expectancy for the twentieth century likewise reveals a steady increase that was unperturbed by the Great War, the Second World War, Korea, or any man-made event. However, a sharp spike downward in 1918 demonstrates the fierce capacity of nature.

Unlike seasonal influenza, the Spanish flu killed a disproportionate number of young, healthy individuals, converting the standard letter V-shaped death profile of influenza into a shape more reminiscent of the letter W.[38] This outcome was assumed at first to be a consequence of the clustering of young men in military camps but later pandemic outbreaks capture the same profile and indicate that young, healthy, and vigorous populations are particularly susceptible to pandemic influenza.

Were such a tragedy to occur today (and recall that pandemics are inevitable and naturally occur every few decades), the death toll in the United States alone could reach almost two million, and the number of people incapacitated for weeks worldwide could reach as high as 2.5 billion (the immobilization figure was determined by extrapolating the number of afflicted from the 1918 to the present population).[39] Such distressing figures might even be conservative given we now live in a world where transcontinental jetliner travel can increase the speed and range of human transport compared to the relative immobility in times of the Spanish flu, which occurred a mere decade after the introduction of the Ford Model-T. Some estimates suggest a flu vaccine would take at least six months and probably could not be made quickly enough to protect most of the population.[40] The modern reliance upon just-in-time manufacturing and inventory control could cause devastating economic disruptions or breakdowns by incapacitating key workers, for example, in sectors such as energy or food production and distribution. The implications are truly sobering.

Out of the Ashes

In the aftermath of the Spanish flu, the medical community embraced the need to understand the causes of this plague and others. These stimuli widened the acceptance of the modern research university, particularly in the United States. One example is personified by Dr. Victor Vaughan, Welch's colleague during the Fort Devens visit. Vaughn returned to the University of Michigan after the Great War and transformed the medical school into one with a research-based approach based on the Johns Hopkins (or more accurately, the von Humboldt) model as practiced by Welch.[41]

Victor Vaughan's son, Henry F. Vaughan, followed in his father's footsteps and was particularly interested in infectious diseases and epidemiology. The father and son copublished the gold-standard book on the epidemiology of infectious diseases in 1922.[42] During the Great War, the younger Vaughan, like his father, had been recruited into the U.S. Army.[43] Henry was assigned to the Sanitary Corps to help oversee the health of the troops, and his specialty was pneumonia and other diseases of the lung. Thus, both father and son found themselves engrossed in the Spanish flu outbreak. In later years, Henry Vaughan was recruited to become the dean of the School of Public Heath at the University of Michigan in 1941. One of his first actions as dean was to recruit a leading expert on influenza, Thomas Francis Jr. to the University of Michigan.[44]

The research interests of Thomas Francis Jr. built upon a seminal 1933 study from the National Institute for Medical Research (U.K.) and the laboratory of Dr. Patrick Playfair Laidlaw.[45] Laidlaw had reported procedures to isolate a virus from an influenza-infected patient. The manuscript conveyed a well-conceived strategy to infect ferrets with the nasal secretions of influenza-infected individuals. Ferrets, the article pointed out, could serve as a model to study and isolate influenza virus. What the article conveniently excluded was that the original intention of this study had actually been to develop a distemper vaccine. In a fortuitous accident, the investigation shifted when one of Laidlaw's researchers became ill with influenza and sneezed on one of the ferrets.[46] That ferret later became ill and the virus was isolated from the infected rodent (as a brief post-script, the ferrets soon evened the score, as evidenced by a 1936 publication from the same institution and one of the same authors, which showed that ferrets could infect humans with influenza virus).

Rather than relying upon a steady line of flu-infected patients to sneeze upon ferrets, Thomas Francis Jr. utilized the relatively new technique of growing viruses in chicken eggs and showed this technique could be used to grow influenza virus.[47] Shortly after moving to Michigan in 1941, Francis hired a newly minted physician by the name of Jonas Salk to work with him to develop a vaccine against influenza. With the looming threat of another world war, Francis and Salk were being funded by the U.S. Army to develop an influenza vaccine that could be used to prevent infection of men in uniform. The army was particularly sensitive to this need, given its experiences at Camp Devens and other bases during the Great War.

Francis and Salk were, in short order, able to develop and test an effective vaccine made from killed influenza virus.[48] However, the two scientists made the poor decision to test their vaccine (as well as less successful ones) on psychiatric patients in Ypsilanti, Michigan, who had been intentionally infected with influenza.[49] Not all of the patients consented to this experiments and the decision to perform the studies in this way would later and rightfully taint the reputations of both scientists. Salk and Francis continued their successful partnership beyond influenza and applied the same approaches to develop a polio vaccine, an accomplishment that was announced to the public on 12 April 1955, exactly ten years to the day after the death of Franklin Delano Roosevelt. FDR is arguably the most famous polio survivor in history, and we now turn our attention to show that Franklin Roosevelt played a pivotal role in the development of the modern American research university by recruiting the former president of MIT and the Carnegie Institute into the federal government.[50]

Growth of the Extramural Program

You may recall from chapter 3 that FDR recruited Vannevar Bush to lead the Office of Scientific Research and Development (OSRD) in the early days of the Second World War.[51] After FDR's death, Bush penned a series of recommendations to President Harry Truman in July 1945 that was forever to change the U.S. economy as well as solidify partnerships among academia, government, and industry. This report, titled *Science: The Endless Frontier*, advocated that basic research was "the pacemaker of technological progress" and proposed to direct federal support for basic research.[52] Though Bush advocated shutting down the wartime activities of the OSRD, he simultaneously advocated the creation of the National Science Foundation to replace it.

Prior to Bush's advocacy, the federal government had passively supported basic biomedical research through mechanisms such as the 1930 Ransdell Act, which reorganized the Laboratory of Hygiene into the National Institutes of Health and authorized the NIH "to accept donations for use in ascertaining the cause, prevention, and cure of disease." Although the government intended to kick-start NIH with a $750,000 endowment, the majority of funding was meant to be raised from private donations.[53] In 1937, the National Cancer Institute (NCI) had been created through an act sponsored by every senator in Congress.[54] The NCI took an innovative approach to fund the training and research of individuals outside of the intramural NIH programs, which included a growing number of research universities. One farsighted aspect of the program was the decision that recipients of extramural grants would be decided by a peer review process to ensure the most promising projects would be prioritized for funding.[55] Vannevar Bush sought to expand this further by ensuring federal support for NIH and by creating the agency today known as the National Science Foundation (NSF).[56] By 1946, the extramural grants program pioneered by the NCI was expanded to all NIH institutes. This program would serve as the fuel for American universities to become the world's "Engines of Innovation."[57]

The funding for NIH experienced a golden period from the 1950s through the mid-1960s. From an initial allotment of $4 million in 1947, annual funding for the grants program had increased to $100 million a decade later.[58] Funding began to stagnate in the late 1960s due to a combination of economic pressures from inflation and the rising costs of the war in Vietnam. Later, Nixon's declaration of a war on cancer helped re-energize NIH and the extramural budget reached $1 billion in 1974. The NIH budget grew modestly through the 1980s and most of the 1990s.

A positive impact of NIH funding was demonstrated by a report that related the amount of NIH funding to declining mortality rates from the four large disease groupings (cardiovascular, stroke, cancer, and diabetes). In recognition that NIH funding positively impacts public health via the creation of new medicines as well as strong economic impact (in terms of creating the foundation for biotechnology, as we will see), a campaign was initiated to double the NIH budget. Indeed, funding from NIH increased from $13.6 billion in FY1998 to $27.1 billion in FY2003. However, this largesse was not to last. Due to further budget cuts and inflation, the NIH budget in 2014 had fallen by 25 percent in terms of purchasing power from its 2003 peak, with obvious implications for the sustainability of future medical improvements.[59]

Having established the roller coaster in NIH funding over time, we will briefly convey how those monies are now distributed. One dollar in ten of the NIH budget is used to support the intramural program, such as the activities performed by Drs. Samuel Broder, Robert Gallo, and others at NIH facilities in Maryland and other locations. Approximately 83 percent of NIH funding supports an extramural grants program. At any given time, more than 300,000 researchers are funded by 50,000 competitive grants awarded to more than 2,500 universities and other research institutions from all fifty states.[60]

The decision to fund one project over another is the result of a rigorous competitive review of grants by scientific peers. These grants comprise the core funding for many American research universities. Grant dollars pay the salaries, equipment, and supplies needed to conduct a study (known as direct costs) but also for the upkeep of their laboratories, such as electricity, Internet connections, and administrative and maintenance costs (known as indirect costs). These indirect costs generally stay in the background but came to the fore as a high-profile scandal when a federal audit in 1991 revealed that Stanford University had utilized indirect funds to support wedding costs and luxury items for its president and, most notoriously, paid the upkeep of the university yacht.[61]

The "Stanford yacht crisis" created considerable and justifiable public concern that some universities were gaming the system to pay for indulgences. After a high-profile inquiry, Stanford quietly paid back the inappropriate expenditures while the NIH initiated comprehensive reform to ensure that their resources were being utilized properly.[62] NIH negotiates the rate of indirect costs on an institution-by-institution basis in recognition that, for example, the cost to support a laboratory at Columbia University in urban Manhattan undoubtedly differs from those incurred by Miami University in rural Oxford, Ohio.

Unlike the Stanford situation, a 2014 investigation by *Nature* magazine revealed that university recovery of indirect costs is much lower than what they pay, indicating that many schools are forced to tap into their endowments, tuition, or other revenues to continue research.[63] The increasing financial losses raise important questions about the sustainability of the research university at a time when these organizations are increasingly the bulwark necessary to ensure future drug discovery, a subject to which we will return in future chapters.

Ironically, the process of applying for and receiving grants is one of the fastest growing reasons for escalating indirect funds. A representative from the Council on Governmental Relations, Tony DeCrappeo, noted that, since the late 1980s, the average size of a grant submission was twenty pages.[64] Increasing federal requirements for assurances of protection from fraud, conflicts of interest, and privacy protection, to name but a few issues, have increased the average size of a grant application to 127 pages. The extra work has caused universities to scale up administrative personnel to track the needed information, thereby increasing indirect costs.

Despite these inefficiencies, NIH funding remains one of the best investments by the federal government. As we will see in the next chapter, funding for university laboratories to conduct basic biology and biomedical research gave rise to the biotechnology revolution, which has become a major contributor to high-paying jobs and taxes back to the federal government. Mazzucato advocates in her eye-opening book, *The Entrepreneurial State*, that public venture capital (her description of funding by NIH and other federal science funding agencies) "is willing to invest in areas with higher risk, while providing greater patience and lower expectations of future returns" and that the government "has often been the source of the most radical path-breaking types of innovation."[65] To convey just one example of the outcomes of publically funded research, we turn to the development of one of the most widely used drugs, the statins.

The Business of Statins

According the U.S. Department of Health and Human Services, heart disease kills about the same number of Americans each year as cancer, influenza, pneumonia, and accidents combined.[66] One in three Americans dies of heart disease and more than one and a half million suffer a heart attack or stroke each year, which equates to one every forty-four seconds. This makes cardiovascular disease the number one killer and also the most expensive health care expenditure, accounting for more than $312 billion dollars in healthcare costs and lost productivity each year. Indeed, almost one dollar of hospital costs in five is devoted to heart diseases. The impact of cardiovascular diseases is even greater than these statistics indicate when you consider that one in three Americans has some form of stroke, heart, or other blood vessel disease, many of whom are unaware of their risk. It is, thus, not surprising that heart disease is a major target of NIH funding, warranting the creation of the National Heart, Lung, and Blood Institute in 1948.[67]

A major cause of cardiovascular diseases occurs when key blood vessels lose their elasticity and either clog or burst. One can think of this like an open water hose in the winter months. As the sun sets on a cold day, ice slowly builds up on the outer edge of the hose and decreases the rush of water. Eventually, the flow will halt altogether or the hose will burst from the steadily accumulating pressure behind the obstruction. When such an event occurs in the human circulatory system, a slowing or halt in blood flow can asphyxiate tissues just beyond the occlusion. If the occlusion occurs in the heart itself, the consequences can include the death of heart tissue, causing an event known as a myocardial infarction or, as it is more commonly known, a heart attack. The back up in pressure on an occluded vessel can ultimately cause a weakening of the blood vessel, known as an aneurysm, which may ultimately burst and cause massive internal bleeding. In other cases, the event that causes the clogging of the vessel could eventually succumb to the accumulating pressure of backed up blood and cause the resulting embolism to break free, only to become entangled again elsewhere in the body. Depending on where the new clog arises, such as the small capillaries of the lung, the outcome can be fatal.

An accumulation of atherosclerotic plaques enriched with cholesterol is a frequent cause of decreased elasticity and blood vessel blockage, much like the ice in our frozen hose. The history of how cholesterol was discovered is at times as thick and occlusive as the substance itself. One often-cited story passed along in the scientific literature is a rather dry story that cholesterol was discovered in 1784 as a result of French scientists studying gallstones. Upon closer inspection, the characters involved become much more interesting.

Antoine François was an ambitious French chemist from middle-class origins, born in 1755, the son of an apothecary in the household of the Duke of Orleans.[68] François chose chemistry as his profession and taught at the Medical School of Paris and then at the Jardin du Roi (the massive botanical garden belonging to King Louis XVI). His lectures were quite popular, in part because François was an early adherent of a new approach of treating chemistry as a science rather than an art, an idea revolutionized by Antoine-Laurent de Lavoisier.

Lavoisier's radical scientific approach to chemistry emphasized objective and quantifiable information over qualitative traits (such as the taste of chemicals, which seems to be a recurring theme in our story). Lavoisier was an aristocrat and respected scientist, widely considered the "Father of Modern Chemistry."[69] However, his highborn background came back to haunt him after the fall of the Bastille. In particular, Lavoisier had purchased a share in a financial company that had collected taxes on behalf of the French Royal government. While Lavoisier espoused reform amidst the turmoil of the French Revolution and its aftermath, Robespierre, leader of the Reign of Terror, ordered the arrest and execution of all individuals involved in tax collection, including Lavoisier.

A popular theory is that Antoine François intentionally implicated Lavoisier while serving as a member of the National Convention. This

speculation is fueled by beliefs that ambition and envy drove François to eliminate the more famous Lavoisier, who was susceptible both because of his financial holdings and his noble birth.[70] Others, such as the famous French
chemist Georges Cuvier, adhere to a version in which Antoine Francoise actively worked to save implicated colleagues but was unable to help the high-
profile Lavoisier.[71] In the end, the indisputable facts are that Lavoisier was
executed by Monsieur Guillotine's new invention on 8 May 1794, whereas
Francois was made Count of Fourcroy on his deathbed in 1809.

Ten years before Lavoisier's execution, François and his colleague, François Paul Lyon Poulletier, had been studying the gall bladder, bile, and gallstones.[72] Their particular interest was to tease out the different substances
that composed gallstones, the excruciatingly painful rocks that can cause
severe infections or life-threatening bouts of pancreatitis. After crushing
and dissolving the gallstones in alcohol (to remove the water), Francois and
Poulletier noted striking, white crystals. Later investigators came to name
this substance after the Greek word for "bile solid" or cholesterine (which
translates to cholesterol in English).

Cholesterol is a lipid (or as it is more commonly known, a fat) and found in
small amounts in every animal cell, where it helps cells keep their shape and
allows them to resist certain chemicals that could otherwise be toxic to the
body, such as water. Completely devoid of cholesterol, the cells in our body
would ooze into oblivion, dissolve in a rainstorm, or shatter into billions of
pieces upon impact with virtually any object. The liver generates large
amounts of cholesterol with the specific purpose of producing bile (also
known as gall), a green or brown fluid that must be produced if we are to digest fats in the small intestine. Cholesterol is itself a type of oil and is a prime
example of the old aphorism that water and oil don't mix. Since blood is essentially a form of water, the cholesterol has to be shuttled about in the blood
by a special type of fat-laden protein known as lipoproteins, the primary car-
rier being known as low-density lipoprotein or LDL.

The problem is that the LDL–cholesterol combination tends to be quite
sticky and adhere to the walls of blood vessels. Once coated, the vessel can
become even stickier and bind ever more LDL–cholesterol, eventually accumulating to the point where the vessel is completely occluded. In 1856,
the modern founder of pathology, the German, Rudolf Virchow, noted that
cholesterol blocked the blood vessels of cadavers who had died of cardiovascular disease.[73] A half-century later, the Russian Nikolay Anichkov fed
rabbits large amounts of cholesterol and noted that their arteries became
occluded and concluded "there is no atherosclerosis without cholesterol."[74]

In a bit of irony (or perhaps justice in the eyes of rodent-lovers), Anichkov himself died as a result of a heart attack in 1964.

Our modern understanding of how cholesterol and diet affect cardiovascular disease was pioneered by a brilliant young scientist by the name of Ancel Keys.[75] Growing up, Keys was evaluated and labeled as "gifted" by the psychologist Lewis Terman, which was quite prescient since Terman at the time was developing a methodology for measuring intelligence that would later become known as the "IQ test."[76] Keys traveled around the world in the early twentieth century, performing odd jobs. His vocations included being an oiler on an ocean liner, a salesclerk at Woolworth's, and an oceanographer at the Scripps Research Institution. Throughout these different career paths, Keys always retained a burning interest and applied science to questions of interest. For example, though not trained in statistics or marine biology, while working an odd job at the Scripps Oceanographic Research Institute, Keys came up with a statistical method to predict the weight of a fish based on its length, and showed how salt water fish were able to survive by passing chloride through their gills.[77]

In 1936, Keys was hired by the Mayo Foundation (now known as the Mayo Clinic) and then the University of Minnesota. In the late 1930s, Keys had become interested in human physiology and diet. According to Keys's colleague, Dr. Elsworth Buskirk:

> When it appeared that the U.S. would be in World War II, Keys went to the Quartermaster Food and Container Institute in Chicago to inquire about emergency rations. The story goes that he was told to go home and leave such things to the professionals. Un-dissuaded, he went to William Wrigley's office and secured $10,000 for the development of an emergency ration. Then, he went to the Cracker Jacks Company. They couldn't supply money, but did provide the water-tight small box concept. The result was the K-ration in sealed Cracker Jacks boxes.[78]

It remains unclear whether the name K-rations was an homage to Keys's last name but, at minimum, we know that the invention, and his initial, were to prove essential for Allied victory (and to be cursed by millions of GIs and sailors in the coming decades).

After the war, Keys remained intrigued by nutrition and noted a seeming paradox that well-fed business executives in the United States had much higher rates of cardiovascular disease than their under-nourished counterparts in post-war Europe. Prior to this, it had been assumed that the health of the heart directly related to overall health. Keys initiated a study in seven countries, which related the level of cholesterol in the blood to the likelihood of suffering from heart disease. Keys further found that a Mediterranean-style diet that is low in animal fat, and avoids saturated fats, seemed to protect against heart disease.[79] These ideas, collectively known as "the lipid hypothesis," were practiced by Keys himself, who died in 2004, two months before his 101st birthday.

Having established that high levels of cholesterol were bad for health, the scientific and medical communities became interested in identifying ways to decrease the levels of serum cholesterol. To know how to block cholesterol, it was important to know how it is produced in the body, which turns out to be a physiologically complex process involving at least thirty different enzymes.[80] The dissection of this process involved many investigators from around the world but was led by two pioneering scientists, Konrad Emil Bloch from Harvard and Feodor Lynen at Munich University, both of whom were awarded the Nobel Prize for their work in the field.[81]

Based on the knowledge gained about how cholesterol is synthesized in the body, armies of academic and pharmaceutical scientists began interrogating the 30-step process. A few semi-successful medicines were developed, including nicotinic acid, clofibrate and cholestyramine.[82] These drugs were designed to remove cholesterol that had already been produced and were marginally effective. Each was limited by side effects and toxicities that minimized their impact. For example, clofibrate caused pituitary disorders and increased the risk of premature death. Cholestyramine caused pronounced bouts of constipation. These were not considered reasonable side effects for a drug that must be taken every day. What was needed was a drug that could prevent the production of cholesterol with a minimal side-effect profile and thus could be useful for the majority of people who have elevated levels of serum cholesterol.

In working through how the body makes cholesterol, Bloch and Lynen identified a precursor molecule, HMG-CoA, which undergoes a chemical modification, known as reduction event, to form a product called mevalonate.[83] This reaction is overseen by an enzyme known as HMG-CoA reductase. In a fortuitous collision that would impact the health of millions, perhaps billions, of people worldwide, two scientists at the University of Texas, Southwestern in Dallas began one of the most productive and durable scientific collaborations in recent history, starting in 1973 and remarkably, continuing to this day. Michael Brown and Joseph Goldstein first met while working at the National Institutes for Health in Bethesda, Maryland.[84] The pair continued their friendship and scientific partnership in Dallas, where they began studying families with an inherited form of hypercholesteremia (excessive cholesterol). This investigation led to the identification of a mutation in HMG-CoA reductase that increased production of cholesterol and the pair hypothesized that by inhibiting this same target, one could lower cholesterol. Their studies ultimately provided conclusive proof that inhibition of HMG-CoA could provide a means of blocking cholesterol, earning the pair a Nobel Prize in 1985 for their work.[85]

The prosecution of HMG-CoA as a target to lower cholesterol was first adjudicated by a Japanese scientist, Akira Endo. Endo was drawn to biomedical research after learning the popular (and, we now know, not entirely accurate) story of how Alexander Fleming discovered penicillin.[86] Inspired by Fleming's approach, Endo began working on projects to discover and characterize new natural products from fungi while working at Sankyo pharmaceuticals in Tokyo. He then became interested in cholesterol and wrote Konrad Bloch to ask if he could study under his tutelage for a time. Bloch did not have an opening at the time, so Endo studied HMG-CoA with Bernard Horecker at the Albert Einstein College of Medicine. Upon his return to Sankyo, Endo combined his interest in fungal natural products with his new understanding of HMG-CoA. After screening almost 4,000 different strains of fungi, a blue-green mold isolated from rice at a grain shop in Kyoto was found to produce a molecule that blocks HMG-CoA reductase. Study of the fungal-derived molecule, known as Compactin, was almost halted after initial studies in animals showed it had no activity in rats. However, Endo persevered and found Compactin was effective in reducing serum cholesterol levels in chickens, dogs, and monkeys. Early clinical trials in humans also showed great promise but Sankyo suddenly cancelled the project in 1980 after a study in dogs suggests very high levels of Compactin (at hundreds of times more than would be used in patients) might cause a rare type of lymphoma. Sankyo immediately dropped the program, while Akira Endo left Sankyo to pursue an academic career at Tokyo Noko University. The story may well have ended here were it not for another scientist who was making the opposite transition, from academia to industry.

Among the academics who contributed greatly to the understanding of cholesterol and fatty acid synthesis throughout this period was Dr. P. Roy Vagelos.[87] Vagelos began his research career at the National Heart Institute, where he became interested in how fatty acids are synthesized, an area of investigation he would continue as a department chair at Washington University in Saint Louis. In 1976, Vagelos joined Merck, Sharp and Dohme Laboratories as head of research and focused the company around the concept of rational drug design, which, as we have seen, is the process whereby knowledge of a disease and its causes can be used to identify particular targets to be perturbed (either blocked or assisted) with potential new drugs. This was a pioneering and radical concept for an industry that had primarily used phenotypic screening, the process whereby one selects drug candidates based on their ability to cause the desired effect without necessarily knowing why the drug worked.

Under Vagelos, Merck focused its energies around a problem near to his heart and with which their scientific leader had much expertise: lipid and cholesterol biosynthesis. Merck had developed its own expertise as the developers of the early cholesterol lowering drug, cholestyramine. However, this particular drug was not sufficiently efficacious and a poor side effect profile led Merck to sell the drug to one of its competitors and start afresh. Using a similar approach as Akira Endo, the Merck team began a campaign to identify fungal-based inhibitors of HMG-CoA. They were successful in identifying a promising drug, which was ultimately named lovastatin.[88] As often happens in science, Endo also discovered the same molecule while working at Tokyo Noko University and at roughly the same time as the Merck team. Vagelos's group progressed from discovery of the compound to testing in people when a rumor began to circulate that Compactin had caused tumors in dogs. Like Sankyo, Vagelos decided to suspend additional work on lovastatin. Ultimately, the FDA encouraged Merck to re-engage in this investigation by allowing the drug to be tested in volunteers from the high-risk familial hypercholesteremia patients that Brown and Goldstein had studied to identify the link to HMG-CoA reductase. The results were remarkable and the side effect profile was highly encouraging. Ultimately, these positive findings, accompanied by lessening concerns about the potential link to cancer, caused Vagelos to re-engage Merck in widespread testing of lovastatin, ultimately leading to its approval by the FDA in September 1987.

As it turns out, an FDA approval to initiate sales was only the first hurdle blocking Merck. Although a quarter of the U.S. population was afflicted with high cholesterol, only a small fraction of patients were being treated for the indication.[89] The limitation arose in part because of a reticence by doctors to prescribe drugs such as cholestyramine, which had many undesirable side effects, to patients who were outwardly quite healthy. To overcome this limitation, Merck launched a widespread advertising campaign, which was a rarity at the time. Working with the American Heart Association, the company conducted cholesterol screening at hospitals and other large venues, complemented by a widespread television commercial campaign to warn Americans of the dangers of high cholesterol. These actions allowed lovastatin to become a relative rarity, a drug that achieved more than a billion dollars in peak sales worldwide. This success helped usher in the age of the blockbuster drug, a subject to which we will return in a later chapter.

At the same time lovastatin was being developed and approved, the entire drug discovery enterprise was being radically reformed through the creation and growth of a new industry: biotechnology.

CHAPTER SIX

The DNA of Biotechnology

In the early 1970s, a new industry was born. Biotechnology was one of the first tangible outcomes arising from the burst in understanding facilitated by NIH's funding of basic and applied research. This was a revolution that would transform human health while generating enormous revenues. It is also a revolution that almost didn't happen and whose continuation is increasingly tenuous. In this chapter, we will provide an overview of the foundations of biotechnology, emphasizing its blending of science and business. This will provide a cornerstone for understanding why the industry is fundamentally at risk at a time when its potential to herald a new generation of medical breakthroughs has been primed by recent gains in understanding the basis of health and disease.

In the years following the traumas of the Great War and the Spanish flu, the British scientist Frederick Griffith was studying two strains of *Streptococcal pneumonia*, a bacterial pathogen of the lung that had delivered the *coup de grace* for many individuals infected with the Spanish flu.[1] One strain of bacteria formed smooth-edged colonies when grown in the laboratory and was quite deadly. The other strain of *Strep* formed rough-edged colonies and was comparatively benign. Griffith's unexpected finding was that if he co-injected a live strain of benign bacteria mixed with a heat-killed sample of virulent bacteria, the mice died. Griffith concluded that something from the dead bacteria had "transformed" the benign bugs into a killer.

Though Griffith had a reputation as a careful scientist, many doubted his claims, including an American scientist from the Rockefeller Institution in New York City by the name of Oswald Avery. Avery repeated his studies and arrived at the shocking conclusions that not only was the finding accurate, but the genetic material responsible for this effect was not a protein (as had been assumed) but instead a substance known as deoxyribonucleic acid, or DNA for short.[2] Avery became a legend in biomedical research and holds the unwanted distinction of being widely regarded as the scientist most deserving of a Nobel Prize who never received the award. As we will see, the birth of recombinant DNA technology, which powered the first wave of biotechnology, is engorged with a surplus of Nobel Prizes.

DNA Research in Six Sentences and Nobel Prizes

Avery's discovery inspired Joshua Lederberg of Columbia University and Edward Tatum of Yale University in 1946 to publish a report that detailed a biological process, termed "conjugation," which allowed bacteria to transmit genetic information to one another via DNA, earning them a 1958 Nobel Prize.[3] Joshua was renowned for his brilliant mind and strong personality while a professor at the University of Wisconsin, where he worked with his wife Esther to describe a small, mobile piece of DNA (termed a "plasmid") that was the vehicle of genetic information exchange during conjugation.[4] Esther discovered phage lambda, a type of virus that infects and inserts its own DNA into a bacterium, and the mechanism by which this occurs led to a 1969 Nobel Prize for three investigators (Max Delbruck, Salvador Luria, and Alfred Hershey, though not Esther herself).[5]

The year after Lederberg published the discovery of plasmids, Francis Crick, James Watson, and Maurice Wilkins used the data from a technology known as X-ray crystallography, developed by Jerome Karle and honored with a 1985 Nobel Prize, to publish their seminal and renowned finding of the double helical molecular structure of DNA in a 1953 article that earned them a 1962 Nobel Prize.[6] Three years later, Arthur Kornberg of Washington University in Saint Louis discovered a protein, DNA polymerase, which allowed DNA to make copies of itself through a process known as replication, which was recognized with a 1959 Nobel Prize.[7] One of Kornberg's fellow Brooklynites was Paul Berg, who received a 1980 Nobel Prize for describing how the genetic information encoded within DNA is translated into proteins.[8]

Ground-Shaking Forces in the Bay Area

The San Francisco Bay region of Northern California in the early 1970s would serve as a crucible where the people, knowledge, and tools gained in the previous half century would coalesce into a scientific upheaval. That disparate people and ideas would be forged together in San Francisco was an amalgam of relationships and happenstance driven by a single far-sighted visionary. Frederick Emmons Terman was the son of Lewis Terman, the man who you may recall from the previous chapter who had popularized the IQ test and identified the genius of Ancel Keys.[9] The son presumably also did quite well on the test, as his brilliance would ultimately outshine his father's.

After obtaining a bachelor's and master's degree at Stanford, Frederick Terman earned a Ph.D. in electrical engineering at MIT.[10] His doctoral mentor was none other than Vannevar Bush, the brilliant scientist and engineer who, among other roles, led the Office for Scientific Research and Development during World War II and penned the note that spawned the founding of the National Science Foundation. Like his mentor, Terman returned to Stanford in 1925 and looked to build the institution into a visionary teaching, research, and technology powerhouse. Among Terman's students were Oswald Garrison Villar Jr., as well as two brothers, Russell and Sigurd Varian, all of whom were early pioneers of radar in the years before the Second World War. Other Terman students included William Hewlett and David Packard, who formed the technology powerhouse that still bears their names.[11] Terman himself played a critical role in the war by leading a team at the Radio Research Laboratory at Harvard, where they developed aluminum strips to block German radar (known as chaff) as well as other radar-based technologies.

Terman returned to Stanford after the war intent upon building the university and the region into a technological powerhouse. To this end, he actively worked to implement the Stanford Industrial Park in 1961 and to recruit technology companies. In doing so, he was broadly credited, along with another Stanford professor, William Bradford Shockley, as the founder of "Silicon Valley."[12] The companies included in the park included some of his students' (Varian Associates and Hewlett-Packard) as well as Eastman-Kodak, General Electric, and Lockheed.

In 1955, Terman was appointed Provost at Stanford, a position he would hold for the following decade. In this role, Terman actively recruited new faculty into the emerging field of recombinant DNA engineering. Among his early successes was the recruitment of Arthur Kornberg, who was leading the Department of Microbiology at Washington University in St Louis. The department was a close-knit group and Kornberg felt it necessary to discuss the potential move with his colleagues prior to accepting. In an amazing demonstration of collegiality, and a coup for Stanford, Kornberg moved his entire department from Washington University to Stanford in the same year Kornberg was tapped for the 1959 Nobel Prize.[13] This close-knit group, already a key force in the emerging recombinant DNA revolution, included Paul Berg and A. Dale Kaiser and formed the nucleus of a much larger effort that led to Stanford's domination of the new field for years to come.

Joshua Lederberg had recently won a Nobel Prize for his work with bacteriophage when he learned of Kornberg's imminent move. Kornberg was well aware of Lederberg's brilliance but considered that his big personality might not be the best fit for the family-like atmosphere established within his Washington University and now Stanford team.[14] Therefore, Kornberg set out on a mission to convince Stanford Provost Terman to create a new department of genetics that Kornberg could lead, allowing Stanford to score two separate Nobel laureates in the span of weeks. Furthermore, the critical mass that centered on Palo Alto would spawn many more laureates in the following decades.

Paul Berg was one of those future laureates. Berg arrived at Stanford from Kornberg's Washington University team in 1959. In 1965, Berg became interested in the biology of bacteriophage lambda after auditing a graduate-level course taught by his colleague, Dale Kaiser. Kaiser and a colleague, Andre Lwoff, had worked together at the Pasteur Institute in the mid-1950s to show that, on occasion, bacteriophage lambda inserts a piece of its own DNA into the genetic material of its host bacteria through a process known as lysogeny. In the lecture, Kaiser noted the analogies between bacteriophage and tumor-associated viruses. You may recall that Rous sarcoma virus caused tumors in chickens and Kaiser considered that this process might arise if the virus inserted DNA into certain cells that, in turn, triggered the malignant process.

Shortly after this eye-opening lecture, Kaiser invited an esteemed colleague, Renato Dulbecco, to give a guest lecture at Stanford.[15] Paul Berg's attendance at this seminar would change his life as well as the course of modern molecular biology. Dulbecco had recently relocated from Caltech to the Salk Institute, where Jonas Salk himself recruited him. Dulbecco was studying one particular tumor virus, simian virus 40 (SV40), which had been shown to cause tumors in certain monkeys.[16] It was becoming clear that certain tumor-causing viruses, like SV40, had the interesting ability to cut out pieces of DNA from cells they infected. These viruses could then drop these off into other cells that they later infected. If the delivery of new DNA occurred at just the right place and time, the changes might be sufficient to cause a normal cell to become cancerous. After meeting with Dulbecco, the two agreed that Berg would take a one-year sabbatical at Salk to learn more about working with SV40.[17] Renato Dulbecco would later share a 1975 Nobel Prize for his work with SV40 while Berg redirected his research to learn more about how DNA might be inserted into mammalian cells.

In the year before Berg's sabbatical, the University of California at San Francisco (UCSF), just up the road from Stanford, hired a new, young professor by the name of Herbert Boyer. Boyer's expertise was in identifying and characterizing restriction enzymes from bacteriophage.[18] Restriction enzymes had recently been discovered as the enzymes that certain viruses (like the bacteriophage discovered by Esther Kornberg) used to cut DNA like a pair of scissors at very specific sites.[19] In another convergence of events, two medical doctors who had trained at the Washington University medical center in St Louis during the mid-1950s, Hamilton Smith and Daniel Nathans, came together a decade later at Johns Hopkins University, where their discovery of restriction enzymes allowed them to share a 1978 Nobel Prize.[20]

As Berg was returning from his sabbatical, Stanford expanded its depth of academic expertise in DNA technology by recruiting a young faculty member by the name of Stanley Norman Cohen. Cohen had recently discovered a means to transform *E. coli* bacteria with plasmids with high efficiency. Though Stanley Cohen and Herbert Boyer worked about thirty miles apart, their path to collaboration took a 2,500 mile detour to Hawaii.[21] While attending a scientific conference at the University of Hawaii on plasmid biochemistry in November 1972, Cohen sat in on a presentation by Boyer, who was discussing his recent discovery of the EcoR1 restriction enzyme. Cohen and Boyer sat in a deli on Waikiki beach until late into the night, discussing the potential use of the enzyme Boyer had discovered to help cut the plasmid DNA that Cohen was studying. Their shared idea was that this approach might allow them to insert a foreign gene within the plasmid and then produce the protein in bacteria transformed with the plasmid. The scientific implications were many but the pair could not have imagined the profound commercial implications.

After Cohen and Boyer demonstrated that the technology worked with bacterial genes, the pair took the unprecedented step of expressing a gene from one species in another. Specifically, genes from *Xenopus laevis*, an aquatic frog native to sub-Saharan Africa, were introduced into the bacterium, *E. coli*. In a seminal 1973 manuscript in the journal, *Proceedings of the National Academy of Science*, they showed that the engineered bacteria could be coaxed into producing a frog protein.[22]

The Boyer and Cohen's discovery of recombinant DNA technology was a fundamental breakthrough that seems worthy of a Nobel Prize, particularly given the myriad prizes awarded to colleagues at Stanford and elsewhere. However, Cohen and Boyer have consistently been overlooked for this honor despite the deep and lasting impact of their finding. Instead, the two have been pilloried by many in the academic community and Boyer was even subject to a faculty senate investigation at UCSF, though ultimately cleared. The reasons for this derision can be summarized in one word: patents.

Before discussing the impact of intellectual property and its role in the foundation of the biotechnology enterprise, it is necessary to take a brief digression to discuss how this revolution was almost stillborn in the days after the discovery of recombinant DNA technology.

Fearing Andromeda

A popular myth of the ancient Greeks centers on Andromeda, a young girl condemned to death following a hubristic boast by her mother that the daughter was more beautiful than the sea nymphs. The hero Perseus ultimately saves Andromeda, chained to a rock and waiting to be killed by a sea monster named Cetus. Like the mythological heroine, the emerging field of biotechnology was almost sacrificed at a young age, near the sea, and with its own share of hubris. By coincidence, Cetus was also the name of the first biotechnology company (formed in 1971) and a tale of Andromeda inspired the forces seeking the destruction of a young biotechnology industry. Fortunately, rational thought and reason ultimately saved the industry from being torn to pieces.

The late 1960s and early 1970s witnessed excitement about technology balanced by fear of what might follow. The anticipation of the Apollo missions to the moon were accompanied by concerns about the rise of technology as evidenced by *2001: A Space Odyssey* in 1968, which was released fifteen months before Apollo XI landed in the Sea of Tranquility.[23] In the book and film, the HAL-9000 computer is unable to resolve a conflict between continuing a deep space mission, which, unknown to the astronauts, is intended to explore evidence of alien intelligence. HAL decides the mission outweighs the lives of the astronauts and disposes of them in a classic technology versus man confrontation, which has become a staple of the science fiction genre. The movie, *2001: A Space Odyssey* was a critical and popular success, being nominated for four 1969 Academy Awards and winning one.

In the following year, the futurist Alvin Toffler released the book *Future Shock*, which sold over six million copies and was itself released as a popular movie, narrated by Orson Welles, in 1972.[24] *Future Shock* detailed Toffler's concerns that technological and societal changes were accelerating at such a pace such that "information overload" (a term popularized by the book) would destroy the psyche of individuals and then the entire civilization. These issues were percolating in the background of those weighing the risks and benefits of recombinant DNA technologies when Andromeda provided an assertive reminder of the complexity and potential dangers of biological research.

The Andromeda Strain, penned by Michael Crichton in 1969, details an outbreak of a deadly organism with the ability, among other things, to kill people instantly.[25] The extraterrestrial pathogen, named Andromeda, is ultimately identified as a contaminant from a military satellite mission that was intended to collect potential new biological weapons in the Earth's atmosphere and in space. The organism had been unintentionally let loose upon the satellite's return and the plague proceeds to kill almost everything and everyone in a remote Arizona town, near where the satellite landed. The protagonist of *The Andromeda Strain* is Dr. Jeremy Stone, a Nobel prize-winning professor and chair of bacteriology at Stanford University. The comparisons to Joshua Lederberg are presumably intentional; particularly when one considers Lederberg's highly publicized interest in astronomy and exobiology, which is the search for life beyond Earth and the impact of space on terrestrial life.[26] Lederberg had penned many articles and memos regarding the need for quarantining astronauts to avoid seeding potential plagues derived from extraterrestrial organisms or chemicals.[27] The need to quarantine returnees from space was adopted in the late 1960s and is maintained by NASA to the present day. The book became a bestseller, establishing a science-gone-wild genre that Crichton would come to dominate with later bestsellers such as *Jurassic Park*, which was adapted into a successful 1993 movie, further piquing the public's interest in concerns about the oversight of scientific research.[28]

In the same summer that the movie version of *The Andromeda Strain* appeared in theaters, Paul Berg received funding from the American Cancer Society to transduce *E. coli* bacteria with SV40 DNA.[29] A Stanford doctoral student tasked to perform the project, Janet Mertz, was attending a summer course at Cold Spring Harbor Laboratory and discussed her planned research. Rather than being impressed, the instructor, Dr. Robert Pollack, expressed great concern.[30] This matter resonated with Pollack, who spent much of his career, before and since, blending science, ethics, and religion.[31] His basis for concern was that SV40 was known to cause tumors. He reasoned that if genes from SV40 were encoded in bacteria, not just any bacteria mind you, but one of the most common microbes in the human gut, then the engineered *E. coli* might cause tumors in people. These bacteria might then spread to other people with devastating results. Such thinking created considerable angst in both the scientific and general populations that was reinforced by daily showings of the film, *Andromeda Strain*. Pollack mobilized many in the scientific community to protest the potential implications of the intended experiment.[32] Even though he knew the risks to be low, Berg volunteered in

1972 to suspend his intended work on recombinant DNA pending resolution of these concerns.[33]

In response to the issues raised by Pollack and others, the NIH and NSF sponsored a meeting of scientific experts in 1973 at the Asilomar Conference Center in Pacific Grove, California.[34] The relative risks were discussed and some common sense procedures were established to minimize the potential risk of infection with tumor viruses or bacteria bearing recombinant plasmids. However, a moratorium on further research remained in place. This seemed to settle nerves a bit, but only for a short time.

A research talk by Herb Boyer at a Gordon Research Conference on Nucleic Acids in the summer of 1973 was followed by publication of the Cohen and Boyer paper in November.[35] Both presentations demonstrated the feasibility of recombinant DNA technology and triggered an avalanche of renewed concern about safety. Cohen and Boyer volunteered to participate in a "who's who" meeting of peers and to suspend their work until questions about the potential biohazards of recombinant DNA were properly addressed. This action was accompanied by a request from the National Academy of Sciences that Berg convene a committee to study the question. These events ultimately led to the International Conference on Recombinant DNA in February 1975, which was again held at the Asilomar Conference Center.[36] The debates about safety and what constituted proper control of the new technology were varied and intense. Within a few days, the scientists concluded the meeting with a series of guidelines, which were codified a year later by the NIH. These rules ensured the safe use of the new technology and eased concerns, both in the scientific and larger communities. The moratorium on recombinant DNA research was then lifted and an explosion in biomedical research began in earnest.

The Birth of Genentech

The controversy surrounding the Cohen and Boyer discovery did not entirely abate with the resolutions of the 1975 Asilomar Conference. A different and arguably even more intense debate now divided the scientific community. The cultural norm among many basic research scientists can be summarized by the well-known phrase from the twelfth-century French abbot, Bernard of Clarivaux: "There are those, who seek knowledge for the sake of knowledge; that is Curiosity . . ."[37] Among other scientific professionals, such as chemists, the idea of patenting an invention was relatively common but this view was not held among all biologists. Thus, the decision by Stanford and UCSF to patent the findings by Cohen and Boyer reso- nated poorly with many of their colleagues. As stated by their Stanford col- league, Paul Berg, years later: "Their claims to commercial ownership of the techniques for cloning all possible DNAs, in all possible vectors, joined in all possible ways, in all possible organisms were dubious, presumptuous, and hubristic."[38] The U.S. Patent Office ruled otherwise and awarded Stan- ford and UCSF a broad patent that would be licensed for the sale of more than 2,000 different products by 468 companies.[39] In total, Stanford and UCSF acquired more than a quarter billion dollars in licensing revenues and set into motion the biotechnology revolution.[40]

An even more challenging concept for their scientific peers to accept was Herbert Boyer's decision to commercialize this new technology in the form of a start-up biotechnology company. Within a year after the second Asilo- mar Conference, Boyer had been approached by Robert Swanson, a twenty- nine-year-old venture capitalist working for a Bay area investment firm that had started just a few years before under the name of Kleiner and Perkins.[41] Swanson proposed to start a company with Boyer to develop new products using Cohen and Boyer's new technology. The company was to be named Genentech.

Within a year, the scientists at Genentech had cloned the human gene for a molecule known as somatostatin into *E. coli* bacteria, thereby showing the utility of using bacteria as microscopic production factories to produce a recombinant protein.[42] While somatostatin did become a product in the years to follow, the scientists had their eyes on a much larger prize: recombi- nant human insulin.[43]

Since its rollout in the 1920s as a consequence of the efforts by Banting, Best, Collip, and Macleod, the primary source of insulin continued to be an extract purified from the pancreas of slaughtered cows and pigs. While the purity of this material had improved considerably over the years, any prod- uct from an animal-derived source runs the risk of being rejected as foreign by the body's immune system. The need for fully human insulin led many companies to try and derive synthetic forms of the hormone, including a fully human version that was prepared in the Basel laboratories of Ciba- Geigy and another from Novo Industri.[44] The clinical results with the syn- thetic material were promising but the costs required to produce the material were relatively high.

The first biotechnology race began as Genentech scientists sought to pro- duce recombinant human insulin in *E. coli*. Boyer initiated a collaboration with Dr. Arthur Riggs and Keiichi Itakura, geneticists at the City of Hope, to isolate the gene for human insulin and to encode this into a plasmid for expression in *E. coli*.[45] Their competitors included other upstart biotechnology companies, most notably a small Cambridge, Massachusetts, company by the name of Biogen, which was also seeking to produce recombinant human insulin. Another synthetic approach was being developed by the Scandinavian company, Novo Industri, that took the approach of converting pig-derived insulin into its human analog. The race to gain FDA approval took place over the late 1970s and into the early 1980s and was ultimately won in 1982 by a partnership involving Genentech and its licensee, Eli Lilly and Co.

Although Genentech had won the race to launch the first recombinant human product, the victory occurred at a high cost to Herb Boyer. In the midst of the competition and on the same day in October 1980 that Genentech launched its initial public offering, Herb Boyer learned that Paul Berg, Walter Gilbert (the founder of Biogen), and Frederick Sanger had received the Nobel Prize. The award credited Berg with the discovery of recombinant DNA technology.[46] Both Boyer and Cohen were overlooked and the decision by the pair to patent the new technology is widely attributed to this snub.

Recombinant DNA technology gave rise to many new scientific and commercial opportunities and founded an entirely new field known as molecular biology. As we have already seen, this included the ability to produce proteins such as insulin. However, an even more impactful application would come from a synthesis of molecular biology and the new understanding of the science of immunology.

Magic Bullets and Smart Bombs: The Rise of Monoclonal Antibodies

The German scientist Paul Ehrlich introduced the concept of a "magic bullet" in a 1906 prediction that chemists would soon be able to produce medicines that could seek out and eliminate the causes of disease.[47] As the immunologist who first described antitoxins (later known as antibodies), one can presume Ehrlich would likely have been pleased with the discovery and application of monoclonal antibodies three-quarters of a century later.

Cesar Milstein was a British scientist of Argentinian descent working at Cambridge University in the late 1970s.[48] His research focused on antibodies, a set of proteins produced by a type of host defense component, known as a B cell. These antibodies circulate in the blood and patrol for and then eliminate foreign pathogens. Each person generates billions of different antibodies but each B cell produces only one type of antibody.[49] In 1957, the

Australian scientist Frank Macfarlane Burnet had conjectured that the immune system remains quiescent until activated by a foreign molecule.[50] One way to think of this is that an antibody can be thought of as a key and the foreign molecule, known as an antigen, as a lock. When the proper combination of key and lock arises, the body's immune system jumps into action.[51] Burnet had limited this "clonal selection theory" to an assumption that the diversity of B cells in the body were determined at birth, but this idea was refined by Joshua and Esther Lederberg, who argued that diversity must continue throughout life.[52]

Milstein wanted to study antibodies produced by normal B cells but needed tools that did not exist. Conventional studies had relied upon antibodies derived from the serum of rabbits, sheep, or goats. The problem was that these antibodies were polyclonal, meaning that they arose from mixtures of B cells. It was far too complicated to study the fate of individual B cells in a polyclonal mixture that may contain hundreds or even thousands of different B cells. Instead, Milstein decided to make use of existing technologies but configured in a way never before seen. Milstein assigned the project to a new post-doctoral fellow recently arrived from Germany, Georges J. F. Kohler.[53] The team of Kohler and Milstein developed a fundamental technology that is still used today, more than three decades after it revolutionized science and biotechnology.[54]

Milstein's work at the time focused on myelomas, a type of B cell cancer that has the ability to produce antibodies. He reasoned that myeloma cells are immortal and could grow forever. If he could physically combine a myeloma cell with a normal B cell that was producing an antibody that he wanted to study, then he might be able to derive a hybrid cell that produced the desired antibody and yet lived forever. In other words, Kohler and Milstein sought to create a Frankenstein-like chimera that blended the immortality of cancer with the antibody secretion of normal cells. These cells would ultimately become known as "hybridomas."[55]

Making antibodies was quite straightforward and techniques for immunization had been practiced and optimized for decades. However, a major challenge was determining how to fuse normal B cells with myeloma cells. In the early 1970s, Dr. Jack A Lucy of the University of London showed that a chemical known as polyethylene glycol, or PEG (which is closely related to the solvent used to manufacture Elixir Sulfanilamide in the 1930s), could fuse the membranes of adjacent cells together, essentially melting two cells into one.[56] Kohler reasoned that this technique might allow the team to develop a hybrid of a myeloma and normal B cell.

Having achieved the ability to fuse cells together, the question then shifted to one of determining how to select for those cells that produce the desired antibody. There were three sets of hybrid cells that could arise from a fusion. The desired outcome was a fusion of a myeloma and a normal B cell. However, there were two other outcomes that could be problematic. The first would occur if two normal B cells fused together. Kohler and Milstein reasoned that these cells were mortal and would eventually die and thus were not a problem.

The other undesired outcome would be a fusion of two myeloma cells together. Kohler and Milstein need a trick to solve this problem and it came from recombinant DNA technology. The team engineered the myeloma cell to no longer produce a protein called HGPRT.[57] Without HGPRT, the myeloma cells, whether fused or not, would die if grown in certain nutrients. However, normal cells have HGPRT, and so a fusion of a myeloma cell with a normal cell would allow the hybridoma uniquely to survive and grow when fed these nutrients.

Putting all these tricks together, Kohler and Milstein first immunized a mouse to sensitize it to an antigen of interest.[58] The B cells from the immunized mouse were then mixed with myeloma cells and treated with PEG such that pairs of cells fused together. The mixed pairs were grown in the special media that killed myeloma cells while the normal cells died if they did not receive the immortality granted to them by a successful fusion with myeloma cells. Thus, the only survivors were those fusions, or hybridomas, of a normal B cell with a myeloma cell. The hybridomas could then be grown as a single clone. The antibody secreted by the hybridomas thus became known as a "monoclonal antibody."

Stacks of Patents

In July 1975, Kohler and Milstein presented their findings to the U.K. Medical Research Council (MRC) and an impressed administrative official, Tony Vickers, immediately recognized the great promise of the technology, and urged action by the National Research Development Corporate (NRDC), which was responsible for patenting ideas generated by the MRC.[59] In an act of extraordinary and wasteful bureaucracy, an NRDC official replied fifteen months later that he had elected not to proceed based on an inability to "identify any immediate applications" of the technology. This decision would ultimately cost the U.K. government billions of pounds in lost royalties and may have contributed to the fact that the United States, rather than the United Kingdom, would dominate biotechnology in the years to come.[60]

Unlike the NRDC, most of the biotechnology industry recognized the value of the Kohler and Milstein monoclonal antibody technology. Quite quickly, monoclonal antibody technology was a cauldron of aggressive discovery and the coin of the realm was the patent. The entire industry was dominated by a core set of patents needed to perform even the most basic activities. A prime example was the aforementioned Boyer and Cohen patent. No work with recombinant DNA technologies could be commercialized without paying Stanford a licensing fee.

Patents were crucial since almost everything about biotechnology was novel. A strong patent position provided a way to separate yourself from the competition or simply to make money by licensing your technology to others without the burden of having to make any tangible product. As a consequence of aggressive intellectual property protection, early adopters of biotechnology often gained insurmountable leads, and in many cases, patent royalties provided the currency for companies, like Genentech, to keep their doors open and develop new products.

Over time, the royalties required to produce a biotechnology product were measured using terms such as "stacks," as in, "Here is a stack of patents that we need to license before we can sell our product."[61] It was not uncommon for the "stacks" on antibody products to exceed 30 or 40 percent of total revenues. In other words, more than a third of gross proceeds might be paid out simply to service patents. These stacks did not include the additional costs of manufacturing, selling, or marketing the product, much less research and development costs. Compounding this, many antibody products were inherently more expensive to manufacture given their larger size and lower yields. Consequently, biotechnology products quickly became associated with high prices.

The high costs of production and licensing, as well as technical limitations, led many early prognosticators to write off the nascent biotechnology industry. However, these critics were soon quieted by an extraordinary rise in biotechnology and its even more extraordinary medical and commercial successes.

A Toxic Start

According to the FDA, the earliest antibody product still sold today is antivenin (*Lactrodectus mactans*), which was approved for use in 1936.[62]

Commercialized by Merck, Sharpe and Dohme, the serum is a sterile solution of venom-neutralizing globulins (antibodies) from the serum of horses immunized with venom from black widow spiders (since horses are not harmed by the venom). The product has been in continuous production for eighty years, which is a testament to its safety and efficacy.

Despite the ability to isolate serum from animals (or in some cases from humans, who have been exposed to a pathogen such as occurred with survivors of the 2014 Ebola outbreak), there are inherent limitations to animal antisera that have been addressed with monoclonal antibodies. Serum collection can be laborious and cost-prohibitive, with significant batch-to-batch variation. Non-human antibodies will eventually be recognized as foreign by the body's defense mechanisms and may be eliminated before they can perform their beneficial actions. In a more extreme version, the animal antibodies may trigger a vigorous immune response that can turn deadly. Returning to the example of the spider antivenin, the administration of a horse antibody is tolerated because the need for the treatment is presumably only once in a lifetime.

The first monoclonal antibody product, Muromonab-CD3, at first glance has the same limitations as the spider antivenin.[63] The product, approved in 1992 and marketed by Jannsen Pharmaceuticals, is a mouse-derived (murine) monoclonal antibody indicated for the prevention of acute rejection in patients in the first days following organ transplantation. The drug eliminates T-cells, the "generals" of the immune system. Thus, Muromonab-CD3 eliminates, albeit temporarily, the same cells that would otherwise cause the drug itself to be rejected. Because of this unique double negative, the drug is still used today.

Although Muromonab-CD3 remains a useful part of the transplantation pharmacopeia, early pioneers in the field of monoclonal antibody drugs recognized it would be important to modify antibodies to make them more human-like. The first step in a long progression was the development of recombinant DNA technologies to create "chimeric" antibodies.[64] Like creatures from mythology, these modern-day chimeras were antibodies comprising both human and non-human sequences.

As a brief summary, an antibody is a complex protein shaped like the capital letter Y. Small portions at the tip of each of the two small arms comprise the sites where the antibodies bind their targets.[65] The concept behind chimerization is to replace the murine portions of the antibody, which are not involved in binding antigens for their analogous sequences in humans. In this way, greater than 90 percent of the murine character of the antibody is eliminated. The first examples of chimeric antibodies demonstrated less immunogenicity but when administered repeatedly, even chimeric antibodies were ultimately rejected. Such findings constrained the use of chimeric antibodies for chronic indications, such as rheumatoid arthritis or certain types of cancer therapy.

A next step in the process was the development of technologies to remove the few remaining murine portions of antibody products. These "humanized" antibodies were even less susceptible to being rejected by the patient's immune system and have become the gold standard.[66] Over time, new techniques have been further developed to allow mice (and even bacteria) to produce antibodies that are fully human and thus do not suffer from the same immunogenicity issues. All this innovation entailed costly research and development activities. The organizations developing the improved antibody products passed along the costs to consumers and payers (for example, insurance companies) through licensing fees and royalties, thereby contributing to the royalty stacks and higher overall prices of antibody products.

Having established the framework for antibody drug discovery and some of the challenges in developing a new product, we turn to one example of how these technologies were applied.

Persistence and Focus: MedImmune

The "barking" sound of an infant's "croup" is familiar to many parents. The name is an Old English term meaning "to cry with a hoarse throat," and the disease is seasonal, occurring like clockwork in the winter months. The symptoms, most notably the barking cough, which sounds remarkably like an enthusiastic seal, might almost sound humorous were its frequency and volume not worse at night. For most children, the symptoms resolve within a day or two and life returns to normal. In a small fraction, including our own healthy daughter, croup can lead to severe bronchiolitis, which in turn increases the risk of childhood asthma.[67] For an even more unfortunate few, most notably premature and immunosuppressed infants, the disease can be deadly. For these children, whose lungs are immature and unable to defend themselves, hospitalization may be required and supportive care may be insufficient.

The frequency and occasional severity of these infections spurred many to try to identify the causative agent. In 1956, two studies of a novel virus linked to croup appeared in the scientific literature. Investigators at the Walter Reed Army Institute of Research (WRAIR) were the first to publish a report of a virus isolated from chimpanzees that caused coughing and other symptoms reminiscent of infantile croup.[68] A second report from Dr. Robert Chanock of the University of Cincinnati isolated a novel virus from infants with croup that caused cells grown in the laboratory to acquire a sponge-like appearance.[69] Both viruses were later shown to be one and the same and were subsequently named respiratory syncytial virus (RSV).

Before returning to the investigation of RSV at Walter Reed, it is worth a brief divergence to convey background on the remarkable Dr. Robert Chanock, who has been described by Anthony Fauci, the current director of the National Institute of Allergy and Infectious Diseases, as "unparalleled in the history of American virology."[70] After obtaining his M.D. at the University of Chicago, Dr. Chanock trained with Dr. Albert Sabin, who was developing the oral vaccine for polio that is widely used today. Chanock contributed to that program and also had a particular talent for identifying novel viruses and bacterial pathogens as he did with RSV while working with Dr. Sabin. Among his accomplishments, Chanock would discover Norwalk virus (now known as Noro virus or the "cruise ship" virus), St. Louis encephalitis virus, western equine encephalitis virus, a bacterial cause and treatment of mycoplasma pneumonia (also known as walking pneumonia), as well as the foundations for an intranasal influenza vaccine, a subject to which we return in a later chapter.[71]

In the years following the initial description of RSV, WRAIR investigators progressed to investigating novel ways to treat infections in infants. Two of the leading investigators were Dr. Wayne Hockmeyer, the chair of immunology, and his boss, Dr. Franklin Top, the commandant of WRAIR. After his retirement, Hockmeyer was asked to lunch by Wally Steinberg, a former executive from Johnson & Johnson who had become a venture capitalist.[72] Hockmeyer and Steinberg discussed opportunities to develop products to treat RSV and on the spot, Steinberg committed $3.5 million dollars to create a new venture. Originally named Molecular Vaccines, the name of the company was soon changed to MedImmune. Hockmeyer and Steinberg were joined shortly by Franklin Top, and the company was located in Gaithersburg, Maryland, a few miles up the road from WRAIR.[73]

Unlike other local companies riding the bubble of euphoria and imagined treasures to be reaped from the human genome project (the subject of a future chapter), the pragmatic Hockmeyer focused MedImmune on the less glamorous slog to develop tangible, revenue-generating products. Army-inspired discipline ultimately triumphed over smoke and mirrors, though not without its own setbacks.

An early impediment almost destroyed the nascent company in late 1993. The company had committed most of its resources into developing a polyclonal antiserum to block RSV from gaining a foothold in the lung of premature infants. After much work and money, the FDA rejected the experimental drug, citing a design flaw in the clinical trials.[74] For many companies, such a setback would have been fatal. Even if the company has the resources to re-engage, a rejection can devastate investor confidence and internal morale. Falling back on his Army training, Hockmeyer called the entire staff together, gave an rousing speech that inspired the troops and focused their attention on the need to regroup and push even harder to obtain an FDA approval for RespiGam.

The FDA approved RespiGam in 1995 and Hockmeyer focused the team on their next mission: a monoclonal antibody product that could outperform RespiGam. This product, which would be known as Synagis, was approved in 1998 for the prevention of RSV infection in premature infants.[75] These smallest of patients were not on the financial radar screen of most large companies, but to a small company like MedImmune, the market was attractive and ultimately proved to be highly lucrative. Building upon the medical and marketing success of RespiGam and increased appreciation of the dangers of RSV infection by pediatricians and parents, Synagis was well received and sales exceeded the one billion dollar mark, allowing Synagis to join the pantheon of "blockbuster" drugs.

In the years following the approval of Synagis, MedImmune's profitability and stock valuation soared. Unlike many biotechnology companies built upon promises rather than products, Hockmeyer had shown that a disciplined focus and tangible product was superior to hype. As we will see in a future chapter, such focus was relatively rare in an industry with as much promise as biotechnology and even proved to be a struggle for MedImmune after Hockmeyer's retirement.

Fuel for the Fire

As we have seen, federal government support for biomedical research soared from the late 1940s through most of the following five decades. The government retained title to patents for inventions supported with federal funding and bureaucracy slowed commercialization. University personnel lacked incentives to pursue partnerships and, according to a 1998 General Accounting Office (GAO) report to Congress, "those seeking to use government-owned technology found a maze of rules and regulations."[76]

A high-profile example was a discovery by Dr. Robert Cade at the University of Florida, who utilized government funds to develop an electrolyte solution to prevent severe dehydration.[77] The project was the result of a 1965 conversation with an assistant coach for the football team, who pointed out that a player could lose eighteen pounds of water weight during a football game. The resulting product was patented and named for the football team. When Cade offered the university rights to the invention, they declined, and Gatorade was licensed to Stokely-Van Camp.[78] As sales increased, the government reminded the university that Cade's research had involved federal funds and encouraged the university to sue Cade and Stokely-Van Camp.[79] The high-profile lawsuit was resolved but left an unpleasant after-taste for all. The accumulation of neglected patents thereafter increased further and a later analysis revealed that, of the 28,000 patents assigned to the federal government, fewer than 5 percent were licensed or commercialized.[80]

The stagflation of the 1970s was a period of prolonged malaise for the U.S. economy. In 1978, engineers at Purdue University had discovered new opportunities in the energy sector, which was strategically important for a country recovering from one oil embargo in 1973 (as punishment for American support of Israel during the Yom Kippur War) and about to enter another (as a result of American support for the recently-deposed Shah of Iran).[81] Ralph Davis, the head of the technology commercialization office at Purdue, began the arduous task of obtaining government approval needed to allow Purdue to begin marketing the energy technology.[82] The glacial pace of federal bureaucracy prompted Davis to contact his senator, Evan Bayh, to express his growing frustration.[83]

Bayh, a Democrat, approached Senator Robert Dole, a Republican, to discuss the latter's long-standing advocacy for health care innovation and translating research from the NIH into new medicines.[84] The pair agreed to sponsor a bill to stimulate economic growth by allowing grant recipients to retain patent rights from federally sponsored research and let them reap the profits thereof. In return to being allowed to prosecute and benefit from their own licenses, the act required universities to update their federal sponsors so that the government could take over the patent if the technology was not being adequately developed by the university or its licensees. Specifically, the Bayh-Dole Act allowed for "march-in" rights such that the federal government could take over the intellectual property if advancement of the technology is not being met by the organization or its licensee.[85] This threat resurfaces every few years, with prominent examples being during the HIV/AIDS crisis, to motivate organizations developing a federally sponsored program for rare or neglected diseases and to override price increases or production shortfalls in HIV drugs.[86]

The Bayh-Dole amendment cleared the Senate in April 1980 but almost died there when a negotiated deal to include it as part of a large omnibus spending bill collapsed after the 1980 elections.[87] The elections had been a landslide for Republicans as many Democrats, including Senator Bayh, were turfed out of office. The hopes that the Bayh-Dole bill would become law were almost extinguished, but the outgoing Congress still needed to pass a budget in a lame-duck session. In a Hollywood-like cliffhanger, the Senate majority leader invoked a procedure that required that the bill be called up on the Senate floor. Evan Bayh was clearing out his office, blocks away from the Capitol building, when one of his aides happened to spot Robert Dole. The Republican from Kansas rushed to the floor and called up the bill, saving it moments before it died. The drama didn't end there, as outgoing Jimmy Carter advocated a different approach to assigning intellectual property rights and had decided to pocket veto the bill. However, a last-minute harangue by presidential aides, buttressed by university and small business leaders, convinced the reluctant president to sign the bill into law as one of his last acts.

Inspired by the twin energy crises of the 1970s, the Bayh-Dole Act itself became the propellant that super-charged the biotechnology industry and ensured American dominance in the decades to come.

From Fad to Sector

While the birth of biotechnology can be traced to the publication of the Cohen and Boyer research on recombinant DNA technology, its growth spurt and adolescence were the direct result of the Bayh-Dole Act. As we will see in an upcoming chapter, the 1980s witnessed an explosion of entrepreneurial activity in the number of start-up companies founded on the basis of translating breakthroughs in the laboratory into new products. Indeed, if we limit ourselves solely to those companies that contributed key activities to an FDA-approved drug, the net number of active and independent biotechnology companies rose from fourteen in 1980 (the year the Bayh-Dole was passed) to 141 organizations by the year 2000.[88] Most of these new companies were propelled by federally-funded research from universities, and most of the founders in these early days, like Herbert Boyer, were from academia. The impact of Bayh-Dole can also be seen in the fact that the vast majority (83 percent) of biotechnology start-up companies were located in the United States.[89]

The extraordinary growth of biotechnology overshadowed the fact that at the same time entrepreneurship from academia was accelerating, the pharmaceutical industry was retreating away from early-stage research. We will turn our attention back to the pharmaceutical industry to witness the pressures that caused many to quietly retreat from drug research, which went largely unnoticed due to the excitement surrounding the rise of biotechnology.

CHAPTER SEVEN

Blockbusters and Bombs

Pressures on the Pharmaceutical Industry

As we have seen in previous chapters, the business of new drug development sprouted from modest beginnings, often sole proprietor apothecaries, into a massive industry with annual sales exceeding $300 billion in the United States alone.[1] The aggregate market capitalization of the ten leading pharmaceutical companies exceeds $1.3 trillion dollars. In this chapter, we detail changes that have taken place over the past three decades that have created powerful pressures on the industry and, as we shall see, fundamentally remodeled the drug discovery enterprise.

Unnatural Trends in Drug Discovery

Nature provides us with a bounty of opportunities to discover new drugs. A natural product from certain *Penicillium* fungi led us to penicillin and other antibiotics, while a chemical constituent of poppies was the basis of morphine. These are but two examples of a much larger role that natural products have played in the history of the modern pharmaceutical industry. In the period spanning the birth of contemporary drug development in the 1930s through the 1970s, more than half of all FDA-approved drugs had as their source a natural biological substance from plants, bacteria, or fungi.[2] In more recent years, the fraction of drugs derived from natural products has shrunk and now stands at less than one quarter.[3] Instead, greater emphasis is placed on "synthetic" drugs, a name representing that these chemicals are derived in the laboratory rather than from a natural source.

What is responsible for this change?

First, nature has a tendency to convey complex structures, which in part reflect the diversity generated by epochs of evolution that have given rise to a multitude of different enzymes. The nonconformity of enzymes and the panoply of molecules they produce can be as dramatically divergent as life itself, which has adapted itself to a myriad of climatic and geographical niches, including venues as varied as volcanic vents and permafrost. From the perspective of a pharmaceutical scientist, such diversity carries forth certain advantages and disadvantages. On the positive side, variety in chemical structures increases the likelihood that a particular structure will eventually be found that has desired properties, such as selectively killing a tumor cell or diminishing cholesterol synthesis. Countering this is the fact that the diversity conveyed by the natural world can craft molecules that simply cannot be efficiently manufactured at levels that are practical for medical or commercial purposes. Such incompatibility means that while a particular molecule may show ideal properties in terms of safety and efficacy, if one cannot reliably produce the compound, it will remain tantalizing but unreachable. A canonical example is seen with the drug paclitaxel (also known as Taxol).

Despite early successes in the development of cancer chemotherapeutic agents in the years following the end of the Second World War, the National Institutes of Health came under considerable pressure from lobbyists advocating a war on cancer.[4] Two of the most vocal advocates were Mary and Albert Lasker. Albert is widely considered the founder of modern advertising, having risen through the ranks to become the CEO of Lord and Thomas, the third-oldest advertising agency in the world.[5] At the helm of the advertising behemoth, Lasker led revolutionary consumer psychology-based campaigns that boosted the visibility and sales of products with an emphasis on the female consumer. Among Lasker's clients were Lucky Strikes cigarettes, Palmolive soap, Kotex tampons, Pepsodent toothpaste, Whirlpool washers, and Van Camp's and Sunkist fruit and vegetable products. To do so, Lasker developed new genres to support his advertising campaigns, such as soap operas, by exploiting the emerging technologies of radio and television.

Albert and Mary Lasker were ardent supporters of health policy issues, including the need for research into cancer (which is rather ironic given Albert's role in almost single-handedly promoting cigarette smoking among women). The Laskers established a foundation bearing their name that still provides the most prestigious American award for medical science. The couple also revitalized a small and struggling nonprofit advocacy group into the modern American Cancer Society.[6] As an ardent Democratic campaign supporter, the Laskers cajoled Congress and the Truman administration to create new resources to promote cancer research.[7] The activism continued into the Eisenhower administration, prodding Congress into passing a $5 million bill to create the Cancer Chemotherapy National Service Center (CCNSC).[8] The mandate of the CCNSC included the creation of a repository of compounds that would be screened for the ability to kill tumor cells in the laboratory. The massive screening effort included a collection of natural products sourced from around the United States, which in turn arose from a challenge to the United States Department of Agriculture (USDA) to collect samples of a thousand different plant species each year.

In August 1962, a United States Department of Agriculture (USDA) botanist, Arthur Barclay, collected some bark from a Pacific yew tree (*Taxus brevifolia*) in a forest near the base of the Mount Saint Helens volcano in Washington state.[9] The location of the tree raises questions as to whether the drug would ever have been found had the volcano erupted a mere two decades earlier (a veritable nanosecond in geologic terms) and devastated the tree responsible for the finding. A crude preparation of this natural material demonstrated potent anti-tumor activity when analyzed in a CCNSC laboratory roughly two years later. The search was then on to identify the particular chemical from this complex extract that conferred the ability to efficiently kill cancer cells. Although quite potent, the compound was present at very low levels in the tree bark and this posed many problems. After a decade-long search involving many samples of *Taxus* bark, a team led by Monroe Eliot Wall at the Research Triangle Institute in North Carolina finally published the discovery of a compound they named Taxol.[10]

The minute levels of Taxol in the tree bark of the Pacific yew meant that excessively large amounts of material were need. For example, more than a ton of tree bark was needed to obtain one-third of an ounce of Taxol.[11] Such yields were unsustainable since the collection of bark was lethal to the yew tree. However, the demand for Taxol mounted with the growing evidence of its ability to kill multiple tumor types, first in laboratory studies and then in clinical trials.[12] Estimates from NCI revealed that the amount of tree bark needed to supply enough Taxol to treat two relatively low-incidence diseases, ovarian cancer and melanoma, would require cutting down more than 360,000 trees a year.[13] These calculations created much consternation within both the environmental and medical communities. To seek assistance from the private sector in addressing this challenge, the National Cancer Institute offered a Cooperative Research and Development Agreement (CRADA) to the pharmaceutical industry. This offer to collaborate entailed a promise that NCI would convey all of its data and stock of Taxol (and massive reserves of tree bark) as well as a low royalty rate in return for a corporate partner willing to continue developing the drug.[14] The corporate partner was also expected to innovate a sustainable way to manufacture Taxol.

Despite lucrative terms, the challenge of taking on the Taxol production problem did not elicit much private sector response to the CRADA. Ultimately, Bristol-Myers Squibb (BMS) was awarded the collaborative agreement in late 1989.[15] Once the program was transferred to Bristol-Myers

Squibb, the company undertook a comprehensive campaign to develop a sustainable approach.[16] The company licensed a process from Robert Holton of Florida State University, who had developed a semi-synthetic route deploying a series of chemical reactions to increase the amount of Taxol isolated from the tree bark.[17] The same chemist later developed a further enhanced process that utilized the needles of yew trees, which are more abundant and do not require killing the trees for collection.[18] The methods were refined further and Taxol is now manufactured using a fermentation process with cells isolated from yew trees combined with a fungal culture (*Penicillium raistrickii*) that altogether eliminates the need for bulk vegetation as a starting point for production of the valuable chemotherapeutic product.[19]

Based on its powerful anti-tumor activities and newfound availability, Taxol was a hit. Bristol-Myers Squibb grew Taxol sales and exceeded $1 billion in 1999, making it the first cancer drug to reach the blockbuster milestone.[20] The implications of this achievement were many-fold and a bit unexpected. Prior to Taxol's crossing the $1 billion landmark in 1999, cancer research was a relative backwater within the pharmaceutical industry. Rather, emphasis was placed on chronic indications, where a patient might need to take a pill each day for the rest of their life. The idea was that a durable market, even at a lower profit margin, was preferable to an acute market such as cancer. Cancer was widely regarded as an unattractive commercial market, as treatment was acute and outcomes were binary. Either the patient was cured and no longer needed to purchase drug or else the patient died and no longer needed to purchase drug. Taxol expanded private-sector thinking about cancer and revealed that a combination of acute therapy with a high profit margin had its own advantages. As of this writing, the pendulum has swung in the opposite direction, with disproportionate emphasis on acute indications.

The high profit margin associated with Taxol also created a firestorm. The high price charged for the drug by Bristol-Myers Squibb was broadly criticized in Congress using the same argument as with AZT, that government investment discovered the drug. A 2003 General Accounting Office (GAO) report agreed with this view and criticized the CRADA process for Taxol, emphasizing the "financial benefits from the collaboration with BMS have not been great in comparison to BMS's revenue from the drug."[21] The GAO report was particularly critical of the fact that the federal Medicare program has been a major payer for Taxol and that Medicare had paid BMS a particularly high price for the drug despite the investment of federal funding in the development of the program.

The story of Taxol manufacturing, while it ends well for patients, typifies the issues experienced by many pharmaceutical companies. Many product candidates based on natural products have had to be abandoned altogether due to inefficient or unsustainable production. Consequently, many companies now actively avoid working with natural products and, instead, focus their activities solely on synthetic chemicals, which are usually easier to generate and scale up to the large amounts needed for commercialization. While these changes have addressed the problem of manufacturing, the fact that synthetic chemicals are generally less diverse than natural products means that the movement away from natural products has decreased the likelihood that truly diverse new medicines will be developed.

Knowledge versus Hubris

The movement away from natural products is but one changing trend impacting drug discovery and development over the past two to three decades. In the first five decades of the modern pharmaceutical era, the primary way new medicines were discovered used a process known as phenotypic screening. These techniques evaluated the ability of compounds to effect a desired change, generally using a laboratory-based experimental model of disease. As we just saw, Taxol was discovered by screening a library of compounds for their abilities to kill tumor cells in the laboratory. Likewise, most antibiotics were found by screening compounds for the abilities to kill bacteria, and AZT was discovered by pulling everything off the shelf and testing for those compounds that stopped the virus. In the case of phenotypic screening, the exact molecule(s) in the diseased (or healthy) cell being impacted may not be known and the choice of the best drug is, instead, based solely on whether the desired outcome is achieved.

The last few decades have witnessed an extraordinary increase in the collective knowledge of disease and health. This information has been deployed effectively to identify molecular targets, where direct intervention is predicted to effect the desired change. We have already seen many successful examples that facilitated the development of effective drug targeting, HMG-CoA, HIV reverse transcriptase, and COX-2 to name but a few. The advantages of the target-based screening included the intellectually reassuring fact of knowing how the target functions in perturbing the disease process. High-profile toxicity failures, such as encountered with Vioxx, have likewise caused the FDA to be more guarded, occasionally crossing over the threshold of excessive caution, to acknowledge every contingency before approving a new drug. Bolstered by increasing knowledge of disease function and toxicity, the drug discovery enterprise, including the academic and private-sector companies and their respective federal overseers, have progressively embraced target-based drug design and migrated away from phenotypic studies.

The catch with regard to target-based screening is the underlying assumption that the target being prosecuted is the most relevant and tractable contributor to the disease process. Such expectations have bred a form of over-confidence that scientists have already unlocked the key to understanding of both normal and diseased function in whatever process they are studying. Almost any scientist will affirm that knowledge is expanding at an exponential rate of acceleration and "scientific truths" are rare and highly plastic. Thus, the assumption that one knows the mechanistic basis to drive new drug development can create a blind over-confidence that, like an ancient Greek tragedy, rarely ends well.

The consequences of a hubristic mindset are many-fold. First, a new approach may monopolize the efforts of entire organizations for years or even decades. Second, the pharmaceutical industry, as well as academia, tends to suffer from a "herd mentality." The perception of a "hot" target family may trigger a disproportionate emphasis by many organizations, and we will see one example of this in the form of "me-too drugs." Given the finite resources available for new drug discovery, an emphasis on one paradigm literally comes at the expense of other past or future breakthroughs in understanding.

In the other extreme, a high-profile failure by one company or with one drug candidate can cause an entire field of investigators to hastily abandon their efforts prematurely. The field of competitive intelligence has burgeoned, and it is generally safe to assume that most large companies who can afford this luxury are well aware of the status of the pipelines of their competitors in something like real time. This aspect of the "herd mentality" is particularly problematic if a drug failure, due to toxicity or lack of efficacy, may have resulted from an "off-target" effect that would not apply to other drugs targeting the same pathway. We witnessed one such example in practice when rumors of a negative result from the earliest statin (toxicities from Compactin during its development by Sankyo Pharmaceuticals) halted the development of all other statins. The field remained frozen until the bold actions of P. Roy Vagelos, encouraged by regulators at the FDA, led Merck to re-initiate clinical investigation of lovastatin.

Compounding this particular problem, the lifetime of any particular pharmaceutical research project routinely exceeds a decade, whereas the tenure of the executive management tends to turn over more rapidly. The biases of new management from their past experiences, combined with a need to brand their new organization with their own programs and ideas, can translate into the premature termination of projects that might otherwise have matured into new medical breakthroughs.

While many of these behaviors are not unique to the pharmaceutical industry, the flight away from phenotypic screening seems to be a collective response by many in the field. Yet, phenotypic screening, by its inherent nature, seeks to identify drug candidates that cause the desired effect, regardless of knowing how this came to be. Moving forward, it will require the type of courage demonstrated by P. Roy Vagelos, ideally incentivized by regulators (that is, FDA), to properly balance the opportunities and risks arising from both phenotype and target-based drug discovery.

In recent memory, the largest perceived threat to the pharmaceutical industry does not arise from inefficiencies in drug discovery but from revenues lost to rivals. This competition increasingly does not take the form of even more innovative and efficacious drugs, but from generic clones of their own products.

The Rise of Generics

Modern Americans are accustomed to the availability of generic medicines but many may not realize this is a relatively recent phenomenon. While the concept of generics has been entrenched from the earliest days of the twentieth century (for example, different brands of aspirin and morphine have been offered for sale for decades), generic medicines did not become an everyday notion until recent years. Indeed, the generic industry almost died altogether in the 1960s before being revived by passage of the Hatch-Waxman Act of 1984.[22]

The 1962 passage of the Kefauver-Harris Amendment in the days following the thalidomide tragedy mandated that drugs demonstrate efficacy, and this same criteria was applied to generic medicines.[23] Even generic medicines that had been sold for decades before 1962 were required to demonstrate proof of efficacy in accordance with Kefauver-Harris. In recognition of the negative burden this critical legislature would place upon generic manufacturers, the Kefauver-Harris Amendment had attempted to soften the blow by allowing these companies to submit "paper new drug applications (NDAs)." This exception allowed the use of pre-existing, published literature to be submitted in lieu of expensive new clinical trials. Even this exemption proved too high a hurdle, as many generics manufacturers were involved solely in manufacturing and sales, not research and development. Therefore, these companies did not have ready access to the expertise or resources needed to support the continuation of their products in light of the new legislation.

Many generic manufacturers simply gave up. An analysis of generic medicines indicated that, whereas 150 drugs were no longer protected by patents in the years after 1962, a mere fifteen "paper NDAs" had been submitted by generic manufacturers.[24] This was welcome news for the innovator companies, who reaped benefits as competition dwindled. Absent generic rivals, these organizations could suddenly increase the price of their products. The rapid escalation in medicine costs caused public outrage and captured the attention of many lawmakers, including Congressman Henry Waxman of California, the chair of the House Health Subcommittee.

Despite the melting away of generic competition, pharmaceutical innovators were themselves anxious about the increasing amount of time required to obtain an FDA approval for a new medicine.[25] The need to evaluate both safety and efficacy increased the financial and time burdens needed to obtain sufficient evidence for a marketing approval. Worse still, the burden on FDA reviewers increased dramatically as these servants were now required to assess efficacy as well as safety, which requires much larger studies and generates considerably more data to review. Unsurprisingly, the time to review a new drug application increased in the years following passage of Kefauver-Harris.[26]

The increased time required for approval means less time for exclusivity (before the patent expires) for innovator companies at the same time that increasing costs of R&D were required to establish efficacy. Such fears created a powerful disincentive for some companies to develop new medicines.[27] The author's own research revealed that the rate of new approvals decreased by at least 20 percent in the years following passage of Kefauver-Harris.[28] By the late 1970s, the time required for clinical trials and review had lengthened to the point where the pharmaceutical industry urged Congress and the president for a dramatic restructuring of the approval process.[29] The issue came to the attention of then-president James Earl Carter, who was sympathetic and initiated a 1978 policy review. Toward the twilight of the Carter administration, the review board verified the increasing costs and time required for clinical testing and review of NDA applications. After Carter's electoral defeat in 1980, concerns about the health of the pharmaceutical industry were comparably shared by the incoming Republicans of the Reagan White House but this issue took a back seat to the malaise caused by stagflation in the late 1970s and early 1980s.

As the economy continued to stagnate toward the end of the first term of the Reagan administration, Senator Orrin Hatch of Utah sponsored a bill to address the disincentives plaguing the pharmaceutical industry. This bill garnered broad support in the Senate and was aided by intensive lobbying from the pharmaceutical industry, which pointed out the large number of jobs and economic activity supported by its activities.[30]

A key provision of Senator Hatch's bill called for "patent term restoration."[31] The concept of "patent term restoration" was a remedy to offset the increasing time needed for clinical development. The Hatch Bill provided that the key patent for an innovator drug will receive a period extension equal to half of the time spanning the time from which the investigational new drug (IND) application has been submitted to the FDA until the time in which the NDA is submitted. Furthermore, the "restoration" captured entire time the FDA needed to review the NDA. To avoid the likelihood that companies might drag their feet during development (to gain more time for patent extensions), the bill required constant due diligence during development and lapses in product development were penalized by subtracting time from the patent term.[32]

Although the bill sailed through the Senate in 1984, the concept of increasing patent time to help pharmaceutical companies was not as popular in the House of Representatives. In a crucial miscalculation, supporters tried to rush the bill through the House via a legislative trick known as a suspension calendar.[33] However, the vote failed and provided enough time to mobilize lobbyists and organizations advocating for generic medicines. These groups found their champion in Representative Henry Waxman of California, who converted the patent restoration legislation into one that also addressed rising medical costs and the need for generic competition. Ultimately, the Hatch-Waxman bill was approved and signed by President Reagan in late 1984. As we will see, the new law was criticized and celebrated by both innovator and generic pharmaceutical companies, and the public at-large shared these mixed sentiments.

Although patent extension was a key provision of the Hatch-Waxman Act and cheered on by innovator companies, the impact of this legislation was ultimately more favorable to generics manufacturers based on the provisions inserted by Representative Waxman.[34] In particular, the new act created a new type of submission category for generic drugs known as an Abbreviated New Drug Application (or ANDA).[35] Rather than requiring extensive and expensive analyses of drug efficacy and safety, the ANDA procedure limited investigation to establishing "bioequivalence."[36] This new term meant that aspiring generic manufacturers were obligated only to present evidence that a generic drug is present in the body at the same relative concentrations and forms as the innovator drug when measured over time.

The controversy over bioequivalence resurfaces occasionally because the ingredients can differ considerably when comparing innovator and generic forms of the same medicine.[37] While FDA approval of an ANDA requires that the drug substance (for example, the part of the pill with the medicinal value) be equivalent, the other components of the pill can also influence where and when the drug works. The majority of a pill consists of substances known as "fillers" that can alter the safety or efficacy of the medicines. These fillers must be composed of chemicals that are "generally regarded as safe" (GRAS) but the components can differ widely.[38] Such differences are loudly trumpeted by innovator companies seeking to defend their markets.[39] For a drug with a narrow therapeutic window (the doses where a drug works versus those where it causes side-effects), even small differences can mean life or death.

Falling Off a Cliff

Returning to the impact of the Hatch-Waxman Act, the lowered hurdles for ANDA approval triggered a blossoming of the generics drug industry.[40] While the act mandated that innovator drugs have a minimum of five years of exclusivity, this time period is often insufficient to gain market acceptance and earn back the investment required for drug discovery and development. The time and costs required for sales and marketing for an innovator drug will ultimately support the generic competitor and, almost invariably, the peak sales of a drug occur just as the drug become subject to generic competition. Almost immediately after facing generic competition, the price of the drug, and net sales drop approximately 70 percent.[41]

Given that drug sales generally peak just before patent expiry, some pharmaceutical companies adopted an approach known as "pay for delay."[42] The idea is that an innovator company will reach an agreement with the first generic competitor to compensate them for delaying the launch of their new product. This approach was facilitated by a provision in the Hatch-Waxman

Act that granted 180 days of exclusive rights to market the generic version for the first company to file an ANDA.[43] Invoking basic math, many innovator companies realized that splitting the profits with the first generic manufacturer was more lucrative than losing its market. The United States Federal Trade Commission had sought to prevent such deal making but a lack of consensus by different appellate courts has created an uncertain future for this questionable practice.[44]

Innovator companies have also invoked a strategy of progressively expanding "patent fences" to hamstring generic competition.[45] The strategy uses a series of patents, filed as late in the development of the drug as possible, to protect critical aspects of the product by just the identity of the active ingredient. Prominent examples include protection of the procedures needed for efficient manufacture of a product or key aspects of its formulation or dosing. The consequence is that while a generic competitor can market a competing product, they may not be able to do so as efficiently as the innovator company if patent fences block key aspects of manufacturing or delivery. The decreased efficiency may mean that the generic version is as expensive as the innovator drug and thus blunts the financial incentives for the generic rival.

The issue of how to balance innovator versus generic competition has remained problematic since the passage of Hatch-Waxman in 1984.[46] The issue has been exacerbated by a trend of stressing "blockbuster" drugs. While an emphasis on high-margin drugs works well in the short term, problems arise when companies depend too heavily on one product or fail to prepare for the day when generic rivals will vaporize incoming revenues. In the years spanning 2006 through 2011, almost $15 billion in sales were lost each year as a result of products falling off "patent cliffs." Worse still, 2012 witnessed the loss of more than $35 billion alone, and a comparable level is slated to be lost in 2015. When one considers that over $120 billion in annual sales were lost in the time spanning 2011 through 2015, the relative growth of pharmaceutical market valuations in recent years is remarkable and it is hard to imagine many other industries that could have survived such losses. To understand how all of this came to be, it is useful to understand how the pharmaceutical industry became addicted to blockbuster drugs.

Blockbusters and Bombs

The promise and the peril of blockbuster medicines are exemplified by the drug called cimetidine. Peptic ulcers have afflicted countless millions over the years, including well known and diverse figures such as the Civil War general Thomas "Stonewall" Jackson, President George Herbert Walker Bush, and Pope John Paul II.[47] In retrospect, ulcers have also been the foundation of various conspiracy theories, such as the untimely death of Napoleon Bonaparte in exile on Saint Helena in the South Atlantic.[48] Many theories have been proposed to explain the premature demise of the fifty-one-year-old emperor, most notoriously one founded on the idea that his British captors poisoned him with arsenic. (A less conspiratorial variation on the theme was that arsenic used to color the wallpaper in Napoleon's house on St. Helena accelerated his early demise.) Recent studies suggest rather conclusively that Napoleon suffered from chronic ulcers and some of these ulcers progressed into a gastric tumor that claimed him.[49]

Charles Darwin also suffered from an undiagnosed malady involving chronic stomach pain that stumped many of the most prominent physicians in contemporary Victorian England. This disease has caused much speculation over the years but recent evidence suggests the infection associated with peptic ulcers contributed to this mysterious affliction.[50] Despite relatively recent breakthroughs in our understanding of and ability to prevent ulcers, an estimated 500,000 Americans still suffer from this indication today.[51] The prominence of peptic ulcer disease, combined with the presumption that treatment would require lifelong intervention, became a Siren song for the pharmaceutical industry. The question was how to intervene.

Histamine is a well-known component of the body's host defenses and was co-discovered by Patrick Playfair Laidlaw (you may remember him as the scientist who also discovered the influenza virus after a colleague sneezed on a ferret).[52] As often happens in biology, nature recycles and allows the same molecule to bind different types of receptors in the body, each of which conveys a different physiological outcome. Histamine is a prominent example. Though histamine is well known to mediate much of the misery associated with allergies, it plays key roles in other bodily functions, such as the transmission of signals to and from the brain and the body, including the critical decision as to whether the body should secrete more stomach acid.[53] In the case of conventional antihistamines that block allergic symptoms, the medicines target a cellular protein known as an H1 receptor (as it was the first histamine receptor identified).[54] However, this H1 receptor is not involved in the decision-making about stomach acid secretion and, therefore, conventional antihistamines used for allergies do not relieve the discomfort of ulcers.

In 1964, Smith, Kline & French pharmaceutical company lured a successful pharmacologist away from Imperial Chemical Industries (ICI, later known as Zeneca).[55] James Black had already made a groundbreaking contribution to medicine by discovering propranolol, a novel inhibitor of adrenalin action.[56] Propranolol was the first in a series of beta-blocker drugs that revolutionized the treatment of a variety of cardiovascular (hypertension, angina, heart attacks), psychiatric (anxiety, tremors, panic) and ophthalmic (glaucoma) indications and became the world's bestselling drug of the time.[57]

Within months after arriving at Smith, Kline & French, Black developed evidence for a second set of histamine receptors that regulated the secretion of stomach acid. His group at Smith, Kline & French set out on a prolonged campaign to prosecute this second class of histamine (or H2) receptors.[58] After considerable effort based on the cutting-edge idea of target-based design (which was just gaining speed), the team identified a potent molecule, known as cimetidine, which displayed strong activity against H2 receptors.[59] Cimetidine was safe to use and could be taken orally as a pill, which could allow patients to self-administer the medicine at home rather than receiving treatment at a doctor's office.

Cimetidine was approved by regulators in the United Kingdom in 1976 and in the United States a year later.[60] The commercial name for the drug was cleverly decided to be Tagamet (for an**tag**onist **and** ci**met**idine) and the new drug was an instant success. By 1979, Tagamet had become the top selling drug in the United States and was marketed in more than 100 countries. Tagamet became the first drug to exceed $1 billion in annual sales, a threshold that had been considered insurmountable just a few years earlier. This milestone set a precedent, and billion-dollar drugs were thereafter known as "blockbusters." In addition to its pioneering role as a blockbuster, cimetidine was also an early example of expanding patent fences to delay generics. Specifically, Smith, Kline & French chemists developed new methodologies to manufacture cimetidine and protected these ideas via patents that forced competitors to use inferior means of production.[61]

The lucrative sales of Tagamet caused its competitors to seek to replicate the success of Smith, Kline & French's blockbuster. Cimetidine was quickly followed by the 1981 approval for another U.K.-based company, Glaxo, of ranitidine (trade name Zantac).[62] In a trend to which we will return, sales of the second-in-class Zantac overtook the first-in-class Tagamet sales by 1988, the same year Black was awarded the Nobel Prize for his work on propranolol and cimetidine.[63]

The treatment of gastric ulcers would foreshadow the vulnerabilities of companies that relied too heavily upon blockbuster drugs. In the same year Tagamet became a blockbuster, Dr. Barry Marshall was appointed Registrar in Medicine at the Royal Perth Hospital in Australia.[64] The year 1981 proved to be critical in terms of gastritis and ulcer treatment, not because of the approval of Zantac but because Marshall had begun collaborating with Robin Warren, a young pathologist who shared an interest in gastritis. This partnership focused on the presence of a bacterium they had cultured from patients with gastritis and ulcers. The pair named this bacterium *Heliobacter pylori (or H. pylori)*,[65] and hypothesized *H. pylori* was the cause (rather than a consequence of) ulcers. This radical idea was met with skepticism and outright ridicule, in large part based on the assumption that no bacteria could survive the highly acidic environment of the stomach.

In one of the most audacious and ill-advised chapters of recent scientific history, Marshall took the extreme measure of swallowing the fetid contents of a culture of *H. pylori*.[66] Before doing so, he had subjected himself to an endoscopy, which showed no sign of gastric disease. Three days later, his only major symptom was a case of bad breath. This minor symptom progressed rapidly to vomiting, and a week after his decision to drink the bacteria-laden broth, an endoscopy confirmed the presence of profound gastritis. His stomach contents were sampled and tested positive for *H. pylori* (demonstrating that the bacterium had survived nicely in the acidic environment). A week later, Marshall capped off his experience as a guinea pig by initiating a course of antibiotics. Marshall assumed the antibiotics would kill *H. pylori*. As anticipated (by Marshall, at least), the bacterium disappeared, followed soon thereafter by the symptoms of gastritis. The experiment was published in 1985 and Marshall and Warren were recognized with a Nobel Prize twenty years later.[67]

The *H. pylori* experiment exposed not just why scientists need to keep an open mind, but also the vulnerable foundations of the pharmaceutical industry. A single experiment devastated the sales of an entire set of blockbuster drugs, including Tagamet and Zantac. Overall, the industry did not seem to learn the expensive lesson about over-reliance upon a small number of blockbuster drugs. If anything, the industry has become even more susceptible to the Siren call of blockbusters. Whereas these drugs represented just over a quarter of revenues for the leading pharmaceutical companies in 1995, the number had grown to almost two-thirds by 2010. As we see in the next chapter, blockbuster drugs are increasingly directed at highly specialized markets that benefit a small population and at great costs.

Me-Too

Just three years after the signing of the 1938 Pure Food and Drug Act, an often-overlooked event would have profound ramifications for the future of the nascent pharmaceutical industry. On 11 August 1941, two and a half years after the approval of Winston Churchill's beloved M&B (the sulfa drug that saved his life), a second sulfa drug entered the marketplace. Recalling an exercise from a preschooler's *Highlights Magazine*, placing pictures of the two molecules next to one another does not immediately reveal the difference to the untrained eye. Upon closer inspection, one of the twenty-eight atoms differs, with the presence of an extra nitrogen atom (denoted by the letter N) on one side of the new molecule. From the perspective of the U.S. Patent Office, this second drug (4-amino-N-pyrimidin-2-yl-benzenesulfonamide) was sufficiently distinct from the original molecule (4-amino-N-pyridin-2-yl-ben zenesulfonamide) to warrant its own patent. This was unwelcome news to Eli Lilly, which had gained FDA approval in the United States for M&B (sulfapyridine) as M&B now faced a competitive challenge from American Cyanamid, whose sulfadiazine gained approval through the presence of that extra nitrogen.

The new upstart was not necessarily any better behaved than the original drug. As might be expected by the similarities in structure, the new sulfa drug performed just about as well as the innovator drug in terms of safety and efficacy. However, the key difference was economic, in that sulfadiazine challenged the potential monopoly that might otherwise have allowed the purveyors of sulfapyridine to dominate the infectious disease market. Over time, closely related drugs would come to be known as "fast-followers" or by the more pejorative term, "me-too drugs."[68] As these designations suggest, such medicines are modeled upon a previously approved innovator drug and convey comparable or incrementally improved activities. These improvements may have a measurable impact (for example, by increasing efficacy, decreasing toxicity, or enhanced delivery) but generally do not convey the orthogonal improvements often observed with first-in-class (also known as first mover or innovator) medicines.[69]

The attractions of fast-follower medicines are obvious. Once proof-of-concept for safety and efficacy has been demonstrated by a first-in-class drug, much of the risk associated with developing a new medicine has been identified and overcome.[70] Fast-follower medicines can then proceed at a more rapid pace, often entailing lower costs of development since lessons learned from the first-in-class medicine can be applied to the upstart. Indeed, analyses of the pharmaceutical industry demonstrate that the average time that a first-in-class drug has the market to itself (before competition from a fast-follower) shrank from more than a decade (in the 1970s) to just over a year (by the 1990s). Indeed, the development of fast-follower drugs often begins even before the approval of the first-in-class medicine.

Decisions about how and when to initiate a campaign to develop me-too drugs, a cottage industry has evolved around competitive intelligence. As mentioned earlier, a small army of intelligence companies canvas the pharmaceutical industry, providing insight about company pipelines, preferred disease areas, sales forecasts, patent claims and expirations. These organizations gather information by reconnoitering scientific conferences and investor meetings, as well as perusing the scientific and medical literature, to develop detailed case reports that often sell for multiple thousands of dollars. This lucrative market appeals to individual pharmaceutical companies, which can keep an eye out for potential competition as well as to investors seeking to predict trends for individuals, companies, and the entire industry.

Less obvious is a curious and counter-intuitive trend characterizing me-too drugs. Second-in-class medicines are often more lucrative than innovator drugs. Beyond lower development costs, second-generation me-too drugs frequently sell for higher prices and book higher sales.[71] In many industries, innovative new products are rewarded with a higher price point and greater sales. A fast-follower will obtain a market by lowering the price and thereby differentiating their market from the innovator. The iPod blazed a trail for portable music, and later, MP3s had to lower their price to compete with the innovator. Something different tends to happen with pharmaceuticals.[72] Products with incremental or no improvements can garner higher, not lower, prices and a larger market. This fact leads many to question why be the innovator and why not, instead, wait for someone else. Such thinking discourages orthogonal innovation.[73]

Why the difference? It is not entirely clear, but we will venture a hypothesis.

Drug development is expensive and arduous, lasting years or decades and involving billions of dollars.[74] The adoption of new medicines by patients and providers can be comparably long and expensive. Whereas we have all become accustomed to crowds of devotees waiting in line for days for the latest iPhone release, patients may be more reluctant to switch medicines. Caregivers may be even more reticent since unfamiliar drugs could

cause unintended side effects, or worse, and thereby render them susceptible to claims of malpractice. The pharmaceutical industry has attempted to
counter such behaviors with intensive and expensive advertising but the
fundamental challenge remains.

One consequence is that first-in-class medicines are increasingly the first
step in a long campaign to achieve market acceptance. Intensive marketing
seeks to gain a toehold for a first-in-class medicine; peak sales may be weak
and inevitably are eroded by generic competition. In contrast, incrementally improved me-too competitors can build upon the work and investment of earlier innovators and reap the rewards as patients and providers
increasingly become familiar with new approaches. Returning to a suite of
products introduced in chapter 5, statins provide a stark example. Mevacor
(lovastatin) was the first-generation statin developed by Roy Vagelos' team
at Merck. The product launched in 1987 and its annual sales peaked in 1994
at $1.3 billion.[75] This innovator drug was challenged by multiple other
statins, each of which has garnered higher peak sales than their predecessor.
Four years after the launch of Mevacor, the third statin, Zocor (simvastatin),
was launched and its sales peaked in 2005 at $4.4 billion.[76] These sales
pale in comparison with the fifth statin, Lipitor (atorvastatin), which was
launched by Warner-Lambert (Parke-Davis) in 1996; its sales peaked in
2006 at $13.7B.[77] Notably, the increasing sales of later-generation statins oc-
curred despite the comparable efficacy of these drugs.[78]

While there has been much debate as to the impact of me-too drugs
upon innovation, it is generally understood that, in a time of shrinking research budgets, investment in follow-on medications occurs at the expense
of innovator drugs.[79] In response to shareholder concerns, many pharmaceutical companies have understandably rebalanced their pipelines to emphasize fast-followers.

Time and Money

Compounding the questions about innovation, me-too drugs are beginning to contribute to the rising costs of drug development. Despite the fact
that a fast-follower approach removes some of the risk associated with drug
development (for example, by establishing that a particular mechanism or
patient population can be useful), this strategy can actually drive up the cost
of drug development. Specifically, an FDA approval requires that the drug
be at least as good as the current standard of care. This obligation increases

the costs of clinical trials in multiple ways. As the standard of care improves over time (for example, from previous approvals), the size of the hurdles increases and a demonstration of comparable activity generally requires the fast-follower to be tested in a larger number of patients than was necessary for its predecessor(s). The larger numbers of patients are essential to establish statistical relevance, which the FDA demands. Furthermore, a follow-on drug is often subject to more extensive testing, both in terms of establishing its efficacy as well as safety. A fast-follower is often burdened by more knowledge of the effects (both positive and detrimental) of the first-in-class innovator.

Another factor that is not intuitively obvious to those outside the field of drug development is that a company sponsoring the next-in-class drug is often required to compare its potential product with the existing standard of care. The would-be challenger is also required to pay the costs of treatment for the control group (treated with the standard of care), including the costs of its competitor's drug. As these drugs are almost invariably still under patent protection, the cost of the competitor's drug can be substantial (for example, cancer drug costs routinely exceed $50,000 per patient). As the drug developer is responsible for paying all relevant medical costs for both the experimental drug and the established standard of care, an aspiring me-too sponsor can find herself in the awkward position of being one of the largest customers for their competitor.

A longer approval time usually imposes a concern greater than cost increases. The higher costs from delays reflect the fact that patent expiration destroys the value of a pharmaceutical product. Each day of delay in FDA approval is more correctly interpreted as one less day that the drug can be sold at premium pricing before the onset of generic competition. Despite remedies conveyed by the Hatch-Waxman Act, any delay in approval ultimately decreases the time of peak sales that a new medicine can be sold. For a drug with a billion dollars in annual sales, each lost day equates to roughly $2.7 million dollars of lost revenue.

An analysis of HIV/AIDS drug development nicely captures a conundrum facing the pharmaceutical industry.[80] As you may recall from an earlier chapter, Jerome Horwitz had developed AZT at the Detroit Cancer Institute in the 1960s as a potential cancer chemotherapeutic.[81] In the mid-1980s, the National Cancer Institute (NCI) initiated a comprehensive program to identify potential therapeutics. Consequently, AZT was tested and ultimately approved four years after the discovery of HIV.

When viewed over time, the development of drugs to combat HIV/ AIDS can be roughly divided into three epochs.[82] In the first epoch, from the mid-1980s through the mid-1990s, the virus was discovered and existing compounds were taken off the shelf and tested using phenotypic screening for their ability to combat the virus. In these early years, the average time from patenting until the initiation of clinical trials exceeded eight years. Thus, the patent clock had been ticking for almost a decade before AZT began to be tested in patients. As every effort was invested to accelerate and expedite the development of new medicines for HIV/AIDS, the time spent in clinical trials for this first generation of HIV/AIDS drugs was measured in months as promising new medicines were expedited through the regulatory process.

As understanding of how HIV/AIDS expanded, a second period of drug development began in the mid-1990s and ran through the mid-2000s. This period witnessed the approval of drugs specifically designed to target HIV protease and integrase. As these medicines were newly created, patents were filed strategically to maximize the time of exclusivity. This was achieved by filing the patents just prior to submitting the IND. However, the increased time needed for clinical trials offset any gains from patenting. Likewise, the costs of clinical trials skyrocketed as more patients were studied to ensure the second generation of drugs were at least as safe and efficacious as the existing standards, such as AZT.

As a consequence of increasing time and costs, the attraction of developing new HIV/AIDS drugs waned. These realities ushered in the third period of HIV/AIDS drug development, which started in the mid-2000s and is characterized by a steep decline in the number of companies developing new HIV/AIDS medicines.[83] From the standpoint of public health, this decision might soon be viewed as shortsighted as the world faces a looming reemergence of drug-resistant HIV.[84]

The rate of new drug approvals for HIV/AIDS has evaporated as many companies have moved on to other challenges. A prominent example was one particular virus, hepatitis C virus (HCV), which would highlight the promise and perils of drug discovery.

High-Profile Failures

Hepatitis is a broad term for a medical condition involving inflammation of the liver. The jaundice associated with hepatitis is well known and its many causes include lifestyle choices (alcoholism and drug addition) and metabolic diseases (non-alcoholic fatty liver disease). However, the most common causes are a variety of pathogenic viruses that target the liver.

For obscure historical reasons, five viruses have been shown to cause hepatitis and were named alphabetically based on when each was discovered. The first discovered, hepatitis A virus, causes an acute infection and is generally transmitted by drinking or eating contaminated food (and is often associated with shellfish).[85] Unlike the acute nature of hepatitis A infections, the hepatitis B virus (HBV), which is transmitted via blood, causes a chronic disease that, in its worst forms, manifests itself as cirrhosis and/or cancer of the liver.[86] It is projected that roughly one-third of the world's population has been infected with HBV at some point in their lives. Infection with HBV is difficult to treat and infection rates are endemic in many parts of East Asia and Sub-Saharan Africa, where HBV kills more than 600,000 people per year.[87] In contrast, the virus has been largely eliminated in many developed countries by vaccines, the first of which were introduced in the early 1980s.[88] Thus, HBV is a current scourge but, over time, should diminish as a result of vaccine development.

In contrast, there is no vaccine for the third viral pathogen, which causes hepatitis C.[89] Originally described in the late 1980s as the causative agent for 90 percent of non-A, non-B hepatitis, a collaboration between the United States Centers for Disease Control and Chiron, a small biotechnology company located in Emeryville, California, discovered the hepatitis C virus (HCV).[90] The blood-borne HCV virus is endemic throughout the world, with an estimated 170 million people (almost one in thirty humans) infected worldwide.[91] In the United States alone, more than 3.2 million people are infected and 17,000 new infections occur each year.[92] Similar to HIV, HCV causes a chronic disease and patients can be infectious for many years without knowing. Compounding this is the fact that HCV has many genetic variations that largely preclude the development of an effective vaccine.[93]

The widespread prevalence of the HCV combined with the fact it was discovered as the world was coming to grips with HIV (and is transmitted by many of the same lifestyle behaviors) brought HCV to the forefront in terms of new drug development. Many of the same scientists and companies that had mobilized to tackle HIV now turned their attentions to HCV. The first drug approved by the FDA for HCV was interferon alfa 2b, recombinant human host defense protein.[94]

Interferon derives its name from the fact that it is among a series of molecules discovered based on their ability to interfere with viral infection. In the early 1950s, two virologists at the University of Tokyo, Yasu-ichi Nagano and Yasuhiko Kojima, were developing a vaccine for smallpox when they noticed a "viral inhibitory factor" produced by tissues exposed to various viruses.[95] Alick Isaacs and Jean Linenmann at the National Institute for Medical Research in London isolated a protein with the same properties while studying influenza-infected cells.[96] Some investigators interpreted these "interferons," as evidence that viruses must convey a factor that "stakes out the turf" of one virus to prevent competition from other viruses that might want to claim the same cell. Later findings demonstrated that the production of interferons was a host defense mechanism to limit the extent and damage from infection. Over time, many interferons have been discovered and grouped into families designated with Greek letters from alpha to omega.

The discovery of interferons captured the public's imagination by the late 1950s as a potential way of combatting the scourge of infectious diseases. In a 1960 edition of the popular Flash Gordon comic strip, the protagonist invokes the use of interferon as a way to save a colleague from infection with a fatal virus from space.[97] Unlike the comic strips, combating infections in the real world proved much more challenging, and interferon alpha 2b was not particularly efficacious in fighting HCV.[98]

The promise of interferons as wonder drugs proved optimistic, and it soon became apparent that additional ways of targeting HCV were needed. This provided a lucrative market for the pharmaceutical industry. The market was particularly appealing as untreated HCV infection will ultimately lead to a costly liver transplant, and so these companies reasoned that payers (insurance companies and Medicare/Medicaid) would be willing to pay a high premium for effective HCV drugs. The combination of a large patient population with a high cost-point triggered a race for new medicines akin to the Oklahoma Land Rush. The winners of this race have reaped considerable fortunes. For example, a ninety-day course of treatment with the two most effective HCV drugs, simeprevir (trade name Olysio) and sofosbuvir (trade name Sovaldi), garner wholesale prices of $733 a day and $1,000 a day.[99]

Unsurprisingly, the race to capture such revenues was enticing to many companies, both large and small, and a virtual feeding frenzy ensued. A prominent example was the acquisition of Inhibitex by Bristol-Myers Squibb in January 2012.[100] Inhibitex was a Georgia-based biotechnology company developing a new drug, INX-189 to compete with sofosbuvir and simeprevir and reap the considerable financial rewards from entering the HCV market. Shortly following the completion of a positive early-stage phase IB clinical trial, Bristol-Myers Squibb offered to buy Inhibitex for $2.5 billion. This might have seemed like a relative bargain at the time because Gilead had acquired Pharmasset (the maker of sofosbuvir) for $11 billion a few months before.[101]

Though data from the early clinical investigation of INH-189 was promising, euphoria would quickly turn into despair. Six months after Bristol-Myers Squibb purchased Inhibitex, the newest clinical data revealed an unanticipated cardiac toxicity that forced discontinuation.[102] Thus, just a half-year later, the company had to write down a $1.8 billion charge. Although this transaction is considered by some to be the worst in recent pharmaceutical industry history, it is indicative of the risks associated with drug development. In some ways, Bristol-Myers Squibb was actually fortunate to identify the issue in Phase II rather than Phase III, which would likely have entailed hundreds of millions of dollars of additional investment.

A lesson learned from a myriad of product failures in recent years is that drug development is quite risky. In reality, the risk has always been present but the ever-escalating prices of development increase the prominence and impact of experimental drug failures. A sobering example arises with oncology drugs. You may recall that a Phase II clinical trial is a moderately sized study designed to identify the best dosing regiment needed to design the pivotal (that is, statistically-significant) Phase III clinical trial. This is often a good investment, as Phase II trials generally involve a few hundred subjects and their costs can be measured in the tens of millions of dollars, whereas Phase III trials often involve thousands of patients and hundreds of millions of dollars. Well-designed Phase III trials are necessarily complex and expensive, often accounting for more than 90 percent of a pharmaceutical company's research and development budget.[103]

A groundbreaking 2005 study by investigators at the University of Toronto cast a long shadow on cancer drug development. These investigators performed a meta-analysis of all Phase III clinical trials between mid-1998 and mid-2003 and compared the results of Phase III findings with identical Phase II studies.[104] The outcome revealed that only 28 percent of positive Phase II clinical outcomes were similarly positive in a Phase III setting. Placed in a proper perspective, this outcome is only slightly better than correctly calling the toss of a coin two times in a row. The ramifications were and remain profound and have created many questions. In each case, highly competent individuals designed and executed state-of-the-art studies.

In large part because of failed late-stage clinical trials, the costs of new drug development have been rising. The Tufts University Center for the

Study of Drug Development has been assessing the costs of drug development and finds that the costs of drug development now exceed $2.6 billion.[105] As we will see in future chapters, such statistics have created a sense of crisis in the boardrooms of many large pharmaceutical companies and changed how the industry operates, threatening the viability of the entire drug discovery enterprise.

CHAPTER EIGHT

Sea Monsters, Immunauts, and Death Panels

In chapter 6, we witnessed the emergence of biotechnology from its early roots in Northern California. Pioneers such as Genentech, Amgen, and Biogen were merely the first notes in a much larger movement. We begin this chapter by defining biotechnology, since the term can be ambiguous. We will then document its growth from a few upstarts to a powerful industry fueled by easy money and increasing confidence. Ultimately, the self-assurance gave way to hubris, and irrational exuberance caused many companies to lose focus. We then conclude the chapter by showing how changes in the macroeconomic climate, combined with a landmark scientific achievement, forced a premature reckoning that threatens to extinguish the entire industry just a few decades after its birth.

Betting the Pharm

Though the term biotechnology is commonly invoked among scientists, clinicians, and investors, its definition varies widely. In describing the field in an earlier chapter, we related biotechnology to the use of recombinant DNA technologies as envisioned and practiced by scientists such as Paul Berg, Stanley Cohen, and Herbert Boyer. Thus, it logically follows that Genentech, founded by Boyer, was the first biotechnology company. Upon closer inspection, the biotechnology industry was already gathering momentum two years prior to Cohen and Boyer's publication of their pivotal 1973 experiment.

The first biotechnology company was founded by a remarkable group of people based on extraordinary science and named after an incredible experience. In 1971, Dr. Peter Farley left the U.S. Navy, where he had served as a surgeon on an early U.S. Navy submarine and enrolled in an MBA program at Stanford University.[1] His entrepreneurial streak led Farley to evaluate potential projects to champion and, in doing so, he met up with Dr. Donald Glaser, a professor at UC Berkeley, who had won the 1960 Nobel Prize in Physics.[2] One of Dr. Glaser's graduate students, Calvin Ward, was working on a second Ph.D. in biochemistry (the first had been in physics) and had developed a technology to automate experiments.[3]

After landing an experienced CEO, Ronald Cape, and venture capital, a new company was founded to advance this technology.[4] Deciding on a company name was elusive at first but was ultimately decided as a result of a misattributed animal attack. While spearfishing with friends off the Northern California coast, Calvin Ward was bitten in the leg and dragged through the water by a large aquatic creature believed to be a killer whale.[5] Armed only with his fishing spear, he prodded the animal until it eventually let go. Believing the incident to be a sign of good luck, the newly formed company decided to name itself Cetus Corporation after the Latin term for a sea monster (or whale). Later, Calvin learned that the aggressive animal was actually a great white shark, but by then, the name Cetus had been adopted.

Cetus became an early biotechnology innovator and followed up on the pioneering work of Gyula Takatsy, stressing the importance of automation and miniaturization to scientific and drug discovery.[6] Their early attention focused on engineering and automation technology from Donald Glaser's laboratory at UC Berkeley. Joshua Lederberg and Stanley Cohen of Stanford were early members of the board of directors and they criticized this focus on technology and instead advocated for recombinant DNA technology. The company was also a master of self-promotion, naming many high-profile members to its board of directors despite their having little scientific or commercial experience. Investor interest in the burgeoning arena of biotechnology was high, and the initial public offering for Cetus in 1981 garnered $108 million, a record level for an IPO at the time.[7]

Cetus invested much of this capital into partnerships with other emerging biotechnology companies. Its first successful therapeutic campaign resulted from a 1985 partnership with Triton Biosciences, a Bay Area biotechnology subsidiary of Royal Dutch Shell, an Anglo-Dutch conglomerate better known for its ventures into fossil fuels.[8] The two companies had intended to develop beta-interferon 1b (trade name Betaseron) for cancer. Cetus plied considerable resources (within the industry, this is known as "betting the pharm") into the development of Betaseron, for cancer but the clinical results were disappointing. Therefore, Cetus doubled-down and spent even more resources to test Betaseron as a means to treat multiple sclerosis. The new drug ultimately did gain FDA approval 1993 and became a blockbuster, not for Cetus but, rather, for its successor.[9]

The development of Betaseron was expensive and ultimately bagged a blockbuster, but Cetus' other effort to develop a new medicine was a greater disappointment that broke the back of the company. The logo for Cetus was a white whale on a blue background. It is, thus, ironic that the company named after a sea monster was a leviathan of its own making. In the early 1980s, Cetus joined a race against Genentech and Immunex to clone and market interleukin-2, a crucial regulator of the immune system.[10] Though Cetus had partnered with a leading IL-2 researcher, Dr. Steven Rosenberg of the National Cancer Institute, the company's initial attempts to gain FDA approval were met with a rejection and requests for more data.[11] The company staked all its remaining capital on the great white whale of IL-2 and, like Melville's Ahab, the trophy sank the boat. Ultimately, Cetus depleted its resources and consented to be bought by a young biotechnology company with a name also recycled from classical mythology.

As a demonstration of the topsy-turvy nature of the highly volatile biotechnology industry, Cetus' acquirer, Chiron Corporation, had been founded in 1981, a full decade after Cetus.[12] Indeed, just a few years before, Chiron had rented some unused laboratory space from Cetus. A year after the acquisition, in May 1992, the IL-2 product, Aldesleukin, was approved by the FDA but the marketing license was awarded to the more nimble centaur from Greek mythology, Chiron, and not the sea monster.

As a final insult to the larger and more mature, but now cowed, Cetus, the $600 million paid by Chiron Corporation in 1991 was mostly in the form of "bio-dollars."[13] Bio-dollars is a pejorative term in which non-liquid assets, such as shares of stock or promises of future earnings, are exchanged to support a partnering or acquisition deal. In the heyday of the biotechnology boom, it was routine to read about billions of dollars in future proceeds (usually based on distant milestones) and these bio-dollars fueled speculative deals that arguably over-emphasized the potential long-term rewards from products that may have been a decade or more from being approved by the FDA and sold to consumers. Thus, the use of bio-dollars in its acquisition of the once-mighty company they had built was a truly bitter pill to the management, employees, and investors of the Cetus Corporation.

While Cetus was striving to gain approvals for Betaseron and Aldesleukin, the company was making seminal contributions that would outshine either therapeutic product. In 1979, Cetus hired a young and rather eccentric Ph.D. biochemist by the name of Kary Mullis, who had earned his PhD from UC Berkeley in 1972 and then left science for a time to become a writer before joining Cetus to help make ends meet.[14] Mullis had been hired to generate strands of DNA to be used by other scientists at Cetus.[15] It was a menial task but it gave Mullis an opportunity to play with equipment in the laboratory. During an April 1983 drive to his cabin in Mendocino County, Mullis developed an idea for a way to use some of the equipment to amplify specific segments of DNA through a process that is now known as the polymerase chain reaction or PCR.[16]

On the evening of 16 December of that same year, Mullis obtained the first positive results and, in his excitement, he told the only other person around at that time of night, a Cetus patent attorney.[17] Recognizing the potential value of the discovery, the patent attorney immediately began working on a set of claims to protect Mullis' findings but was warned by Cetus management not to let this become a distraction. Mullis presented his findings at the annual company retreat in May 1984, but the finding was largely ignored and the meeting is best remembered for a fistfight involving Mullis and another Cetus employee.[18] The company struggled with whether to fire the brilliant but unstable Mullis, but he was, instead, given a chance to work with a small team to optimize PCR. By November 1984, the team obtained definitive evidence of the utility of the new technology and Cetus applied for a patent in March 1985.[19]

PCR became a multi-billion dollar franchise, but the earnings were not realized by Cetus but by Hoffman La Roche. The reason comes back to Cetus' interest in IL-2. Roche had key patents relating to IL-2 that Cetus sought to license.[20] The two companies agreed to a swap, in which Cetus gained access to Roche's IL-2 technology while Roche did the same for PCR. Ultimately, Cetus ended up selling its entire PCR portfolio to Roche for $200 million, which infuriated Mullis, who had been compensated a mere $10,000 for his development of this technology. Roche then marketed its PCR assets for more than $10 billion. Mullis, on the other hand, quit Cetus in 1986 and continued his eccentric ways, at one point starting a company intent on selling molecular souvenirs consisting of DNA isolated from deceased celebrities including Elvis Presley and Marilyn Monroe.[21]

Failing to Produce

Many biotechnology companies have shared a similar experience as Cetus. Startup companies often lack the resources of experience to execute or anticipate and thereby avoid potential problems. A prominent example is the experience of Immunex.

Immunex was a Seattle company founded in 1981 by two immunologists from the newly formed Fred Hutchinson Cancer Research Center at the University of Washington. Drs. Steven Gillis and Christopher Henney were studying the growth of key cells of the human immune system using state of the art laboratory methods.[22] The late 1970s and early 1980s witnessed an upwelling in understanding about the cells and chemicals of the body's host defenses, those components that prevent infectious diseases and many cancers.

A subset of the molecules secreted by white blood cells, known as cytokines, had been discovered and shown to govern critical choices about cell growth and death. These molecules literally made life-or-death decisions as the key arbiters of the body's host defense mechanisms, governing whether the immune system should attack a particular target or not. The importance of such decisions can be seen by considering two extremes. In cases where the immune system should attack but does not, laxity can allow foreign pathogens, such as viruses or bacteria, to thrive and propagate deadly infections. On the other hand, an inappropriate decision to attack can cause an equally deadly range of autoimmune diseases. Thus, the system must be finely balanced and tightly controlled by an array of cells and molecules, such as cytokines.

Gillis and Henney were leading experts in the expanding field of cytokine biology. As such, they were frequently asked to consult with or otherwise assist pharmaceutical industry companies who sought to underwrite their studies as part of a partnership to develop new drug leads for the range of diseases linked to inappropriate host defense decision making.[23] Instead of succumbing to these enticements, the two investigators opted for the riskier choice of leaving their jobs at the university and starting a new company in Seattle.

Immunex Corporation focused on the discovery of cytokines that controlled the growth of key cells in the human immune system. The company intended to use recombinant DNA technology for an academic-like approach to continuously develop new products and then to license those products to established pharmaceutical companies. Rather than compete with established pharmaceutical companies, which Gillis and Henney assumed were far ahead of them in terms of sophistication and expertise, the idea was to function as a middleman between academic research and pharmaceutical application by constantly investing in new generations of products. This idea is a logical extension of the approaches used by academic researchers and is based on the fundamentals of how NIH-funded research is conducted. The science performed by Immunex was quickly recognized to be of the highest quality and the company developed a reputation for strong science and highly motivated employees, famed for their *esprit de corps*, in which they referred to one another as "Immunoids."[24]

The company learned quickly that established pharmaceutical companies themselves had struggled with newly emerging recombinant DNA technologies and that, in many ways, their Immunoids were more sophisticated and experienced. Immunex learned to pivot and, ironically, ended up creating one of the first vertically integrated biotechnology companies.[25] Vertical integration is an approach of performing all aspects of drug research, development, manufacturing, sales, and marketing. Building a vertically integrated company can be an expensive and distracting prospect. To fund these expansion capabilities, the company licensed away many of its early discoveries and marketing rights to others. Despite sizeable revenues from out-licensed products, the company had lost nearly $30 million by 1990 and did not yet have a single approved drug.[26] Additional challenges of becoming a fully integrated company later became apparent with the approval of Immunex's first product, GM-CSF (trade name Leukine).

GM-CSF is a cytokine that promotes the growth of many cells of the immune system. As such, the scientists at Immunex realized that recombinant forms of GM-CSF could be used to repopulate a patient's immune system following certain types of chemotherapy or bone marrow transplants. The resulting product, Leukine, was approved in 1991 but challenged by a competing product, G-CSF (trade name Neupogen) from Amgen, which had gained FDA approved a mere two weeks before Leukine.

Immunex devoted considerable attention and resources into promoting the manufacturing, sales, and marketing of Leukine, including the construction of a new manufacturing facility in Bothell, Washington, to support what was anticipated to be a blockbuster drug.[27] However, the sales of Leukine had been essentially hobbled by the fact that FDA had approved its use only for bone marrow transplantation, whereas the competing Amgen drug was approved for a broad range of indications associated with immunosuppression from cancer chemotherapy. Therefore, while Neupogen gained blockbuster status, Immunex's manufacturing capabilities built for Leukine went largely unused. As we will see, manufacturing issues would again haunt the company in the coming years and ultimately deliver a fatal blow.

Compounding the disappointment surrounding Leukine, Immunex soon found itself being forced to deprive resources for its other activities and programs, including a novel way to block a different cytokine known as tumor necrosis factor alpha (TNF-alpha). For more than a century, it had been observed that some bacterial infections had the unexpected properties of causing tumors to shrink.[28] In the early 1960s, a study from the National Cancer Institute showed that a certain sugar isolated from a rather notorious bacterium, *Serratia marcescens*, was able to shrink tumors in experimental models of cancer in mice.[29]

The notoriety of the bacterium *Serratia marcescens* was based on its ability to grow on bread, where it caused bright red colonies to make the bread appear as if it were bleeding.[30] This striking, and seemingly "miraculous" feature was noted in the thirteenth century during a Eucharist ceremony in 1263 and purportedly compelled Pope Urban IV to initiate the Feast of Corpus Christi. Less miraculous was a demonstration by Memorial Sloan Kettering scientists that the bacterial-derived sugar, known as an endotoxin, had caused host defense cells to begin manufacturing a soluble factor that had the remarkable property of shrinking tumors.[31] This finding initiated a search for this so-called "tumor necrosis factor" (necrosis being the Greek word for "death").[32]

In 1980, the budding biotechnology company Genentech recruited a young scientist from nearby University of California, San Francisco, named Bharat Aggarwal.[33] One day shortly after his arrival, the non-scientific founder of Genentech challenged Aggarwal to find "a cure for cancer" by isolating and cloning the tumor necrosis factor that was stimulated by bacterial endotoxins.[34] Despite a complete lack of familiarity with the subject, Dr. Aggarwal took the challenge and within four years had identified and characterized tumor necrosis factor (known as TNF-alpha) as a novel cytokine.

Over time, TNF-alpha had been linked not only with cancer but also as a key mediator of inflammation associated with autoimmune, cardiovascular, metabolic, and neurological diseases.[35] Sepsis was a particularly enticing disease, associated with high levels of TNF-alpha since this indication is a whole-body form of inflammation that causes catastrophic damage during infection and is usually fatal. While TNF-alpha plays a beneficial role in terms of shrinking tumors in mice, the overall impact of sustained high levels in people is negative, as elevated TNF causes the body's defense cells to turn on their hosts and trigger various autoimmune diseases. Thus, the therapeutic opportunities quickly evolved to inhibit, rather than promote, the expression and function of TNF-alpha.

Returning to the situation at Immunex, the Seattle scientists had followed the TNF story and came up with a novel solution to block TNF in diseased patients. Immunex scientists combined their expertise in understanding cytokines with a basic understanding of rapidly emerging monoclonal antibody technologies. Their elegant solution was to create a so-called "TNF decoy receptor," which consisted of a Frankenstein-like artificial fusion of the TNF receptor with the framework of an antibody.[36] This "decoy" could be injected into patients, where it would bind to and remove TNF circulating in patients with autoimmune diseases. The drug was named etanercept (trade name Enbrel) and showed exceptional promise in early testing.[37]

Despite the promising findings with Enbrel, Immunex had exhausted most of its available resources in supporting the sales, marketing, and manufacturing of Leukine.[38] To address this issue, Immunex formed a strategic partnership with an established pharmaceutical company, American Cyanamid, which provided a new source of capital. Specifically, American Cyanamid would purchase a majority stake in Immunex (53.5 percent of the company's stock) in exchange for a $350 million payment plus a 50 percent premium to Immunex shareholders.[39] American Cyanamid also detached its oncology subunit from its pharmaceutical division, Lederle Laboratories, and assigned it to the new Immunex.

Since TNF-alpha had been implicated in sepsis, the new Immunex invested its proceeds into clinical trials for this indication.[40] Sepsis has among the worst reputations for being resistant to therapeutic intervention and Enbrel proved not to be an exception. A clinical trial failed abjectly and executives in American Cyanamid pressured the management of Immunex to abandon further Enbrel development. Immunex managed to persuade American Cyanamid to continue development for other autoimmune indications but only if the FDA agreed to this further development, which it did. The company then redirected its energies toward rheumatoid arthritis, and obtained an FDA licensure in November 1998.[41]

Although Leukine was Immunex's first product, the company had been forced to out-license much of its value. The remaining value of Leukine was diluted by a limiting FDA approval (an attempt to expand its use to cancer chemotherapy was rejected by the FDA in 1995) and competition from its rival, Amgen. However, the blockbuster potential of Enbrel looked to be worthy of the past misfortunes, and Immunex was set for a breakout in the years following its approval in 1998. At the time, there were few effective treatments for rheumatoid arthritis (beyond steroids, which have notoriously bad side-effects) and Enbrel sales reached $10 million within days after product launch.[42] Beyond arthritis, Immunex had also obtained promising data with Enbrel for treating Crohn's disease and chronic heart failure. In 1999, Enbrel sales reached $367 million and Immunex stock soared, splitting twice that year.[43] By 2000, the market capitalization of Immunex had even exceeded its Seattle neighbor, the Boeing Aircraft Company.[44]

Though reaching a zenith in product sales and stock price, the foundations of Immunex were built upon Enbrel and the company had not developed sufficient manufacturing capabilities to support the level of demand. Though the company broke ground on the construction of an Enbrel manufacturing plant in 1999, this was too little and too late. It isn't clear whether the delayed manufacturing strategy was a direct consequence of the Leukine experience (where manufacturing had been over-built), but soon, Enbrel was scarce and had to be distributed by lottery.[45] The inability to meet demand crippled the much-needed development of the trust that a new product launch requires. Furthermore, other TNF-based medicines were being approved by competitors (such as Remicade, for which Centocor received FDA approval in 1998) and the opportunity for market dominance was forever lost.[46]

Largely as a consequence of these outcomes, Immunex agreed in late 2001 to be purchased by Amgen, its rival for Leukine and the world's largest biotechnology company.[47] By this time, Immunex had initiated a large expansion, and not only of its manufacturing capabilities. It had built a new Helix campus on the Seattle waterfront, as well. Amgen permitted the completion of this construction but by mid-2014 had decided to shutter the Seattle site altogether, thus ending once and for all the Immunex legacy.[48]

Well, not quite.

Cold Reception for a Hot Drug

The cofounder of Immunex, Steve Gillis, started a second biotechnology company, Corixa, in 1994.[49] At this particular time, the investor community was recovering from a vigorous period of new biotechnology startups and negative sentiment was growing since rather few biotechnology companies were posting profits. Prominent examples of this malaise included the fact Genentech was forced in 1990 to accept majority ownership by Roche in exchange for a $500 million cash infusion.[50] Just as Gillis was establishing Corixa, Chiron (the company that acquired Cetus three years before) sold a 49.9 percent share of its stock to the drug giant Ciba-Geigy in exchange for the promise of additional equity and debt guarantees.[51]

Despite this difficult environment, Gillis built Corixa around a business model that would again emphasize great science and build value by licensing its findings to a subset of strategic partners.[52] It is not clear whether a return to this middleman approach was a direct response to the experiences at Immunex but Corixa clearly intended to avoid the trap arising from vertical integration. Given the tough capital markets, the strategy at Corixa also sought to avoid the need for future venture capital by raising an initial pile of money and using this to license products to partners, who would thereafter underwrite the future costs of research and development for the next generation of new products. In such a way, iterative cycles of discovery and licensing would serve to continuously increase value.

Within a few short years, this strategy had built a market capitalization that exceeded a quarter billion dollars and the company undertook a series of mergers to further expand its capabilities. Prominent among these was the October 2006 acquisition of Coulter Pharmaceuticals, which caused investor confidence to surge to a point where the Corixa market capitalization exceeded $2 billion.[53]

The key driver of enthusiasm behind the acquisition of Coulter was a drug that would become known as tositumomab (trade name Bexxar). Bexxar was a monoclonal antibody product that targets a molecule known as CD20, which is present on the surface of all B lymphocytes.[54] As such, this molecule provides a way to eliminate cancerous versions of B lymphocytes, and a prominent example is a disease known as non-Hodgkin's lymphoma (or NHL). NHL is a term that captures a broad range of blood cancers all of which are derived from B lymphocytes that express the CD20 antigen. As such, this provided an opportunity for selective targeting of CD20 with monoclonal antibodies. In 1997, a small San Diego biotechnology company named IDEC had received FDA approval for a monoclonal antibody known as rituximab (trade name Rituxan) that binds CD20 on tumor cells and kills them via a natural process known as antibody-dependent cellular cytolysis (ADCC).[55] Despite less-than-spectacular clinical data, Rituxan was well received by the medical community and propelled by the dire need for new therapeutic options for NHL. With this in mind, Corixa pushed harder to develop its own CD20-based monoclonal antibody, Bexxar.

Investors were excited since Bexxar was hot. Literally.

The key feature distinguishing Bexxar from Rituxan was the fact that Bexxar's antibody had been irreversibly linked to a "warhead" consisting of a radioactive form of iodine (iodine-131).[56] The idea was that the antibody would function as a hybrid between a guided missile and a microwave oven. Memories of the Gulf War in the early 1990s were instilled, with spectacular images of individual, targeted missiles precisely destroying individual targets during the First Gulf War. While this is the basis for all monoclonal antibodies, Bexxar had the added feature of being able to irradiate the area immediately around the tumor cells, thereby killing other tumor cells in the vicinity. This radiation-directed damage did, indeed, improve the magnitude and duration of patient responses in an unprecedented manner. For example, the pivotal study for Bexxar was conducted using a small sample of forty patients with non-Hodgkin lymphoma, each of whom had exhausted all their clinical options.[57] Perhaps most important, these patients had already failed rituximab and were facing imminent death. Despite long odds, Bexxar worked in almost two-thirds of these patients and the therapeutic benefit lasted for more than two years. Indeed, almost one-third of the patients experienced a complete remission and were alive more than a decade later.

The road to FDA approval of Bexxar, however, was not without its bumps. While reviewing the clinical data, the FDA made it know it was concerned about the introduction of a radioactive substance into a patient's body. In September 1999 and again in March 2001, the FDA requested additional safety information from Corixa. These delays forced the company to restructure its workforce, reducing the number of employees by almost one-sixth.[58] Ultimately, however, Corixa was vindicated and the superior efficacy of Bexxar allowed it to gain FDA approval in June 2003.[59]

Corixa and its investors anticipated massive sales. Rituximab had already broken through the blockbuster ceiling in 2002 (with more than a $1 billion in annual sales) and exceeded the $2 billion mark in 2006.[60] Given superior clinical findings, it logically followed that Bexxar would fare even better in the market. For example, whereas rituximab required a patient to be repeatedly treated, sometimes for many years, a single shot of Bexxar was sufficient to obtain a meaningful and long-lasting clinical benefit, and in almost three-quarters of all patients. Those oncologists who saw the data from clinical trials were surprised at how well the drug worked.[61]

Despite the superiority of the drug, Bexxar was a dismal flop for one simple reason: doctors did not prescribe the drug for their patients. Bexxar sales peaked in 2008 at $25 million, which was one percent of the revenues generated by the inferior rituximab in that same year.[62] The poor showing caused Corixa to be dismantled and ultimately sold to GlaxoSmithKline (GSK) pharmaceuticals for a paltry $300 million. Indeed, the motivation for GlaxoSmithKline to acquire Corixa was not Bexxar but another product Corixa had developed to increase the efficacy of vaccines being developed by the British pharmaceutical company. Bexxar was formally withdrawn from the market in 2013 and is not longer available to the many cancer patients, who might benefit from its use.[63]

What went wrong? Despite the fact that Bexxar demonstrated superior activity, the marketing of the drug had a fatal flaw. In the world of cancer treatment, there are three types of doctors, known pejoratively as "cutters," "burners," and "pushers." "Cutters," unsurprisingly are surgical oncologists, who are tasked with physically removing tumor masses from patients. "Burners" refers to radiation oncologists, who generally use imaging devices and radioactive beams to target cancerous masses. The third and largest groups consist of "pushers," who are medical oncologists. These cancer doctors generally design and oversee (or push for) chemotherapeutic medicine regimens, most of which are infused intravenously into patients while being overseen by a trained medical staff.

Pushers almost invariably treat patients with NHL. Medical oncologists make most of their money from infusion clinics, and prescribing a single dose of Bexxar would jeopardize their revenue stream. This is because Bexxar must be prescribed by radiation oncologists (due to the radioactive iodine warhead on the antibody). Thus, the pushers either did not want to lose their patients to burners or otherwise encountered logistical or reimbursement hurdles in the healthcare management system that precluded decisions to recommend Bexxar. In particular, reimbursement issues usually dictate if and how a radiation oncologist is paid for their services (and the medicines they prescribe). The relative novelty of Bexxar meant that reimbursement issues were continually problematic and this helped push the doomed Bexxar into the dustbin.[64]

Despite the fact that Steve Gillis remains highly regarded as a pioneering scientist and an outstanding entrepreneurial leader, this one man's experiences in founding and leading Immunex and Corixa demonstrates impediments that can unravel otherwise brilliant scientific and commercial strategies. One lesson learned is that logistics are crucial and manufacturing too much (Leukine) or too little (Enbrel) product can be devastating. Furthermore, these experiences show the danger that breakthrough biomedical products can encounter from unanticipated logistical issues (for example, prescribing decisions and reimbursement). As we will see, these issues were not unique to Immunex or Corixa, yet the lessons from these pioneers are still not fully appreciated, even by many of their peers.

Learning from the Mistakes of Others

William Bowes was an early biotech venture capitalist whose investments included Cetus Corporation, where he sat on its board of directors from 1972 until 1978, before leaving in exasperation.[65] From his vantage point, Bowes witnessed experiences he would internalize and seek to rectify in his future ventures. In particular, he was concerned that Cetus had emphasized hype over basic science and felt this was a fundamental oversight that contributed to its struggles.

In 1979, Bowes sought to correct this oversight by starting with outstanding science. To this end, Bowes sought out a professor at UCLA, Winston Salser, to help him build a high-caliber scientific advisory board as the first step in creating a new company.[66] The resulting organization was to be located in Thousand Oaks, California, a location selected for its affordability (at the time) and the fact it was roughly equidistant from UCLA, Caltech, and UC Santa Barbara. Thousand Oaks also had the advantage of being a relatively sleepy backwoods, which was helpful given lingering concerns by the general public spurred by *Andromeda Strain* perceptions that were still associated with recombinant DNA technologies. Teaming up with Bowes was Franklin (Pitch) Johnson, a classmate from when the two were earning their MBAs from Harvard. Bowes also hired George Rathmann to become the founding CEO of the new company, which was named Applied Molecular Genetics (later shortened to Amgen).

George Rathmann was a precocious student who had earned a bachelor's degree from Northwestern University at the age of eighteen.[67] Too young to matriculate into medical school, he instead obtained a Ph.D. in physical chemistry from Princeton before joining 3M to practice a new passion in polymer chemistry.[68] After a stint working in the field of medical devices, Rathmann accepted a job at Abbott Laboratories in 1975 to lead research into new diagnostic agents, growing that division into one of its most successful subsidiaries within a few short years.

A few years later, the still-precocious Rathmann sought to learn more about the budding recombinant DNA technology and decided to take a six-month leave of absence to learn about the new phenomenon. He chose as a mentor the former professor of one of his Abbott scientists, the UCLA faculty member Winston Salser.[69] Salser explained that he didn't have time to help Rathmann learn the basics of the field because he was working on starting a new company based on the technology. Salser then convinced Rathmann to come to Los Angeles, where Bowes and Johnson talked with him about Amgen. Intrigued by the promise of the new technology, Rathmann agreed to lead the embryonic company.

In its early years, Amgen began the arduous process of researching new proprietary therapeutics while paying the bills by developing enzymes and designing hormones for livestock. Following on the heels of a successful IPO from its soon to be perennial rival, Genentech, Amgen company raised $42 million in its IPO in 1982, just one year after its formal founding.[70] These resources allowed Rathmann to focus the considerable energies and talents of the company on a single product, erythropoietin (also known as EPO).

Erythropoietin is a natural protein in the body that controls the production of red blood cells.[71] Though perhaps better known as the doping drug abused by Lance Armstrong and other Tour de France cyclists and athletes, Amgen developed EPO to address the profound anemia associated with cancer chemotherapy and other diseases. In a remarkable feat of scientific and drug development acumen, Amgen scientists cloned the gene for human EPO and progressed to developing and testing the drug such that it gained a 1989 FDA approval within five years after the project was first conceived.[72]

In a move reminiscent of that taken by Immunex with Leukine but with a much more positive outcome, Rathmann invested Amgen's limited capital into the construction of a $20 million manufacturing facility that was completed three years before FDA approved EPO.[73] In doing so, Amgen was positioned for a rapid launch of the product and profited from an early and strong establishment of the Epogen brand.

Amgen's next great challenge was to emerge from a successful first product launch and overcome the sophomore slump that has plagued many early-stage biotechnology companies. Amgen's second product was a recombinant form of another growth factor, human G-CSF, which promotes the growth of neutrophils, a vital subset of bone marrow cells that are depleted following cancer chemotherapy or bone marrow transplantation. This product, Neupogen, began early-stage clinical trials for severe chronic neutropenia in 1987, and based on positive findings in which 90 percent showed positive results, Amgen investigators designed a pivotal Phase III clinical trial in late 1988.[74] Likewise, the Phase III clinical trial demonstrated strong positive data. These findings allowed Amgen to gain a broad FDA approval for both cancer and bone marrow transplantation, and this strong foundation allowed Neupogen to eclipse the competing product, Leukine (the Immunex drug approved in the same year).[75]

Amgen avoided the temptation to emphasize hype and rapid growth that characterized many of its biotechnology rivals, vying instead to become a more disciplined and stable company. In this way and others, Amgen compared itself from the outset with conventional pharmaceutical companies rather than other biotechnology upstarts, albeit with a more aggressive and nimble biotech-like approach. To ingrain discipline and further distinguish it from other biotechnology companies, Amgen cultivated a stable management team and succession strategy using expertise drawn from large, established industries. This strategy contrasted with its peers, who tended to recruit high flyers with a comparably high turnover rate. The combination of hiring senior talent from other industries and cultivating them internally to learn the system before taking the helm helped Amgen, unlike many of its peers, to become and remain a successful and independent biotechnology company. For example, Amgen's chief financial officer, Gordon Binder, had been in management in Litton Industries (a large defense contractor) and the Ford Motor Company.[76] Likewise, following the 1988 retirement of its first CEO George Rathmann, Amgen elevated Binder to CEO, a position he held for more than a dozen years. A nuclear engineer and retired U.S. Navy officer, Kevin Sharer, worked at AT&T, McKinsey & Company, General Electric, and MCI Telecommunications before joining Amgen in 1992.[77] Sharer retired at the end of 2012 and was replaced by the company's president and COO, Robert Bradway, whose experience before Amgen was building corporate finance activities while employed at Morgan Stanley.[78] The unorthodox approach of hiring quite orthodox executives has distinguished Amgen from many of the other less conventional biotechnology companies and is but one reason why many in the investment and pharmaceutical industries tend to regard Amgen more as a pharmaceutical than a biotechnology company.

Embracing Orphans

Amgen's EPO product was an early example of a so-called "orphan drug," a meaningful designation developed coincident with the rise of biotechnology.[79] In the early 1980s, the U.S. Congress was on its way to passing a piece of legislation that would revolutionize first the biotechnology and then the pharmaceutical industries. As we saw in an earlier chapter, the Kefauver-Harris Act passed overwhelmingly after the thalidomide disaster. Although conveying many benefits, this legislation increased the cost of pharmaceutical research and development by requiring that the FDA verify that new drug candidates demonstrated both safety and efficacy as compared with the standard of care. The increased complexity and size of clinical trials drove up the price of new drug development and Congressional lobbying organizations, such as the National Organization for Rare Disorders, argued that the private sector would actively avoid low-incidence diseases in favor of large indications with vast number of potential customers.[80]

Representative Henry Waxman, who would function as a key driver of 1984 legislation aimed at increasing the availability of generic medicines, sponsored a bill in late 1982 to incentivize the development of new medicines for orphan indications through the creation of tax breaks, increased patent terms, expanded marketing rights, and clinical research subsidies.[81] President Reagan signed the bill into law in early 1983 and the new Orphan Drug Act (ODA) allowed companies developing drugs and vaccines to receive these incentives if they were used to prevent or treat a disease that affected fewer than 200,000 Americans. The details of the ODA included a seven-year period of marketing exclusivity from the time the drug was approved (regardless of its patent status) as well as the ability for qualifying companies to receive tax credits equal to half of the drug's development costs. The incentives were further sweetened in later years by excluding drug sponsors from having to seek approval under the ODA, which precluded the requirement to pay PDUFA fees to expedite FDA approval.

The provisions of the ODA could be applied either to new or existing drugs that might be repurposed for orphan indications.[82] The first drug approved under the ODA was levocarnitine (trade name Carnitor), which was approved by the FDA in 1986.[83] The new medicine was a nutritional supplement directed at a small population of patients who suffer from a genetic defect that deprives them of a substance known as carnitine, which is necessary for the metabolism of fatty acids.[84] The rare illness, which affects one in 10,000 newborn infants, causes severe brain dysfunction and can place individuals at risk for sudden heart or liver failure. Carnitor also is effective for treating other indications that cause low levels of carnitine, including patients undergoing frequent kidney dialysis or taking certain drugs (such as AZT for HIV/AIDS maintenance).[85]

Starting with Carnitor, the incentives created by the 1983 legislation have inspired many companies to seek initial FDA licensure under the ODA.[86] Since its inception through the end of 2013, the FDA has designated 185 medicines that received an approval under ODA provisions.[87] The rate of new drug approvals for orphan indications has skyrocketed, from an annual average of three in the 1980s to a current rate of twelve per year as of this writing. Indeed, the year 2015 marked a milestone in which more drugs were approved for orphan indications than for all other indications combined. Biotechnology companies, in particular, have particularly embraced this approach, none more than the company known as Genzyme.

Costly Enzymes

In 1981, the world's most accomplished chemist teamed up with a pioneer of the modern package shipping industry to found a company dedicated to saving the lives of patients with rare diseases.[88] Sheridan Snyder was a serial entrepreneur who, in 1971, founded a company that developed Instapak, an expanding urethane foam that can be used to package and ship fragile items. Almost ten years later, Snyder was looking for his next chance to start a new company and hired an investment agency to find him a great prospect. In the course of evaluating opportunities, the investment team met a young enzymologist, Henry Blair, who was being supported by an NIH grant to research Gaucher's disease, a rare genetic disease that afflicts one in 20,000 newborns and is particularly prevalent in Ashkenazi Jews.[89] Snyder hired Blair in 1981 but since he was relatively junior, he reached out to a group of eight Harvard and MIT professors and offered them a 10 percent stake in the company in return for scientific guidance. George Whitesides, an entrepreneurial chemist, who was transitioning from MIT to Harvard at the time, took him up on the offer.[90] Two years later, the new company began to crystallize around Blair's scientific research on Gaucher's disease but needed an experienced executive. They found their candidate in the form of Henri Termeer, who was recruited from Baxter Travenol.[91] 1983 was also a pivotal year for the new company, named Genzyme, based on the passage of the Orphan Drug Act.

Termeer adopted a conservative approach of using NIH research dollars in general, and funding earmarked for orphan indications in particular as a means to delay or preclude the need for external capital.[92] Putting this conservative approach into practice, Genzyme located its headquarters into a decrepit building in Boston's "Combat Zone" (a.k.a. Kendall Square) and forced the company to focus on products rather than manuscripts (which is always a temptation for scientists trained in academia). The company's first treatment for Gaucher's disease, Ceredase, was approved by the FDA in 1991 and later replaced by another Genzyme product, Cerezyme, a recombinant protein that was approved in 1994.[93]

Starting with Gaucher's disease, Genzyme began demonstrating via success the opportunities of transforming cures for rare diseases from a backwater to commercially attractive opportunities. The company contributed to the approval of more than twenty products, generated annual revenues in excess of $4.5 billion, and built a market capitalization of $15 billion by 2010.[94] Genzyme's growth was also fundamental to the emergence of Cambridge, Massachusetts, and Kendall Square as a hub for innovation and entrepreneurship.[95]

Further contributions to the development of biotechnology included the fact that George Whitesides became one of the most impactful scientists in history, with more than 1,200 publications and fifty patents. Whitesides has founded no fewer than a dozen different companies that, collectively, captured a market capitalization that exceeded $20 billion, including GelTex Therapeutics, Theravance, Surface Logix, Nano-Terra, and WMR Biomedical. Having been infected with biotechnology entrepreneurial fever based on his experiences at Genzyme, Sheridan Snyder also went on to found four additional biotechnology companies.

Beyond being one of the few drugs approved for orphan indications and its impact on the growth of the Cambridge and Kendall Square, Cerezyme was also destined to set a precedent that would reverberate throughout the entire medical profession. Since the drug addresses an orphan indication, the executives at Genzyme recognized that a high price would be required to offset the relatively small market. They also gambled that insurance companies and other payers (for example, the federal government) would tolerate high prices since the number of people affected (and thus the overall economic impact) would be small. High prices could also be defended by the argument that alternatives for these patients would include costly hospitalizations, lost productivity, and/or death. With this in mind, the price for Cerezyme was set at an annual cost to patients of $200,000.[96] This high price point would come to fundamentally change both the biotechnology and pharmaceutical industries.

Compendia Games

It is not widely known by the general population, but any physician in the United States can prescribe any FDA-approved drug to any patient for any indication (with the rare exception of certain controlled substances). While the FDA controls the "label," this largely limits what the distributor is able to state or advertise about the efficacy and side effects of the drug. Thus, a drug approved only for a pediatric condition can be prescribed "off-label" for an elderly patient, and *vice versa*. Indeed, most drugs are not approved for use in children because of the perils, both medical and reputational, associated with studies of experimental medicines in children. Yet many medicines approved for adults are used off-label in minors.

A key distinction is that the payers, mostly insurance companies or federal programs such as Medicaid/Medicare, are not required to pay for off-label uses. Thus, while a doctor can prescribe any drug for any patient, the insurance company does not necessarily have to pay for this medicine.

The word "compendium" is derived from a Latin term meaning to weigh together or balance. Within the medical community, a compendium is a brief summary for each of the inventory of medicines available for use. Compendia are generally used to decide what drugs will or will not be covered by insurance programs, thus the compendia often dictate or heavily influence reimbursement decisions. The practical importance of compendia cannot be overstated, but these are also sources of considerable confusion. In part, problems arise because there are several different compendia and each is constantly changing. Among the most prominent compendia are the American Hospital Formulary Service Drug Information (AHFS-DI), the American Medical Association Drug Evaluations (AMA-DE), the National Comprehensive Cancer Care Network (NCCN), the United States Pharmacopeia Drug Information (USPDI) to name just a few. Differences between compendia frequently arise and can confuse or delay the outcome of decision-making by insurers to determine what medicines will be covered by their policies.

A view of the decision-making process can be seen by focusing on how one particular insurer, Medicare, determines whether it will cover the costs of drugs for one particular field, oncology.[97] This particular field was selected because the standards of cancer care change rapidly, with the introduction of new knowledge of the disease and the ceaseless entry of new products. The choice of oncology for this example was also based on a 1997 survey conducted by the American Enterprise Institute for Public Policy Research and the American Cancer Society, which showed that 60 percent of medical oncologists prescribed off-label medicines to their patients.[98] Consequently, reimbursement decisions in this particular clinical specialty have undergone considerable scrutiny and changes in the past few years. At present, Medicare will provide coverage for a particular drug if at least one of the following criteria are met: 1) the drug has been approved by the FDA for the relevant indication; 2) the use of the drug is supported by one of the Medicare-approved compendia; or 3) the use is supported by peer-reviewed publications of clinical-stage research and in respected medical journals.[99]

The National Comprehensive Cancer Network (NCCN) is the most commonly cited cancer compendium. The NCCN is an organization consisting of nineteen hospitals; it began in 1995 to develop a comprehensive set of guidelines to support cancer detection and treatment.[100] Each guideline in the NCCN compendium provides detailed information about the drug as well as the investigators making the recommendations (to provide transparency about any conflicts or interests that might impact the judgment of the reviewers).

Returning to the subject of orphan drugs, an increasing fraction of new cancer drugs have gained their initial approval for an orphan indication.[101] As we have seen, an orphan drug approval conveys many financial and marketing advantages and often allows a drug to be approved more rapidly than may be possible with a non-orphan indication. Many companies have gamed the system by conducting additional studies beyond the intended orphan indication through a process known as "compendia expansion." To provide an example, the approval for a new drug addressing a widely known cancer (for example, breast, lung, or colon cancer) may require clinical trials involving thousands of volunteers and many years (or even decades) to gain approval. In contrast, a properly executed strategy within an orphan indication may require a fraction of the volunteers, which decreases both the costs and time required for FDA approval. The sponsor may then conduct small-scale Phase II clinical trials to provide sufficient information to support the publication of a manuscript in a relevant medical journal.

In doing so, "a compendium expansion strategy" can gain an initial FDA approval (for the orphan indication) while also providing a path to a larger market with the publication of a modestly sized (and thus relatively inexpensive) study. Many insurance companies are reticent about questioning the price of an orphan indication (given the reputational and political implications of denying coverage based on cost) and thus the cost of the drug for an orphan indication generally can tolerate a much higher set point than might be allowed for a non-orphan drug.[102] Since the same price must be charged to all customers, this means that the off-label use of the drug via the compendium expansion will often generate more revenues than might have been possible via a standard approval strategy.

Unsurprisingly, many biotechnology and pharmaceutical companies have embraced this concept of a "compendium expansion" strategy. A study recently published by the author demonstrated that whereas one in five drugs approved by FDA for cancer in the 1990s did so for an orphan indication, the rate of orphan approvals for oncology doubled in the most recent decade (starting in 2011).[103] On one hand, the strategy of seeking an initial approval for an orphan indication is quite legal and allows the biotechnology and pharmaceutical industries to develop new cancer drugs in a less expensive and timely manner. Consistent with the letter of the 1983 Orphan Drug law, these drugs are deployed to assist orphan indications that may not have been tested using standard procedures to gain FDA approval. On the other hand, the exploitation of the ODA to set a higher price is not consistent with the intended goal of reducing medical costs. Furthermore, the compendium expansion strategy skirts around the fundamental scientific, medical, and regulatory rationale for conducting large-scale clinical trials to assure that new medicines are at least as safe and efficacious as the current standard of care.

In some ways, cancer is unusual, as increasing knowledge reveals that each patient's disease is different and unique from all others (though some underlying themes resonate). Thus, rules regulating oncology have necessarily been less rigid to provide sufficient flexibility to allow oncologists and payers to agree upon approaches that benefit their patients. However, the use of the compendium expansion strategy is not unique to oncology and has been implemented for other indications. From the standpoint of regulating both the quality and costs of medical care, it will be important to determine if and how such strategies alter medical care and affordability. Perhaps more importantly, the use of such strategies raises important questions about how the FDA regulates the approval of new medicines as such "loopholes" as compendia expansion could obviate the execution of future Phase III clinical trials (a subject to which we return in the final chapter).

There is another potential implication arising from the use and potential misuse of the Orphan Drug Act. As we will see, the resources available to conduct drug discovery and development are quite finite and, in reality, have been shrinking. As more resources are devoted to the development of orphan indications, this necessarily reduces their availability for more widely experienced indications such as metabolic and neurodegenerative diseases. Whereas the rationale behind the 1983 Orphan Drug Act appropriately conveyed concern that rare disease were not being adequately addressed due to a lack of incentive, it may now be time to ask if the pendulum might have swung too far in the opposite direction.[104]

The boisterous and very public demonstrations for and against the 2010 Affordable Care Act, which invoked previously unheard of premonitions such as "death panels," revealed the public's sensitivity to any discussion of finite resources. Nonetheless, it may be time to re-engage in an objective and rational discussion of the need to properly husband the resources of both private-sector enterprises and the public-sector entities that regulate them. A key question to be explored includes whether the more efficient FDA approvals associated with orphan drugs, which are subsequently used in the larger population via a compendium expansion strategy, outweigh any potential risks in terms of reduced evaluation of safety or efficacy. Likewise, there are questions as to whether the investment of finite resources toward a subset of low-incidence diseases outweighs the needs for new therapeutic options for indications that impact millions.

CHAPTER NINE

Drama on the I-270 Tech Corridor

In the previous chapter, we saw examples of success and failure in the development of a sustainable biotechnology company. The promises of technology in general and the growth of Cambridge, Massachusetts, and South San Francisco, California, as centers of innovation have motivated governmental and regional groups across the United States to create "technology corridors" or "technology parks," and examples can be found in virtually every state. An interesting and still ongoing example can be seen in the Interstate 270 Tech Corridor just outside Washington, D.C.

The Capital Beltway is a ring road surrounding the District of Columbia. Interstate 270 projects like a spoke from the Capital Beltway and runs for more than thirty miles through the rolling suburban Maryland countryside, connecting the legislative heart of the nation to one of its main arteries, Interstate 70, which itself winds more than two thousand miles from Baltimore through Utah. Like the biotechnology industry itself, the I-270 technology corridor begins near the Bethesda campus of the National Institutes of Health (NIH), the primary agency of the federal government tasked with promoting biomedical innovation. Nine miles up the road is an exit for Sam Eig Highway that separates the suburban towns of Gaithersburg and Rockville in Montgomery County, Maryland.

An early distinction of this part of Montgomery County, Maryland, was its role as a watering hold and overnight rest stop for the Braddock Expedition of 1755.[1] More than two and a half centuries ago, the egotist British Major General of the Coldstream Guards, Edward Braddock, camped with his two regiments of regular army and colonial militia in Rockville during the French and Indian War (known as the Seven Years War in Europe). The general was on his way to attempt the capture Fort Duquesne at the fork of the Ohio River, a fort that protected a town that would soon be named after the British prime minister, William Pitt (the elder).[2] After trudging through the woodlands of the Maryland and Pennsylvania colonies, Braddock would ignore warnings from a young colonial, Colonel George Washington, and be cut down in a sudden ambush. Washington would survive the battle, rallying the troops and establishing a reputation that would carry him to even greater leadership roles in the years to come. Two and a half centuries later, in the same area that Washington had decamped (and mere miles from the eponymous capital of the United States), the biotechnology industry witnessed an episode of egotist-driven hubris that was similarly cut down by a sudden ambush.

Speculation

Just three decades after Francis Crick and James Watson solved the structure of DNA and a decade after the beginnings of the era of biotechnology, a discussion began about cataloging the human genome. An expert in DNA research and Chancellor of the University of California, Santa Cruz, Dr. Robert Sinsheimer organized a 1985 workshop to promote the idea of sequencing all the letters of the DNA alphabet in people, also known as the human genome.[3] These discussions continued in another workshop the following year, led by Dr. Charles DeLisi, Director of the Department of Energy (DOE). The DOE had maintained a long-standing interest in understanding the effects of ionizing radiation on DNA mutations ever since its creation, in 1977, and a government-issued mandate to regulate the nuclear power industry.[4] With this in mind, DeLisi initiated a long conversation that culminated in funding from the final 1988 budget of the Reagan administration to begin projecting the framework and costs for how this project might look.[5] In the following year, the NIH created the National Center for Human Genome Research and appointed none other than James Watson himself as its first director. The first laboratory experiments to map the human genome (and identify major components of the project before sequencing could begin in earnest) began in late 1990.

In parallel with this planning, the NIH and Department of Energy created a program to assess the ethical, legal, and social implications (ELSI) of genomics research.[6] The ELSI program continues today and remains committed to addressing complex issues associated with increased knowledge of how genetic and genomic research can impact individuals, communities, business, and society.[7] The program's role remains the elucidation of the genome and, particularly, the potential to link genetic differences in individuals with their prospective susceptibility to disease. Knowledge of these links can have profound implications for an individual's awareness of his or her mental and physical wellbeing, employment status, and insurability. Another question on the docket for the ELSI program from the beginning was the role of patenting and intellectual property and, specifically, whether inherent genetic information should be patented as a result of genomic re-search, a thorny issue that recurs repeatedly in our story.[8]

By mid-1996, the genome had been mapped and the actual elucidation of the DNA sequence of the human genome project (HGP) had kicked off at six different American universities and nonprofit institutions.[9] The project time-lines sought to complete an initial sequence of the human genome by 2003. One site that was not selected was The Institute for Genomics Research (TIGR) just off the I-270 corridor in Rockville, Maryland. This institute was founded by former NIH scientist and DNA sequencing expert, Craig Ven-ter.[10] Venter had frequently found himself at the center of controversy in the early 1990s, when he tried to patent genes he had isolated while functioning as an NIH employee.[11] The action spurred a highly volatile congressional hear-ing in 1992 and, ultimately, the NIH took a firm stance that it would not seek to patent genes.[12] A frustrated and ardent Venter quit his NIH post and founded TIGR in 1992 to continue work on genomics. In his post at the helm of this non-profit institution, Venter lobbed much criticism upon the NIH's genome project, which he felt was moving too slowly, and Venter took it as a personal affront when TIGR was excluded from the list of organizations that would do the bulk of the sequencing.

In May 1998, Venter formally pronounced the Human Genome Project a debacle and announced he was now starting a new, for-profit company to compete with the NIH program.[13] Beginning with this statement and re-peated many times in the years to come, Venter suggested the NIH program should be shuttered or focus its energies on sequencing the mouse genome. In its place, his new company would out-perform the federally-backed pro-gram.[14] He further claimed, it turns out correctly, that he could sequence the genome for one-tenth of the cost and years faster than the human ge-nome project (although, in fairness, the prior work by the NIH had pro-vided a springboard for Celera). Indeed, the name Celera was based on the Latin word for "speed," and Venter meant to move faster and more effi-ciently than the NIH. Furthermore, Venter planned to leverage this speed so that Celera could patent the genes as they were sequenced and before NIH could discover them. Then, Celera would charge others to get access to the genomic data or otherwise put into practice any learning they might find in the form of new diagnostic tests or insights into the design of new medicines.

The formation of Celera was one action within a genomic frenzy among investors and budding entrepreneurs as they formed one company after another to sequence the genome and carve out critical genes with patent protection. By the time Celera had formed, the I-270 corridor had already become a hub of genomics activity and played host to the nonprofit TIGR as well as multiple for-profit genomics-based companies such as Human Genome Sciences (founded in 1992), GenVec (1992), and Gene Logic (1994). These companies were each established to extract bits of knowledge from the genome and sell it, either as a subscription for access to data or to develop a keystone of patents that they could license to companies developing tangible products (for example, drugs or diagnostics).

By the time Venter formed his rival organization, much of the genome had been mapped or sequenced by the NIH project and openly provided by the government to all interested parties. Celera used this information to accelerate its own sequencing project. Venter's strategy centered upon an approach known as "shotgun sequencing," a preference he had conveyed repeatedly in his criticisms of the more leisurely NIH program.[15] The NIH took an approach known as chromosome walking, which is analogous to reading a book from cover to cover, starting at the beginning and carefully reading word-for-word the story to its end. In contrast, the shotgun approach encompassed a rapid-fire series of sequencing efforts to decode multiple, random, and overlapping short strands of DNA all throughout the genome. Extending upon the book analogy, it is comparable to obtaining multiple, overlapping paragraphs on random pages and then using computer-aided systems to reassemble the words into a single, continuous book.

Ultimately, the challenge from Celera caused NIH to reconsider its own approaches and later to adopt a shotgun approach as well. The race was joined and, on a positive note, the competition promoted efficiencies for all parties.[16] Whereas the Human Genome Project had set an initial 2003 goal, the sequencing was completed and announced in mid-2000. On a less constructive note, the animosities grew and frequently became public and seemingly personal at times.[17] The leadership of the NIH's National Center for Human Genome Research transitioned from James Watson (of Crick and Watson fame) to Francis Collins in 1993. Collins was another large personality, known for riding a motorcycle and playing in a rock band. Collins had a deep philosophical conviction about the genome project that fundamentally differed from Venter's.[18] Collins believed that the information about the genome should be available to all and that no one should seek a patent on such god-given materials. Unlike Venter, a publically avowed atheist, Collins had a deep spiritual conviction and published a book detailing the compatibilities between science and religion.[19] Thus Collins was deeply concerned and personally affronted that Celera sought to outrun NIH in an effort to capture and patent all the DNA in the human genome.

The rivalry between Collins and Venter played out on the public stage, and their different styles and beliefs and their obvious mutual disdain served to feed the headlines for years to come.[20] These actions often undermined the credibility of both Celera and the NIH and created destructive partisan divides. To weaken Celera, the National Center for Human Genome Research and its academic partners published data online almost as quickly as it was obtained. This approach created what is known in the legal world as "prior art," which prevented Celera from staking out these genes with patents.[21] Celera and Venter would counter in the media by lobbing self-pitying responses or caustic invectives, sometimes personal, against Collins and other federally-supported scientists. In doing so, this melodramatic back and forth often overshadowed the critical and fundamental impact being made through increased knowledge of the human genome.[22]

Under pressure, Celera ultimately agreed to open up a portion of its results to the scientific community but set limits that were criticized by some as exclusionary and evidence of even more profiteering. Animosity between the two competing projects remained the subject of media interest, punctuated by occasional high-profile and arrogant pronouncements by Venter about the superiority of his approaches and equally vehement rebuttals from the government team.

The personalizing of the competition and its link to Venter's ego was later reinforced by the revelation that the genome being sequenced by Celera was from Venter's own DNA.[23] In a later interview, Venter expressed concern that Collins or others at NIH might use knowledge of perceived defects in his DNA to create "a circus" and use certain biological information to raise questions about Venter's character or behavior.[24] Ultimately and appropriately, the credit for solving the human genome was shared by NIH and Celera. Like sausage making, the process was unpalatable at times but the rivalry between Collins and Venter undoubtedly increased the speed and efficiency of the larger project. Ultimately, the media linked this odd couple as the two individuals shared multiple accolades, such as awards from the Harvard University Center for Public Leadership, the "Biography of the Year" from A&E Networks, and "America's Best Leaders" by *US News and World Report*. These two large personalities who did not particularly like to be in the same room with one another are, ironically, destined to live together forever in history.

While Celera and the National Center for Human Genome Research battled it out, the genomics-based biotechnology revolution generated extraordinary interest from investors and speculators. Celera stock peaked at an aggregate value that exceeded $6 billion in February 2000 (just two years after its founding), while the market capitalization of Human Genome Sciences rose past $8.5 billion.[25] Speculation and frenzy grew around all things related to genomics. For example, Gene Logic, a company that sold subscriptions to view the genome (which was available for free on the NIH website) reached a market capitalization in excess of $5 billion dollars in early 2000.[26] As a consequence of a vast inflow of investment dollars, the I-270 technology corridor experienced an extraordinary period of growth and employment. Relatively humdrum biotechnology companies focused on product development unrelated to genomics, such as next-door neighbor MedImmune, found themselves losing valuable personnel to Celera and Human Genome Sciences, who often paid more than twice the going rate to obtain high quality talent. More insidiously, the genomics companies often lured new recruits with promises of lucrative stock options, many of which were known to be overvalued as a result of a bubble that grew with irrational investor exuberance that surrounded the field of genomics in the closing days of the twentieth century. The question was when and how the bubble was to burst.

The speculation ended with a sudden crash that emanated from a surprising source. Rather than a financial market-based correction as the source of a much-needed reality check, the bubble-popping event was a joint announcement by the American president and British prime minister. In March 2000, President William Jefferson Clinton and Prime Minister Tony Blair issued a statement of principles that clearly supported the free use and availability of genomic data. Shortly thereafter, Celera and the National Center for Genomic Research issued a joint declaration that human DNA should be patentable only after one has shown potential utility (as opposed to the sequence itself).[27] The investor community reacted sharply in a swift recognition of the speculation that had built up around genome-based companies. In a short period, the market recognized that simple knowledge of a series of letters in the genomic alphabet might not necessarily translate into actionable intelligence. Consequently, share prices of genomics companies crashed sharply with many losing more than 90 percent of the value they had held just days before.[28]

Due to the concentration of genomics-based companies in the I-270 corridor, the region was hit particularly hard. Highly flying companies like

Celera suddenly struggled to make payroll while "passé" companies that developed tangible products (rather than concepts) like MedImmune were suddenly flooded with resumes. The attrition was felt at all levels, as Craig Venter himself was turfed out of Celera in 2002 and William Haseltine was removed from the helm of Human Genome Sciences in 2004 amid an announcement of a 20 percent reduction in force.[29] Despite and because of these senior-level changes, the two companies did manage to survive these transitions for a time, though neither would ever live to see their fortunes rise to even a fraction of the speculative levels seen at the turn of the millennium.

Ever the paragon of self-promotion, Venter returned to TIGR (renaming it the J. Craig Venter Institute) and sequenced the 18,473 genes of his own dog, a standard poodle named Shadow.[30] Venter later initiated an around-the-world expedition on his luxury yacht to identify new organisms and sequence them.[31] His plans were to rival Charles Darwin by creating a "catalog of all genes on the planet" and, thereby, organize a new and comprehensive view of evolution.[32] Venter's second declared motive for this voyage was to derive information that could be used, via recombinant DNA engineering, to create new and artificial forms of life and, thus, undoubtedly, to ignite new and even more interesting controversies in the years to come.

Too Many Targets

The large amounts of venture capital that flowed into the biotechnology industry in the 1990s and early 2000s were not limited to genomics companies. As the first waves of biotech companies went public via IPOs, many were acquired or began generating revenues, both of which provided value to their investors. As a consequence, venture funding recycled back into the industry and supported new generations of startup companies.

As we saw repeatedly with Amgen, Genentech, MedImmune, Immunex, and other early biotech pioneers, a laser-like focus was essential to gain an FDA approval for the first product. A laser focus often meant avoiding the distractions associated with developing a pipeline. Thus, once the key hurdle of launching a new product was surmounted, company management could suddenly realize there was nothing left in the queue to provide an encore performance. This outcome could be fatal in an industry that so highly treasured the idea of future growth. The need to create and maintain a sustainable pipeline was a never-ending priority for biotechnology companies. Were a company to remain laser focused and go it alone, the long times required to develop a drug could mean that a gap of a decade or longer might separate the marketing of a first product and the FDA approval of the second. Compounding this chasm, limited patent life generally means that a company has a limited time, usually less than a decade, before its patent expires and generic competition begins to carve up its revenues.

For many biotechnology upstarts, creating a pipeline meant transitioning from a disciplined laser focus to a more chaotic expansion into multiple therapeutic areas and technologies, all at once. A frenetic drive to populate vigorous pipelines gave rise to a common practice known as the "shots on goal" approach. Inspired by the hockey (or soccer) statistic, the rationale is buttressed by the high attrition rate of projects from preclinical research through FDA approval. In practice, this strategy created the need for aggressive business development to repopulate the pipeline with enough product opportunities, and at different stages of preclinical and clinical development, to ensure that the interval between product approvals was sufficiently short to preclude investor worries that a particular growth-based company had gone stale. Given the high failure rate of drug candidates at all stages of the R&D process, ensuring that the gap between approvals did not widen too far meant that multiple pipeline products were needed for each stage of development. The duplication itself translated into a greater need for resources and necessarily engendered a loss of focus.

It is, therefore, unsurprising that a key trait for a successful startup biotechnology company, a laser-like focus, could actively undermine their transition from a "one-hit wonder" to an organization supported by a growth-oriented pipeline. A different type of discipline and mindset was required to generate revenues from approved products and invest the largesse to build a sustainable pipeline. To populate a sustainable pipeline, many companies quickly scaled up their size from a handful to hundreds or even thousands of employees in research and development. This created not only logistical problems but raised issues with regard to management as the styles and actions to lead a growing, diversified, and vertically integrating organization were quite different from those of a small, laser-focused startup.

The need to maintain a robust pipeline bred competition among biotechnology companies for finding and acquiring new targets and technologies. Demand drove up prices and created a "bubble" in valuation for early-stage technologies and created unrealistic expectations. The bubble was also driven by the fact that early-stage deals often were sealed using "bio-dollars" that promised overblown expectations of future revenues or traded stock in exchange for milestones that might never be achieved.

The benefactors included academia, which could readily find partners to license promising ideas. Indeed, many university administrators began to believe the revenue opportunities arising from academic inventions could be limitless and such incentives led some to overvalue their intellectual property while holding out for more aggressive terms that increasingly aped their private-sector counterparts. In parallel, the lure of biotechnology drove investors to underwrite early-stage academic ideas to establish new waves of "feeder" biotechnology companies that could mature the ideas and concepts arising from universities into more developed programs.

An insidious consequence of the "shots on goal" approach was a gradual loss of discipline. The idea of gaming the system by prosecuting multiple projects created an almost-fatalistic notion that quantity trumped quality. Some drug candidates were knowingly advanced into clinical trials though they may not have been fully optimized. Other organizations and individuals rationalized the advancement of unworthy or suboptimal drug candidates with their fingers crossed for luck but remained fully aware of their limitations.

The lack of discipline was poisonous for the entire system. The erosion in discipline was not limited to R&D teams, as shareholder pressure could lead management to make unrealistic projections. For example, senior executives might seek to increase shareholder sentiment through public announcements of an unrealistic increase in the number of investigational new drug applications (in effect, the shots on goal). Given the time and money needed for early-stage research and development, such an outcome often required ever-more aggressive and expensive business development activity (licensing and acquisitions). Another way to achieve such a goal is to increase the quantity of new drugs entering clinical trials by cutting corners and thus decreasing the overall quality of new candidates.

Unsurprisingly, many suboptimal drug candidates were doomed to fail. Poor decision-making and inferior experimental product candidates had a profound impact on the entire research and development enterprise. The rush to advance new drugs into the clinic meant that failure would arise at a later-stage, often during expensive clinical trials. Indeed clinical trials generally add as much as a decade and hundreds of millions, if not billions of dollars more than would have been needed if the weak projects had been culled before the initiation of human testing. In this light, it is perhaps unsurprising that the years to come would witness high-profile failures of experimental medicines in late-stage clinical trials. Time will tell whether drug candidates developed in this period of time will ultimately suffer a higher attrition rate than those developed before or after the period spanning the 1990s and early 2000s. As we will see, waves of notorious failures undoubtedly fueled recent skepticism by company management and investors as to the value of research and development. However, in the early years of the new millennium, the emphasis on finding new and different targets fed a frenzy and created a bubble.

The ultimate source of new targets was believed to come with the sequencing of the human genome. As we have seen, the valuation of companies such as Celera, GeneLogic, and Human Genome Sciences expanded rapidly based on expectations that these companies would be able to leverage knowledge into value-driving partnerships that would lead to new targeting opportunities for drugs to prosecute. Over time, the effect of the genomics revolution was to squelch, rather than promote, biotechnology. The flood of new data and target projections arising from the human genome project flooded pipelines and, ultimately, broke the back of the "feeder" sub-industry formed to meet a seemingly-insatiable need for targets just months or years before.

Careful What You Wish For

A few miles up the Great Seneca Highway from the J. Craig Venter Institute is the corporate headquarters of MedImmune, Inc. Rather than emphasize genomics like its neighbors down the road in Rockville, Celera and Human Genome Sciences, MedImmune's corporate strategy was devoted to developing and selling tangible products. This old-fashioned business plan was less glamorous than its neighbors' approaches and the company paid the price in terms of losing employees over the years to its local rivals. However, MedImmune was to thrive while its competitors fought simply to survive; but in doing so, MedImmune would face its own challenges.

The difficulties encountered by many biotechnology companies reflect, in part, the idea introduced in the previous chapter of the "sophomore slump." Amgen took a disciplined approach to focus on one product, then a second, and a third, ultimately building a powerful pipeline that ensured its continued growth and independence. This outcome tends to be the exception in biotechnology, and a prominent example of a very different outcome can be seen with MedImmune. As discussed, MedImmune was founded in 1988 with the goal of developing a novel therapy to prevent respiratory syncytial virus infection of premature babies. The company first introduced a polyclonal antibody-based product, known as Respigam, in 1996 and re-placed this in 1998 with a monoclonal antibody product known as palivi-zumab (trade name Synagis).[33] Synagis sales in its first full year (1999) reached $116 million and by 2004, its annual sales had exceeded the block-buster threshold of one billion dollars.[34]

In some ways, Synagis was as much a curse as a dream, as it set an unrealis-tic precedent for the organization. Unlike Respigam, which suffered an FDA rejection that almost shuttered MedImmune altogether, Synagis sailed through clinical trials. The total time of clinical testing (the time period from submission of the investigational new drug application to the FDA approval of the drug was three and a half years, which is toward the top of the league charts. This rapid time to approval is all the more remarkable because Synagis was targeted toward the most vulnerable and sensitive population, premature infants, where the FDA is particularly prone to caution given the risk and in-evitable visibility of unwanted side effects with pediatric populations (and particularly neonates). MedImmune accomplished this feat by exploiting the fact that RSV is a seasonal infection, occurring primarily in the late autumn and early winter months in the northern hemisphere and six months later in the southern hemisphere.[35] Like a well-trained military unit (and recalling MedImmune's founders had been career Army officers), the clinical trials for Synagis were expertly designed and executed. The clinical investigation of Synagis was truly an international affair involving both northern (USA, Pan-ama, Costa Rica) and southern (Australia, New Zealand and South Africa) hemisphere nations.[36] In doing so, the company effectively doubled the rate of investigation, thereby allowing Synagis to gain a rapid approval.

SYNAGIS WAS ALSO QUITE well behaved in other ways. The high cost of producing a biologics product is a common problem with monoclonal anti-body drugs.[37] Unlike small molecule drugs, which can be synthesized by chemists in laboratories and scaled-up for mass production, most biologics are produced by living cells, which tend to be rather fickle. This constraint creates a multitude of challenges, including batch-to-batch variations, and can impede the ability to manufacture a product in large quantities. Through a combination of skill and luck, the manufacture of Synagis exceeded expec-tations.[38] The procedures used to manufacture Synagis were routinely ten to one hundred times more efficient than other monoclonal antibody prod-ucts of the era.

Synagis also established a high standard by not being rejected by patients or eliciting an immune response.[39] It is essential to remember that biologics-based drugs are generally quite large and, thus, are carefully scrutinized by the patient's host defenses. Often, an antibody drug is seen as foreign (as in fact, it is) and could be mistaken for a disease-causing bacterium or virus.[40] When such safeguards are tripped, the drug is generally rendered ineffective as the body learns to clear out the drug before it can do its beneficial job. Worse still, an exaggerated immune response can reject the drug and trigger a deadly process known as anaphylaxis, comparable to the response some individuals experience following a bee sting. For these reasons, drugs like Synagis are often administered in infusion clinics (recall the situation encountered by rituximab), where doctors are on call and able to identify and intervene at the first signs of anaphylaxis. Despite being administered to thousands of children, Synagis has remained relatively unscathed by this form of rejection.

On Guard

To avoid the "sophomore slump" following the approval of its RSV therapeutics (Respigam and Synagis), MedImmune began building its early-stage research and development capabilities even before FDA granted approval for these drugs. An early program included the licensing of patents from the National Cancer Institute and the University of Rochester for virus-like particle (VLP) technology.[41] VLP technology permits the manufacture of structures that resemble the empty shells of viral particles but lack the genetic material that allows viruses to propagate disease. The idea championed by MedImmune and their academic collaborators was to implement VLP technology to generate novel vaccines. Having procured the patents and know-how, MedImmune scientists began the process of developing a novel vaccine to protect against human papillomavirus (HPV).[42]

According the Centers for Disease Control and Prevention (CDC), HPV is the most common sexually transmitted virus in the United States.[43] There are at least 120 different types of HPV, and virtually every sexually active person has been exposed to at least one.[44] Condoms are unreliable, as the virus can infest not only the genitals but the upper thigh and hands (after touching pubic areas). Thus, the rates of HPV infection continue to remain at high levels even after precautions are taken to avoid other sexually transmitted diseases, such as HIV. Given the many variants of HPV, the infection can manifest itself in many ways. Like other papillomaviruses, which generally cause small growths (such as common warts), HPV can cause a small tumor mass known as a genital wart.[45] Certain variants of HPV can cause a much more consequential disease. In particular, two HPV variants, HPV16 and HPV18, cause almost three-quarters of all cervical cancers.[46]

Based on this finding, MedImmune scientists implemented the VLP technology to create a vaccine to prevent HPV infection.[47] A nearly identical project was initiated at Merck Pharmaceuticals and a race began to create the first vaccine to prevent cancer.[48] MedImmune developed its own vaccine and tested it in preclinical and clinical trials in women, demonstrating potent efficacy.[49] However, communications with the FDA convinced the company that final approval of its vaccine would require a very large clinical trial that would cost more revenue than even the lucrative Synagis could support. Therefore, MedImmune licensed its technology and product to SmithKline Beecham in 1997. Thereafter, SmithKline Beecham (and its successor organization, GlaxoSmithKline) carried the project forward and underwrote the cost of clinical trials. The race between SmithKline Beecham and Merck was ultimately won by Merck in 2006 after the approval of a vaccine known as Gardasil.[50] However comforting coming first had been, the victory was somewhat pyrrhic as Merck was required to take a license from GlaxoSmithKline (and MedImmune) in acknowledgement that MedImmune controlled the dominant patent for the VLP technology.[51] As the two rivals were now partners on this project, the GlaxoSmithKline product, known as Cervarix, was first targeted to Europe, whereas Gardasil was initially marketed in the United States.

Thus, while Gardasil was a commercial success, it still did not fulfill the need for a robust pipeline, and MedImmune remained hungry to build an arsenal of potent new medicines.

Inhaling

Flush with cash from increasing sales of Synagis and the out-licensing of the HPV vaccine, MedImmune accelerated efforts to build a sustainable pipeline. The company decided to go shopping with its new revenues.

MedImmune's first major purchase was U.S. Bioscience in 1999.[52] The Conshocken, Pennsylvania, company had just gained an FDA approval for amifostine (trade name Ethyol), a drug designed to reduce treatment-induced side effects in patients being treated with radiation for head and neck cancers.[53] Scientists at the Walter Reed Army medical center had originally discovered amifostine during the Cold War in a desire to find ways to protect soldiers from radiation poisoning in a battlefield setting following a nuclear attack. In later studies, amifostine was found to have beneficial effects in cancer patients.[54] The drug selectively accumulated in normal tissues and functioned as a powerful anti-oxidant that prevented radiation-mediated damage. The treatment of head and neck cancers often includes the use of external beam therapy from focused x-rays or proton beams. Radiation therapy can cause severe damage to the salivary glands, which in turn, causes multiple side effects, from a moderate sore throat to extreme dryness that warrants the use of a feeding tube, which in turn, increases the potential for infection by fungal and bacterial pathogens. Clinical studies by Walter Reed, and then U.S. Biosciences, demonstrated Ethyol could ameliorate these symptoms, and these studies formed the basis of its 1999 FDA approval of the drug and a reason why MedImmune decided to acquire U.S. Bioscience later that year.

U.S. Biosciences had a marketed niche product and was reportedly building a robust pipeline of cancer drugs. Despite a failed clinical trial that followed almost immediately in the wake of the announcement that MedImmune was acquiring U.S. Bioscience, the transaction, worth more than a half billion dollars continued unimpeded.[55] Upon closer inspection but after the deal had closed, it was determined the acquisition had largely been based upon conjecture and hype. U.S. Bioscience lacked substance in terms of creating a meaningful oncology pipeline for MedImmune. This type of disappointment was not uncommon in a time when inflated stock prices and corporate valuations propelled a mania of mergers and acquisitions based on speculation and fueled by future promises of revenues. Over time, such bio-dollar transactions gained a well-earned reputation for being risky and volatile.

With continuing strong revenues from Synagis, MedImmune was still on the prowl for its next big product. In late 2001, the company announced it was spending $1.5 billion to acquire Aviron.[56] The Mountain View, California, biotechnology company was well known to MedImmune, in part because the two companies shared multiple members of their respective boards of directors (including MedImmune's founder Wayne Hockmeyer). Both companies also shared an interest in respiratory viral infections.[57] In particular, Aviron had developed a live, attenuated version of the influenza virus vaccine that was delivered intranasal administration rather than as a needle-borne shot.[58]

The concept behind an attenuated vaccine has its origins in a 1798 report by the English physician, Edward Jenner, who described the use of a naturally-attenuated form of a benign pox virus (*Vaccinia* virus) to prevent the much more deadly smallpox infection.[59] The concept of attenuation came to the forefront again in the 1950s as the result of a terrible tragedy. As you may recall from the discussion in chapter 5, poliovirus infection can cause paralysis of muscles in the leg, head, neck, or diaphragm. Fear of polio was endemic due largely to ignorance of how it was transmitted and because children were frequent victims.[60]

In a bit of irony, it is now believed the incidence of polio blossomed in the twentieth century as a result of increased sanitary standards. Polio virus infection of infants generally causes mild symptoms but rarely leads to paralysis.[61] However, the danger increases with age. Thus, poor hygiene throughout history had the unintended side effect of exposing people to the pathogen when they were least impacted (although clearly, poor sanitation increased susceptibility to many other pathogens). Thus, polio rates increased with improved sanitary conditions, which began in earnest in the late nineteenth and early twentieth centuries. However, delayed exposure to the virus until later in life, when the victims were at greater risk of developing life-long paralysis, increased the dangers of poliovirus infection.

The sheer panic and blind fear engendered by a local polio outbreak was arguably as debilitating as the infection itself and could shut down entire cities or regions for weeks or months at a time.[62] Upon learning of a local outbreak, health departments would routinely quarantine the homes of the infected, close local and regional schools, swimming pools, movie theaters, camps, and other places of potential congregation, while warning citizens to minimize contact with one another. Thus, the world breathed a deep sigh of relief upon learning of the creation of a vaccine to prevent the dreaded disease in a 12 April 1955 speech given by Jonas Salk, who had trained with Thomas Francis and later moved to the University of Pittsburgh.[63] Quite literally, the church bells were rung in many towns upon learning the news. Jonas Salk became a media idol and rock star (in the days before actual rock stars), standing above Gandhi, Albert Einstein, and the Pope in rankings of contemporary heroes.[64]

In contrast, the medical and scientific communities did not embrace Salk's findings and many actively scorned him.[65] For one thing, the "Salk vaccine" to prevent polio, like virtually all scientific discoveries, was the consequence of considerable effort by earlier generation of scientists, most notably Maurice Brodie, a researcher at New York University, who utilized formaldehyde to kill polio virus in the mid-1930s. Though the efficacy of the Brodie vaccine was minimal, Jonas Salk and Thomas Francis had improved the techniques by 1952, and three years later, a grateful world learned of the success of the killed "Salk vaccine."[66] Resentment and, in some cases, petty jealousy caused colleagues in the medical profession to accuse Salk of glory seeking.[67] Others in the scientific world believed that a killed vaccine was a less elegant approach than an attenuated vaccine. This latter group was, thus, prepared to pounce when news broke of a terrible tragedy.

In the fervor to expedite the distribution of the newly discovered Salk vaccine, five companies across the United States were licensed by the U.S. government to distribute polio vaccine in 1955.[68] Unfortunately, Cutter Laboratories, a family-owned pharmaceutical company in Berkeley, California, did not sufficiently inactivate the polio vaccine it was processing and thus the vaccine unintentionally introduced a deadly virus, rather than a life-saving vaccine, directly into many unsuspecting people.[69] Within two weeks after its distribution, Cutter realized the mistake and stopped selling the product.[70] Upon closer inspection, an NIH inspection revealed the processes used by Cutter were consistent with the standards of production and that the four other companies (Eli Lilly, Parke-Davis, Wyeth, and Pitman-Moore) producing the vaccine experienced similar problems. In total, 120,000 doses of polio vaccine had live vaccine and at least forty thousand people were infected, with fifty-six developing paralysis. Five children died from the disease.[71]

The repercussions were swift and severe.[72] The heads of the NIH, the Microbiology Institute and the Assistant Secretary for Health resigned and the country faced waves of congressional hearings and lawsuits. The "Salk vaccine" had been irreversibly tainted and was replaced by an attenuated oral vaccine developed by Dr. Albert Sabin of the University of Cincinnati. This attenuated vaccine was rushed into clinical trials in 1957 and gained licensure five years later.[73] While the Sabin vaccine and its signature delivery via sugar cube was a tremendous success, the attenuated virus itself occasionally causes an iatrogenic (vaccine-induced) and mild form of the disease. In a case of turn-about, the admittedly rare but very real risk of iatrogenic polio re-invigorated the use of a killed virus vaccine and enhanced-potency versions have now gained favor over the oral vaccine in the United States and elsewhere.

Of Boutique and Commodity Products

Returning to the story of MedImmune and its attenuated virus vaccine, the Mountain View, California, company Aviron had licensed a vaccine from the laboratory of Hunein "John" Maassab at the University of Michigan.[74] Maassab had trained with Thomas Francis (who, you may recall, not only hired Jonas Salk but also developed the killed influenza vaccine) and was in the auditorium for the 1955 speech in which Salk relayed the positive findings with his killed polio vaccine.[75] Inspired by Francis, Salk and Sabin, Maassab devoted most of his career to developing an attenuated form of influenza for use as a vaccine.[76] His novel approach was to develop a cold-adapted influenza virus vaccine (CAIV). As the name suggests, Maassab's team optimized a procedure by which a wild-type virus (literally, a virus that exists in the wild) can be efficiently modified such that it can grow only at room temperature (25° C). These viruses convey an attenuated, subclinical disease when introduced into people (whose temperatures normally hover at 37° C) and functions as a vaccine.[77]

The vaccine captured considerable press attention and awards (for example, the 1997 *Popular Science Magazine* Award for Science and Technology) in part because it used an intranasal instillation as a dispersed spray rather than a needle injection into muscle.[78] Part of the advantage of the CAIV vaccine (later named FluMist) was its localized delivery to the respiratory system, which would elicit a more physiologically-relevant host defense response for a disease of the lung.[79] Indeed, a 1996 announcement from NIH indicated Maasab's CAIV protected more subjects from influenza as compared with standard vaccines.[80]

Positive findings led to a surprise move in 2001, when MedImmune announced it would pay $1.7 billion to purchase Aviron.[81] Although MedImmune had been devoted to vaccine research from its early founding, its focus tended toward high-impact products for small specialty markets that could command boutique prices. For example, Synagis commanded a price near $5,000 for a full season of RSV protection, which was quite pricey for the early 2000s.[82]

In contrast to Synagis, FluMist was a commodity product that would be marketed to a large customer base that was accustomed to paying a few dollars for an influenza vaccine. The acquisition of Aviron was based on an assumption that superior efficacy, combined with the lack of a needle, would command boutique pricing. Given the prevalence of annual influenza vaccinations, including sixty million to ninety million people each year in America alone, MedImmune management were convinced of its blockbuster potential. The product was presumed to have particular attraction for the parents of small children and the many adults who dread needles.

MedImmune was also banking on an assumption that the FDA would approve FluMist in time for a 2002 product launch. The influenza vaccine market is seasonal, with vaccinations beginning in late fall and generally tapering off in the first weeks of the new year. In mid-2002, a disappointed but optimistic MedImmune management team announced the FDA had delayed approval of FluMist pending the resolution of a series of more than five dozen questions about its manufacturing and clinical data.[83] The company had already invested millions of dollars to develop and package a year's worth of vaccine, which could not be distributed absent an FDA approval. In a July teleconference with investors, company management indicated it was not giving up on the possibility the product would be approved in time for FluMist to compete for sales in the 2002–03 influenza season. However, that was not to be and the company later had to abandon that season and dispose of the costly materials it had produced. Given the hype around the product, the effect on investor and employee morale was devastating, with frequent references to the German translation of the notorious product's name (which would ultimately be sold in Europe using the moniker, FluEnz).

FluMist was ultimately approved almost a full year later, on 17 June, 2003.[84] This late approval date (relative to the start of the annual flu immunization cycle) meant that MedImmune would get a late start on the 2003–04 season, as advertising and marketing could not begin until FDA had approved the marketing campaign materials. The company was further hamstrung by a series of unfortunate but avoidable issues. First, the clinical trial design used to gain licensure had not included enough children under the age of five years to convey information about safety and efficacy data to support an FDA approval for this group. Likewise, the company had made a conscious decision not to seek an initial approval for individuals over the age of forty-nine, out of concern that federal retirement programs might not reimburse the intended boutique price tag of FluMist.

Multiple judgment errors further handicapped the launch of the innovative new vaccine. Most visibly, FluMist was burdened with a wholesale price of $46 a dose, which was many times the $6 price of a conventional flu shot.[85] Consumers balked at this exorbitant price and the company quickly offered a $25 rebate as an incentive, but to no avail.[86] Compounding the issue was a fundamental business challenge that is not widely known. Most patients (and, indeed, investors) were not aware that doctors purchase vaccines from a wholesale supplier and then sell this in their offices. If a vaccine is not used, the physician's practice loses money. In a haphazard attempt to appeal to physicians, MedImmune marketed FluMist to doctors with the promise that any unused product would be bought back from the physicians.[87]

While this might seem at first glance to be a reasonable approach, the strategy created the unintended consequence that doctors sold all their conventional flu shots before recommending FluMist. The vaccine also required frozen storage, and the lack of freezer space in most doctors' offices (not to mention local pharmacies and health fairs) diminished product availability.

The most devastating impact came from public health providers. FluMist contained live, albeit attenuated, virus and this caused some state and local health departments to require that the vaccine be administered by specially trained pharmacists.[88] Panic about the use of live virus even caused some hospitals to bar any employees or visitors from visiting immune-compromised patients and, in some cases, forbad anyone immunized with FluMist to enter the hospital.[89] Such negative publicity counteracted a costly $25 million advertising campaign by MedImmune and its marketing partner, Wyeth Pharmaceuticals.[90] A high-profile announcement by Wal-Mart that it would not offer FluMist in its more than 1,000 venues conveyed the dénouement for the 2003–04 product launch.[91] By mid-November 2003, MedImmune had lowered its sales forecast from four million doses to 400,000 (which itself was over-optimistic) and analyst estimates of FluMist sales for its inaugural year were lowered by 97 percent, from $90 million to $3 million.[92]

The malaise continued. FluMist did not perform much better in its sophomore 2004–05 season despite the fact that the wholesale price had been cut in half to $23.50 per dose.[93] Even the fact that the flu shot was in short supply that year could not save the product. As flu season approached, the major manufacturer, Chiron (the organization that purchased Cetus), announced that its entire stock of flu vaccine had been deemed unsafe by the FDA.[94] This announcement caused mild panic among the population. In response, MedImmune publicized it would increase production of FluMist from a planned one million doses to three million doses. Even the combination of panic and the absence of competition did not permit FluMist to break out of its slump, and the year ended with a relatively paltry sale of one million doses.[95]

MedImmune continued to double-down on the product and invested even more valuable resources into the struggling FluMist program. In March 2004, the company broadcast a strategy to achieve $500 million in sales in the United States and $800 million worldwide by 2009.[96] Despite these efforts, sales continued to sputter and totaled only $36 million in 2006 and $55 million in 2007, by which time the company had ceased to exist as an independent entity.[97]

In the days before MedImmune announced its acquisition of Aviron in late 2001, MedImmune stock was trading at a price of roughly $40 per share.[98] The excitement generated by the news drove the stock up near $50. By the time MedImmune had submitted its responses to the FDA's inquiries regarding FluMist in August 2002, the luster was lost and shares were trading at closer to $29 a share. Poor sales following product launch depressed share prices further, and MedImmune stock closed at $24 in November 2003 and remained near the $20 mark through at least August, 2006.

While most of the attention on the company continued to focus on the ongoing FluMist debacle, MedImmune's flagship product, Synagis, was booking record sales, and the company had developed a strong pipeline of product opportunities in the fields of infectious diseases, autoimmunity, and oncology.[99] Speculation then began to grow that the company might be acquired, which allowed the stock price to rebound in the closing weeks of 2006. By February 2007, the billionaire and shareholder activist Carl Icahn had purchased a large stake in MedImmune and the share price rose to more than thirty dollars per share.[100] On 12 April 2007, the company that had prided itself as an independent maverick leaked news it was exploring a potential sale with several large investors, including Icahn. The stock price soared on speculation and the company agreed to be purchased for $58 a share (a total of $15.6 billion and an extraordinarily high premium) by the British pharmaceutical giant, AstraZeneca.[101]

Along with MedImmune, other biotechnology flagship companies in Montgomery County were to lose their independence amid waves of industry consolidation. The acquired organizations included Human Genome Sciences, which was bought by GlaxoSmithKline for $3 billion in 2012 and the once-mighty Celera (whose market capitalization had exceeded $6 billion in 2000), which was finally put out of its misery by Quest Diagnostics for $344 million in 2011. Gene Logic likewise divested its genomics portfolio, which had once been priced in the billions of dollars, to Ocimum for a mere $10 million in 2008.[102]

Such acquisitions were not limited to Montgomery County but instead reflected a larger trend that was reshaping the pharmaceutical and biotechnology industries. Montgomery County would again play a role in this new trend, as just a few miles up Sam Eig Highway, midway between the former headquarters of MedImmune and Human Genome Sciences, is a building sandwiched between a movie theater and a series of chain restaurants in the RIO Washingtonian Center. The nondescript building houses a company with the name of Sigma-Tau, and is one example of a new trend that could fundamentally threaten our ability to continue generating new medicines, a subject to which we now turn.

CHAPTER TEN

Autophagy

The tendency toward increased mergers and acquisition has not been limited to Maryland or the East Coast but reflects a much larger trend that has literally consumed both the biotechnology and pharmaceutical industries.

Although a goal of this book has been to avoid complex scientific terminology, an exception is the title of this chapter, the foreign term "autophagy." Autophagy is a Greek word that literally translates into "digesting oneself." As a brief background, each cell in the human body (and there are roughly 37 trillion in each of us) has a complex array of little factories, known as organelles, which produce the proteins, fats, sugars, energy, and other components needed for survival. Sometimes, cells must recycle organelles to acquire energy or building blocks to construct something else. This process has been dubbed autophagy.[1]

In many ways, autophagy captures the recent history of the pharmaceutical industry. The last two decades have witnessed an unprecedented fervor for consolidation that has substantially shrunk the number of organizations able to participate in drug discovery and development. Given the intense scrutiny that bloated pharmaceutical companies face in the financial markets, there is strong pressure for companies to better control spending. Such examination often culminates in cutbacks that eliminate the people or entire divisions that are involved in the most speculative or risky activities. Each new drug requires intensive investment for more than a decade and is fraught with risk and high-profile failures. Thus, it is unsurprising that attempts to cut the bottom line within pharmaceutical companies often curtail research and development activities. When viewed collectively, the cutbacks threaten to impede the ability of the entire industry to develop new medicines.

The paradox is that pharmaceutical companies utterly depend upon pipeline replenishment for future revenues since patent terms (and the consequent generic competition) invariably limit the duration that even the most successful product can generate income. The absence of a pipeline is fatal and so most established pharmaceutical companies have instead refilled pipelines by acquiring one another or by implementing an outsourcing approach built around the purchase of late-stage products or companies. This strategy created a burgeoning but shortsighted market in corporate acquisitions of successful biotechnology companies. However, the supply of products and companies is finite and insufficient to continue the enterprise in its current form. Consequently, some multi-billion dollar companies have undoubtedly already passed the point of no return, effectively rendering them into "walking dead."

Returning to the theme of "how did we get here" that opened this book, we will now turn to factors responsible for how industry autophagy came into being.

Everything Old Is New Again

Like the title of the hit Peter Allen song, the promise of biotechnology caused the established pharmaceutical industry to reinvent itself. One of the earliest adopters of this approach was the Colonel's company.

Eli Lilly and Co. had an extraordinary track record developing new drugs throughout most of the twentieth century. The leading innovator in the pharmaceutical industry consistently invested its proceeds to push the envelope and identify new opportunities. In the 1970s, the company expanded for a time into cosmetics, purchasing Elizabeth Arden, Inc. and later ventured into medical instrumentation, diagnostics, and agriculture.[2] In doing so, the company lost its focus and, in the early 1990s, posted its first quarterly loss. The resulting internal and shareholder uproar led to the ouster of its CEO and recruitment of its first CEO who was not promoted from within.

Randall Tobias had served as vice chairman of the telecommunications behemoth AT&T but was recruited to Eli Lilly in 1993, where he focused Eli Lilly on drug development and shed many of the outside activities that were viewed as a distraction.[3] In doing so, Tobias emphasized the opportunity for Eli Lilly to reinvent itself as a progressive biotechnology company rather than a stodgy pharmaceutical giant. Tobias later went onto serve in the U.S. government, first as the first Global AIDS Coordinator in 2003 and then at the helm of the U.S. Agency for International Development (USAID), but was forced out of government as the result of a sex scandal involved a notorious Washington, D.C. madam.[4]

By the time Tobias took the helm at Eli Lilly, the company had already scored its first biotechnology product with the 1982 approval of recombinant human insulin, a product it had licensed from Genentech.[5] As you may recall, this move extended the franchise of the company that had first entered the diabetes market as a result of collaborating with Banting, Best, and Collip.

Thus Eli Lilly was the first company to pioneer the sale of animal-derived insulin back in 1923. Similar to the Genentech partnership, Eli Lilly was progressive in actively seeking out partnerships with startup biotechnology companies and established a track record of leveraging these partnerships into new products.[6] One prominent example of a successful partnership was with a company from Bothell, Washington.

ICOS Pharmaceuticals was founded in 1989 by a seasoned group of professionals including George Rathmann, the recently departed CEO of Amgen, Christopher Henney (a founder of Immunex), and Robert Nowinski, who had founded an earlier Seattle-based biotechnology company.[7] These accomplished founders were underwritten by funding from Bill Gates and soon initiated a partnership with the pharmaceutical giant Glaxo to begin testing a series of inhibitors of a molecule implicated in the control of blood pressure and angina in heart patients. PDE5 had recently been described in the scientific literature and was the fifth member of a larger protein family that included targets that had demonstrated great promise in the treatment of various cardiovascular diseases. Based on this information, pharmaceutical and biotechnology companies began testing the possible efficacy of PDE5 inhibitors to treat angina.[8]

Pfizer was the first company to initiate clinical trials with a PDE5 inhibitor, sildenafil, which had been discovered at its Sandwich laboratories in the United Kingdom.[9] The clinical investigation initiated with older men suffering from angina but the study investigators quickly concluded the drug was not particularly effective for that disorder. However, many subjects noted a rather unusual side effect of gaining and maintaining strong erections. Some subjects had previously been diagnosed with penile erectile dysfunction and asked if they could continue on the study. The results were published in 1996 and impelled Pfizer to pivot from developing the new drug for heart disease and, instead, focus on erectile dysfunction. Later investigation revealed that the PDE5 target was particularly enriched within sponge-like structures of the corpus cavernosum of the penis.[10] Sildenafil inhibited the PDE5 and thereby increased blood flow to these sites. The resulting drug, named Viagra, was approved in 1998 and became a commercial blockbuster almost immediately.[11] Sales of what became known as "the little blue pill" had exceeded a billion dollars a year after product launch.

Seeking to surpass Pfizer's newest blockbuster, ICOS had its own PDE5 inhibitor, tadalafil, and this drug conveyed the added advantage of remaining in the body for a longer time.[12] The drug also demonstrated efficacy in erectile dysfunction, and its long resident time in the body caused it to gain the nickname of "the weekend pill."[13] At roughly the same time the first Viagra clinical results were published, GlaxoWellcome (by this time, Glaxo had merged with Burroughs-Wellcome) had decided to abandon the ICOS partnership altogether (which might have allowed the company to share in 50 percent of the profits).[14] ICOS continued developing the weekend pill and later signed a co-development agreement with Eli Lilly.[15] The new, long-lasting erectile dysfunction drug, Cialis, was approved in 2003 and sales exceeded the "blockbuster" threshold of $1 billion in 2007.[16] Based on these outcomes, Eli Lilly decided that rather than sharing its proceeds with ICOS, it would simply buy them out for $2.1 billion.[17]

Two Ways Selling Drugs Can Lead to Jail

A second Eli Lilly acquisition was of a biotechnology company that became a household name, but not necessarily for reasons that were intended.[18]

ImClone Systems Incorporated was a biotechnology company founded in 1984 by two brothers, Samuel (Sam) and Harlan Waksal, who had emigrated from Paris, France, to Dayton, Ohio, in the 1950s.[19] Generally acknowledged for his charm and intelligence while obtaining his bachelors and doctoral degrees from The Ohio State University, Sam performed a brief post-doctoral fellowship in Israel before returning to the United States and working at Stanford University.[20] In this capacity, Waksal quickly gained a dodgy reputation for deception and outright lies, culminating in his termination in 1974.[21] Sam later claimed to be under the care of a psychiatrist and had overcome his issues enough to land another job, this time at the National Cancer Institute in Maryland. He was again asked to leave his position in 1977 after a series of suspicious "accidents" that seemed to interfere with his ability to reproduce critical findings. Sam Waksal then moved to Tufts University, where he was, again, perceived by his peers and supervisors as brilliant but was repeatedly accused of fabricating data and misleading his colleagues.

Meanwhile, the younger Waksal, Harlan, had gone on to receive an M.D. from Tufts University. As a medical resident still at Tufts, he was arrested in 1981 at the Fort Lauderdale, Florida, airport and charged with possession of more than two pounds of cocaine, which was hidden in his underwear and carry-on bag.[22] In an attempt to cover for his now-jailed brother, Sam, who was still at Tufts but not an M.D., reportedly saw patients while performing rounds in place of his brother. Upon learning of this blatant indiscretion, both Waksals were asked to leave Tufts. Sam again landed on his feet, accepting a job to run a laboratory at Mt. Sinai Hospital in New York. Soon thereafter, Sam was accused of financial improprieties and he agreed to leave his position in 1985, though the covenant by which Samuel Waksal left Mt. Sinai Hospital remains sealed.

In 1984, the two brothers had decided to found a biotechnology company to be located in Manhattan. According to a later interview, their goal was "to make some money, get rich, and retire early."[23] Within months, the two had lined up $4 million in venture capital funding and named the company Im-Clone (as a contraction of immunology and cloning). Among the investors in the new biotechnology company were Martha Stewart and Carl Icahn. Sam's social status within Manhattan benefitted greatly from these relationships.[24] Despite the fact ImClone did not yet have a lead product, Waksal lived the high life and began borrowing money from the company (reportedly more than $300,000 in the early 1990s alone) to cover a lavish lifestyle, which included the costs of becoming a movie producer and restaurateur.[25]

Around the same time Waksal was opening his second restaurant, he connected with a well-respected cancer researcher at the University of California, San Diego, who had developed a monoclonal antibody that might be useful for the treatment of cancer by binding a molecule known as the epidermal growth factor receptor (EGFR). Despite a decline in investor interest in biotechnology during the mid-1990s, the Waksal brothers managed to keep ImClone afloat and to develop its antibody product, known as cetuximab (trade name Erbitux). The results of clinical trials with a variety of tumor types, including colon, pancreatic, head, and neck cancers, were promising and this prompted a lucrative September 2001 partnership with Bristol-Myers Squibb (BMS), who acquired the rights to sell Erbitux, should it be approved by FDA.[26] In the deal, BMS would earn 40 percent of the profits in Erbitux in exchange for billions of dollars of cash and investment into ImClone.

On Christmas Day, just three months after signing the pact, a panicked Bristol-Myers Squibb executive called Harlan, who was vacationing at a ski resort in the Rocky Mountains. The pharmaceutical executive informed Harlan of conversations with the FDA, which indicated the application for Erbitux approval would be rejected.[27] According to a later investigation conducted by the Securities and Exchange Commission, Sam Waksal immediately began calling family, friends, and his stockbroker to warn them to sell their stock before the imminent FDA announcement. The stock broker, Peter Bacanovic, in turn called their mutual friend, Martha Stewart, to warn her. Once the FDA did, indeed, formally announce the drug had been rejected, Waksal began a high-profile campaign designed to convince investors that the setback was temporary and based on minor issues whereas, in reality, the FDA concerns were much more substantive.

In light of the sensitivities around the Enron collapse, which had occurred just months before, and given the high visibility of Samuel Waksal and Martha Stewart, regulators and prosecutors were particularly sensitive to charges of malfeasance.[28] By January 2002, the House of Representatives had launched hearings, revealing Waksal had forged a signature of the company's lead attorney on multiple occasions.[29] Waksal and Stewart were later arrested and charged with insider trading.[30] Sam was ultimately sentenced to more than seven years in prison and ordered to pay millions of dollars in fines. After his release from jail, Waksal admitted: "I did something that was just stupid. And wrong. Stupid and wrong is a bad combination."[31]

Ultimately, additional clinical investigation addressed the FDA concerns and Erbitux was approved for the treatment of colon cancer, first in Europe and then in the United States.[32] By this time, Harlan, who had succeeded Sam as CEO, was himself removed for a separate transgression.[33] (Harlan had apparently tried to obtain from the company a legal opinion that would have allowed Harlan to avoid paying personal taxes on certain financial transactions.) Having achieved their goal of gaining Erbitux approval, the long-assailed and weary leadership of ImClone put the company on the selling block after it was seized by the activist-investor, Carl Icahn, who had acquired a majority of the stock.[34] A failed attempt by Bristol-Myers Squibb to retain the remaining ownership of the company was followed by a bidding war with Eli Lilly, which the latter ultimately won for the sum of $6.5 billion.

From Colonel to Major to Minor

A brief overview of the modern pharmaceutical industry, which began in earnest in the 1940s, demonstrates that Eli Lilly dominated the field in terms of introducing new medicines into the U.S. market. By 1950, Eli Lilly had gained approvals for nine different medicines, which was more than double that of its closest rival. Within this same time period, Merck had introduced only four new medicines into the United States.[35] When viewed over the following decades, Eli Lilly & Co. continued its role as a dominant pharmaceutical company, leading the field in terms of number of drugs gaining FDA approvals when viewed in 1960, 1970, 1980, and 1990. In contrast, a look at the league tables in 2000, 2010, and today reveals Eli Lilly ranks no higher than ninth place, and the company today is generally not considered a major pharmaceutical company, but a middling or even minor actor.

What happened?

From the last two vignettes, it may appear that Eli Lilly & Co. made a habit of picking off competitors, like ImClone and ICOS. Yet while the Colonel's company has been one of the most successful companies in terms of internal development, it has been one of the least prolific pharmaceutical companies in terms of mergers and acquisitions. Indeed, its major deals are generally limited to modest-size biotechnology companies.

In contrast, let's look at who now leads the pharmaceutical field. In an earlier chapter, we described the growth of the Charles E. Pfizer & Co. (Pfizer), a Brooklyn-based company founded in 1849.[36] In terms of introducing new FDA-approved drugs to the U.S. market, Pfizer ranked no higher than seventh place at any point throughout the twentieth century.[37] In contrast, Pfizer vaulted to the fourth largest number of newly introduced drugs by 2000 and is the dominant pharmaceutical player today, controlling twice as many new medicines as its closest rivals, U.S.-based Merck, Swiss-based Novartis, France-based Sanofi, and England-based GlaxoSmithKline. Reviewing the pharmaceutical industry over its modern history at twenty-year intervals, the number of drugs controlled by the modern Pfizer, Inc. (or its subsidiaries) rose from one (in 1950) to fifteen (in 1970) to twenty-nine (in 1990) to 196 (in 2010).

Pfizer was able to achieve this extraordinary growth largely as a result of mergers and acquisitions. The company was not the originator of the waves of consolidation that have come to symbolize the pharmaceutical industry since the 1990s but it has been its largest benefactor in terms of sheer size. Arguably, the year that kicked off the modern era of industry consolidation was 1989, which witnessed two mega-mergers (though in 1970, the first major merger was the combination of the Swiss-based Ciba and Geigy). First, Bristol-Myers and Squibb were two New York companies founded in the late nineteenth century that shared interests in both pharmaceuticals and consumer products.[38] The CEOs of the two companies, Richard Gelb of Bristol Myers and Richard Furlaud of Squibb, were long-time friends and reportedly had mused for years about the potential for merging their respective companies.[39] The 1989 merger briefly catapulted the newly formed Bristol-Myers Squibb company to the number two spot (after Eli Lilly) but this elevation was to be short-lived.[40]

In the same year, the American drug giant Smith, Kline & French announced a merger with British-based Beecham.[41] The Beecham Group was known both for pharmaceutical products such as Augmentin® but even more so for consumer brands such as Aquafresh toothpaste, Aqua Velva, and Geritol vitamins. Reflecting back on an earlier vignette, Beecham had also purchased Memphis-based S.E. Massengill Company in 1971. (Massengill, you may recall, was responsible for the Elixir Sulfanilamide tragedy in 1937 that gave rise to modern pharmaceutical regulation.) Smith Kline & French was best known for marketing drugs such as thorazine, which revolutionized the care of psychiatric patients, and Tagamet (which competed with Glaxo's Zantac). In 1982, Smith Kline & French diversified into both the medical diagnostic equipment and pharmaceutical sectors, including the acquisition of Allergan and Beckman instruments, thereafter changing its name to Smith-Kline Beckman, a name that would remain relevant for less than a decade, when SmithKline Beecham was formed in 1989 by the combination of this already-complex company with the Beecham Group.[42]

By the turn of the new millennium, the merger mania had taken hold of the pharmaceutical industry.[43] In 1996, two companies located in Basel, Switzerland, Ciba-Geigy and Sandoz, merged into a new company named Novartis.[44] Ciba-Geigy, as the hyphen separating the names suggests, was formed in 1971 after the merger of Basel-based Ciba and its hometown rival, J.R. Geigy. Ciba (an acronym for the mouthful of a name, Gesellschaft fur Chemische Industrie Basel) was founded in 1859 to create synthetic dyes for coloring silk. Geigy (founded in 1901) not only developed comparable dyes but also expanded into other chemicals, amongst which was the discovery of the insecticide, dicholorodiphenyltricholoroethane, or as it is more commonly known, DDT. Both companies eventually expanded into pharmaceuticals, which came to dominate their businesses.

An even more complex mega-merger occurred in 2004. Sanofi was a medium-size Paris-based pharmaceuticals spinoff of the French oil conglomerate, Total. Hoechst Marion Roussel was itself the outcome of a series of mergers amongst German Hoechst, Paris-based Roussel Uclaf, and Kansas City, Missouri-based Marion Merrell Dow (which was, in turn, a merger of three other American companies, including Richardson-Merrell, the Cincinnati-based company that had attempted to pressure FDA's Frances Kelsey into approving thalidomide). In 1970, Sanofi merged with another middling French pharmaceuticals company, Synthelabo.[45] The new Sanofi-Synthelabo ventured into the U.S. marketplace with the purchase of Sterling-Winthrop from Kodak in 1994 (Kodak had acquired the prior merger of Sterling Drug with Winthrop Stearns in 1988). In 1999, another French company, Rhone-Poulenc, merged with the German-led conglomerate Hoechst

Marion Roussel to form Aventis.[46] Five years later, the company merged again with Sanofi-Synthelabo to form Sanofi-Aventis (later known simply as Sanofi).[47]

The wave of European pharmaceutical mergers was not yet exhausted. Another example of the trend toward consolidation is seen with a series of English company mergers. Burroughs Wellcome was one of the most storied pharmaceutical companies in the industry, founded in the nineteenth century but arguably claiming its greatest renown in the 1980s and 1990s.[48] Burroughs Wellcome contributions to medicine included the development of AZT and the adoption of rational design of medicine via Nobel-winning pioneers such as Gertrude Elion and George Hitchings. Just down the road was the R&D hub of another English company. Glaxo's history reached back to the late nineteenth century but it came to the forefront with the approval of Zantac, a me-too drug based on James Black's Smith, Kline and French drug, cimetidine, which you may recall was a histamine H2 inhibitor for the treatment of ulcers. In 1995, Glaxo and BurroughsWellcome announced a merger to form Glaxo-Wellcome. This new entity soon thereafter combined with another English company, SmithKline Beecham to form the behemoth pharmaceutical company now known as GlaxoSmithKline.

Growth of a Behemoth

Returning to North America and Pfizer, the 1980s and 1990s were good to the company in terms of developing blockbuster drugs. Examples included new medicines for depression (Zoloft®), hypertension (Norvasc®), infectious diseases (Zithromax® and Diflucan®), Alzheimer's disease (Aricept®), high cholesterol (Lipitor®), and of course erectile dysfunction (Viagra®).[49] By the turn of the century, Pfizer was sitting on a large pile of cash and was intent to deploy it.

By 2000, Pfizer had itself gained FDA approvals for thirty-six different drugs.[50] That same year, it paid $90 billion to acquire Warner-Lambert.[51] The Warner-Lambert acquisition added an additional thirty-three medicines, since Philadelphia-based Warner-Lambert had itself acquired Ann Arbor, Michigan-based Parke-Davis & Company in 1970.[52] Before this major acquisition had been fully digested, Pfizer acquired a second pharmaceutical conglomerate with complex roots.

Upjohn was another well-known Michigan company, founded in 1886. In 1995, Upjohn merged with Pharmacia, a nineteenth-century pharmaceuticals company with roots in Milan, Italy (where it had been known as Farmacia

Carlo Erba, after its pharmacist founder), was formed in 1837.[53] The new entity, Pharmacia-Upjohn, became an emerging giant in the pharmaceutical industry. Ten years before the Pharmacia-Upjohn merger, the chemical giant Monsanto had acquired the storied G.D. Searle & Co., a Chicago-based pharmaceutical company. Searle was another pharmaceutical company named for its founding pharmacist, Gideon Daniel Searle, who started the company in 1888. Searle developed Celebrex®, the COX-2 inhibitor detailed in a previous chapter, as well as many other well-known products, such as Metamucil (a laxative), Dramamine (a motion sickness medicine), and aspartame (an artificial sweetener).

In 2000, Monsanto and Pharmacia-Upjohn merged to form a behemoth known simply as Pharmacia. Though the waters had not calmed following the absorption of Warner Lambert, Pfizer acquired Pharmacia in 2003 for $60 billion.[54] Given the overall size of the deal and the high premium (36 percent over the trading price), this acquisition raised many eyebrows among investors and disturbed the morale of Pfizer staff, who were still adapting to the uproar and layoffs from the Warner-Lambert acquisition.

The waters churned further as Pfizer initiated a second merger tsunami. As the nation began a long, slow recovery from the Great Recession, rumors circulated on Wall Street that Pfizer was again on the prowl. Pfizer was facing a litany of patent expirations in the next few years that would threaten some of its most lucrative products, most notably the cholesterol lowering medicine, Lipitor®.[55] Pfizer management confirmed these rumors with the January 2009 acquisition of Wyeth.[56] The New Jersey company, which had been known as American Home Products until 2002, had a strong pipeline of late-stage products, including a much anticipated monoclonal antibody product, bapineuzumab, targeting Alzheimer's disease. However, this robust pipeline meant Wyeth needed resources to complete the clinical trials required for FDA approval. The need was particularly problematic at the time, as Wyeth was recovering from a rough stretch with lawsuits emerging from the 1997 withdrawal of the diet drug known as Fen/Phen.[57] Ironically, the acquisition of Wyeth based on its strong pipeline of research and development candidates was followed shortly thereafter by layoffs totaling more than 30,000, which included large swathes of both the Pfizer and Wyeth R&D teams.

Pfizer was not yet done. In 2010, Pfizer announced the acquisition of King Pharmaceuticals, which added a strong portfolio of generic medicines and an experimental new pain medication, Remoxy.[58] Unfortunately for Pfizer, and as another indication of the inherent risk associated with drug development, both bapineuzumab (from Wyeth) and Remoxy (from King) failed to be approved by the FDA and Pfizer was forced to abandon the products in 2012 and 2014, respectively.

The 2009–10 wave of mergers generated repercussions that resonated throughout the pharmaceutical and biotechnology industries. Pfizer was growing so large many competitors decided they needed to counter this growth with their own mergers. A few weeks after the Pfizer acquisition of Wyeth, Roche purchase Genentech in a $47 billion deal.[59] Roche had already owned a majority holding in Genentech after a 1990 deal, which had given the biotechnology pioneer a cash infusion to develop more products.[60] Likewise, Merck had largely shunned the merger mania of the past two decades. Just six weeks after Pfizer purchased Wyeth, Merck & Co. announced a dramatic shift in tactics with a $41 billion acquisition of its New Jersey neighbor, Schering-Plough.[61] The new and more aggressive strategy later led Merck to purchase Idenix Pharmaceuticals in June 2014 and Cubist Pharmaceuticals in December 2014.[62]

Most recently, Pfizer announced the acquisition of Allergan in late 2015. As you may recall, in its first instantiation, Allergan was a pharmaceutical that had been formed in 1948 and was later acquired by SmithKline Beckman in 1980. In 1989, the newly formed SmithKline Beecham had spun off some non-core assets (for example, ophthalmology and cosmetics products) into a new company, also named Allergan. Best known for the later development of botulinum toxin (Botox), the neurotoxin responsible for a fatal form of food poisoning, the company initial gained FDA approval for the use of Botox for focal dystonia, an involuntary spasm of the muscles around the eye. Like its natural bacterial counterpart, the active ingredient of Botox was able to paralyze the nerve endings responsible for these contractions, but the company soon realized even more gains from paralyzing other nerves on the face that are the cause of cosmetic wrinkling.

Botox quickly grew into a blockbuster drug and cultural icon and Allergan grew into a multibillion-dollar pharmaceutical giant. Like many large pharmaceuticals, the company grew in part by acquiring other companies and itself became the target of others. In 2014, the company was courted by Actavis, a corporation largely known for the sale of generic pharmaceuticals, as well as Valeant Pharmaceuticals, to which we will return shortly. Ultimately Actavis prevailed in acquiring Allergan in November 2014 though the new company, ultimately named Allergan, was to be short lived, as the Pfizer acquisition one year later ended the short independent run of this new organization.

As of this writing, it is too early to determine the impact of the Pfizer-Allergan merger. In the period of speculation after it was learned that the two companies were in discussion, a report in *Forbes* suggested that the new company would be headed by Brent Saunders, the Allergan CEO.[63] Mr. Saunders had built a reputation for shunning drug development and, instead, focusing on sales and marketing. Were such a strategy to continue at the new corporation, it would effectively eliminate the largest research and development franchise in the pharmaceutical industry, particularly in consideration of the legacy companies represented by Pfizer. Furthermore, it is unclear whether the Pfizer-Allergan merger would trigger a fresh new frenzy of pharmaceutical consolidation, but as we have seen, this trend is likely to persist until autophagy exhausts itself of new blood.

Everything Old Is New Again, Part 2

Biovail was founded in the early 1970s as a manufacturer of generic medicines.[64] For the following two decades, the company languished in obscurity, with insignificant sales until 1983, when the company was purchased by a twenty-four-year-old Toronto resident. Eugene Melnyk had owned a medical publishing company and from this vantage point learned of an interesting discovery by Biovail scientists. Their controlled release technology allowed drugs to be taken on a less frequent basis.

After surviving a few financial near-death experiences, Biovail broke out in the mid-1990s with an FDA approval to market a new version of an old drug. Using its patented controlled-release of medicines, Biovail could improve the safety and preclude the need for frequent dosing. Its first application of this technology was to dilitiazem, a calcium-channel blocker for which Merrell Dow Pharmaceuticals gained an FDA approval in 1982 for the treatment of hypertension and angina. Although the drug was effective, its consumers suffered frequent side effects, including dizziness, flushing, a rapid heartbeat, and passing out after standing.[65] Biovail could preclude these side effects by controlling the drug's release of medicine in the body with their technology.[66]

The resulting product, Tiazac® was approved in September 1995. The drug was a quick success, with Biovail reporting higher than expected sales by the end of the year.[67] From a low of $2.75 per share in November 1994, Biovail stock climbed to more than $200 per share by the following September.[68] The company applied its time-release technology to other products, both branded and generic drugs, and created many partnerships.[69] By 1998, Biovail had thirteen products on the market and the stock split twelve times between 1996 and 2001.[70]

The company was to suffer various literal and figurative bumps in the road. The company experienced slow growth and disappointing earnings in 2003. In October, a supply of Wellbutrin XL, one of its newest drugs, was being transported from Canada to the United States when the tractor-trailer hauling it was involved in a multi-vehicle pileup outside of Chicago.[71] Eight people died in the accident and, while the truck was damaged, its cargo remained intact.[72] Nonetheless, Melnyk reported the accident would decrease sales of Wellbutrin XL by $15 million to $20 million. This announcement raised many eyebrows about exploiting a deadly accident for a struggling product. Canadian authorities were the first to investigate and found Biovail's actions were "contrary to the public interest" and Melnyk was required to pay more than $500,000 for the costs of the investigation.[73] The American SEC was less accommodating, slamming him with more than $1 million in fines and barring Melnyk from participating on the board or in the management of public companies for five years.

Biovail was again in the spotlight in 2008, when Melnyk and other company officials claimed in the televised news magazine, *60 Minutes*, that high-profile hedge funds were spreading negative news to drive down Biovail stock price."[74] Any public (or investor) sympathy that might have been elicited by the segment was short-lived as allegations emerged about shady accounting practices from the *New York Times* and the *Columbia Journalism Review*.[75]

Two years later, the intrigue associated with Biovail dissipated as the company disappeared in a creative way.

Valeant or Nefarious?

As we have seen repeatedly throughout this book, drug discovery is inherently risky. In recent years, a new means to avoid risks has emerged within the pharmaceutical industry: eliminate research and development. The exemplar of this new approach was the Canadian company Valeant, which, in reality, is a new incarnation of Biovail.

The story of Valeant begins in the 1960s with the formation of ICN Pharmaceuticals by a Serbian immigrant to the United States.[76] Milan Panic was born in Belgrade in 1930 and served with Tito's partisans before becoming an Olympic-caliber bicyclist.[77] Panic defected and came to the United States in 1960. Shortly after arriving in California, he invested $200 to found International Chemical and Nuclear (ICN) Pharmaceuticals and located the head-quarters in his garage.[78] Over time, Panic purchased a series of small companies, creating a collection described by *Business Week* as "a ragtag collection of acqui-sitions, selling everything from generics to laboratory supplies."[79]

In 1970, ICN received an FDA approval for is first drug, levodopa (trade name Bendopa®).[80] This drug is perhaps best known for its role in the book and Oscar-nominated film, *Awakenings*, in which the late neurologist Oliver Sacks recounts the use of levodopa (also known as L-dopa) on patients suf-fering from encephalitis lethargica.[81] The rare disease, also known as "sleepy syndrome," leaves its victims in a statue-like condition and unable to move or speak. While the causes of this disease remain unknown, an epidemic of the disease occurred worldwide in the years spanning 1915 through 1926.[82] Dr. Sacks found that levodopa caused a dramatic, but sadly only transient, "awakening" of patients, some of whom had been completely unresponsive for five decades.[83] Milan Panic's $200 investment paid off nicely, with Panic becoming a multi-millionaire.

ICN scientists later discovered ribavirin, a drug with broad activity against many viruses. Panic touted the strengths of ribavirin, claiming it could cure HIV/AIDS. These false claims earned him a $600,000 fine from the FDA for inappropriate promotion.[84] In a move reminiscent of Sam Waksal's 2001 Christmas Day fiasco, the FDA declined to approve ribavirin for use against hepatitis C virus infection but ICN waited until Panic and others had sold millions of dollars in stock before disclosing this information to shareholders. This earned Panic another $6 million in fines.[85]

With upheavals shattering the Balkans in the early 1990s, Serbian Presi-dent Slobodan Milosevic asked Milan Panic to become the first Prime Min-ister of the new Federal Republic of Yugoslavia.[86] The Federal Republic of Yugoslavia was short-lived and consisted of present-day Serbia, Montene-gro, and Kosovo. Potentially overstepping the legal–ethical border, Yugo-slavia quickly became one of the ICN's main markets in the years before and during Panic's tenure as prime minister. His appointment as prime minister and election campaign also created stress for the U.S. government, whose citizens are not allowed to accept an office in a foreign nation. The falling out with Milosevic occurred when Panic failed in an attempt to run against Milosevic for the presidency of Yugoslavia. However, these concerns were short-lived, as Panic's tenure in the office lasted just over six months, as he and Milosevic became dire enemies.[87] Milosevic later confiscated the assets of ICN as an act of retribution against his dire enemy.[88]

Even while Panic governed in Yugoslavia, he remained at the helm of ICN, which created problems both for ICN and his adopted country. A few years after his return, Panic faced a series of sexual harassment suits from multiple women, one of whom gave birth to Panic's illegitimate son.[89] The company portrayed their founder and executive as a victim of extortion and provided Panic with loans to settle the lawsuits but, ultimately, these were settled out of court in late 1998.[90] To the relief of its beleaguered shareholders, Panic was ultimately removed from his role as chairman of the board and chief executive in 2002.[91]

With Panic's high-profile departure, ICN rebranded itself as Valeant Pharmaceuticals, but the aftertaste continued. The company established measures to improve transparency but its image was not improved by its aggressive approach to mergers and acquisitions. After the departure of its founder, Valeant began an extraordinary campaign of corporate acquisitions. Its business development activities were tireless and the company acquired three companies and announced two major partnerships in 2008, four acquisitions and two partnerships in 2009, and five acquisitions and another major collaboration in 2010.[92] Whereas the company controlled only four novel drugs in 2000, the number had escalated to twenty-four different medicines by 2010.[93] The worm turned later in 2010, with Valeant becoming the target rather than the perpetrator of its latest acquisition.

In June 2010, Biovail announced it was paying $3.3 billion to acquire Valeant.[94] Given the poor repute of Biovail and its management, the newly merged company retained the Valeant name and its CEO. However, the company would domicile in Canada (to gain preferred tax treatment), move its headquarters to Mississauga, Ontario, and retain a board of directors dominated by Canadians. The new Valeant retained its aggressive tendencies and doubled down on acquisitions. In 2011, Valeant acquired eight companies and announced three more license agreements; 2012 witnessed six new acquisitions and five licenses.[95]

An interesting comparison is to liken Valeant to Eli Lilly. Both companies are evenly ranked in the number of drugs under their control.[96] The market capitalizations of both companies, as of this writing, are similar, with Lilly at $77 billion and Valeant at $67 billion. However, here the comparison ends, as the fundamental business strategy differs. Eli Lilly is a conventional pharmaceutical company that invested 23.8 percent of its revenues on research and development expenses. In contrast, Valeant has taken an approach of avoiding R&D altogether and spends a mere 2.7 percent on R&D. Indeed, most of

Valeant's R&D expenses are directed at activities required by FDA for approved products rather than for new product development.

Valeant's approach is quite canny in actively avoiding risk by acquiring companies after they have obtained an FDA approval. In doing so, Valeant removes costs associated with research and development risk and eliminates costly late-stage failures. On the other hand, its strategy requires that Valeant pay a premium for the companies it acquires. Valeant's bottom line shrank from losses of $116 million in 2013 versus losses of $866 million in 2014 despite a revenue increase from $3.5 billion to $5.8 billion. Consequently, Valeant's earnings per share (EPS) are negative, whereas Eli Lilly is profitable. Despite this, investors generously rewarded Valeant's strategy and its share price grew year-over-year, twice as fast as Eli Lilly over the decade ending in 2015.

Noting how the market has rewarded Valeant's model of avoiding R&D and focusing on manufacturing and distributing medicines, other investors and companies have embraced the model. Valeant has been joined by Jazz Pharmaceuticals, MEDA, and Sigma-Tau Pharmaceuticals (the Montgomery County, Maryland, company nestled midway between the former corporate headquarters of MedImmune and Human Genome Sciences), which manufacture, sell, and market medicines but do not research new drugs. For example the administrative costs of Jazz Pharmaceuticals in 2014 exceeded R&D expenses by five-fold. Organizations like these that emphasize sales and marketing and minimize or eliminate R&D have gained a larger foothold in terms of controlling new medicines. Whereas such organizations controlled only two (0.26 percent) drugs as of 1990, their prominence had swelled to 215 new molecular entities (or almost 15 percent of all new medicines) by the end of 2013.[97]

Most recently, the Valeant model has encountered turbulence. In early 2016, Valeant revealed it was under investigation by the U.S. Securities and Exchange Commission (SEC) and the U.S. Attorney General's office. Waves of accusations followed, including drug price inflation, as evidenced by the fact the company increased the costs of all of its medicines by two-thirds in 2015 alone, a topic of particular interest in an election year. The company also faced charges of improper accounting, with implications for supporting the criminal charges being investigated by the SEC and Attorney General's office. As of this writing, the company stock was in free fall and the fate of the CEO overseeing company operations, as well as the viability of the company's business model, was increasingly bleak.

Throughout this and the following chapters, it is important to recognize that, independent of Valeant, most of the decisions to decrease research and development activities were thoughtfully considered and quite rationale. Whereas there has been much recent criticism of the industry and its leadership, some of which is warranted, the overall strategies and impacts detailed here were not premised on dark motivations, but rather on the need for increased efficiencies.

Slow Motion Destruction

The dilemma moving forward is if and how the multi-trillion dollar pharmaceutical and biotechnology industries will survive the coming years. Stated plainly: Who will develop the next generation of medicines?

In an attempt to address this question, the author's own research has been devoted to identifying and determining the fates of organizations and individuals who have contributed to the approval of new medicines. This work focused on new molecular entities (NMEs), which are the active ingredients in medicines introduced over the years. The discovery of how many different drugs have been approved brought a surprise, as even the FDA did not have a complete list. The FDA publishes a resource known as the *Orange Book*, which identifies all medicines that can be prescribed by physicians. However, this database does not include medicines that have been withdrawn over time, either because the drug is no longer useful (outdated by newer medicines) or due to safety concerns (for example, Vioxx). Our team at Yale developed a comprehensive list and we then began the arduous process of assessing the scientific and research background on these drugs.

This information identified trends that generated considerable interest when shared with experts at Yale and other organizations. These investigators encouraged us to publish a series of twenty articles in the scientific journal, *Drug Discovery Today*, in 2014 through 2015. One of the most striking outcomes pertains to sustainability of the pharmaceutical and biotechnology industries.

When viewed over time, 275 companies have been granted an FDA approval to market a new active ingredient or NME.[98] We then tracked these companies over time, with emphasis on both the entry and exit of companies. An entry was defined as a company that entered the list of organizations that gained an FDA approval, whereas an exit indicated a company that no longer is actively involved in research and development.

The number of companies actively involved in drug discovery grew steadily from the 1930s through the end of the twentieth century. Something unexpected occurred as the net number of active and independent companies with drug discovery and development capabilities reached 100; it began to plateau.[99] While the number of organizations stalled, the number of new drugs continued to accumulate. More and more drugs ended up being controlled by fewer companies, and a small subset of very large pharmaceutical companies increased their dominance. Most troublingly, we noted the growth of companies, like Valeant, that lacked a commitment to new drug discovery.

One of the starkest findings suggested that the biotechnology enterprise may be on its last legs.

The End of Biotechnology?

One of the most sobering findings from our studies of FDA-approved drugs suggested the precarious state of the biotechnology industry. In the midst of organizing how to write twenty different papers within a year, the author found himself spending virtually every free hour compiling the data into information. One day it might be the number of new antibiotics approved and the next would be a compiled list of mechanisms by which chemotherapy drugs kill cancer. Our goal was to let the data reveal trends without bias toward pre-conceived notions. One of our first goals was to assess the role of biotechnology in drug discovery and development and the fate of "successful" biotechnology companies.

Over the past decade, almost half of new drug approvals were awarded to biotechnology companies.[100] Looking more closely, biotechnology companies also contributed research or development activities to more than a third of FDA approvals that were ultimately awarded to pharmaceutical companies. Altogether, the biotechnology sector is directly or indirectly responsible for more than two-thirds of all new medicines.

We also assessed the fate of "successful" biotechnology companies. For the purposes of the analysis being conducted, a "successful" biotechnology company was broadly defined as any private-sector organization that contributed to at least one FDA-approved drug and was founded coincident with or after Cetus Corporation in 1971.[101] We sifted through multiple public sources to identify organizations from both public and private sectors that had contributed to an approved drug. Our data revealed that the number of "successful" biotechnology companies took the shape of a perfectly symmetrical bell curve. In the early years after 1971, the number of companies accumulated slowly, but then began to grow logarithmically. By 1980, there were just over a dozen "successful" companies and more than eighty a decade later. By the year 2000, the number of active and independent biotechnology companies that had contributed to an FDA-approved drug reached an apex at just over 140.

The net number of active and independent biotechnology companies that have contributed to an FDA approved drug plateaued in the late 1990s and the early years of the new millennium, much as we had seen with the pharmaceutical industry. Then something peculiar happened. A substantial uptick in the number of corporate acquisitions began to shrink the net number of biotechnology companies. Whereas only seven companies had been acquired in the quarter century from the birth of biotechnology through 1995, waves of mergers and acquisitions occurred thereafter.

Since 2000, an average of more than seven companies each year has been lost from a shrinking population of active and independent biotechnology companies. Digging deeper, we found these companies were being purchased to gain access to a single product, usually a recently approved drug. The research and discovery capabilities of these companies are then dismantled. As of the end of 2014, the number of active and independent companies had declined from a peak of 141 to 60.[102] Twelve companies were acquired in 2014, meaning that, were the present rate of acquisitions to continue, there will no longer be any active and independent biotechnology companies by the end of the decade.

Given its potential impact on public health and the economy, it is rather surprising that the data questioning the sustainability of the biotechnology industry had not been observed previously. The fact that large pharmaceutical companies have digested many of the most impactful biotechnology companies is particularly troubling. As we have already seen, pharmaceutical companies have been progressively moving away from early stage research and development and dismantling their research and development capabilities. It seems highly unlikely, therefore, that these pharmaceutical companies will leave the R&D infrastructures of their acquisitions intact. Rather, these acquisitions are simply being carried out to gain access to already-approved products or late-stage pipeline candidates.

We cannot yet know for certain that the remaining pharmaceutical companies have irreversibly dismantled their R&D capabilities or those of the companies that they have acquired. Indeed, AstraZeneca has elected to boost the size and capabilities of its MedImmune subsidiary. However, even in this rare case, the gains at MedImmune occurred at the expense of AstraZeneca's other R&D activities around the world.[103] Rarely do other large pharmaceutical companies leave their acquisitions intact and retain the high-performing groups that were responsible for the emergence of the biotech company in the first place.[104]

Genentech will provide an interesting case study. Although the company had been majority owned by Roche for years, the relatively recent and complete assimilation of Genentech into Roche in 2009 will bear watching to see if Roche implements staff cuts or a curtailment of research and development. Of all the major pharmaceutical companies, Roche devotes the highest fraction of its revenues to R&D, and so Genentech may be spared the pruning that has characterized so many other acquired biotechnology companies.

Clearly, the biotechnology industry in general and R&D activities in particular are in the midst of a dramatic overhaul, and perhaps the entire industry is fading to black. Were present trends to continue, other types of organizations will necessarily have to fill the void created first by the retreat of conventional pharmaceutical companies away from R&D followed later by the dismantlement of the biotechnology industry. With this in mind, we will now convey the present "state of the union" in terms of research and development, including an introduction to some non-traditional players that may hold a key to the future of new medicine discovery.

CHAPTER ELEVEN

Three Views of a Train Wreck

As we have seen throughout this book, over the past eight decades, the drug development enterprise has made extraordinary contributions to public health and the economy. In that time, the FDA has approved more than 1,500 different active ingredients and public health has benefited greatly. The rate of introduction for new medicines generally ranges from twenty to forty per year, and this rate has remained largely stable since the 1980s. The exception is that the rate of approvals spiked briefly in the late 1990s following passage of the Prescription Drug User Fee Act (PDUFA), which cleared a backlog of new drug applications, but then settled back to its long-term average.[1]

New medical options have fundamentally improved the quantity and quality of life for those individuals who have been able to access them.[2] As seen by numerous examples herein, the introduction of new medicines to treat infectious and cardiovascular diseases increased average life expectancy by an impressive 29.2 years in the period spanning 1900 through 1997.[3] According to statistics meticulously curated by the U.S. Centers for Disease Control and Prevention (CDC) for more than a century, pneumonia, tuberculosis, and diarrhea/enteritis were the leading causes of mortality in 1900, accounting for one-third of all American deaths. Infectious diseases were particularly prominent among the youngest population, accounting for 40 percent of premature deaths in children.[4] By the end of the century, none of these causes were anywhere to be found in the top five leading causes of American mortality. In particular, child mortality shrank dramatically as a result of improved hygiene, vaccinations, and antibiotics. Likewise, the rate of deaths from heart disease and stroke shrank from a peak of 307.5 (per 100,000 Americans) in 1950 to less than half that amount (134.6 per 100,000) by the end of the century. In large part, these achievements arose because of improved control of blood pressure, arrhythmia, and circulating cholesterol levels.[5] According to the CDC, "In 1996, 621,000 fewer deaths occurred from coronary heart disease than would have been expected had the rate remained at its 1963 peak."[6]

From an economic perspective, the growth and impact of the pharmaceutical and then biotechnology industries has been equally extraordinary. Companies collectively worth trillions of dollars generate billions of dollars in annual profits and employ millions of high-paid workers. The impact of the pharmaceutical industry can be seen in many aspects of American life. The healthcare industry is among the fastest growing and most impactful in terms of economic drivers and jobs, not to mention the fact that most major retirement vehicles (for example, 401K plans) contain a sizeable proportion of pharmaceutical industry stocks.

Based on the fact that the pharmaceutical industry requires constant pipeline replenishment, the evaporation of biotechnology companies suggests the whole enterprise is teetering and could conceivably collapse within a few short years. Were this to happen, the implications would be devastating, both in terms of the economy and public health. As we will see, the looming crisis in early-stage drug research and development has been widely anticipated and the dangers have been building for decades. With the continuing goal of addressing the question of "how did we get here," we will look at the crisis from multiple perspectives and show that, ironically, the present dilemma is largely the result of past success and developed as a consequence of well-reasoned and highly defensible decision making.

A View from the Boardroom

A 2012 article from a team of former scientists and economists at the equity research firm Sanford C. Bernstein outlined a prescient study that highlighted the plummeting efficiency of pharmaceutical industry research and development.[7] Their report asked how many new drug approvals a billion inflation-adjusted dollars could have purchased over the past six decades. In the early 1950s, a billion dollars was sufficient to gain approvals for something on the order of ninety new drugs. By the start of the new millennium, the same billion dollar investment in R&D (again, removing the effects of inflation), translated into a single approval. As of 2012, a billion dollars could purchase about one-third of a new drug. Recent and independent findings from Tufts University confirm this result, with the average cost of drug development exceeding $2.6 billion.[8] The decline in efficiency has consistently occurred on a logarithmic scale and continues today

The Sanford C. Bernstein team termed the declining efficiency "Eroom's Law."[9] This nomenclature is a grim inversion of the famous dictum from Gordon E. Moore, a cofounder of Intel Corporation who, in 1965, predicted that computing power doubles roughly every two years.[10] Technically, Gordon E. Moore predicted that the number of transistors in a dense integrated circuit doubles every two years, but the advent of microprocessors allowed for a bit of a "fudge" in its application. In contrast to the gains in efficiency associated with the nesting of semiconductors onto silicon chips, the costs of pharmaceutical research and development have increased about as dramatically and, thus, the "Moore's Law" of computing lore is inverted into the "Eroom's Law" for biotechnology and pharmaceuticals.[11]

There are many explanations for the declining efficiency in drug development. Among these, the original 2012 article conveyed a challenge humorously named the "better than the Beatles" problem.[12] This title nicely conveys the conundrum faced by the pharmaceutical industry to introduce new products that are superior to the current standard. The title of this explanation reflects the insuperable challenge that musicians would face were they constrained by regulators only to release songs that would be better than anything created by the Fab Four. If successful, then this new song would set the standard beyond which the next aspiring artist would have to surpass in order to be available in your local record store (or its online equivalent). In such a system, the growth in musical selections would quickly be stymied, but this exact fate is standard practice for the practitioners of pharmaceutical research and development.

As we have seen with statins and other follow-on (or me-too) drugs, the tenets of Eroom's Law are accurate to a degree but perhaps modified: "As good as the Beatles and better paid than Beyoncé." This change might reflect the reward that next-in-class drugs reap from being introduced to the market at a later time. This scenario seems rather unique to the pharmaceutical industry. Continuing with a music industry analogy, the iPod was a classic example of a disruptive technology that could command a higher price point as a reward for innovation. In the years following the introduction of the iPod, a flurry of MP3 players followed that were able to slice into Apple's market share only by lowering costs, thereby increasing the attractiveness of their product over the original innovator. This is generally the way markets work. A different paradigm seems to dominate in the pharmaceutical industry, where later-generation drugs demand higher price points and consumers (doctors and insurance companies) are willing to pay more as time progresses. We saw this with statins and, sadly, the model applies to other "me-too" drugs as well.

Innovator organizations may find themselves being punished for investing resources into a breakthrough product that is unfamiliar only to find that a later comparable or marginally improved product outperforms them financially. A well-known example of this outside the pharmaceutical industry is the introduction of the Ford Edsel, which was loaded with new technologies unheard of at the time, like seatbelts, child-proof rear doors, a rolling dome speedometer, warning lights (for oil and engine temperature), as well as many ergonomic improvements.[13] Though technologically superior to its competition the Edsel was destined to become a paragon for commercial failure. Too often, the innovative pharmaceutical products (recall the situation with Bexxar) are more likely to share the fate of Edsels than iPods.

Such messages have been heard loud and clear in executive boardrooms throughout the industry. The pipelines of virtually all major pharmaceutical companies are increasingly skewed toward next-generation products that convey little or no additional benefit as compared with the innovator's drug. The author experienced this first hand when a leadership change at a former biotechnology company concluded that the company's pipeline of future products was too innovative and focused on promising breakthrough medicines. The new executive scaled back on potential groundbreaking programs to facilitate an influx of me-too opportunities to compete with already-approved products on a purely economic basis. Unsurprisingly, such actions caused many of the most innovative scientists in the company to seek employment elsewhere, thereby fating that organization to future mediocrity.

For organizations advancing first-in-class products, a question has centered on how to capture markets in a way that minimizes the punishing "me-too" effect. One opportunity was provided by passage of the 1983 Orphan Drug Act. The law grants powerful financial and exclusivity provisions to hold off competition, both from generic and follow-on rivals. Furthermore, the low incidence of orphan indications within the population, by definition, allows for a higher price point. Whereas it was almost unheard of to charge (or gain reimbursement for) hundreds of thousands of dollars for a particular medicine, payers now routinely face such price pressures with the knowledge that refusal could have substantial repercussions in terms of unfavorable publicity (recalling the "death panels" invoked during discussions of the Affordable Care Act).

The charges for orphan drugs are reaching ever higher and there are mumbled expressions of million-dollar price tags for certain medicines, particularly those used to treat debilitating pediatric indications (which are the most photogenic and, thus, most damaging to the reputation of payers). Because of these costs, the adoption of orphan indications is rising quickly. According to the author's own research, the average annual number of new drugs approved with an orphan indication has risen from 14 percent in the 1980s to more than 50 percent in 2015.[14]

Another response is a sudden decline in research and development investment. For the many decades from the 1930s through the 2010, research and development budgets had been rising quickly simply to keep pace with Eroom's Law. Troublingly, more recent results suggest that overall pharmaceutical industry investment in research and development is no longer keeping pace with inflation. Given that the costs of developing a new medicine continue to expand at a rapid rate, the net overall effect of decreased R&D spending will inevitably mean that the number of medicines must fall. Over time, such a trend will have massive repercussions on the economy and for individual health. For example, a decreased flow of innovative new products will decrease the profitability of the pharmaceutical industry, which is already sensitive to a rising loss of sales as a result of the patent cliffs and inevitable generic competition. The generics industry itself will eventually be impacted as well, because a decrease in innovative new medicines means will halt the flow of new products for this downstream industry.

Beyond the economic impact on multi-trillion dollar industries, the decreased pharmaceutical research and development spending is beginning to show itself in terms of negative impacts on individual and public health. A rather well publicized example is the ongoing antibiotics crisis. As is increasingly appreciated by the popular press, a rise in drug-resistant bacteria is rapidly out-pacing the introduction of new medicines meant to combat infectious agents. Indeed, many esteemed scientists maintain that we already live in a "post-antibiotic world."[15] This is not a new event, as articles warning of such an outcome were published more than two decades ago.[16] Were this trend to continue, it is unavoidable that the league tables of mortality causes will soon witness the return of scourges such as pneumonia and tuberculosis.

A separate but related example of how a faltering pharmaceutical research and development enterprise could negatively impact individual and public health can be seen with the dearth of effective medicines to prevent or treat neurodegenerative diseases. The world's population is aging at an unprecedented rate, with the inevitable outcome that neurological disorders will continue their degenerate rise. A 2004 Alzheimer's Association report predicted a 44 percent increase in the disease by 2025.[17] Yet, ever fewer pharmaceuticals companies are focused on this indication.[18] Likewise, and notwithstanding the fact that we are presently experiencing a remarkable renaissance in our understanding of the brain and how it works, the fields of neurology, psychiatry, pain, and itch have all experienced dramatic downturns despite unprecedented gains in understanding of brain function.[19] At first glance, this seems counter-intuitive and shortsighted but a review of recent history reveals this is a defensible reaction. To illustrate this, we will focus upon the situation with Alzheimer's disease.

The field of neurosciences is a veritable graveyard of drugs that failed in clinical trials and approved drugs that never lived up to expectations. A prominent example is donepezil (trade name Aricept®), which was approved for the treatment of Alzheimer's disease in 1996 amid much fanfare. However, an increasing body of medical literature suggests that while some short-term benefits can be observed, these dissipate within weeks or months. Unfortunately, other Alzheimer's drugs fare little better, including rivastigmine (Exelon), galantamine (Razadyne), and memantine (Namenda), and worse still, the minimal efficacy comes at the cost of non-trivial side effects.[20]

One might conclude that the low bar set by these past Alzheimer's drugs provides a fertile pasture for a disruptive new innovation. Indeed, a rapidly expanding market potential has motivated many pharmaceutical companies over the years. Sadly, the outcomes of millions of dollars and many years of scientific research and development investment have almost invariably culminated in disappointment. A December 2013 report from the Boston Consulting Group revealed that R&D activities in the field of neurosciences had the greatest negative predictive impact as to whether a company will succeed in drug development.[21] This dismal forecast was confirmed months later by a discouraging report from the Cleveland Clinic, which demonstrated that 99.6 percent of experimental drugs intended to treat Alzheimer's disease had failed in clinical trials.[22] As if on cue, Roche announced the failure of a highly anticipated Alzheimer's drug immediately on the heels of the publication of the Cleveland Clinic study.[23]

As a consequence of these experiences, many pharmaceutical executives have objectively evaluated the risks and rewards conveyed by continuing neuroscience product development and have reduced or completely eliminated programs, teams, and entire portfolios that had been focused on Alzheimer's disease and other neuroscience indications. Once dismantled, complex research and development engines are virtually impossible to reassemble, suggesting the public health impact of such well-reasoned financial decisions could have ramifications for decades to come.

Even for successful drug candidates that gain FDA approval, the costs associated with their development are increasing dramatically and this, along with a high failure rate, has caused many biopharmaceutical companies to progressively retract their activities in all aspects of drug research and development. The author's past peer-reviewed and published studies have found that companies first cut back on the earliest discovery activities, which included efforts meant to understand why diseases arise. Examples of such studies include fundamental mechanistic studies of the key features distinguishing normal and disease processes and the identification of targets that might be prosecuted to restore or prevent disease. Such basic work is essential for determining the mechanisms by which one might manipulate the body to create new breakthrough medicines. However, as these efforts focused on products that were the furthest from realizing any market impact, they were the most susceptible to cuts. Furthermore, such research is rarely reported in quarterly investor calls, as concept-stage research and development is generally not a driver of market performance. Thus, the flight away from early-stage mechanistic studies rarely reached the level of discussion by many of the largest companies.

Over the years, the pullback was not to stop at the most basic research activities. Instead, the retreat from early-stage research progressed further and began to include retrenchment away from early stage efforts to prosecute new targets, the high staffing and infrastructures costs needed to screen for early-stage "hits." A "hit" is a pharmaceutical vernacular meaning a chemical that had the desired activity in a laboratory screen. Hits rarely themselves become drugs but instead form the basis for future improvement to find other molecules that might eventually lead to a new medicine. Thus, the management of pharmaceutical companies could justifiably defend decisions to curtail these expenses given the vast majority of these compounds would never progress into a saleable product. As time progressed, many corporate executives cut a bit deeper into the muscle of their R&D activities by reducing or eliminating the chemistry activities needed to advance a hit into a potential drug that might be explored in clinical trials. This decision, again, was defensible in part because a decreasing emphasis on identifying hits meant there was less need to maintain an infrastructure to mature these hits into drug candidates. Indeed, a single drug development research project routinely requires the efforts of dozens, if not hundreds, of chemical and biological scientists. Thus, an active decision to resource such early-stage drug discovery projects from external partners translated into considerable cost savings in terms of the employment burden required to maintain an active early-stage R&D program. Instead, it was reasoned, such efforts would be left to upstart companies found within the biotechnology sector.

This process is nothing new and began in the 1970s and 1980s. Indeed, the decision to outsource these early-stage efforts was not coincidentally linked with the rise of the biotechnology industry. Hardly anyone appreciated that there could be any negative impact from such outsourcing, and if they did so, one could readily appreciate that the cost cutting and efficiencies gained from outsourcing were simply part of a prudent fiscal policy. Based on the industry's intimate experiences with Eroom's Law, many large pharmaceutical companies transitioned their early-stage expertise to external partners and focused their strengths on later-stage preclinical activities, such as packaging investigational new drug (IND) applications as well as clinical trial design and execution. Preclinical research is defined herein as the activities required to advance a known "clinical candidate" molecule through specialized assessments of its toxicology and pharmacology to the point where it can begin testing in people. It generally does not include the large amount of research needed to identify that candidate or optimize it via laboratory studies.

As costs and risk continued to rise, particularly for clinical trials, many companies began to emphasize later-stage partnerships. Their reasoning was based on the fact that the biotechnology industry was maturing throughout the 1980s and 1990s and some of the upstart biotechnology companies, such as Amgen or Genentech, were gaining experience in advancing clinical candidates to and beyond the submission of an IND. Indeed, Amgen was one of the first biotechnology companies to announce an intention to transition into a more pharmaceutical-like approach, and this coincided with the staffing of many senior-level positions with executives formerly employed by the pharmaceutical industry.

Rather than simply resign themselves to be the middle-men in the decade-long relay race required for new drug development, many maturing biotechnology companies became ever more eager to develop their own pipelines and market their products directly to consumers. As we saw with the example of Immunex, such decisions required the raising of large infusions of investor dollars. The expenses needed to staff a sales and marketing enterprise often constrained the ability of these same companies to perform the early-stage research and development activities that had led them to success in the first place. Thus, established biotechnology companies were, in effect, evolving into the pharmaceutical giants, albeit smaller and with shorter institutional memories, that they had intended to supplant and, in doing so, inherited many of the same traits of their predecessors.

The trend continued. It is generally non-controversial to state that the early stage activities in preclinical (that is, IND preparation) and clinical trial are quite mundane, and Phase I clinical trials are often described within the industry as "cookie-cutter." Therefore, a successful argument was made that a large pharmaceutical company should not focus its limited resources on such activities. Instead, these companies either contracted this work to a set of companies known as contract research organizations (CROs) or waited to license or purchase programs that already had been approved to begin Phase I clinical trials.

Thus, the progression continued with two outcomes. First, the pharmaceutical side of the equation changed as more and more preclinical and early-stage clinical investigation was performed outside the four walls of the company.

Second, the biotechnology companies were increasingly required to provide their larger pharmaceutical partners with more mature programs, often including projects in which the lead candidate had been selected and undergone initial testing in people. Again, such activities often require considerable investment in people and the resources required to identify the lead candidate and complete the gauntlet of tests required for a successful IND application, not to mention the Phase I clinical trial itself. Each of these commitments not only required considerable resources but posed a distraction for fledgling companies that had been founded based on their particular strengths focused on unique scientific or early-stage discovery expertise.

Hardly anyone outside the drug research and development community noticed these changes, as biotech companies increasingly filled the void left by the retreat of established pharmaceutical companies first from discovery, then preclinical research, and, finally, early-stage clinical research. So long as investor monies continue to flow freely, the progressive retreat of the pharmaceutical industry from early stage research and development activities was viewed as a tremendous opportunity to tap into a well of much-needed licensing revenues and cash infusions.

In the heady years of the 1980s and 1990s, early speculation on successes such as Genentech, Biogen, and Amgen, led many to invest heavily into biotechnology, and the money flowed into both established as well as startup biotechnology companies to feed the activities needed to establish a partnership (and thus a likely and lucrative acquisition) for biotechnology companies. The evolution of these companies continued and these organizations began to become the buyers of technologies, as well. Specifically, companies that had been known as research powerhouses increasingly began to source their new programs from a newer generation of startup companies. In the years leading up to the new millennium, there was no lack of opportunities to do so.

For many years, the promise of new biotechnology companies remained a darling of the venture investor community. Many early-stage biotechnology companies, many of which were based on concepts lacking tangible products, were nonetheless perceived as valuable opportunities for initial public offerings (IPOs). Furthermore, the industry's hunger for targets often meant that early-stage biotechnology companies, both public and private, presented attractive targets for acquisition. As this particular trend accelerated throughout the 1990s, a particularly interesting variation on the theme became apparent. Whereas the earliest generation of biotechnology companies fought fiercely to remain independent and grow vertically (for example, Amgen, Genentech, and MedImmune), the newer generation of companies were built with the ultimate goal of being sold. Many of these new biotechnology organizations were founded with sole goal of "flipping" the company within a few years. At the extreme, there were often cases in which the founders sought to flip a company within a few months or even weeks. Unsurprisingly, many of these companies used a "smoke and mirrors" approach to create attractive perceptions that often did not correspond with reality. Much like their counterparts in the real estate sector, the biotechnology industry increasingly was attracted to the idea of investing the minimum needed to dress up a property in preparation for a quick sale.

All the while, the target needed for a successful biotechnology exit (that is, being acquired by a strategy partner) was changing as the industry continued to pull further away from research and development. At present, the conventional wisdom suggests that a partnership with an established pharmaceutical company requires a previous demonstration at least of human proof of concept. In other words, a company must not only identify the target, but they must successfully prosecute the target with the intended therapeutic, file a successful IND application with FDA, conduct successful Phase I clinical trials, obtain promising data, and importantly, demonstrate some evidence that the intended drug works as planned in clinical trials. This understanding sets a high bar for pharmaceutical partnering such that a biotechnology partner must not only demonstrate that an experimental drug is safe in people but also effective in ameliorating disease and in a manner that would anticipate superior efficacy in a larger clinical trial. Long gone are the days when a company like ICN (Valeant) can launch in a garage with a $200 investment or that upstart companies such as Celera could cobble deals based on early-stage technology (that is, DNA sequencing) with diffuse concepts that might one day lead to a saleable products.

Like the larger economy, the biotechnology industry had been subject to "irrational exuberance" as evidenced by looking at the amount of capital raised and number of initial public offerings by biotech companies. The boom periods included the initial euphoria associated with recombinant DNA technology in the 1980s and a sustained period of speculation throughout much of the 1990s.[24] However, a crescendo was reached in the year 2000. The first quarter of that year witnessed six new biotech IPOs and almost a billion dollars in capital raised. The pace quickened further in the second quarter with almost $1.5 billion in capital, and the third quarter was busier still with more than $2 billion raised. The excitement generated by news of the genome project, and all the miracle breakthroughs it would foster, led many to believe that biotechnology was exceptional and could sustain such momentum indefinitely.

Busted

The bursting of the dot.com bubble changed everything. The second quarter of 2001 was the first since 1989 not to experience a single biotech IPO. The years following likewise recorded lower activity, with roughly half as many IPOs as 1990. The industry was also tarnished by a variety of issues including egocentric leadership and high-profile ethical meltdowns at places like Celera, ICN, and Imclone. While the number of IPOs did recover somewhat in the first half decade of the new century, the global financial turmoil that began in 2007 dealt what may have been the fatal blow to biotechnology as it is presently configured. The level of venture capital invested into biotechnology fell by almost half and, interestingly, did not re-engage with the industry after the recovery began or since. Instead, new venture capital dollars were more likely to be invested in startups focused on software and other technologies.

Why the flight of venture capital away from biotechnology? The answers are complex but a few explanations come to the fore.

First, the completion of the human genome project seemed to inject some reality into the euphoria that had accompanied the high-profile, multi-billion-dollar program. Perhaps it was inevitable that public attention would shift elsewhere (as NASA experienced following the completion of the initial Apollo moon landings) and as, we have seen, the completion of the project corresponded with the realism that knowledge of the human genome was simply the first step in a long process that might someday translate into products that could be sold (other than genomic information itself). The more rational scientists and companies also began to distinguish between correlation and causality. Whereas a causative role increases the likelihood that targeted intervention with a new drug will derive a beneficial effect, a correlative change in the expression of a target (as was often conveyed) did not necessarily translate into an efficacious product. Compounding this, demonstrating causality was often a long, arduous, and expensive proposition.

Second, the genome project itself slaked the thirst of the biotechnology and pharmaceutical industries for new targets. Whereas just a few years before, a company formed around a new target might perform a minimal set of studies and then offer itself as a candidate for acquisition (or perhaps on IPO), even an amateur with minimal background in research could access data from the publically available (NIH-based) genome project and start a new biotechnology venture (in theory). Thus, the supply and demand equation shifted to create a perception that the industry was now awash with new targeting opportunities.

Third, venture capital investors also began looking at the formation of new companies in a different way. As we have already discussed, the time required for the development of a new medicine is often measured in decades rather than years. For example, the period of clinical testing for new medicines (the time period from filing and IND until the FDA award) averaged more than eleven years. Contrast this against the lifetime of a typical venture capital fund, which is generally capped at ten years. Thus, subscribers to venture capital funds may be forced to hold shares at a time when they would prefer to clean their books and liquidate the stock and take a loss to offset capital gains from other investments. The need to wind-down a fund can cause a shareholder to prefer a loss rather than continuing to hold shares, much less adding more funds.

Another reason many investors have fled is that new drug development is resource-intensive. The costs include the need for expensive equipment, highly skilled personnel, and specialized space (most biotechnology cannot or should not be performed in a garage, unlike other technology industries). The millions of dollars required to support a single biotech company could, instead, be used to underwrite dozens of software-based companies (and spreading the risk in doing so).

Those companies that did receive venture funding in recent years have been bombarded with terms such as "capital efficiency." This concept reflects the investor goal of minimizing the need to build infrastructure within newly formed company. The R&D model for execution rapidly evolved from buying to renting. In other words, a lean company could become capital efficient by out-sourcing as many activities as possible to CROs. This transition did indeed increase efficiency, as the key infrastructure needed to advance a product from a mere concept to an IND-enabled drug candidate could be performed by companies with little (and in rare cases no) internal technical staffing.

"Focus" is a second term associated with biotechnology formed since the dawn of the new millennium. Focus reflects the idea that a company should select one product and emphasize a single indication. Whereas companies like Genentech, Immunex, and Amgen enhanced their valuation through the creation of wide-ranging portfolios, the newer biotechnology entries are crafted to advance a single product to the point where the company either fails to establish proof of concept (and thus is shuttered) or is sold and disbanded to replenish the pipeline of a more established partner.

In this new generation, "lambs to the slaughter" companies are designed to be acquired and disassembled as quickly and efficiently as possible. The minimal staffing associated with capital efficiency facilities the rapid dissolution of those companies fortunate enough to be acquired. One consequence of this approach is that it seems to preclude the creation of a new generation of biotechnology companies that can emerge to replace the losses in past "successful" biotechnology companies. As we have seen, the likes of past independent and successful biotech pioneers such as MedImmune and Genentech have themselves been acquired, and these are not being replaced by comparably-sized organizations (other than the few remaining active and independent companies created in the 1980s and 1990s like Biogen and Celgene).

In a series of reports for *Forbes* magazine, the analyst Bruce Booth revealed the number of early-stage investors has fallen by half since 2006.[25] This commenter further notes new biotech company formation has fallen to such a level that it cannot sustain the number of IPOs necessary to continue to biotech bubble that began in 2013 and continued in 2014.[26] It logically follows that a lack of new startups is also threatening the pipeline needs of larger organizations.

The ecosystem of the biotechnology food chain is, therefore, being eroded from the bottom. Meanwhile, atop of the food chain, large pharmaceutical giants have irreversibly dismantled their capabilities. As one example, the author received a call from a senior executive at a major pharmaceutical company. It seems this company had been consistently cutting R&D and ultimately decided to shutter its North American research and development operations. After the requisite layoffs and selling off of buildings and equipment, the company realized it had cut away so many core capabilities that it had rendered itself unable to continue some later-stage projects. Recognizing the threat, company management was at a loss as to how to proceed and reached out to academic organizations to help staunch their internal bleeding. It is unclear (to the author at least) if or how the company will ultimately manage to overcome this self-inflicted wound.

Having established the effects of rising costs on the pharmaceutical industry, we will begin to explore some of the reasons for these increased costs by turning our attention to the next pivotal player in the ongoing play: the federal government.

Payer, Regulator, and Investor

The United States federal government has many and varied interests related to the subject of drug discovery and development, including their roles as largest payer, key regulator, and dominant investor in new medicines.

The federal government is the planet's largest employer. According to statistics updated annually by the *BBC*, *The Economist*, and others, the Department of Defense alone employs with 3.2 million personnel.[27] This figure eclipses the Chinese People's Liberation Army (at 2.3 million) and the largest private sector employer, Walmart, at 2.1 million. Beyond defense, the United States Federal Civil Service employs an additional two million, excluding more than 600,000 employed by the U.S. Postal Service.[28] Importantly, all these individuals have access to federal health insurance, which includes prescription medicine coverage. With these numbers alone, the U.S. federal government is by far the world's largest payer for medicines.

These direct employment numbers are dwarfed by the 1965 amendments to the Social Security Act, which created Medicare and Medicaid.[29] Medicare provides insurance to Americans age sixty-five and older, regardless of income or medical history, which amounts to an enrollment estimated at forty-seven million as of 2010.[30] In the case of Medicaid, the federal government provides matching funds to states to enable medical assistance to low-income residents. As of 2009, over fifty million Americans were enrolled, and the passage of the 2010 Patient Protection and Affordable Care Act is estimated to increase the number of covered individuals by an additional 32 million.[31]

The heft of the federal government as an employer and payer of prescription benefits is particularly interesting when considering how other aspects of the federal structure impact decisions guiding drug pricing, approval and withdrawal, and creating the infrastructure and incentives that impact decisions regarding the discovery and development of new medicines.

One controversy concerns the ability of some programs, but not others, to set prices on drugs. The Department of Veterans Affairs (VA) is able to negotiate with pharmaceutical companies to establish a formulary, which can substantially lower the costs paid for pharmaceuticals. In contrast, under Medicare Part D, the prescription drug benefit, the federal government is not permitted to negotiate with pharmaceutical companies.[32] In a 2007 report from Families USA, the VA often pays lower prices for medicines, such as an estimated $782.44 for a year's supply of Lipitor (a fifth-generation statin) while Medicare pays $1,120 to 1,340 for the same drug. The same report stated:

> Although generic versions of drugs are now available, plans offered by three of the five insurers currently exclude some or all of these drugs from their formularies. . . . Further, prices for the generic versions are not substantially lower than their brand-name equivalents. The lowest price for simvastatin (generic Zocor) 20 mg is 706 percent more expensive than the VA price for brand-name Zocor. The lowest price for sertraline HCl (generic Zoloft) is 47 percent more expensive than the VA price for brand-name Zoloft.[33]

Although an extensive discussion of pricing disparities is well beyond the scope of this book, these examples raise understandable questions that have tended to hijack discussions of how the federal government interacts with the pharmaceutical industry.

Despite being the world's largest payer for pharmaceuticals, the regulatory arm of the U.S. federal government contributes substantially to the increasing costs of new medicines. The subject has been raised elsewhere in this book; the higher costs of drug development largely reflect the increasing costs of clinical trials, which, in turn, echo increasing demands for safety data by the FDA. The FDA holds the unenviable position of trying to find an ever-moving balance between facilitating the introduction of innovative new medicines against the potential threats that new approaches might impose.

Unsurprisingly, the agency comes under attack from both the left and right of the American political spectrum, and its judgment can be swayed by shifts in popular opinion. The FDA tightened policies for monitoring drug safety during clinical trials in the shadow of high-profile withdrawals based on safety concerns. For example, the agency required more intensive assessments of potential cardiovascular harm following the revelations of the

Vioxx tragedy in the early 2000s. Consequently, the costs of clinical trials rose as a result of the increased monitoring of heart function. The thalidomide tragedy, likewise, increased the sensitivity of both the general public and the FDA in terms of assessing potential carcinogenicity or birth defects. Such examples reflect increased experience gained over time as side effect profiles of medicines are compiled and efforts taken to avoid future occurrences. Thus, these activities are a logical extension of the FDA mandate to assure the public. Nonetheless, the collective experiences threaten to create a situation in which excessive caution hampers or entirely excludes the development of new medicines.

Like science in general, our understanding of safety constantly shifts and requires nimbleness and flexibility to ensure a balance between necessary and unnecessary regulation. Instead, the path to drug approval must contend with a steady accretion of new regulations. Many of regulations may no longer be relevant or necessary. For example, the Ames test was developed in the 1970s to ask if experimental drugs might be mutagenic. Despite evidence that the test is not accurate and can require unnecessary follow-up testing to distinguish safe from unsafe drugs, the FDA continues to require Ames testing before human clinical trials can commence.[34] While Ames testing is a relatively minor contributor to the costs of drug development, it provides one example of the need for a comprehensive reassessment of the regulatory pathway guiding new drug development.

Likewise, the requirement to demonstrate efficacy following passage of the 1962 Kefauver-Harris amendment increased the average time of clinical investigation from an average of seven months (in the early 1960s) to more than a decade today. This issue was famously raised by an executive at Eli Lilly in 2008, who noted the volume of information submitted to the FDA to support their New Drug Application for Prasugrel, if printed out, would be taller than the Empire State Building in Manhattan.[35] Were the standards of today applied to many cornerstone medicines approved in the not-too-distant past, it seems unlikely that the FDA would have granted approvals to quite useful drugs such as the cardiovascular drug warfarin or the cancer drug 5-fluorouracil, to name just two. While it is essential to ensure proper regulation to safeguard that new medicines are safe and effective, it is difficult to believe that the process couldn't become more efficient. As we will see in the last chapter, there are some tangible and reasonable opportunities for improvement.

Shifting gears, Mazzucato points out in her captivating book, *The Entrepreneurial State*, that the federal government has consistently been the largest source venture capital for biotechnology.[36] Some of the greatest value derives from NIH, which generates considerable scientific and monetary value. These organizations place relatively little pressure on funded projects to produce tangible products, especially in the short term. While this might seem to be a recipe for wastefulness, Mazzucato argues that the opposite is the case. For example, the growth of the biotechnology industry starting in the 1970s is largely the outcome of public investment by NIH rather than venture firms such as Kleiner Perkins, which often receive disproportionate credit relative to their meager input.[37] The returns on federal investments include high-paying jobs, innovative new products, and the utter dominance that the United States has enjoyed in biotechnology from the birth of the new industry.

In recent years, the tide has begun to change and in different ways. First, the amount of federal regulation has grown logarithmically over the past quarter century.[38] This growth started as a rational response to high-profile improprieties being performed by a very small subset of universities and nonprofit organizations (recall the Stanford yacht incident related in chapter 5). In response to the recognition of such malfeasance, the federal government introduced a series of modifications to federal funding policy, and nine new regulations were introduced between 1991 and 1995. By 2012, the cumulative number of new regulations had exceeded eighty, and on average, almost six new regulations are now introduced each year.[39] These changes have created a tsunami of additional paperwork, as pointed out in a 2015 report from the Federation of American Societies for Experimental Biology (FASEB). As a result, universities have begun creating their own self-sustaining bureaucracy needed to ensure compliance with the new mandates and this has caused an upsurge in administrative costs. The growth in administrative costs has come at the cost of the research itself, since a larger fraction of federal funding must now be directed to supporting the ever-growing paperwork and infrastructure.

The inefficiency in utilizing federal research dollars is exacerbated by the fact that federal funding itself is shrinking at an alarming rate. A long view of federal support in the National Institutes of Health reveals that budget is falling. When measured as a share of gross domestic product, NIH funding remained relatively constant from the early 1960s through the mid-1990s, at a level ranging from roughly 1.1 to 1.4 percent.[40] By the late 1980s, the popular media resonated with considerable fears that non-U.S. countries, most notably Japan, surpass the United States in terms of capturing a larger market share of the burgeoning biotechnology industry.[41]

Many of the concerns about the NIH budget came to a head in 1998 when the Clinton administration announced a plan to double NIH funding over the following five years.[42] The succeeding George W. Bush administration continued this commitment, and the budget almost doubled from $14 to $27 billion annually (though the increase in reality was 66 percent when accounting for cost increases).[43] Such a rapid budget expansion unsurprisingly meant inefficient decision making across the board that largely blunted the impact of the well-intentioned doubling of the NIH budget.

One example was the 2001 announcement by NIH of a plan to dramatically increase the stipends provided to graduate and post-doctoral students supported by NIH grants.[44] On one hand, this was a much-needed and commendable action. The amount of time spent as a post-doctoral on research had been steadily increasing. Originally conceived as an interim period of a year or two to allow newly-minted Ph.Ds. an opportunity to gain a different kind of experience in another setting before setting out on their own, the post-doc experience was accompanied by a low salary to discourage complacency. However, stiff competition for academic positions and shrinking federal research dollars forced some scientists to remain at the post-doctoral level for years or even decades longer than intended. Thus, the decision to increase salaries was meant in part as a way to encourage post-doctoral scientists to remain committed to the field and to discourage academic institutions from taking advantage of a low-cost and highly trained labor pool. The abrupt and rapid increase in stipends, however, absorbed a substantial portion of increased NIH funding in the days of "the doubling."

Compounding this, another unintended consequence of the highly publicized doubling of the NIH budget was a perception by the public and many lawmakers that the critical fix had been made to ensure future continuation of medical advances. It is now widely appreciated that the steep short-term increase in funding of the Apollo program to land a man on the moon and return him safely to the Earth had the unintended consequence of devastating NASA. Having accomplished the mission, the public and their tax dollars moved on to other things. A similar albeit less dramatic malaise has seemed to afflict NIH in the years following "the doubling."

Since its peak in 2003, the NIH budget has not kept pace with inflation, and as of this writing, real spending is down by 25 to 30 percent.[45] Fiscal pressures from multiple international conflicts and economic declines have negatively impacted all aspects of the federal budget. In particular, the federal "sequester," which started in 2013 and continued today has negatively squeezed the NIH budget particularly hard. Budget decreases for research and development are problematic in part because most projects, and therefore grants to support them, are multi-year endeavors. Thus, even a single year of a budget decrease could disproportionately limit or preclude value that might have been building over years of previous investment. For example, key individuals are now furloughed due to budget constraints and this destroys momentum but also risks that the needed talent will abandon the project. Large projects cannot be quickly restarted, particularly as critical infrastructure erodes and personnel rapidly disperse to find employment elsewhere (often in other fields altogether).

The social, health, and economic impacts of the NIH are consistently the strongest investment resulting from federal spending. NIH funding generates many types of value, including useful inventions, innovative startup companies, breakthrough medicines, as well as having a strong impact on society and economy. Viewed purely in terms of economic growth, President Barack Obama announced in his 2013 State of the Union address that a $4 billion investment into the human genome project has already yielded a 178-fold return on investment according to NIH figures.[46] Likewise, a 2012 report from the Milken Institute recently indicated that every dollar of NIH funding generates a return ranging from $1.70 and $3.20 of output from the bioscience industry.[47] Independent of the financial impact of NIH funding on the broader economy, the consequences of the doubling and then retraction of the NIH budget have in the short term had their greatest impacts on the academic enterprise, to which we will now turn our attention.

If You Build It, the Bills Will Come

In the early days of "the doubling," academia relished the infusion of cash from NIH that was anticipated to occur in the coming years. One example can be seen in the amount of space created and devoted to research activities within colleges and universities. According to a report from the National Science Foundation, the academic sector collectively had approximately twenty-eight million square feet of research space in 1994. Over the following years, this number has almost doubled, and stood closer to fifty-five million square feet as of 2011.[48]

Administrative decisions to construct new space were founded upon the inaccurate assumption that Congress and taxpayers were durably committed to continuing strong NIH budget increases. Most of these decisions were made many years in advance due to the time- and resource-intensive construction required for modern R&D laboratories. The expense and time needed to build new research facilities was compounded since the commitment extends well beyond the initial construction of buildings and includes their long-term maintenance. The burden increased further as pharmaceutical and then biotechnology companies began to reduce the level of preclinical discovery and research directed toward universities (as these companies were exiting the early R&D space altogether) and this added to the flight of dollars needed to support university research.

A prime example of the impact of such decisions can be seen with the Scripps Research Institute. Founded in 1924 by the newspaper heir and philanthropist, Ellen Browning Scripps, the La Jolla, California, foundation is widely regarded as one of the most impactful non-university research institutes in the world.[49] Its contributions to the field of medicine include the development of the rheumatoid arthritis drug adalimumab (trade name Humira), the lupus drug belimumab (trade name Benlysta), the purification schema for a drug that addresses the major cause of hemophilia (Factor VIII), as well as three other FDA-approved drugs. The institute currently hosts four Nobel Prize Laureates as well as some of the most respected biologists and chemists in the world. Despite this outstanding lineup of talent and extraordinary track record, the future of the Scripps Institute is in jeopardy. In 1987, the institute appointed Richard Lerner, an outstanding scientist and the developer of Humira and Benlysta. Lerner proceeded to recruit the highly acclaimed staff and quadrupled the size of the institute in La Jolla.

In 2003, Scripps also announced a deal with the state of Florida to build a second campus in the town of Jupiter for $310 million.[50] Although the state of Florida covered many of the costs of the new campus, the spending by Scripps on this campus was not sustainable, particularly in light of declining federal research support. NIH grants are responsible for 86 percent of the Scripps operating budget and budgetary cutbacks were harmful and may ultimately prove fatal.[51] Much of the remaining budget depended on sponsored research from the pharmaceutical and biotechnology industries, which also is drying up.

In mid-2014, the Scripps Research Institute was running a $21 million operating deficit when its new president, Dr. Michael Marletta, announced it would be bailed out by being absorbed into the University of Southern California.[52] In the days that followed, the faculty revolted and scuppered the deal, removing Dr. Marletta in the process.[53] At present, the institute's ability to survive in the face of continuing NIH budget cuts is unclear, and many in the academic community are resigned to the likelihood that the venerable Scripps Research Institute may soon be forced to close its doors. If or when this occurs, it will send shockwaves throughout both the private and public sectors.

Beyond funding the construction and maintenance of research buildings, funding from the NIH has increasingly been used to support the salaries of those working within those laboratories. As we have seen, graduate students and post-doctoral fellows are primary engines of new research discoveries, and the cost of supporting these investigators has increased substantially in the past few years.

The entire academic infrastructure has also been rocked by a redefinition of tenure at most institutions. In the middle part of the twentieth century, the awarding of tenure meant that a faculty member had a position and salary for life. The rationale for tenure has changed with recognition that it is politically unpopular (particularly at state-supported institutions) and often wasteful, risking the accumulation of "dead wood" professors, who come to work only to read the newspaper or check their mail. Consequently, tenure today has undergone many changes and this often means that a professor can retain his position but not most, if any, of her salary. Many schools have limited the tenure commitment to a small fraction, if any, of total salary, leaving the professor to generate the remainder from research grants. Thus, shrinking NIH funding will mean that the loss of a grant deprives faculty members of a sizeable portion of their income. Unsurprisingly, this outcome has repelled many of the best and brightest individuals from considering academia as part of their future plans. If this trend in shrinking grants persists, it could have the unintended consequence of resigning academia to settle for mediocrity. Such an outcome is not in the best interest of the United States, as universities, and the technologies they create, are the leading economic products in the nation and the engines of future American innovation.[54]

Research studies in academia have also come to rely heavily upon less conventional personnel, such as research associates and research, many of whom are refugees from shrinking public and private sector institutions. Corporate downsizing caused many furloughed investigators to turn to local research universities, and these investigators often enrich the academic environment with their decades of experience. In the author's own experience of building a research center focused on drug discovery at Yale University, advertisements for open positions in the center were often answered by extraordinary individuals with unparalleled experiences. For example,

Ph.D. scientists with multiple decades of experience and established track records of success in developing new drugs in the pharmaceutical industry applied to fill relatively junior openings at Yale. One example occurred when the university advertised a position for a junior-level applicant in medicinal or computational chemistry. One individual, a leader in his field, ultimately was hired for the position, bringing decades of experience at Pfizer, Parke-Davis, and Sterling-Winthrop. Although the talented candidate was in many ways over-qualified for the advertised position, it was nonetheless a substantial improvement over his job at the time, which was teaching high school chemistry in the Groton (Connecticut) public school district. A later job opening was filled by another fifty-something chemist with comparable credentials, who was recruited from another Yale laboratory, where he had been serving as a post-doctoral researcher (a position normally offered to students immediately after receiving their Ph.D.).

These individuals, each with an extraordinary career in the private sector before downsizing forced them to become under-employed, provide evidence of an emerging problem that has not yet been discussed outside the corridors of a few elite institutions. Whereas universities have historically provided the cradle to teach basic chemistry skills to undergraduate, pre-doctoral, and post-doctoral students, the type of expertise conveyed tends to be more esoteric and less utilitarian. However, these chemists are rarely in a position to be able to contribute to real-world activities such as developing a new drug. Rather, outstanding medicinal chemists have historically learned their craft as a result of hands-on experiences in the private sector. Within industry, a typical chemist often works on multiple projects at any given time and, via discussions and collaborations with more senior mentors, becoming exposed to deep knowledge based on long institutional experience that is not possible to acquire in a conventional academic setting. The fact many companies have downsized or altogether eliminated their capabilities in medical chemistry has the unintended consequence of disrupting the chain of training of the next generation of scientists. These disruptions in a mentoring process needed to create experienced medicinal chemists threaten to preclude or greatly delay the discovery of new medicines.

As detailed, an increasing number of regulations, up eighty-fold since 2012, have increased the bureaucracy of research universities and thereby decreased efficiency.[55] According to a 2015 study conducted by FASEB, more than one-third of faculty time is consumed by administrative tasks, and the support staff needed to manage a grant and ensure compliance with the myriad new rules has increased exponentially. Furthermore, faculty members now find themselves spending virtually all of their time fund-raising by writing grants rather than focusing their energies on training students or conducting research. These inefficiencies are particularly problematic for public universities since state support for these schools has, likewise, been under pressure for many years. The local news of virtually every state in the Union is replete with stories about the impact of cutbacks on post-secondary education, and in response to such pressures, administrators understandably find it politically expedient to cut back research activities.

A final pressure, and one that threatens to break the back of the academic research enterprise, is an increase in demand for research grants. At the same time that the number of grants funded by NIH is shrinking, the number of applications and applicants is increasing. Recent years have witnessed ever more applicants competing for a diminishing pot of research grant funding.[56] The larger number of applicants and applications in part reflects the fact that universities had built up laboratories and research infrastructure and needed investigators to occupy this valuable space. Compounding this, fewer faculty openings (for example, professorships) has meant that academia is being reshaped by a pronounced and prolonged increase in the number of "super post-docs" and research associates, who often spend decades, rather than years, working in a non-tenure-track positions in academia. These junior investigators are increasingly competing with established professors, and the result is that the funding rate of the conventional NIH grant (known as an R01 grant) declined from 36 percent in the year 2000 to 22 percent in 2013.[57]

Competition is generally the finest way to identify and support the strongest ideas, and the NIH has been a paragon of this virtue. However, the impact of hyper-competition arising from a combination of fewer grants and more applicants has traversed the threshold separating constructive from destructive. For senior faculty members, who often have the largest laboratories, grant funding threatens the continuity of research that may have begun decades before. The blow may be even more profound for junior investigators seeking to establish their careers. An inability to obtain or maintain funding may jeopardize their employment and force them out of the system. The shock of these changes is already being felt. For example, the number of M.D.-trained physician–scientists is in steep decline.[58] This population of scientists is particularly important because they blend much-needed ability to understand both scientific concepts and clinical application. Unlike many of their Ph.D. peers, physician–scientists have the option of focusing on clinical work and many have opted to leave research as evidenced by a drop from 24,000 participants in the mid-1980s to fewer than 14,000 in 2011.[59]

Washington's War on Drugs

As recognition grew that the private sector was retreating from early-stage research and development, the federal government in the form of the NIH began to step in. In 2003, the NIH created the Molecular Libraries Program (MLP), which provided a central source of drug research capabilities for investigators throughout the country to screen for chemical probes, the earliest stage of new drug discovery.[60] A major part of the program involved the use of approximately $70 million annually, starting in 2005, to create the Molecular Libraries Screening Centers Network (MLSCN), a collection of eight institutes or universities with capabilities to perform aspects of the biology and chemistry activities that were being abandoned by the private sector.[61] Each of the eight institutions received a multi-million contract to perform screening and they responded by increasing staffing, often recruiting experienced scientists newly released by major pharmaceutical and biotechnology companies. Among the centers selected was a group at the Scripps Research Institute, which reportedly staffed hundreds of new investigators to support the MLSCN under an assumption of its continuance. The MLSCN program was fully underwritten through 2011 and expectations were high that it would continue thereafter. The NIH announced this was not to be. In a move reminiscent of the private sector, the dissolution of the MLSCN forced a new round of layoffs in the drug discovery community, and many believe it might have been the proverbial straw that broke the camel's back in terms of the increasing the financial burden on the Scripps Research Institute.

The abandonment of the MLSCN network presaged the creation of a different system. In January 2012, Dr. Francis Collins, (the former head of the federal genome project and then-director of NIH) oversaw the launch of the National Center for Advancing Translational Sciences (NCATS).[62] Much was written in the press about how the new center would create a new mechanism to emphasize translation, the actions needed to advance from the concepts arising in basic science research to turning them into something tangible that can improve public health. In reality, NCATS largely consisted of a rebranding of an existing program, the Clinical and Translational

Science Awards (CTSAs). Nonetheless, the program and Francis Collins were skewered in Congressional hearings with comments mirroring that of Roy Vagelos (the former head of Merck), who asked: "Does anyone in the audience believe that there is something that NCATS is going to do that the industry thinks is critical and that they are not doing? That is incredible to think that. If you believe that, you believe in fairies."[63] The questioning of Collins continued with particular emphasis over concerns that support for later-stage translational activities would necessarily come at the expense of earlier-stage basic research grants, which have been the bread-and-butter of the NIH since its inception.

So, where do we stand?

Death Valley

In summary, the pharmaceutical industry has largely retrenched away from early-stage drug discovery and research. This process has occurred over decades and was largely unnoticed due to the visibility of the emerging biotechnology industry, which quickly filled any gaps left by the departure of the pharmaceutical industry. However, the majority of successful biotechnology companies (in terms of contributing to an approved drug) have now been acquired by large pharmaceutical companies, and in most cases, their R&D capabilities have been restructured in a way that emulates their acquirers. Such outcomes might not be overly problematic were the management and staff to recycle and re-form a new company. However, venture capital seeks the fastest and highest return on its money and capital-intensive biotechnology investments are now less attractive than funding a few twenty-somethings to type code in their parents' basement. Furthermore, the "seed corn" of biotech arises from the nation's universities, which are being squeezed financially by a combination of funding cuts from the NIH and private sector combined with an over-built infrastructure and personnel commitments.

Altogether, these issues have created what is known as the "Valley of Death" in drug development. This dramatic term captures the fact that, while the flow of ideas from basic science have never been more vigorous, the ability to efficiently translate these into new breakthrough medical products has never been more in doubt. Large pharmaceutical companies increasingly rely on replenishment of their pipelines from the rivers of products that biotechnology provided, which in turn were gleaned from academic laboratories. However, the river has been dammed at many stages of preclinical and clinical research and the resulting trickle is insufficient to water the ever-increasing desert.

To cross this chasm, we will need to fundamentally reconsider all aspects of how new medicines are created. This will require creative new ideas and experimentation but the potential rewards and opportunities might be unprecedented from the perspective both of financial gain and public good.

CHAPTER TWELVE

Bridging the Valley

Will the Next Mr. Gates Please Stand Up?

In his fourth-century B.C.E. lecture, *Physike Akroasis* (which translates into "Lectures on Nature," more commonly known simply as "Physics"), Aristotle introduced the concept of *horror vacui* or, as it is more widely known, "Nature abhors a vacuum."[1] The flight of the private sector away from early-stage research and development is a fine example of such a vacuum and this author firmly believes the truth spoken millennia ago by the ancient Greek philosopher. With great certainty, we can assume something will fill the vacancy actively left behind by the retreat of the pharmaceutical industry and the decline of new biotechnology startups. Though inevitable, it is important to minimize the delay in filling this vacuum, as the lives of millions literally depend upon the steady introduction of new medical breakthroughs.

Beyond the public health implications of minimizing the time and extent of the vacuum, extraordinary incentives impel the creation of new approaches for discovering and advancing medical innovations. The market capitalization of just the top seven pharmaceutical companies collectively exceeds $1 trillion, and this does not include the remaining pharmaceutical companies and the entire biotechnology industry. Thus, the humanitarian goals of promoting continued advancements in public health are perfectly aligned with the Keynesian concepts of "animal spirits" that instinctively drive financial markets. In short, those individuals who can identify and implement new models for drug discovery and development will realize considerable personal wealth and professional advancement.

In this final chapter, we convey some ideas to accelerate and broaden the conversation around how best to bridge the proverbial Valley of Death in drug discovery. While the humanitarian and financial stimulus for developing new ideas are united, the urgency of such changes is not broadly appreciated. Indeed, a quick glance at the financial section of any major news or financial website will reveal continued stories of commercial success. As of this writing, the biotechnology IPO market is currently in the midst of a two-year bubble that shows no sign of abating. Nonetheless, the foundations needed for continued growth are fundamentally at odds with the basic fact that the feed material for new pharmaceutical products is waning.

A key word that should be remembered throughout this conversation is "incentive." Consistent with Newton's first law of motion, the present momentum will continue until an external force changes its rate and direction. While many, if not all, of the ideas proposed below may not be applicable, and there are undoubtedly comparable or superior remedies, these are intended simply to stimulate conversation and motivate thought beyond the current conventions. Such new thinking is necessary to identify and implement new ways to resurrect the fundamental enterprise of future drug development.

Challenges and Assets

As we saw in the previous chapter, new venture capital is being directed toward computer and software technology rather than biotechnology start-ups. These highly rational and defensible decisions are based on two properties that fundamentally distinguish biomedical research from software development: time and money. The development of a new drug is capital-intensive, requiring millions of dollars simply to identify which product to advance, and can require years and even decades of intensive investigation.

Compounding the cost of research and development, new medicines have the potential to do great good and, if toxic, to convey equally severe harm. Thus the introduction of new medicines and the continued availability of existing drugs must continue to be carefully regulated by the governments of the world. This regulation adds considerable cost and time to drug development and also means that decades can pass from the epiphany moment of discovery until the marketing of a new medicine can commence. In this context, it is entirely understandable that many investors have elected to place their bets on small groups of software developers working out of a garage with minimal overhead in their quest to develop a product whose success is determined simply by market demand. Contrast this with the average pharmaceutical or biotechnology product, which requires billions of dollars and years of investment before the question of market demand can even be tested. Thus, the reluctance to invest in new medicine development is understandable and helps explain how we have reached the present impasse.

Likewise, the academic sector is experiencing an ever-increasing strain of federal distraction away from basic and applied science research. As pointed out by Dr. Holden Thorp in his landmark book, universities have been the "Engines of Innovation," not just for the biomedical sciences but across all areas of technology.[2] However, these engines are running low, not in terms of the questions and technologies that could be addressed (which are at an all-time high) but in the fuel needed to propel them. NIH budgets are not keeping pace with inflation, and this exacerbates the problem that the academic sector overbuilt their R&D infrastructures during the period of "the doubling" under an unrealistic assumption that the federal largesse would maintain its upward acceleration.

An additional challenge pertains to the sustainability of the human component of drug discovery and development. Historically, drug development was the outcome of a myriad of decisions and, despite being fundamentally based in the sciences, there is also a component of drug discovery and development that is more an art and grounded in past experiences. As one example, the decision-making conveyed by the fields of pharmacology as well as computational or medicinal chemistry address the "drug-ability" of a potential pharmaceutical candidate. The term "drug-ability" captures in part the question of whether a molecule can be administered in a manner that allows it to get to the right parts of the body in method that is both safe and effective. While technology assists this process, key decisions are almost invariably not driven by computer-based data analysis but most heavily impacted by past experiences with related projects and the remembrance of molecules that may have been tested in the past. Little quirks that led to beneficial or detrimental outcomes from past drugs tested in bygone years or decades ago are often recalled and applied to improve future decision-making.

As an art, the knowledge gained over decades is passed along to a new generation through a mentoring process. A Ph.D. in chemistry from the nation's finest universities provides merely the shallowest foundations to initiate a career of lifelong learning, which includes direct experiential learning accelerated by interactions with colleagues.

A fundamental issue is that the mentors and colleagues needed to pass along their wisdom to a new generation have gradually been allowed to evaporate. As the private sector has eased away from early-stage research, companies have furloughed the individuals armed with the expertise to convey long-accumulated wisdom to guide activities such as pharmacology and computational and medicinal chemistries. As we saw in the previous chapter, unemployment and under-employment have created an exodus of highly-trained scientists and many of the most accomplished researchers have either retired or given up, moving to other fields altogether. In doing so, these changes have disrupted the chain of mentors and colleagues needed to continue propagating the field.

Taken together, these challenges also convey unprecedented opportunities.

New Hope in New Haven

The fact that universities have overbuilt their R&D capabilities combined with an under-employment of critical holders of unique knowledge would seem to convey clear opportunities for a fruitful contribution to bridging the Valley of Death in drug development. One issue is that most universities do not have the expertise, resources, proper mindset, or local environment to exploit the opportunity. Through the engines of technological innovation, academia has historically been averse to commercialization, which is humorously referred to internally as turning to the "dark side." However, as evidenced by individual such as Phil Needleman (who developed Celebrex at Searle), P. Roy Vagelos (who led Merck), and Herbert Boyer (who founded Genentech), academicians can successfully contribute to the private sector and succeed. Unfortunately, these three individuals were only able to do so by leaving academia for industry and, thus, their otherwise contagious entrepreneurial zeal was taken away from academia.

Greater emphasis needs to be placed upon university contributors who bestow their expertise to new drug development yet remain in academia and, therein, pass along their experiences to others. A paragon of this virtue is found in the person of Joseph (Yossi) Schlessinger of Yale. Schlessinger was born swaddled in a British military parachute in Croatia during the closing hours of the Second World War.[3] His parents were each on their second marriage (both prior spouses had been murdered by the Nazis or their collaborators) and the couple joined the Yugoslav partisans to fight against the Nazis before moving to Israel in 1948. Growing up in Israel, Yossi was tough, smart, and disciplined, serving in the elite Golani Brigade during the Six Day War and the Yom Kippur War, while at the same time earning his Bachelor, Master's and a Ph.D. from the Weizmann Institute during this tumultuous period. In the years following the Camp David Peace Accord, Schlessinger was on the faculty of the Weizmann Institute for more than a decade, during which time he also directed research at Rorer Pharmaceuticals in Pennsylvania. Schlessinger's field of expertise centered on the study of a class of signaling molecules within cells known as protein kinases.

In his academic and commercial ventures, Schlessinger helped pioneer the concept that protein kinases could serve as targets for medicines to treat cancer and other indications. Schlessinger moved to New York University in 1991 and at the same time cofounded a biotechnology company named Sugen to target cancer kinases with highly selective inhibitors. Sugen succeeded, developing a renal cancer drug named Sutent (approved by FDA in 2006) and was ultimately acquired by Pharmacia and Upjohn in 1999.[4] Pharmacia and Upjohn were later acquired by Pfizer in 2002, and Sugen was yet another victim of the layoffs that often characterize pharmaceutical mergers. In 2001, Schlessinger became restless and moved to Yale University, cofounding another biotechnology company, Plexxikon, in 2001. Plexxikon continued Schlessinger's passion for targeting cancer-associated kinases, culminating in the discovery and FDA approval of Zelboraf for the treatment of melanoma.[5] Plexxikon was later acquired by Daiichi Sankyo Pharmaceuticals in 2011.[6] Bucking the trend, the Japanese parent company has left the company largely intact and independent. Schlessinger also founded Kolltan Pharmaceuticals in 2007, which develops monoclonal antibody-based therapeutics for cancer.[7]

In this extraordinary career, Schlessinger stands in rare company as a successful academician and entrepreneur. His experiences have enriched the environment around him and, unsurprisingly, Schlessinger's gravitas led a private sector company to call on Yossi's team at Yale to help develop new drugs. In 2011, Gilead Sciences, a California-based company best known for developing drugs targeting HIV, HCV, and other viral indications, announced a broad and deep partnership with a Yale team led by Schlessinger.[8] The company recognized the opportunities for developing oncology drugs but its expertise was largely focused upon infectious diseases. Rather than take a standard go-it-alone approach to commit the considerable resources and time needed to develop the expertise all at once internally, Gilead, instead, sought to develop an oncology portfolio by working with existing expertise at Yale. Essentially, the idea was that the established and outstanding cancer research at Yale University would provide a virtual research department for Gilead Sciences.

Many in the biotechnology and pharmaceutical communities simply rolled their eyes upon learning the news of the Yale-Gilead partnership, presuming that this collaboration would suffer the same fate as most corporate-academic partnerships. This history of academic-corporate collaborations in drug discovery is fraught with frustration inevitably leading to failure. Indeed, the oil-water mix of academia and the private sector has largely not worked due to mutual misunderstandings of the goals, motivations, and processes. Indeed, many academic-corporate partnerships might be better characterized as "mutual parasitism." The initial announcement of the Yale-Gilead partnership indicated that it was structured as a three-year deal that would be reviewed for the possibility of extending the relationship for an additional three years and for up to a decade. Almost all the eye rollers in both the academic and private sectors assumed the relationship would be best characterized by the American football term for an ineffective offense: "three and out."

What the naysayers did not count upon was the singular force that is Yossi Schlessinger. With his mix of academic smarts and entrepreneurial savvy (mixed with Israeli special forces toughness), Schlessinger navigated a large and complex partnership (funded at a level of $10 million per year) that was quite successful and, to the amazement of many, the relationship was, indeed, renewed in late 2014 for another three-year period and at the same high level of financial commitment.[9] This remarkable and unprecedented outcome was the result of constant and relentless communication of the goals and expectations of all individuals and organizations involved in the partnership.

The Yale-Gilead partnership conveys but one example of how the private and public sectors can work together in a spirit of mutual respect, appreciate the unique pressures on each other, and work together toward shared goals. The success of this example, which basically took the form of a high-stakes experiment, provides new insight into one new model for bridging the Valley of Death.

More than a Cliché

To fully recognize the opportunities arising from the chance to bridge the ever-expanding divide separating basic research and commercial development, both academic and private-sector organizations must strive to become "partners of choice." This hackneyed descriptor is often invoked and rarely achieved. The Yale-Gilead partnership shows one, but certainly not the only, way in which true partnerships can succeed. The Yale partnership depended upon Yossi Schlessinger and, thus, may not be feasible or even desirable for other organizations. Yet it does demonstrate a means by which interdependence can be achieved, and there are undoubtedly many other models, some of which have not yet even been contemplated, that can be applied to promote academic–private-sector partnerships around the globe to begin addressing the Valley of Death in a more generalized way.

As evidenced by the plights of both academic organizations (such as the Scripps Research Institute) and the accelerating erosion in the number of private sector biotechnology companies, developing the skills to become "a partner of choice" could soon transition from being an aspiration to a basic survival skill. Many universities and companies will fail to do so and the future will undoubtedly witness unprecedented bankruptcies by universities and nonprofit research institutes.

The first high-profile bankruptcy has already occurred, Antioch College in Ohio, a prestigious private school founded by the politician and reformer Horace Mann in 1852.[10] The school was the alma mater for a diverse group of alumni that included *Twilight Zone* creator Rod Serling, civil rights leader Coretta Scott King, actors Leonard Nimoy and Cliff Robertson, as well as scientist Stephen Jay Gould.[11] However, the much-lauded school was forced to shutter its doors in 2008. As of this writing, Antioch College is attempting to re-open and gain accreditation, but its future is uncertain, as is the future of many other institutions of higher learning.

What is needed to allow universities to meet their obligations as educational institutions and yet become a partner of choice to help bridge the Valley of Death? The answers are many-fold, but three prominent answers are to shed bureaucracy, embrace partnering, and, ironically yet most needed, educate the educators.

As discussed in the previous chapter, the nation's universities have become increasingly bureaucratic. This counter-productive trend in part reflects increasing demands from federal funding agencies such as NIH, which have heightened the extent of regulatory requirements for institutions accepting federal funds. As pointed out in a 2015 FASEB report, academic institutions have responded by increasing staffing and directing their faculty to spend more time on the requisite paperwork.[12] All of this has come at the expense of the actual work needed to develop new medicines. Therefore, leadership from the government and academic sectors need to come together to identify what activities are mission-critical versus what activities have been rendered outdated or unnecessary. This mission could be overseen by a neutral but interested party such as the National Academy of Sciences, if granted the power to invoke binding but reasonable new policies in place of the existing quagmire of superfluous regulation. Among the policies to be reviewed should be guidance on issues such as conflicts of interest (both at the individual and the institutional level) as well as indemnification policies (for when things go wrong), and how to distribute royalties such that it creates both sustainability for the institutions and incentives for aspiring inventors.[13]

Inherent bias against the application of knowledge remains a high hurdle that many university communities must overcome. A long-held view of universities as ivory towers that garner knowledge for the sake of knowledge remains the dominant theme for some individuals, departments, and even entire universities.[14] This view must be respected, but the entire institution cannot be held hostage to a view that is increasingly inconsistent with the future of the modern research university. Outdated attitudes toward tenure policies convey one such example.

Collaboration with the private sector was cited as a prominent reason why the author was granted tenure by Purdue University in the late 1990s. Purdue University has, indeed, been quite progressive in private-sector outreach, in part because of its prominence in the highly practical fields of engineering.

Much more common is the approach exemplified by another high-profile organization, where a high-performing assistant professor was denied tenure based on the fact that, while he had exceeded the minimal amount of external (NIH) funding needed to gain tenure, he had elected to work on a drug development project with industry rather than pursue additional federal grants. The irony was that his institution realized higher royalties from this commercial partnership than would have been achieved from yet another grant. As one can imagine, the message received by the rest of the faculty community was heard loud and clear, and this undermined the ability of that institution to credibly claim that applied research was valued. This Manichean view of applied research is outdated but held by a significant fraction of faculty and administrators. The inherent conservatism and high politics that occur behind the closed doors of many ivory tower institutions are accurately evinced by former Harvard professor and United States Secretary of State Henry Kissinger, who voiced: "I formulated the rule that the intensity of academic politics and the bitterness of it is in inverse proportion to the importance of the subject they're discussing. And I promise you at Harvard, they are passionately intense and the subjects are extremely unimportant."[15]

To become viable and reliable partners, academic institutions must also expand beyond merely protecting intellectual property to actively seeking and facilitating the translation of new ideas into meaningful applications. Such a change extends well beyond the esoteric and into practical measures. As one example, technology transfer offices are consistently among the most despised and misunderstood organizations at many research institutions. Like an ogre from mythology, technology transfer offices are accused of gobbling up the babies (the precious ideas birthed by faculty often after incubating for years or decades) and either selling them for pennies on the pound or burying them altogether such that they suffer a gruesome death, neglected and unappreciated.

To overcome such perceptions (and some cases, the realities), universities should advocate for or facilitate the translation of new opportunities as opposed to protecting intellectual property. The former approach conveys that the job of the dreaded technology transfer office is to separate the wheat from the chaff and actively carry forward the most promising ideas, whereas the idea of "protecting" ideas brings to mind the vision of building a moat around the concept or keeping the idea locked away in a tower. As the resources available to most technology transfer offices are limited (and declining), this necessarily means that most ideas will not be advanced.

A key to success, much as Yossi Schlessinger found with external interactions, is a need for constant communication. Faculty submitting ideas for new product concepts should be counseled and well-informed as to the status of their ideas and projects as they move forward or the rationale for why "their baby isn't yet pretty enough" and then encouraged to help mature their concepts. Such actions can overcome perceptions that the technology transfer office locks away their babies in at tower or buries them in a pit.

Given the purview of the organizations in question, an ironic fact is that many academics remain largely ignorant of the need or opportunity to translate their research. In the course of writing this book, the author recently joined Washington University in St. Louis (WashU) to assist in the development of a community that embraces innovation and entrepreneurship. As we have seen several times throughout this book, this university has an extraordinary track record in training or recruiting exceptional scientists and educators and consistently ranks as one of the nation's elite medical schools. Despite and, indeed, because the faculty are at the top of the NIH league tables, Washington University had ranked among the lowest in terms of sponsored research and licensing.

While deciding whether to leave his position at Yale and move to WashU, the author performed a non-scientific survey of the most prestigious faculty and found that surprisingly few (on the order of 5 percent) of this rarified group was actively involved in translating their work. Upon his arrival at WashU, the author met with a large and representative population of the most highly regarded of the faculty to assess whether such under-performance indicated an institutional bias against translation, or an ivory tower mindset, that is generally impossible to overcome. Instead, the response to the question of why the investigators had not moved to translate their research or partner with the private sector was almost invariably met with, "I simply don't know where to start." The respondents consistently remarked that the need to write and manage their grants, oversee the training of students and post-doctoral fellows, as well as their other responsibilities simply did not leave enough time in the day to consider expanding into other areas.

This perception of increasing time pressures on faculty is certainly not unique to Washington University and is shared by virtually all universities across the globe. This issue can be managed both directly and indirectly. Successful universities have and will continue to identify ways to incorporate training in innovation, entrepreneurship, and translation (of ideas into products) as part of crafting their work environment. For example, short presentations on the importance of intellectual property can be conveyed in the regular staff meetings that all faculty attend. Likewise, individuals with translational experience could be embedded within the community, both to stay abreast of the most promising projects as well as to serve as a sounding board for investigators who have an idea and simply want to pressure test the concept. Another approach is to train the students and post-doctoral fellows, who are the lifeblood of many research institutions, in the basic aspects of entrepreneurial theory and practice. These individuals are generally eager to learn more about translational opportunities (as they look to craft their future career paths) and these valued but often overlooked contributors of the academic community can be useful to facilitate a bottom-up approach to educate the educators. Using these approaches and others, the hurdle of addressing the "I don't know where to begin" concern can begin to be addressed.

The growth of biotechnology in the latter quarter of the twentieth century caused a subset of universities to reap a windfall of royalties, but like the curse of natural resource wealth that plagues many developing nations, the largesse was largely squandered.[16] If anything, the gushers of cash arising from the licensing of a new drug created an assumption that others will soon follow, but the reality was that the promise of future wealth was largely illusory. Moving forward, universities should be careful to adopt an evergreen approach, much like that of the private sector, where a substantial fraction of income earned from royalties is reinvested to create the next wave of opportunities.

A successful example of an approach for how a university can underwrite the costs of translational discoveries can be seen with the Trask Innovation Fund created by Purdue University.[17] The fund provides short-term cash infusions to help mature individual technologies to the point where they can be licensed or otherwise monetized. The criteria used to determine whether a project will be funded are based solely on the translational value of the project rather than on the political gravitas of the applicant or the in-novativeness of an idea (that lacks immediate translation potential). Like a conventional venture capital fund, the Trask Innovation Fund is designed to realize future profit, but a key difference is that a substantial portion of the profits are reinvested into the next generation of projects.

Another opportunity to more actively engage the academic community in addressing the Valley of Death in drug development is to incentivize such research.

Incentivizing Change

The decrease in NIH funding over the past decade has greatly increased the stress level of the average biomedical researcher, and this provides an op-portunity to enlist them into the fight to discover new medicines. The obvi-ous question is how to find the resources to provide the incentive. One idea is to tap into existing resources and increase the efficiency of developing new medicines.

One opportunity for addressing the Valley of Death involves a partnership with non-profits and philanthropy. According to the Urban Institute, the growth rate of the nonprofit sector has overtaken both the private and public sectors. In 2010, nonprofit organizations added more than 887 billion dollars (or 5.4 percent) to the U.S. gross domestic product.[18] Historically, public health and medical research have been a favorite of philanthropy, and this relationship could be modified and expanded in ways that help bridge the Valley of Death in drug development. Much as Gilead worked with Yale University to develop a pipeline of new products, nonprofits could establish deep relationships with a select number of universities to meet their goals of addressing unmet needs.

As an example that could literally improve the lives of millions, the grow-ing public health dangers of Alzheimer's disease could provide a means to test new strategies to address the Valley of Death. As we have already seen, Alzheimer's disease has been the graveyard of many potential new drugs and, as a result, countless pharmaceutical and biotechnology companies have restructured to actively avoid neuroscience research.[19] These actions are un-derstandable but further widen the chasm of the Valley of Death for this particular set of indications. The aging of the population means that this flight away from neurodegenerative disease drug development is fundamen-tally at odds with their inevitable increase in incidence and severity in the coming years.[20] The problem simply will not go away.

From the perspective of the private sector, the problem with neurosciences includes the fact that the models used to prioritize drug candidates in the laboratory have not been predictive of efficacy that will be encountered in patients. While this stimulated the exodus of companies away from diseases like Alzheimer's, it presents a tangible challenge that could be taken up by universities and nonprofit organizations focusing on aging or neurodegenerative diseases. Specifically, these nonprofits could team up with universities to develop infrastructure, from basic research through drug design and testing via clinical trials. The expertise for the full range of activities generally does not exist within any one institution. Canny nonprofits could either provide the resources to fill the gaps within a single organization or create consortia that provide a seamless transition such that an idea generated in one institution can be advanced by others, ultimately reaching a point where the drug either can gain FDA approval or be partnered with an established private-sector company that will carry it forward.

Nonprofits achieve these goals by promoting grand challenges akin to X-Prizes. While X-Prizes have gained much public and media attention over the past two decades, the approach was pioneered almost a century ago when the French hotelier Raymond Orteig offered a $25,000 prize for the first non-stop flight between New York and Paris, a challenge that was won by a dashing young pilot, Charles Lindbergh, flying the now-legendary Spirit of St. Louis.[21]

Similar to the model for academia exemplified by the Purdue Trask Fund, the Cystic Fibrosis Foundation (CF Foundation), recently realized a substantial profit from the development of Kalydeco, a product licensed to Vertex Pharmaceuticals.[22] In November 2014, Vertex Pharmaceuticals announced that it had sold the licensing rights of Kalydeco to Royalty Pharma (a private-sector company that operates in much the same way as Valeant Pharmaceuticals). The nonprofit had invested as much as $150 million dollars to support the development of Kalydeco, which was consistent with its mission to develop new drugs to treat cystic fibrosis, and licensed the drug to Vertex. In the 2014 deal with Royalty Pharma, the CF Foundation received a one-time cash payment of $3.3 billion. It remains to be seen if the foundation will treat this as an opportunity to reinvest in a new generation of therapeutics consistent to further address its mandate to improve patient care, but regardless, the transaction demonstrates the potential that nonprofits, similar to universities, could develop evergreen approaches to support continual improvement in clinical care and new medicines.

Public Venture Capital

The largest and most consistent pool of funding for biomedical research has been provided by the U.S. federal government, largely in the form of grants from the National Institutes of Health. However, since the completion of "the doubling" in 2004, the amount of NIH funding has effectively decreased by at least a quarter, and what remains is increasingly blunted by bureaucratic compliance. Regarding the latter, a substantial revision to eliminate duplicative or outdated regulations could provide a straightforward way to effectively increase the amount of funding available to conduct biomedical research without any increase in spending.

Although the federal budget is admittedly under pressure from all sources and parties, lawmakers should consider that multiple and consistent studies have demonstrated a strong return on investment from NIH funding.[23] While the magnitude of return varies from report to report, all concur that NIH funding is efficiently managed and that the return comes in many forms, including revenues from new companies staffed by well-paid professionals but also in the form of public health benefits, including new medicines and vaccines.

Were Congress and the executives to recognize and address the decline in research spending through agencies such as the NIH, the execution must be carefully considered. The experience of "the doubling" revealed that a rapid increase in funding was not, in retrospect, spent in the most constructive way. For example, the rapid increase in the acquisition or construction of research space translated into the creation of empty or under-utilized resources.[24] A prominent example is the West Campus of Yale University, which was purchased from Bayer Pharmaceuticals when the German company underwent another round of downsizing and entirely shuttered its North American research operations in 2007.[25] Yale University purchased this site in anticipation of staffing it with NIH-funded investigators. Eight years later, the site remained largely empty, in part because of decreasing availability of NIH research funding to support staffing.

Another issue that frequently confronts the administrators of the NIH centers is the need for balance between basic and applied research. In a time of declining budgets, any effort to support applied research and development must necessarily come at the expense of basic research. This point was raised most recently in Congressional hearings about the creation of NCATS and by dignitaries such as P. Roy Vagelos.[26] Such viewpoints are grounded on past and present reality. Moving forward, a durable approach would be to define a level of spending for basic medical sciences that will not decrease and, more important, assure that this level will at least keep pace with an inflation rate linked to the costs of performing research and development.

Beyond a guaranteed floor that is set aside for basic research, additional funding for applied or translational research could focus on unmet needs. Such needs could take the form of unmet clinical challenges (for example, Alzheimer's disease for an aging population) or technical challenges that impede future biomedical sustainability. We have already demonstrated that the private sector has shed much expertise crucial for the development of new medicines as a means to cut costs or as a result of abandoning early-stage research and development. A prominent example is the decline in training for future biomedical researchers in the fields of applied pharmacology, computational chemistry, and medicinal chemistry. NIH might sponsor or underwrite regional centers where the tradecraft needed to sustain these vital fields could be passed along to new generations. Such concentrations of talent could then be made available, on a fee-for-service basis, at a reduced fee (which would be supplemented by the NIH using a competitive approach to select the most impactful projects) for projects emerging from the public or private sectors that promise to address unmet medical needs.

Such ideas require a pragmatic approach that recognizes unmet needs and future opportunities but is grounded in a market-driven process. Mazzucato argues convincingly that the instruments of the federal government in general, and the NIH in particular, have done an outstanding job in "picking the right horse."[27] While this support has stoked American innovation in many technical fields, ultimately, the market, by which we mean the unmet medical needs rather than the most financially lucrative products, is the most efficient means to identify and prioritize the needs and opportunities. Prominent among these are the need for new generation of drugs to combat infectious diseases (including the ongoing antibiotics/antibacterial crisis as well as a looming threat of new pathogens, such as a return of HIV that is resistant to conventional therapies).

The mechanisms to allow the NIH and other organizations to kick-start such operations are already in place, albeit these were not necessarily constructed for this particular purpose. For example, the National Cancer Institute has a cadre of cancer centers throughout the nation that include basic and applied scientific expertise. Likewise, the vast majority of funding for the newly formed National Center for Advancing Translational Sciences (NCATS) consists of an existing program known as Clinical and Translational Science Awards (CTSAs). These networks could provide a staging ground both to identify and prioritize unmet medical needs as well as to identify and disseminate ideas and projects to create a portfolio of projects to address these needs.

Private-Sector Engagement

It is worth repeating the comment by P. Roy Vagelos during 2012 Congressional hearings about the creation of NCATS: "Does anyone in the audience believe that there is something that NCATS is going to do that the industry thinks is critical and that they are not doing? That is incredible to think that. If you believe that, you believe in fairies."[28] As we have seen throughout this book, the pharmaceutical industry brings an extraordinary track record of drug development. In decades past, the expertise of any given pharmaceutical company was vertically integrated such that a company could deploy expertise in any stage of drug development, from target identification and validation through preclinical development, clinical evaluation, FDA approval, product launch, sales, marketing, manufacturing, and distribution. However, market realities have combined with increasing regulatory burdens to cause a fundamental restructuring that has progressively moved away from early stage activities. While Dr. Vagelos correctly pointed out that the industry is well versed in identifying critical issues, the steady trend of withdrawing from early stage discovery and research is an increasing and presumably irreversible problem. Conventional wisdom suggests the most likely scenario is that most companies will continue not to engage in drug development until some demonstration of human proof of concept has been achieved. The key problem is the need to develop the data necessary to re-engage the private sector and, thus, bridge the divide between conventional NIH funding and the point at which the baton can be passed to the private sector.

The federal government largely lacks the ability to address this issue alone or in combination only with academia, which lacks the "boots on the ground" expertise and the instincts needed to develop meaningful medicines. To avoid an inefficient use of federal funding, the federal government needs to engage the private sector in a manner that is mutually beneficial. The private sector should be deployed in a style that works to their strengths. Although pharmaceutical companies have withdrawn from some areas of the drug development process, their experience and institutional memory for activities such as late-stage clinical design and execution remain unparalleled. Thus, a partnership to develop new medicines should be inclusive and build upon the strengths of all parties (government, academia, and industry).

A series of successful and attempted mergers over the past few years have brought to the fore a challenge and opportunity associated with the pharmaceutical industry. The relatively high corporate income tax rate in the United States at 35 percent (as compared to the United Kingdom at a peak rate of 26 percent or Ireland at 12.5 percent) has created at least two prominent problems.[29] First, many companies have sought to avoid higher U.S. taxes through tax inversions, in which an American company acquires an overseas competitor in an effort to relocate its legal domicile to a country with a lower tax rate.[30] Another approach has led to the accumulation of untaxed profits from product sales outside the United States, which would be taxed by the United States were the monies to be brought into the country. For example, Pfizer is estimated to have $73 billion dollars offshore, with Abbott at $40 billion, and other pharmaceutical companies not far behind.[31]

Tax reform is a hot button issue on both the political left and the right, and the goal of this discussion is not to address this volatile issue directly. However, in reconsidering how taxes are assessed, the incentives to invest in research and development activities could be increased. A research tax credit already exists in the United States and stands at roughly 20 percent. This level might be tiered such that higher levels apply to monies repatriated to the United States, and even higher credits might be applied to areas determined to be unmet medical needs (for example, antibiotics or neurosciences) or certain training activities (for example, educating pharmacologists or computational chemists).

Coca-Cola and Pepsi

The pharmaceutical industry necessarily is amongst the most highly regulated industries on Earth. Episodes such as thalidomide and Vioxx reinforce the need to identify and regulate "bad drugs" that are toxic. However, as we saw with the failed prosecution of Coca-Cola by Harvey Washington Wiley, excessive regulation can stymie innovation and create unnecessary hurdles. High levels of regulation convey practical limitations, such as the need to perform certain studies that may have been useful in the past but are not so in the future. The idea that a New Drug Application (NDA), if printed out, would stack higher than the Empire State Building raises questions about the efficiency of the process. The cost savings could be manifold because it not only requires time and money to prepare all of these studies but additional time and money by the FDA to review them.

A practical approach would be to appoint a neutral committee to propose binding rules as to what tests and procedures are necessary to protect the public from "bad drugs." Outdated or unnecessary tests should be eliminated altogether and the timing of certain investigations might be altered to encourage early-stage research. Particular emphasis might be placed on studies needed in the earliest stages of drug development, since this seems to have become the fastest growing chokepoint over the past two decades.

In discussions with colleagues about the future of the pharmaceutical industry, a frequently cited analogy is that enterprise has been moving toward a resemblance of Coca-Cola versus Pepsi. This comparison most often means that pharmaceuticals are moving to the point where advertising, marketing, manufacturing, and distribution are emerging as the activities, where "big pharma" both excels at and is directing most of its attention. For example, Johnson & Johnson spent twice as much on sales and marketing ($17.5 billion) than on research and development ($8.2 billion), and the trend was much the same for many of its peers.[32] Anyone who has been in front of a television for more than fifteen minutes can attest to the extraordinary rise in direct-to-consumer advertising by the pharmaceutical industry. The ethics and impact of such advertising can and does impel much debate and is not the focus of this discussion but does become relevant to our final proposal, which suggests a radical approach that could substantially modify how drugs are approved, sold, and marketed.

Two and Out

In thinking through the implications that the industry is moving toward a Coca-Cola versus Pepsi model, a logical extension of this idea struck the author one day in the shower (admittedly a cliché but technically accurate). The idea was that the market ultimately decides who will win (Coca-Cola versus Pepsi) by the amount of product sold. Specifically, if a product meets the demand, then it will notch the greatest sales.

Taking this to an extreme, we suggest a model in which the market decides which drugs will succeed and which will fail by launching drugs at an earlier stage than is presently done. Currently, the market does decide winners from losers, but only after a drug has gone through a multi-billion dollar development cycle that assures the new entry is at least as good as the current standard (the "better than the Beatles" approach recounted in an earlier chapter). FDA approval hangs almost entirely upon the successful completion of Phase III clinical trials that entail multiple clinical trials with large numbers of subjects, years and even decades of clinical research, and hundreds of millions of dollars for each trial. While many drugs fail to reach the standard of "better than the Beatles" in the large population, retrospective analyses often reveal subsets of patients, perhaps based on a key genetic or environmental variable, where the experimental drug was superior to the standard of care. By this time, however, the project may have been discontinued (or the company already been forced to shutter its doors, in the case of resource-constrained biotechnology companies) and this may preclude the availability of resources available to repeat the study with the more narrowly defined patient population.

An alternative approach could be to eliminate the requirement for costly Phase III clinical trials altogether. Rather, the goal would be to allow the post-approval market to identify the best opportunities for newly-approved drugs. In this scenario, even greater emphasis would need to be placed upon safety studies in Phase I and Phase II to preclude toxic drugs (for example, Vioxx). Moreover, candidate drugs would need to demonstrate some evidence of efficacy in Phase II trials. However, once evidence of efficacy is achieved, the post-approval market would determine the best use for the drug.

Indeed, as we have already pointed out, such a strategy has already been in practice for decades in oncology. Specifically, the strategy associated with a "compendium expansion" invokes drugs that have been approved for other indications and uses a simple Phase II trials (and the resulting peer-reviewed publication to justify to payers (insurance companies) that the product should be reimbursed for the off-label indication. The strategy we propose is a simply extension of this idea beyond the field of oncology. The only other change is to make more drugs available for such opportunities by making these drugs available after a positive finding from a Phase II clinical trial.

There could be many advantages to this program. As Phase III clinical trials capture the largest proportion of the costs of drug development and time, the prices of drugs approved under this model would necessarily be reduced (theoretically by up to 90 percent). Likewise, the reduced amount of information needed for review should expedite and sharpen reviews by the FDA of an NDA package.

A variation on this theme would be to allow companies an option to obtain FDA approval with a more conventional Three Phase approach and to provide incentives for them to do so. For example, a Three Phase clinical development program could allow the developer to charge a higher premium for having demonstrated conclusive efficacy relative to the current standard versus a Two Phase development program, which would require them to lower the price charged. A two-tier pricing strategy might also appeal to providers, distributors, or payers in efforts to manage the costs of healthcare.

Let's return to the proposal for a Two Phase approval schema. Unlike most consumer products, the post-approval product evaluation would not rely upon the advertisement or packaging but, rather, on objective reporting of safety and efficacy. Specifically, an independently managed nonprofit (comparable to the Consumer Union) would manage and analyze databases of drug safety and efficacy. This organization would need to ensure its independence from industry pressure of incentives while remaining nimble and shunning partisan politics and bureaucracy. Although such a mechanism might sound and, indeed, be far-fetched, companies are already required to conduct extensive monitoring of post-approval safety and report their findings to the FDA. The key difference is that our strategy would require that an impartial third party be responsible for ensuring compliance and analyzing data that included evidence of efficacy as well as safety.

The era of personalized medicine is already upon us and vast amounts of information suggest the many roles of diverse factors such as genetics and the environment on disease and responses to treatment. For example, scientists are learning more about the roles of metabolism on safety and efficacy of certain drugs and how these vary when comparing different individuals or defined patient populations. As this knowledge grows, it could be compared with the findings from efficacy to *a priori* predict which medicines are most likely to work in which patients. In doing so, the market could be defined based on objective data rather than the whims (or biases) of health providers or patients.

A caveat to this model is that special attention would need to be placed upon the role of sales and marketing. The personal preference of the author would favor the elimination altogether of direct-to-consumer advertisement of pharmaceutical products. Even if allowed to continue, advertisement should advise potential prescribers, payers, and patients that the drug may be promising for its indication but refer these individuals to their healthcare provider or others who could utilize the compendium to determine the patient's best options.

Such a system, were it to be adopted, would need to begin as an experiment and should focus on relatively benign or chronic indications. Stated another way, the adoption of such as system should not begin with the evaluation of life-threatening acute indications (for example, cancer treatment or new treatments for sepsis) that entail critical and potentially irreversible decisions.

Given the conservatism in regulation that currently typifies the pharmaceutical industry, it seems more likely that the Cincinnati Reds will play the Cleveland Indians in the World Series than that these ideas will be adopted as recommended. Nonetheless, unconventional thinking will be required to identify new ways of thinking and acting to ensure a continued pipeline of new medicines that adds to the public health successes of the past century.

Notes

Chapter One

1. L. Gandhi, "A History of 'Snake Oil Salesmen,'" *Code Switch* (blog), 26 August 2013, http://www.npr.org/blogs/codeswitch/2013/08/26/215761377/a-history-of-snake-oil-salesmen.

2. N. Siriwardhana, N. S. Kalupahana, and N. Moustaid-Moussa, "Health Benefits of n-3 Polyunsaturated Fatty Acids: Eicosapentaenoic Acid and Docosahexaenoic Acid," *Advances in Food and Nutrition Research* 65 (2012): 211–22.

3. C. Graber, "Snake Oil Salesmen Were on to Something," *Scientific American*, 1 November 2007, http://www.scientificamerican.com/article/snake-oil-salesmen-knew-something.

4. Gandhi, "History of 'Snake Oil Salesmen.'"

5. R. Mestel, "Snake Oil Salesmen Weren't Always Considered Slimy," *Los Angeles Times*, 1 July 2002, http://articles.latimes.com/2002/jul/01/health/he-booster1.

6. D. Winterman, "History's Weirdest Fad Diets," *BBC News Magazine*, 2 January 2013, http://www.bbc.com/news/magazine-20695743.

7. C. Rance, "'Eat! Eat! Eat!' Those Notorious Tapeworm Diet Pills," *The Quack Doctor* (blog), 2 January 2015, http://thequackdoctor.com/index.php/eat-eat-eat-those-notorious-tapeworm-diet-pills.

8. J. D. Smyth and D. P. McManus, *The Physiology and Biochemistry of Cestodes* (New York: Cambridge University Press, 2007).

9. J. C. Munger and W. H. Karasov, "Sublethal Parasites and Host Energy Budgets: Tapeworm Infection in White-Footed Mice," *Ecology* 70 (August 1989): 904–21.

10. W. Nyberg, R. Grasbeck, M. Saarni, and B. von Bonsdorff, "Serum Vitamin B12 Levels and Incidence of Tapeworm Anemia in a Population Heavily Infected with *Diphyllobothrium Latum*," *American Journal of Clinical Nutrition* 9 (1961): 606–12.

11. S. P. Stabler, "Vitamin B12 Deficiency," *New England Journal of Medicine* 368 (2013): 149–60.

12. L. Szinicz, "History of Chemical and Biological Warfare Agents," *Toxicology* 214 (2005): 167–81.

13. T. A. Shragg, T. E. Albertson, and C. J. Fisher Jr., "Cyanide Poisoning after Bitter Almond Ingestion," *Western Journal of Medicine* 136 (1982): 65.

14. S. I. Baskin, J. B. Kelly, B. I. Maliner, G. A. Rockwood, and C. K. Zoltani, "Cyanide Poisoning," *Medical Aspects of Chemical Warfare* 11 (2008): 372–410.

15. V. Herbert, "Laetrile: The Cult of Cyanide. Promoting Poison for Profit," *American Journal of Clinical Nutrition* 32 (1979): 1121–58.

16. A. G. Rauws, M. Olling, and A. Timmerman, "The Pharmacokinetics of Amygdalin," *Archives of Toxicology* 49 (1989): 311–19.

17. N. M. Ellison, D. P. Byar, and G. R. Newell, "Special Report on Laetrile: The NCI Laetrile Review. Results of the National Cancer Institute's Retrospective Laetrile Analysis," *New England Journal of Medicine* 299 (1978): 549–52.

18. R. W. Moss, "Patient Perspectives: Tijuana Cancer Clinics in the Post-NAFTA Era," *Integrative Cancer Therapies* 4 (1) (2005): 65–86.

19. Baskin et al., "Cyanide Poisoning."

20. B. Harmon, *Technical Aspects of the Holocaust: Cyanide, Zyklon-B, and Mass Murder* (1994), http://www.nizkor.org/ftp.cgi/camps/auschwitz/cyanide/cyanide .001, accessed 20 March 2015; P. Longerich, *Heinrich Himmler: A Life* (Oxford, England: Oxford University Press, 2011).

21. G. Sonnedecker, "The Founding Period of the U.S. Pharmacopeia," *Pharmacy in History* 35 (4) (1993): 151.

22. M. A. Flannery, "Building a Retrospective Collection in Pharmacy: A Brief History of the Literature with Some Considerations for U.S. Health Sciences Library Professionals," *Bulletin of the Medical Library Association* 89 (2) (2001): 212.

23. D. Barton, *Benjamin Rush: Signer of the Declaration of Independence* (Aledo, Tex.: Wallbuilders Press, 1999.

24. A. B. Jaffe and J. Lerner, *Innovation and Its Discontents* (Princeton, N.J.: Princeton University Press, 2004).

25. Ibid.

26. W. H. Cole, "That Amazing Man Beck," *Journal of the Rutgers University Libraries* 30 (2) (2012): 32–39.

27. Erika Janik, *Marketplace of the Marvelous: The Strange Origins of Modern Medicine* (Boston: Beacon Press, 2014).

28. M. Pendergrast, *For God, Country, and Coca-Cola: The Definitive History of the Great American Soft Drink and the Company That Makes It* (New York: Basic Books, 2013).

29. Ibid.

30. A. Niemann, "Ueber eine neue organische Base in den Cocablättern," *Archiv der Pharmazie* 153 (2) (1860): 129–55.

31. F. Allen, *Secret Formula* (New York: HarperCollins Publishers, 1994).

32. Pendergrast, *For God, Country, and Coca-Cola*.

33. A. W. Bingham, *The Snake-Oil Syndrome: Patent Medicine Advertising* (Hanover, Mass.: Christopher Publishing House, 1994).

34. S. H. Adams, *The Great American Fraud* (New York: PF Collier & Son, 1907).

35. W. F. Janssen, "The Squad that Ate Poison," *FDA Consumer* 15 (10) (1981): 6–11.

36. C. A. Coppin and J. C. High, *The Politics of Purity: Harvey Washington Wiley and the Origins of Federal Food Policy* (Ann Arbor: University of Michigan Press, 1999).

37. Ibid.

38. B. Watson, "The Poison Squad: An Incredible History," *Esquire*, 27 June 2013, http://www.esquire.com/blogs/food-for-men/poison-squad; C. Lewis and S. W. Junod, "The 'Poison Squad' and the Advent of Food and Drug Regulation," *FDA Consumer* 36 (6) (2002): 12–15.

39. Watson, "Poison Squad."

40. Ibid.; Lewis, "The Poison Squad and the Advent of Food and Drug Regulation."

41. Watson, "Poison Squad."

42. W. F. Janssen, "Outline of the History of U.S. Drug Regulation and Labeling," *Food Drug Cosmetic Law Journal* 36 (1981): 420.

43. Coppin and High, *Politics of Purity*.

44. B. A. Weinberg and B. K. Bealer, *The World of Caffeine: The Science and Culture of the World's Most Popular Drug* (New York: Psychology Press, 2001).

45. H. A. Robertson and J. E. Steele, "Activation of Insect Nerve Cord Phosphorylase by Octopamine and Adenosine 3′, 5′-monophosphate," *Journal of Neurochemistry* 19 (6) (1972): 1603–6.

46. P. C. A. Kam and S. Liew, "Traditional Chinese Herbal Medicine and Anaesthesia," *Anaesthesia* 57 (11) (2002): 1083–89.

47. Coppin and High, *Politics of Purity*.

48. M. M. King, "Dr. John S. Pemberton: Originator of Coca-Cola," *Pharmacy in History* 29 (2) (1986): 85–89.

49. L. T. Benjamin Jr., "Pop Psychology: The Man who Saved Coca-Cola," *Monitor on Psychology* 40 (2009): 18.

50. Pendergrast, *For God, Country, and Coca-Cola*.

51. Benjamin, "Pop Psychology."

52. L. T. Benjamin Jr., "Harry Hollingworth: Portrait of," *Portraits of Pioneers in Psychology* 2 (1991): 119.

53. L. T. Benjamin Jr., "Coca-Cola, Caffeine, and Mental Deficiency: Harry Hollingworth and the Chattanooga Trial of 1911," *Journal of the History of the Behavioral Sciences* 27 (2006): 42–55.

54. Ibid.

55. Ibid.

56. Coppin and High, *Politics of Purity*.

57. S. Johnson, *The Ghost Map: The Story of London's Most Terrifying Epidemic— and How It Changed Science, Cities, and the Modern World* (New York: Penguin, 2006).

58. B. J. Ford, "From Dilettante to Diligent Experimenter," *Biology History* 5 (3) (1992).

59. A. van Leeuwenhoek, "Part of a Letter from Mr. Antony van Leeuwenhoek, FRS Concerning Green Weeds Growing in Water, and Some Animalcula Found about Them," *Philosophical Transactions* 23 (1702): 1304–11.

60. D. A. E. Shepard and John Snow, *Anaesthetist to a Queen and Epidemiologist to a Nation: A Biography* (Cornwall, PE: York Point Publishing, 1995).

61. Johnson, *Ghost Map*.

62. A. M. Silverstein, *Paul Ehrlich's Receptor Immunology: The Magnificent Obsession* (Cambridge, Mass.: Academic Press, 2001).

63. A. Gelpi, A. Gilbertson, and J. D. Tucker, "Magic Bullet: Paul Ehrlich, Salvarsan and the Birth of Venereology," *Sexually Transmitted Infections* 91 (1) (2015): 68–69.

64. S. H. Lindner, *Inside IG Farben: Hoechst during the Third Reich* (New York: Cambridge University Press, 2008).

65. B. Witkop, "Paul Ehrlich and His Magic Bullets, Revisited," *Proceedings of the American Philosophical Society* (1999): 540–57.

66. C. Koonz, *The Nazi Conscience* (Cambridge, Mass.: Harvard University Press, 2003).

67. Lindner, *Inside IG Farben*.

68. W. L. Shirer, *The Rise and Fall of the Third Reich: A History of Nazi Germany* (New York: Random House, 1991).

69. R. Proctor, *Racial Hygiene: Medicine Under the Nazis* (Cambridge, Mass.: Harvard University Press, 1988).

70. H. Friedlander, *The Origins of Nazi Genocide: From Euthanasia to the Final Solution* (Chapel Hill: University of North Carolina Press, 1997).

71. J. Bankston, *Gerhard Domagk and the Discovery of Sulfa* (Newark, Del.: Mitchell Lane Pub Incorporated, 2002).

72. Ibid.

73. G. Domagk, "Chemotherapie der Bakteriellen Infektionen," *Angewandte Chemie* 48 (42) (1935): 657–67.

74. J. S. Haller, "The First Miracle Drugs: How the Sulfa Drugs Transformed Medicine," *Journal of the History of Medicine and Allied Sciences* 63 (1) (2008): 119–21.

75. E. Crawford, "German Scientists and Hitler's Vendetta against the Nobel Prizes," *Historical Studies in the Physical and Biological Sciences* (2000): 37–53.

76. Haller, "*First Miracle Drugs*."

77. C. Ballentine, "Taste of Raspberries, Taste of Death: The 1937 Elixir Sulfanilamide Incident," *FDA Consumer* 15 (5) (1981): 1–2, http://www.fda.gov/AboutFDA/WhatWeDo/History/ProductRegulation/SulfanilamideDisaster/default.htm.

78. Ibid.; P. M. Wax, "Elixir Sulfanilamide-Massengill Revisited," *Veterinary and Human Toxicology* 36 (6) (1994): 561–62.

79. L. Bren, "Frances Oldham Kelsey: FDA Medical Reviewer Leaves Her Mark on History," *FDA Consumer* 35 (2) (2001): 24–29.

80. Ballentine, "Taste of Raspberries, Taste of Death."

81. Ibid.

82. P. M. Wax, "Elixirs, Diluents, and the Passage of the 1938 Federal Food, Drug, and Cosmetic Act," *Annals of Internal Medicine* 122 (6) (1995): 456–61.

Chapter Two

1. S. Johnson, *The Ghost Map: The Story of London's Most Terrifying Epidemic—and How it Changed Science, Cities, and the Modern World* (New York: Penguin, 2006).

2. J. Snow, *On the Mode of Communication of Cholera* (London, UK: John Churchill Publishing, 1855).

3. P. M. Dunn, "James Lind (1716–94) of Edinburgh and the Treatment of Scurvy," *Archives of Disease in Childhood,* Fetal and Neonatal edition 76 (1) (1997): F64–F65.

4. K. J. Carpenter, *The History of Scurvy and Vitamin C* (New York: Cambridge University Press, 1988).

5. J. Lind, *A Treatise of the Scurvy* (Edinburgh: Sands, Murray and Chocran, 1772).

6. G. Donald, *The Accidental Scientist: The Role of Chance and Luck in Scientific Discovery* (London, UK: Michael O'Mara Books, 2013).

7. E. D. Pellegrino, "The Nazi Doctors and Nuremberg: Some Moral Lessons Revisited," *Annals of Internal Medicine* 127 (4) (1997): 307–8.

8. G. J. Annas and M. A. Grodin, "The Nazi Doctors and the Nuremberg Code," *Journal of Pharmacy & Law* 4 (1995): 167–245.

9. J. Folkman, "Tumor Angiogenesis: Therapeutic Implications," *New England Journal of Medicine* 285 (21) (1971): 1182–86.

10. M. S. O'Reilly, L. Holmgren, Y. Shing, C. Chen, R. A. Rosenthal, M. Moses, W. S. Lane, Y. Cao, E. H. Sage, and J. Folkman, "Angiostatin: A Novel Angiogenesis Inhibitor that Mediates the Suppression of Metastases by a Lewis Lung Carcinoma," *Cell* 79 (2) (1994): 315–28.

11. J. Folkman, presented at the Seminars in Oncology, 2002 (unpublished).

12. R. Cooke, *Dr. Folkman's War: Angiogenesis and the Struggle to Defeat Cancer* (New York: Random House, Inc.).

13. E. Dorey, "Entremed's Stock Seesaws," *Nature Biotechnology* 17 (3) (1999): 212–13.

14. S. Devi, "U.S. Health Agencies Take Stock After Federal Shutdown," *Lancet* 382 (9902) (2013): 1391.

15. T. Hünig, "The Storm has Cleared: Lessons from the CD28 Superagonist TGN1412 Trial," *Nature Reviews Immunology* 12 (5) (2012): 317–18; N. Somberg and J. Somberg, "First-in-Man (FIM) Clinical Trials Post-TeGenero: A Review of the Impact of the TeGenero Trial on the Design, Conduct, and Ethics of FIM Trials," *American Journal of Therapeutics* 14 (6) (2007): 594–604.

16. L. Farzaneh, N. Kasahara, and F. Farzaneh, "The Strange Case of TGN1412," *Cancer Immunology, Immunotherapy: CII* 56 (2) (2007): 129–34.

17. R. English, "'Elephant Man Couldn't Resist Drug Test Money,'" *Daily Mail,* 20 March 2006, http://www.dailymail.co.uk/news/article-380395/Elephant-Man-resist-drug-test-money.html.

18. L. Farzaneh, N. Kasahara, and F. Farzaneh, "The Strange Case of TGN1412"; G. Suntharalingam, M. R. Perry, S. Ward, S. J. Brett, A. Castello-Cortes, M. D. Brunner, and N. Panoskaltsis, "Cytokine Storm in a Phase I Trial of the Anti-CD28 Monoclonal Antibody TGN1412," *New England Journal of Medicine* 355 (10) (2006): 1018–28.

19. Somberg and Somberg, "First-in-Man (FIM) Clinical Trials Post-TeGenero."

20. J. R. Tisoncik, M. J. Korth, C. P. Simmons, J. Farrar, T. R. Martin, and M. G. Katze, "Into the Eye of the Cytokine Storm," *Microbiology and Molecular Biology Reviews* 76 (1) (2012): 16–32.

21. I. A. Clark, "The Advent of the Cytokine Storm," *Immunology and Cell Biology* 85 (4) (2007): 271–73; M. T. Osterholm, "Preparing for the Next Pandemic," *New England Journal of Medicine* 352 (18) (2005): 1839–42.

22. R. Stebbings, S. Poole, and R. Thorpe, "Safety of Biologics, Lessons Learnt from TGN1412," *Current Opinion in Biotechnology* 20 (6) (2009): 673–77.

23. M. I. Zia, L. L. Siu, G. R. Pond, and E. X. Chen, "Comparison of Outcomes of Phase II Studies and Subsequent Randomized Control Studies Using Identical Chemotherapeutic Regimens," *Journal of Clinical Oncology* 23 (28) (2005): 6982–91.

24. C. Downs, "The Medicare Prescription Drug Improvement and Modernization Act and the Delivery of Cancer Chemotherapy," *American Journal of Health-System Pharmacy: AJHP; Official Journal of the American Society of Health-System Pharmacists* 64 (15 Suppl 10) (2007): S13–15, quiz S21–S23; American Society of Clinical Oncology, "Reimbursement for Cancer Treatment: Coverage of Off-Label Drug Indications," *Journal of Clinical Oncology* 24 (19) (2006): 3206–8.

25. InVivo, "The REMS Pioneers: Amgen's Nplate Sets Another New Standard," *InVivo*, 2008, http://invivoblog.blogspot.com/2008/09/rems-pioneers-amgens-nplate-sets.html.

26. S. K. Teo, "Properties of Thalidomide and its Analogues: Implications for Anticancer Therapy," *AAPS Journal* 7 (1) (2005): E14–E19.

27. J. Botting, "The History of Thalidomide," *Drug News Perspectives* 15 (9) (2002): 604–11.

28. T. Stephens and R. Brynner, *Dark Remedy: The Impact of Thalidomide and Its Revival as a Vital Medicine* (New York: Basic Books, 2009).

29. G. J. Annas and S. Elias, "Thalidomide and the Titanic: Reconstructing the Technology Tragedies of the Twentieth Century," *American Journal of Public Health* 89 (1) (1999): 98–101.

30. M. Fair, "GSK Hit with Thalidomide Birth Defect Suit," *Law360.com*, 9 August 2012, http://www.law360.com/articles/368575/gsk-hit-with-thalidomide-birth-defect-suit.

31. L. Bren, "Frances Oldham Kelsey: FDA Medical Reviewer Leaves her Mark on History," *FDA Consumer* 35 (2) (2001).

32. M. Mintz, "Remembering Thalidomide," *Washington Post National Weekly Edition*, 22–28 July 1996, p. 21.

33. Botting, "*History of Thalidomide*"; Stephens and Brynner, *Dark Remedy*.

34. L. Layton, "Physician to be Honored for Historic Decision on Thalidomide," *Washington Post*, 13 September 2010, http://www.washingtonpost.com/wp-dyn/content/article/2010/09/13/AR2010091306279.html.

35. H. Davis Graham, "Kefauver: A Political Biography," *Tennessee Historical Quarterly*, 1971, 413–18.

36. W. W. Goodrich, "FDA's Regulation under the Kefauver-Harris Drug Amendments of 1962," *Food, Drug, Cosmetic Law Journal* 18 (1963): 561.

37. S. S. Sanbar, *Legal Medicine* (Philadelphia: Elsevier Health Sciences, 2007).

38. J. Sheskin, "Thalidomide in Lepra Reaction," *International Journal of Dermatology* 14 (8) (1975): 575–76.

39. D. P. Cavalcanti, J. Correa-Neto, J. L. Delgadillo, N. L. G. Dutra, and T. Felix, "Thalidomide, a Current Teratogen in South America," *Teratology* 54 (1996): 273–77.

40. F. S. L. Vianna, L. Schüler-Faccini, J. C. L. Leite, S. H. C. de Sousa, L. M. M. da Costa, M. F. Dias, E. F. Morelo, M. J. R. Doriqui, C. M. Maximino, and M. T. V. Sanseverino, "Recognition of the Phenotype of Thalidomide Embryopathy in Countries Endemic for Leprosy: New Cases and Review of the Main Dysmorphological Findings," *Clinical Dysmorphology* 22 (2) (2013): 59–63.

41. J. B. Zeldis, B. A. Williams, S. D. Thomas, and M. E. Elsayed, "STEPS™: A Comprehensive Program for Controlling and Monitoring Access to Thalidomide," *Clinical Therapeutics* 21 (2) (1999): 319–30.

42. R. J. D'Amato, M. S. Loughnan, E. Flynn, and J. Folkman, "Thalidomide Is an Inhibitor of Angiogenesis," *Proceedings of the National Academy of Sciences* 91 (9) (1994): 4082–85.

Chapter Three

1. M. S. Kinch, A. Haynesworth, S. L. Kinch, and D. Hoyer, "An Overview of FDA-Approved New Molecular Entities: 1827–2013," *Drug Discovery Today* 19 (8) (2014): 1033–39.

2. F. Hawthorne, *The Merck Druggernaut: The Inside Story of a Pharmaceutical Giant* (New York: John Wiley & Sons, 2004); P. R. Vagelos and L. Galambos, *Medicine, Science, and Merck* (New York: Cambridge University Press, 2004).

3. A. D. Krikorian, "Were the Opium Poppy and Opium Known in the Ancient Near East?," *Journal of the History of Biology* 8 (1) (1975): 95–114; M. Booth, *Opium: A History* (London, UK: St. Martin's Press, 1999).

4. Z. Chovanec, S. Rafferty, and S. Swiny, "Opium for the Masses," *Ethnoarchaeology* 4 (1) (2012): 5–36.

5. M. Thevis, G. Opfermann, and W. Schänzer, "Urinary Concentrations of Morphine and Codeine after Consumption of Poppy Seeds," *Journal of Analytical Toxicology* 27 (1) (2003): 53–56.

6. Booth, *Opium*.

7. P. G. Kritikos and S. P. Papadaki, *The History of the Poppy and of Opium and their Expansion in Antiquity in the Eastern Mediterranean Area* (Vienna, Austria: United Nations Office on Drugs and Crime, 1967).

8. T. E. Cone, "On the Etymologic Derivation of Some Commonly Used Words in Pediatrics: Infant, Cretin, Meconium, and Incterus," *Pediatrics* 46 (6) (1970): 870.

9. Booth, *Opium*.

10. M. P. Hall, *Paracelsus, His Mystical and Medical Philosophy* (Los Angeles: Philosophical Research Society, 1980).

11. T. U. Hoogenraad, "History of Zinc Therapy," in *Copper and Zinc in Inflammatory and Degenerative Diseases*, ed. K. D. Rainsford, R. Milanino, J. R. J. Sorenson, and G. P. Velo (New York: Springer, 1998), 1–5.

12. H. C. Binswanger and K. R. Smith, "Paracelsus and Goethe: Founding Fathers of Environmental Health," *Bulletin of the World Health Organization* 78 (9) (2000): 1162–64.

13. H. E. Sigerist, "Laudanum in the Works of Paracelsus," *Bulletin of the History of Medicine* 9 (1941): 530–44.

14. M. Polo, *The Travels of Marco Polo* (London, UK: J. M. Dent & Sons, 1918).

15. D. O. Flynn and A. Giráldez, "Cycles of Silver: Global Economic Unity through the Mid-Eighteenth Century," *Journal of World History* 13 (2) (2002): 391–427.

16. J. Lovell, *The Opium War* (Tuggarah: Picador Australia, 2011).

17. J. Ch'ên, *State Economic Policies of the Ch'ing Government, 1840–1895* (New York: Garland, 1980).

18. R. Karl, "The Burdens of History: Lin Zexu and The Opium War," chap. 7 in *Whither China?*, ed. Xudong Zhang (Durham, N.C.: Duke University Press, 2001).

19. W. T. Hanes and Frank S., *The Opium Wars: The Addiction of One Empire and the Corruption of Another* (Naperville, Ill.: Sourcebooks, Inc., 2004).

20. Ibid.

21. Lovell, *Opium War*; Karl, "The Burdens of History: Lin Zexu and The Opium War."

22. R. Schmitz, "Friedrich Wilhelm Sertürner and the Discovery of Morphine," *Pharmacy in History* (1985): 61–74.

23. R. J. Huxtable and S. K. W. Schwarz, "The Isolation of Morphine—First Principles in Science and Ethics," *Molecular Interventions* 1 (4) (2001): 189; P. J. Hanzlik, "125th Anniversary of the Discovery of Morphine by Sertürner," *Journal of the American Pharmaceutical Association* 18 (4) (1929): 375–84.

24. Huxtable and Schwarz, "Isolation of Morphine"; Hanzlik, "125th Anniversary."

25. I. Possehl and K. Loew, *Merck, Heinrich Emanuel* (Berlin, Ger.: Duncker and Humblot, 1994).

26. Ibid.

27. T. A. Henry, *The Plant Alkaloids* (London, UK: J. & A. Churchill, 1913); F. Hawthorne, *The Merck Druggernaut* (London, UK: Wiley, 2005).

28. Merck & Co. and Merck Sharp, and Dohme, *The Merck Manual of Diagnosis and Therapy* (Darmstadt, Ger.: Merck, 1899).

29. S. Coben, *A. Mitchell Palmer: Politician* (Boston: Da Capo Press, 1972).

30. P. Avrich, *Sacco and Vanzetti: The Anarchist Background* (Princeton, N.J.: Princeton University Press, 1996).

31. H. G. Cohen, "The (Un)favorable Judgment of History: Deportation Hearings, the Palmer Raids, and the Meaning of History," *New York Urban League Review* 78 (2003): 1431.

32. T. Weiner, *Enemies: A History of the FBI* (New York: Random House Incorporated, 2012).

33. W. d'A. Maycock, "Sir Lionel Ernest Howard Whitby," *Vox Sanguinis* 2 (1) (1957): 79–80.

34. M. Wainwright, "How Two Antimicrobials Altered the History of the Modern World," *Microbiology Today* 34 (1) (2007): 16.

35. J. S. Haller, "The First Miracle Drugs: How the Sulfa Drugs Transformed Medicine," *Journal of the History of Medicine and Allied Sciences* 63 (1) (2008): 119–21.

36. A. Fleming, "The Discovery of Penicillin," *British Medical Bulletin* 2 (1) (1944): 4–5.

37. F. Diggins, "The True History of the Discovery of Penicillin by Alexander Fleming," *Biomedical Scientist* (2003): 246–49.

38. K. Keyes, M. D. Lee, J. J. Maurer, M. E. Torrence, and R. E. Isaacson, "Antibiotics: Mode of Action, Mechanisms of Resistance, and Transfer," in *Microbial Food Safety in Animal Agriculture: Current Topics*, ed. M. E. Torrence and R. E. Isaacson (London, UK: Wiley, 2008), 45–56.

39. B. Ebbell, *The Papyrus Ebers: The Greatest Egyptian Medical Document* (Copenhagen, Denmark: Levin & Munksgaard, 1937).

40. W. Lednicki, *Henryk Sienkiewicz: A Retrospective Synthesis* (The Hague, Holland: Mouton, 1960).

41. S. Selwyn, "Pioneer Work on the 'Penicillin Phenomenon,' 1870–1876," *Journal of Antimicrobial Chemotherapy* 5 (3) (1979): 249–55.

42. Ibid.

43. S. Duckett, "Ernest Duchesne and the Concept of Fungal Antibiotic Therapy," *Lancet* 354 (9195) (1999): 2068–71.

44. E. P. Abraham, "Howard Walter Florey. Baron Florey of Adelaide and Marston. 1898–1968," *Biographical Memoirs of Fellows of the Royal Society* (1971): 255–302.

45. E. Chain, H. W. Florey, A. D. Gardner, N. G. Heatley, M. A. Jennings, J. Orr-Ewing, and A. G. Sanders, "Penicillin as a Chemotherapeutic Agent," *Lancet* 236 (6104) (1940): 226–28.

46. R. Evans, "Norman Heatley," *The Guardian*, 8 January 2004, http://www.theguardian.com/news/2004/jan/08/guardianobituaries.highereducation.

47. Ibid.

48. H. Harris, "Howard Florey and the Development of Penicillin," *Notes and Records of the Royal Society* 53 (2) (1999): 243–52.

49. D. C. Hodgkin and E. N. Maslen, "The X-Ray Analysis of the Structure of Cephalosporin C," *Biochemical Journal* 79 (2) (1961): 393.

50. J. P. Glusker, "Dorothy Crowfoot Hodgkin (1910–1994)," *Protein Science* 3 (12) (1994): 2465–69.

51. G. J. Fraenkel, "Penicillin at the Beginning," *Annals of Diagnostic Pathology* 2 (6) (1998): 422–24.

52. W. Shaw, "The Miracle of the Mould," *Nature* 428 (6985) (2004): 801–2.

53. A. N. Richards, "Production of Penicillin in the United States (1941–1946)," *Nature* 201 (1964): 441.

54. Ibid.

55. C. M. Grossman, "The First Use of Penicillin in the United States," *Annals of Internal Medicine* 149 (2) (2008): 135–6.

56. F. Guthrie, "XIII.—On Some Derivatives from the Olefines," *Quarterly Journal of the Chemical Society of London* 12 (1) (1860): 109–26.

57. A. Niemann, "Ueber eine neue organische base in den Cocablättern," *Archiv der Pharmazie* 153 (2) (1860): 129–55; A. Niemann, "Ueber die Einwirkung des Braunen Chlorschwefels auf Elaylgas," *Justus Liebigs Annalen der Chemie* 113 (3) (1860): 288–92.

58. M. Freemantle, *The Chemists' War: 1914–1918* (London, UK: Royal Society of Chemistry, 2014).

59. P. D. Anderson, "Emergency Management of Chemical Weapons Injuries," *Journal of Pharmacy Practice* 25 (1) (2012): 61–68.

60. E. B. Krumbhaar, "Role of the Blood and the Bone Marrow in Certain Forms of Gas Poisoning: I. Peripheral Blood Changes and their Significance," *JAMA* 72 (1) (1919): 39–41.

61. R. J. McElroy, "The Geneva Protocol of 1925," in *The Politics of Arms Control Treaty Ratification*, ed. Michael Krepon and Dan Caldwell (New York: St Martin's Press, 1992).

62. T. T. Marrs, R. L. Maynard, and F. Sidell, *Chemical Warfare Agents: Toxicology and Treatment* (Chichester, UK: John Wiley & Sons, 2007).

63. F. D. Roosevelt, "Letter to the Senate on Chemicals in Warfare, "*The American Presidency Project*, www.presidency.ucsb.edu/ws/?pid=15443.

64. S. Mukherjee, *The Emperor of All Maladies: A Biography of Cancer* (New York: Simon and Schuster, 2010).

65. R. K. Bassett, *Endless Frontier: Vannevar Bush, Engineer of the American Century* (Baltimore, Md.: Johns Hopkins University Press, 1999).

66. P. Christakis, "The Birth of Chemotherapy at Yale. Bicentennial Lecture Series: Surgery Grand Round," *Yale Journal of Biology and Medicine* 84 (2) (2011): 169.

67. L. S. Goodman, M. M. Wintrobe, W. Dameshek, M. J. Goodman, A. Gilman, and M. T. McLennan, "Landmark Article Sept. 21, 1946: Nitrogen Mustard Therapy. Use of Methyl-bis(beta-chloroethyl)amine Hydrochloride and Tris(beta-chloroethyl) amine Hydrochloride for Hodgkin's Disease, Lymphosarcoma, Leukemia, and Certain Allied and Miscellaneous Disorders," *JAMA* 251 (17) (1984): 2255–61.

68. J. Schiff, "Pioneers in Chemotherapy," *Yale Alumni Magazine*, 2011, http://www.yalealumnimagazine.com/articles/3173/pioneers-in-chemotherapy.

69. G. B. Infield, *Disaster at Bari* (London, UK: Hale, 1974).

70. R. Harris and J. Paxman, *A Higher Form of Killing: The Secret History of Chemical and Biological Warfare* (New York: Random House, 2007).

71. R. Price, "A Genealogy of the Chemical Weapons Taboo," *International Organization* 49 (01) (1995): 73–103.

72. Infield, *Disaster at Bari*.

73. J. Corum, *Wolfram von Richthofen* (Lawrence: University Press of Kansas, 2008).

74. Infield, *Disaster at Bari*.

75. Ibid.

76. Ibid.

77. Ibid.

78. G. B. Faguet, *The War on Cancer* (New York: Springer, 2005); R. Rettig, *Cancer Crusade: The Story of the National Cancer Act of 1971* (Princeton, N.J.: Princeton University Press, 1977).

79. J. C. Dacre and M. Goldman, "Toxicology and Pharmacology of the Chemical Warfare Agent Sulfur Mustard," *Pharmacological Reviews* 48 (2) (1996): 289–326; A. Gilman, "The Initial Clinical Trial of Nitrogen Mustard," *American Journal of Surgery* 105 (1963): 574–78.

80. Lilly Archives, "Colonel Eli Lilly," *Indiana Government*, 2008, http://www.in.gov/governorhistory/mitchdaniels/files/Press/lillybio.pdf.

81. Indiana Historical Society, "Eli Lilly & Co.," *Indiana Historical Society*, 1999, http://www.indianahistory.org/our-services/books-publications/hbr/eli-lilly.pdf.

82. J. H. Madison, "Manufacturing Pharmaceuticals: Eli Lilly and Company, 1876–1948," *Business and Economic History* (1989): 72–78.

83. M. E. Krahl, "George Henry Alexander Clowes 1877–1958," *Cancer Research* 19 (3) (1959): 334–36; G. H. A. Clowes, "George Henry Alexander Clowes, Ph.D., D. Sc., LLD (1877–1958): A Man of Science for All Seasons," *Journal of Surgical Oncology* 18 (2) (1981): 197–217.

84. S. Jolles, "Paul Langerhans," *Journal of Clinical Pathology* 55 (4) (2002): 243.

85. P. Langerhans, "Über die Nerven der Menschlichen Haut," *Virchows Archiv* 44 (2) (1868): 325–37.

86. M. Patlak, "New Weapons to Combat an Ancient Disease: Treating Diabetes," *FASEB Journal* 16 (14) (2002): 1853e–64e.

87. O. Minkowski, "Historical Development of the Theory of Pancreatic Diabetes by Oscar Minkowski," *Diabetes* 38 (1) (1989): 1–6.

88. L. J. Sanders, "From Thebes to Toronto and the 21st Century: An Incredible Journey," *Diabetes Spectrum* 15 (1) (2002): 56–60.

89. R. Luft, "Oskar Minkowski: Discovery of the Pancreatic Origin of Diabetes, 1889," *Diabetologia* 32 (7) (1989): 399–401.

90. M. Bliss, *Banting: A Biography* (Toronto, Ontario: University of Toronto Press, 1993).

91. E. L. Opie, "The Relation of Diabetes Mellitus to Lesions of the Pancreas. Hyaline Degeneration of the Islands of Langerhans," *Journal of Experimental Medicine* 5 (5) (1901): 527–40.

92. E. A. Schafer, "Address in Physiology," *British Medical Journal* 2 (1806) (1895): 341–48.

93. M. F. Chaplin, "Developments in Enzyme Technology," *Journal of Biological Education* 18 (3) (1984): 246–52.

94. M. Barron, *The Relation of the Islets of Langerhans to Diabetes with Special Reference to Cases of Pancreatic Lithiasis* (Chicago: Franklin H. Martin Memorial Foundation, 1920).

95. E. P. Cathcart, "John James Rickard Macleod, 1876–1935," *Obituary Notices of Fellows of the Royal Society*, 1935, 585–89.

96. M. Bliss, "The Discovery of Insulin: The Inside Story," *Publication: American Institute of the History of Pharmacy* 16 (1997): 93–99.

97. F. G. Banting, C. H. Best, J. B. Collip, and J. J. R. Macleod, "The Preparation of Pancreatic Extracts Containing Insulin," *Transactions of the Royal Society of Canada* 16 (1922): 27–29.

98. M. Bliss and R. Purkis, *The Discovery of Insulin* (Chicago: University of Chicago Press, 1982).

99. A. Hardy, "Recalling the Medical Officer of Health. Writings by Sidney Chave, London, King Edward's Hospital Fund, 1987," ed. M. Warren and H. Francis, *Medical History* 32 (04) (1988): 478–79.

100. Bliss, "Discovery of Insulin."

101. O. H. Warwick, "James Bertram Collip: 1892–1965," *Canadian Medical Association Journal* 93 (9) (1965): 425–26.

102. L. Rosenfeld, "Insulin: Discovery and Controversy," *Clinical Chemistry* 48 (12) (2002): 2270–88; J. B. Collip, "The Original Method as Used for the Isolation of Insulin in Semipure Form for the Treatment of the First Clinical Cases," *Journal of Biological Chemistry* 55 (1922): 40–41.

103. D. T. Karamitsos, "The Story of Insulin Discovery," *Diabetes Research and Clinical Practice* 93 (2011): S2–S8; B. E. Hazlett and J. R. Davidson, "Historical Perspective: The Discovery of Insulin," *Clinical Diabetes Mellitus: A Problem-Oriented Approach* (1986): 2–10.

104. Rosenfeld, "Insulin"; Karamitsos, "Story of Insulin Discovery."

105. Rosenfeld, "Insulin"; Karamitsos, "Story of Insulin Discovery."

106. Bliss, "Discovery of Insulin."

107. Ibid.

108. Ibid.

109. Rosenfeld, "Insulin."

110. G. Alberti, "Lessons from the History of Insulin," *Diabetes Voice* 46 (2001): 33–34.

111. J. H. Madison, "Manufacturing Pharmaceuticals."

Chapter Four

1. I. Dömök, "Dr. Gyula Takátsy (1914–1980)," *Orvosi Hetilap* 121 (37) (1980): 2273.

2. G. Takatsy, "The Use of Spiral Loops in Serological and Virological Micro-Methods," *Acta Microbiologica Academiae Scientiarum Hungaricae* 3 (1–2) (1955): 191.

3. H. Fenniri, *Combinatorial Chemistry* (Oxford, UK: Oxford University Press, 2000).

4. C. J. Cramer, *Essentials of Computational Chemistry: Theories and Models* (London: John Wiley & Sons, 2013).

5. M. S. Kinch and E. Patridge, "An Analysis of FDA-Approved Drugs for Infectious Disease: HIV/AIDS Drugs," *Drug Discovery Today* 19 (10) (2014): 1510–13.

6. N. R. Faria, A. Rambaut, M. A. Suchard, G. Baele, T. Bedford, M. J. Ward, A. J. Tatem, J. D. Sousa, N Arinaminpathy, and J. Pépin, "The Early Spread and Epidemic Ignition of HIV-1 in Human Populations," *Science* 346 (6205) (2014): 56–61.

7. Ibid.

8. V. Ellerman and O. Bang, "Experimental Leukemia in Chickens," *Zentr. Bakteriol. Parasiterik* Abt 1 (1908): 595–609.

9. P. Rous, "A Sarcoma of the Fowl Transmissible by an Agent Separable from the Tumor Cells," *Journal of Experimental Medicine* 13 (4) (1911): 397–411.

10. H. M. Temin and D. Baltimore, "RNA-Directed DNA Synthesis and RNA Tumor Viruses," *Advances in Virus Research* 17 (1972): 129–86.

11. H. M. Temin and S. Mizutani, "RNA-Dependent DNA Polymerase in Virions of Rous Sarcoma Virus," *Nature* 226 (27 June 1970): 1211–13.

12. E. Batschelet, E. Domingo, and C. Weissmann, "The Proportion of Revertant and Mutant Phage in a Growing Population, as a Function of Mutation and Growth Rate," *Gene* 1 (1) (1976): 27–32.

13. S. Alizon and C. Fraser, "Within-Host and Between-Host Evolutionary Rates across the HIV-1 Genome," *Retrovirology* 10 (1) (2013): 49.

14. T. Gojobori, E. N. Moriyama, Y. Ina, K. Ikeo, T. Miura, H. Tsujimoto, M. Hayami, and S. Yokoyama, "Evolutionary Origin of Human and Simian Immunodeficiency Viruses," *Proceedings of the National Academy of Sciences* 87 (11) (1990): 4108–11.

15. Ibid.

16. Faria et al., "Early Spread and Epidemic Ignition of HIV-1."

17. S. K. Gire, A. Goba, K. G. Andersen, R. S. G. Sealfon, D. J. Park, L. Kanneh, S. Jalloh, M. Momoh, M. Fullah, and G. Dudas, "Genomic Surveillance Elucidates Ebola Virus Origin and Transmission during the 2014 Outbreak," *Science* 345 (6202) (2014): 1369–72.

18. D. S. Wilkie and J. F. Carpenter, "Bushmeat Hunting in the Congo Basin: An Assessment of Impacts and Options for Mitigation," *Biodiversity and Conservation* 8 (7) (1999): 927–55.

19. Faria et al., "Early Spread and Epidemic Ignition of HIV-1."

20. D. van Reybrouck, *Congo: The Epic History of a People* (New York: Ecco Press, 2014).

21. A. E. Durrant, A. A. Jorgensen, and C. P. Lewis, *Steam in Africa* (Durrington, UK: Littlehampton Book Services Ltd., 1981).

22. World Health Organization, "50 Facts: Global Health Situation and Trends 1955–2025," *World Health Organization,* 1998, http://www.who.int/whr/1998/media _centre/50facts/en.

23. Faria et al., "Early Spread and Epidemic Ignition of HIV-1."

24. M. Worobey, M. Gemmel, D. E. Teuwen, T. Haselkorn, K. Kunstman, M. Bunce, J-J. Muyembe, J-M. M. Kabongo, R. M. Kalengayi, and E. Van Marck, "Direct Evidence of Extensive Diversity of HIV-1 in Kinshasa by 1960," *Nature* 455 (7213) (2008): 661–64.

25. A. W. Dorn and D. J. H. Bell, "Intelligence and Peacekeeping: The UN Operation in the Congo, 1960–64," *International Peacekeeping* 2 (1) (1995): 11–33.

26. R. O. Jackson, "The Failure of Categories: Haitians in the United Nations Organization in the Congo, 1960–64," *Journal of Haitian Studies* 20 (1) (2014): 34–64.

27. M. T. P. Gilbert, A. Rambaut, G. Wlasiuk, T. J. Spira, A. E. Pitchenik, and M. Worobey, "The Emergence of HIV/AIDS in the Americas and Beyond," *Proceedings of the National Academy of Sciences* 104 (47) (2007): 18566–70.

28. A. Bruś-Chojnicka, M. Bura, M. Chojnicki, W. Śmieińska, M. Pawlaczyk, and I. Mozer-Lisewska, "The History of the Human Immunodeficiency Virus Research," *Journal of Medical Science* 1 (2014): 62.

29. J. L. Ziegler, R. C. Miner, E. Rosenbaum, E. T. Lennette, E. Shillitoe, C. Casavant, W. L. Drew, L. Mintz, J. Gershow, and J. Greenspan, "Outbreak of Burkitt's-Like Lymphoma in Homosexual Men," *Lancet* 320 (8299) (1982): 631–33.

30. J. W. Curran and H. W. Jaffe, "AIDS: The Early Years and CDC's Response," *Morbidity and Mortality Weekly Report* Surveillance Summaries 60 (Suppl 4) (2011): 64–69.

31. H. W. Haverkos, D. P. Drotman, and M. Morgan, "Prevalence of Kaposi's Sarcoma among Patients with AIDS," *New England Journal of Medicine* 312 (23) (1985): 1518.

32. R. F. Garry, M. H. Witte, A. A. Gottlieb, M. Elvin-Lewis, M. S. Gottlieb, C. L. Witte, S. S. Alexander, W. R. Cole, and W. L. Drake., "Documentation of an AIDS Virus Infection in the United States in 1968," *JAMA* 260 (14) (1988): 2085–87.

33. R. Shilts, *And the Band Played On: People, Politics, and the AIDS Epidemic* (New York: St. Martins, 1987).

34. L. Montagnier, "A History of HIV Discovery," *Science* 298 (5599) (2002): 1727–28.

35. R. C. Gallo and L. Montagnier, "The Discovery of HIV as the Cause of AIDS," *New England Journal of Medicine* 349 (24) (2003): 2283–85.

36. R. Straus, *Medical Care for Seamen: The Origin of Public Medical Service in the United States* (New Haven, Conn.: Yale University Press, 1950).

37. J. Parascandola, "History, Commissioned Officers Association of the USPHS, Inc.," *Commissioned Officers Association of the USPHS*, 2010, http://www.coausphs.org/phhistory.cfm.

38. F. H. Garrison and A. R. Hasse, *John Shaw Billings: A Memoir* (New York: GP Putnam's Sons, 1915).

39. C. B. Chapman, *Order out of Chaos: John Shaw Billings and America's Coming of Age* (Boston: Science History Publications, 1994).

40. C. Luiggi, "Foundations: One-Man NIH, 1887," *Scientist* 25 (6) (2011): 80.

41. J. J. Kronenfeld and M. R. Kronenfeld, *Healthcare Reform in America: A Reference Handbook* (Santa Barbara, Calif.: ABC-Clio, 2004).

42. R. Rettig, *Cancer Crusade: The Story of the National Cancer Act of 1971* (Bloomington, Ind.: iUniverse, 2005).

43. T. A. Waldmann, "Disorders of the Expression of the Multichain IL-2 Receptor in HTLV-I-Associated Adult T-Cell Leukemia," *Haematology and Blood Transfusion* 32 (1989): 293–98.

44. R. C. Gallo, "Research and Discovery of the First Human Cancer Virus, HTLV-1," *Best Practice & Research: Clinical Haematology* 24 (4) (2011): 559–65.

45. S. Broder, "Interview with Dr. Samuel Broder," *In Their Own Words. NIH Researchers Recall the Early Years of AIDS, Office of History National Institutes of Health,* 1997, http://history.nih.gov/nihinownwords/docs/broder_01.html.

46. E. Langer, "Researcher Jerome P. Horwitz, 93, Created AZT, the First Approved Treatment for HIV/AIDS," *Washington Post,* 9 September 2012, http://www.washingtonpost.com/national/health-science/researcher-jerome-p-horwitz-93-created-azt-the-first-approved-treatment-for-hivaids/2012/09/19/0c08c38a-0280-11e2-9b24-ff730c7f6312_story.html.

47. J. P. Horwitz, "Design of Some Nucleic Acid Antimetabolites: Expectations and Reality," *Investigational New Drugs* 7 (1) (1989): 51–57.

48. The Henry J. Kaiser Family Foundation, "A History of HIV/AIDS in North America and the World," *HIV/AIDS Connection,* 2011, http://www.hivaidsconnection.ca/sites/default/files/images/RedScarf/A History of HIV AIDS in North America and the World.pdf.

49. Washington Post, "Researcher Jerome P. Horwitz, 93, Created the First Approved Treatment for HIV/AIDS," *Washington Post,* 19 September 2012, https://www.washingtonpost.com/national/health-science/researcher-jerome-p-horwitz-93-created-azt-the-first-approved-treatment-for-hivaids/2012/09/19/0c08c38a-0280-11e2-9b24-ff730c7f6312_story.html.

50. T. S. Lin, Z. Y. Shen, E. M. August, V. Brankovan, H. Yang, I. Ghazzouli, and W. H. Prusoff, "Synthesis and Antiviral Activity of Several 2, 5'-anhydro Analogs of 3'-azido-3'-deoxythymidine (AZT), 3'-azido-2', 3'-dideoxyuridine (AZU), 3'-azido-2', 3'-dideoxy-5-halouridines, and 3'-deoxythymidine against Human Immunodeficiency Virus (HIV-1) and Rauscher-Murine Leukemia Virus (R-MuLV)," *Journal of Medicinal Chemistry* 32 (8) (1989): 1891–95.

51. P. Vitello, "Jerome Horwitz, AZT Creator, Dies at 93," *New York Times,* 20 September 2012, http://www.nytimes.com/2012/09/21/health/jerome-p-horwitz-creator-of-azt-dies-at-93.html.

52. R. Yarchoan, K. J. Weinhold, H. K. Lyerly, E. Gelmann, R. M. Blum, G. M. Shearer, H. Mitsuya, J. M. Collins, C. E. Myers, and R. W. Klecker, "Administration of 3'-azido-3'-deoxythymidine, an Inhibitor of HTLV-III/LAV Replication, to Patients with AIDS or AIDS-Related Complex," *Lancet* 327 (8481) (1986): 575–80.

53. Langer, "Researcher Jerome P. Horwitz, 93, Created AZT."

54. Yarchoan et al., "Administration of 3'-azido-3'-deoxythymidine."

55. G. Kolata, "FDA Approves AZT," *Science* 235 (4796) (1987): 1570.

56. Langer, "Researcher Jerome P. Horwitz, 93, Created AZT."

57. Editor, "AZT's Inhuman Cost," *New York Times,* 28 August 1989, http://www.nytimes.com/1989/08/28/opinion/azt-s-inhuman-cost.html.

58. V. A. Harden, *AIDS at 30: A History* (Dulles, Va.: Potomac Books, Inc., 2012).

59. D. B. Gould, *Moving Politics: Emotion and ACT UP's Fight against AIDS* (Chicago: University of Chicago Press, 2009).

60. D. G. Katz, A. Dutcher, T. A. Toigo, R. Bates, F. Temple, and C. G. Cadden, "The AIDS Clinical Trials Information Service (ACTIS): A Decade of Providing Clinical Trials Information," *Public Health Reports* 117 (2) (2002): 123.

61. Kinch and Patridge, "An Analysis of FDA-Approved Drugs."

62. S. M. Hammer, K. E. Squires, M. D. Hughes, J. M. Grimes, L. M. Demeter, J. S. Currier, J. J. Eron, J. E. Feinberg, et al., "A Controlled Trial of Two Nucleoside Analogues plus Indinavir in Persons with Human Immunodeficiency Virus Infection and CD4 Cell Counts of 200 per Cubic Millimeter or Less," *New England Journal of Medicine* 337 (11) (1997): 725–33; R. M. Gulick, J. W. Mellors, D. Havlir, J. J. Eron, C. Gonzalez, D. McMahon, D. D. Richman, F. T. Valentine, et al., "Treatment with Indinavir, Zidovudine, and Lamivudine in Adults with Human Immunodeficiency Virus Infection and Prior Antiretroviral Therapy," *New England Journal of Medicine* 337 (11) (1997): 734–39.

63. R. D. Moore and R. E. Chaisson, "Natural History of HIV Infection in the Era of Combination Antiretroviral Therapy," *AIDs* 13 (14) (1999): 1933–42.

64. J. Henkel, "Attacking AIDS with a 'Cocktail' Therapy?," *FDA Consumer* 33 (4) (1998): 12–17; A. Williams and G. Friedland, "Adherence, Compliance, and HAART," *AIDs Clinical Care* 9 (7) (1997): 51.

65. B. Roca, "Adverse Drug Reactions to Antiretroviral Medication," *Frontiers in Bioscience* landmark edition 14 (2008): 1785–92.

66. Williams and Friedland, "Adherence, Compliance, and HAART."

67. G. F. Vanhove, J. M. Schapiro, M. A. Winters, T. C. Merigan, and T. F. Blaschke, "Patient Compliance and Drug Failure in Protease Inhibitor Monotherapy," *JAMA* 276 (24) (1996): 1955–56.

68. T. Horn, "Transmitted HIV Drug Resistance on the Rise in U.S.," *AIDSmeds*, 21 March 2012, http://www.aidsmeds.com/articles/hiv_drug_resistance_1667_22118 .shtml.

69. Kinch and Patridge, "An Analysis of FDA-Approved Drugs."

70. R. Pear, "Faster Approval of AIDS Drugs is Urged," *New York Times*, 16 August 1990, http://www.nytimes.com/1990/08/16/us/faster-approval-of-aids-drugs-is-urged.html.

71. D. J. Cantor, "Prescription Drug User Fee Act of 1992: Effects on Bringing New Drugs to Market," *University of Maryland*, 12 September 1997, http://www.law .umaryland.edu/marshall/crsreports/crsdocuments/97-838_E.pdf.

72. M. S. Kinch, A. Haynesworth, S. L. Kinch, and D. Hoyer, "An Overview of FDA-Approved New Molecular Entities: 1827–2013," *Drug Discovery Today* 19 (8) (2014): 1033–39.

73. J. A. DiMasi, C. P. Milne, and A. Tabarrok, "An FDA Report Card: Wide Variance in Performance Found among Agency's Drug Review Divisions," *Manhattan Institute*, 23 April 2014, http://www.manhattan-institute.org/html/fda-report-card -wide-variance-performance-found-among-agencys-drug-review-6015.html

74. A. C. Vlot, D. A. Dempsey, and D. F. Klessig, "Salicylic Acid, a Multifaceted Hormone to Combat Disease," *Annual Review of Phytopathology* 47 (2009): 177–206.

75. I. Raskin, "Role of Salicylic Acid in Plants," *Annual Review of Plant Biology* 43 (1) (1992): 439–63.

76. C. Gerhardt, "Recherches sur les Acides Organiques Anhydres," *Annals Chimie et de Physique* 37 (1853): 285–42.

77. Encyclopedia, "Gerhardt, Charles Frederic," *Encyclopedia.com*, 2008, http://www.encyclopedia.com/topic/Charles_Frederic_Gerhardt.aspx.

78. D. Jeffreys, *Aspirin: The Remarkable Story of a Wonder Drug* (London, UK: Bloomsbury Publishing USA, 2008).

79. Bayer Pharmaceuticals, "Biographies: Felix Hoffmann," *Bayer*, http://www.bayer.com/en/felix-hoffmann.aspx.

80. W. Sneader, "The Discovery of Aspirin: A Reappraisal," *British Medical Journal* 321 (7276) (2000): 1591.

81. E. Vaupel, "Arthur Eichengrün: Tribute to a Forgotten Chemist, Entrepreneur, and German Jew," *Angewandte Chemie* international edition 44 (22) (2005): 3344–55.

82. Sneader, "Discovery of Aspirin."

83. J. S. Goodwin and J. L. Ceuppens, "Effect of Nonsteroidal Antiinflammatory Drugs on Immune Function," *Seminars in Arthritis and Rheumatism* 13 (1 Suppl 1) (1983): 134–43.

84. C. Sakamoto, "Roles of COX-1 and COX-2 in Gastrointestinal Pathophysiology," *Journal of Gastroenterology* 33 (5) (1998): 618–24.

85. P. Needleman and P. C. Isakson, "The Discovery and Function of COX-2," *Journal of Rheumatology* Suppl 49 (1997): 6–8.

86. W. L. Xie, J. G. Chipman, D. L. Robertson, R. L. Erikson, and D. L. Simmons, "Expression of a Mitogen-Responsive Gene Encoding Prostaglandin Synthase Is Regulated by mRNA Splicing," *Proceedings of the National Academy of Sciences* 88 (7) (1991): 2692–96; D. A. Kujubu, B. S. Fletcher, B. C. Varnum, R. W. Lim, and H. R. Herschman, "TIS10, a Phorbol Ester Tumor Promoter-Inducible mRNA from Swiss 3T3 Cells, Encodes a Novel Prostaglandin Synthase/Cyclooxygenase Homologue," *Journal of Biological Chemistry* 266 (20) (1991): 12866–72.

87. C. Bombardier, L. Laine, A. Reicin, D. Shapiro, R. Burgos-Vargas, B. Davis, R. Day, M. B. Ferraz, C. J. Hawkey, M. C. Hochberg, T. K. Kvien, and T. J. Schnitzer, "Comparison of Upper Gastrointestinal Toxicity of Rofecoxib and Naproxen in Patients with Rheumatoid Arthritis. VIGOR Study Group," *New England Journal of Medicine* 343 (21) (2000): 1520–28, 1522, p. following 1528.

88. S. Prakash and V. Valentine, "Timeline: The Rise and Fall of Vioxx," *NPR*, 2007, http://www.npr.org/templates/story/story.php?storyId=5470430.

89. D. Mukherjee, S. E. Nissen, and E. J. Topol, "Risk of Cardiovascular Events Associated with Elective Cox-2 Inhibitors," *JAMA* 286 (8) (2001): 954–59.

90. History Commons, "Context of 'March 2000: VIGOR Study Ends; 20 Deaths among Patients Taking Vioxx,'" *History Commons*, www.historycommons.org/context.jsp?item=VIGOREnds.

91. J. Yates, "Important Prescribing Information," *U.S. Food and Drug Administration*, 2002, http://www.fda.gov/downloads/Safety/MedWatch/SafetyInformation/SafetyAlertsforHumanMedicalProducts/UCM171089.pdf.

92. "Merck reiterates flat 2006 earnings guidance," *CNN Money*, 6 December 2006, http://money.cnn.com/2006/12/06/news/companies/merck/index.htm.

93. A. Berenson, "Jury Finds Merck Liable in Vioxx Death and Awards $253 Million," *NBC News*, 19 August 2005, http://www.nbcnews.com/id/9006921/ns/health-arthritis/t/jury-finds-merck-liable-landmark-vioxx-case.

94. D. J. Graham, D. Campen, R. Hui, M. Spence, C. Cheetham, G. Levy, S. Shoor, and W. A. Ray, "Risk of Acute Myocardial Infarction and Sudden Cardiac Death in Patients Treated with Cyclo-Oxygenase 2 Selective and Non-Selective Non-Steroidal Anti-Inflammatory Drugs: Nested Case–Control Study," *Lancet* 365 (9458) (2005): 475–81.

95. P. Loftus and B. Kendall, "Merck to Pay $950 Million in Vioxx Settlement," *Wall Street Journal*, 23 November 2011, http://www.wsj.com/articles/SB10001424052970204531404577054472253737682.

96. C. Grassley, "Chairman Grassley Questions Merck about Communication with the FDA on Vioxx," *U.S. Senate*, 15 October 2004, http://www.finance.senate.gov/newsroom/chairman/release/?id=d83c8c4e-4773-444d-a72b-b6ccf6aace16.

97. "Drug Safety Oversight Board," *U.S. Food and Drug Administration*, 2014, http://www.fda.gov/AboutFDA/CentersOffices/OfficeofMedicalProductsandTobacco/CDER/ucm082129.htm.

98. "Food and Drug Administration Amendments Act (FDAAA) of 2007," *U.S. Food and Drug Administration*, 2007, http://www.fda.gov/RegulatoryInformation/Legislation/SignificantAmendmentstotheFDCAct/FoodandDrugAdministrationAmendmentsActof2007/default.htm.

99. Kinch et al., "Overview of FDA-Approved New Molecular Entities."

100. "Executive Summary: Strategic Plan for Regulatory Science," *U.S. Food and Drug Administration*, 2013, http://www.fda.gov/ScienceResearch/SpecialTopics/RegulatoryScience/ucm268095.htm.

101. J. Dupont, "FDA Overview: November 2011," *U.S. Food and Drug Administration*, 2011, http://www.fda.gov/downloads/Training/ClinicalInvestigatorTrainingCourse/UCM283299.pdf.

102. D. Brancaccio, "PBS Now: January 7, 2005," *PBS*, 7 January 2005, http://www.pbs.org/now/transcript/transcriptNOW101_full.html.

103. D. Graham, "Senate Finance Committee: Testimony of David J. Graham, MD, MPH, November 18, 2004," *U.S. Senate*, 18 November 2004, http://www.finance.senate.gov/imo/media/doc/111804dgtest.pdf.

104. Ibid.

105. M. Angell, "Taking Back the FDA," *Boston.com*, 26 February 2007, http://www.boston.com/yourlife/health/diseases/articles/2007/02/26/taking_back_the_fda.

106. UCSUSA, "Voices of Scientists at FDA: Protecting Public Health Depends on Independent Science," *Union of Concerned Scientists*, 2006, http://www.ucsusa.org/sites/default/files/legacy/assets/documents/scientific_integrity/fda-survey-brochure.pdf.

107. "FDA Science and Mission at Risk," *U.S. Food and Drug Administration*, 2007, http://www.fda.gov/ohrms/dockets/ac/07/briefing/2007-4329b_02_01_FDA Report on Science and Technology.pdf.

108. Pew Charitable Trusts, "The State of the FDA Workforce," *Washington Post*, 2012, http://www.washingtonpost.com/r/2010-2019/WashingtonPost/2012/11/19/National-Politics/Graphics/PEW_FDA_Public_19112012.pdf.

109. M. Hamburg, "50 Years after Thalidomide," *U.S. Food and Drug Administration*, 7 February 2012, http://blogs.fda.gov/fdavoice/index.php/2012/02/50-years-after-thalidomide-why-regulation-matters.

Chapter Five

1. D. J. De Solla Price and T. Page, "Science since Babylon," *American Journal of Physics* 29 (12) (1961): 863–64.

2. P. Martin and J. Melville, *The Chrysanthemum Throne: A History of the Emperors of Japan* (Honolulu: University of Hawaii Press, 1998); J. Hitchcock, *History of the Catholic Church* (San Francisco, Calif.: Ignatius Press, 2012).

3. *Guinness Book of World Records*, 2015, http://www.guinnessworldrecords.com/world-records/oldest-university; UNESCO, World Heritage Convention, 2015, http://whc.unesco.org/en/list/170.

4. E. Tamkin, "Keeping It in the Family," *Slate*, 20 October 2014, http://www.slate.com/articles/business/continuously_operating/2014/10/world_s_oldest_companies_why_are_so_many_of_them_in_japan.html.

5. D. Fallon, *The German University. A Heroic Ideal in Conflict with the Modern World* (Boulder: Colorado Associated University Press, 1980).

6. Humboldt-Universitat zu Berlin, "Short History," 2011, https://www.hu-berlin.de/ueberblick-en/history/huben_html/huben_html?set_language=en&cl=en.

7. J. K. Hill, *Universities in the U.S. National Innovation System*, 2006, http://www.ausicom.com/filelib/PDF/ResearchLibrary/US%20research%20data.pdf.

8. H. H. Thorn, *Johns Hopkins: A Silhouette* (Baltimore, Md.: Johns Hopkins University Press, 2009).

9. A. Flexner, *Daniel Coit Gilman: Creator of the American Type of University* (San Diego, Calif.: Harcourt, Brace and Company, 1946).

10. S. Flexner and J. T. Flexner, *William Henry Welch and the Heroic Age of American Medicine* (New York: Dover Publications, 1941).

11. A. W. Crosby, *America's Forgotten Pandemic: The Influenza of 1918* (New York: Cambridge University Press, 2003); J. M. Barry, *The Great Influenza: The Story of the Deadliest Pandemic in History* (London: Penguin, 2005).

12. C. Gerdil, "The Annual Production Cycle for Influenza Vaccine," *Vaccine* 21 (16) (2003): 1776–79.

13. A. Lode and F. Gruber, "Bakteriologische Studien über die Aetiologie einer Epidemischen Erkrankung der Hühner in Tirol," *Centralblatt für Bakteriologie, Parasitenkunde, und Infektionskrankheiten* 1 (1901): 593–604.

14. P. J. Crutzen and E. F. Stoermer, "The 'Anthropocene,'" *Global Change Newsletter* 41 (2000): 17–18.

15. W. W. Thompson, D. K. Shay, E. Weintraub, L. Brammer, N. Cox, L. J. Anderson, and K. Fukuda, "Mortality Associated with Influenza and Respiratory Syncytial Virus in the United States," *JAMA* 289 (2) (2003): 179–86; Centers for Disease Control and Prevention, "Estimates of Deaths Associated with Seasonal Influenza: United States, 1976–2007," *Morbidity and Mortality Weekly Report* 59 (33) (2010): 1057.

16. M. S. Pereira, "The Effects of Shifts and Drifts on the Epidemiology of Influenza in Man," *Philosophical Transactions of the Royal Society of London* B, Biological Sciences 288 (1029) (1980): 423–32.

17. "Selecting the Viruses in the Seasonal Influenza (Flu) Vaccine," *Centers for Disease Control*, www.cdc.gov/flu/professionals/vaccination/virusqa.htm.

18. B. Dennis, "Why Scientists Guessed Wrong on this Year's Flu Vaccine, and Why It Could Happen Again," *Washington Post*, 8 January 2015, http://www.washingtonpost.com/national/health-science/from-an-uncertain-process-of-guesses-and-science-each-years-flu-vaccines-emerge/2015/01/08/efc6e010-9744-11e4-aabd-d0b93ff613d5_story.html.

19. R. G. Webster, W. J. Bean, O. T. Gorman, T. M. Chambers, and Y. Kawaoka, "Evolution and Ecology of Influenza A Viruses," *Microbiological Reviews* 56 (1) (1992): 152–79.

20. M. A. Miller, C. Viboud, M. Balinska, and L. Simonsen, "The Signature Features of Influenza Pandemics: Implications for Policy," *New England Journal of Medicine* 360 (25) (2009): 2595–98.

21. M. Worobey, A. Rambaut, O. G. Pybus, and D. L. Robertson, "Questioning the Evidence for Genetic Recombination in the 1918 'Spanish flu' Virus," *Science* 296 (5566) (2002): 211–13.

22. A. T. Price-Smith, *Contagion and Chaos: Disease, Ecology, and National Security in the Era of Globalization* (Cambridge, Mass.: MIT Press, 2009; G. Kolata, *Flu: The Story of the Great Influenza Pandemic of 1918 and the Search for the Virus that Caused It* (New York: Simon and Schuster, 2001); J. K. Taubenberger, "The Origin and Virulence of the 1918 'Spanish' Influenza Virus," *Proceedings of the American Philosophical Society* 150 (1) (2006): 86.

23. Price-Smith, *Contagion and Chaos*.

24. M. O. Humphries, "Paths of Infection: The First World War and the Origins of the 1918 Influenza Pandemic," *War in History* 21 (1) (2014): 55–81.

25. J. M. Barry, "The Site of Origin of the 1918 Influenza Pandemic and Its Public Health Implications," *Journal of Translational Medicine* 2 (1) (2004): 3.

26. W. H. Frost, "The Epidemiology of Influenza," *JAMA* 73 (5) (1919): 313–18; Barry, *Great Influenza*.

27. W. H. Frost, "The Epidemiology of Influenza"; Barry, *Great Influenza*.

28. I. A. Clark, "The Advent of the Cytokine Storm," *Immunology and Cell Biology* 85 (4) (2007): 271–73.

29. J. R. Tisoncik, M. J. Korth, C. P. Simmons, J. Farrar, T. R. Martin, and M. G. Katze, "Into the Eye of the Cytokine Storm," *Microbiology and Molecular Biology Reviews* 76 (1) (2012): 16–32.

30. Barry, *Great Influenza*.

31. J. J. Keegan, "The Prevailing Pandemic of Influenza," *JAMA* 71 (13) (1918): 1051–55.

32. Barry, *Great Influenza*.

33. A. M. Stern, M. S. Cetron, and H. Markel, "The 1918–1919 Influenza Pandemic in the United States," *Public Health Reports* 125 (Supply 3) (2010): 6–8.

34. Barry, *Great Influenza*.

35. E. O. Jordan, *Epidemic Influenza: A Survey* (1927); K. D. Patterson and G. F. Pyle, "The Geography and Mortality of the 1918 Influenza Pandemic," *Bulletin of the History of Medicine* 65 (1) (1991): 4–21.

36. N. P. A. S. Johnson and J. Mueller, "Updating the Accounts: Global Mortality of the 1918–1920 'Spanish' Influenza Pandemic," *Bulletin of the History of Medicine* 76 (1) (2002): 105–15.

37. W. Rosen and B. Whitener, *Justinian's Flea: Plague, Empire, and the Birth of Europe* (New York: Viking, 2007).

38. Barry, *Great Influenza*.

39. D. M. Morens and A. S. Fauci, "The 1918 Influenza Pandemic: Insights for the 21st Century," *Journal of Infectious Diseases* 195 (7) (2007): 1018–28.

40. WHO, "Pandemic Influenza Vaccine Manufacturing Process and Timeline," *World Health Organization*, 6 August 2009, http://www.who.int/csr/disease/swineflu/notes/h1n1_vaccine_20090806/en.

41. R. Adler, *Victor Vaughan: A Biography of the Pioneering Bacteriologist, 1851–1929* (Jefferson, N.C.: McFarland & Company, 2015).

42. V. C. Vaughan, H. F. Vaughan, and G. T. Palmer, *Epidemiology and Public Health: Respiratory Infections* (Maryland Heights, Mo.: C. V. Mosby Company, 1922).

43. Adler, *Victor Vaughan*.

44. J. R. Paul, "Thomas Francis Jr.," *Biographical Memoirs. National Academy of Sciences* 44 (1974): 57–110; H. E. Griffin, "Thomas Francis Jr., M.D.: Epidemiologist to the Military," *Archives of Environmental Health* 21 (3) (1970): 252–55.

45. W. Smith, C. H. Andrewes, and P. P. Laidlaw, "A Virus Obtained from Influenza Patients," *Lancet* 222 (5732) (1933): 66–68.

46. R. Carver and J. Skehel, "Distemper and Influenza at Mill Hill," *Mill Hill Essays 2000*, 2000, http://www.historyofnimr.org.uk/mill-hill-essays/essays-yearly-volumes/2000-2/distemper-and-influenza-at-mill-hill/.

47. S. L. Plotkin and S. A. Plotkin, "A Short History of Vaccination," *Vaccines* 5 (2004): 1–16.

48. T. Francis Jr., J. E. Salk, H. E. Pearson, and P. N. Brown, "Protective Effect of Vaccination against Induced Influenza A," *Journal of Clinical Investigation* 24 (4) (1945): 536.

49. M. Walter, "Human Experiments: First, Do Harm," *Nature* 482 (7384) (2012): 148–52.

50. H. Markel, "April 12, 1955: Tommy Francis and the Salk Vaccine," *New England Journal of Medicine* 352 (14) (2005): 1408–10.

51. G. P. Zachary, *Endless Frontier: Vannevar Bush, Engineer of the American Century* (Cambridge, Mass.: MIT Press, 1999).

52. J. M. England, "Dr. Bush Writes a Report: "Science: The Endless Frontier," *Science* 191 (4222) (1976): 41–47.

53. C. Luiggi, "Foundations: One-Man NIH, 1887," *Scientist* 25 (6) (2011): 80.

54. J. T. Kalberer, "Impact of the National Cancer Act on Grant Support," *Cancer Research* 35 (3) (1975): 473–81.

55. J. A. Shannon, "The Advancement of Medical Research: A Twenty-Year View of the Role of the National Institutes of Health," *Academic Medicine* 42 (2) (1967): 97–108.

56. J. M. England, *A Patron for Pure Science: The National Science Foundation's Formative Years, 1945–57* (Washington, D.C.: National Science Foundation, 1983).

57. H. Thorp and B. Goldstein, *Engines of Innovation: The Entrepreneurial University in the Twenty-First Century* (Chapel Hill: University of North Carolina Press, 2013).

58. K. G. Manton, X-L. Gu, G. Lowrimore, A. Ullian, and H. D. Tolley, "NIH Funding Trajectories and Their Correlations with U.S. Health Dynamics from 1950 to 2004," *Proceedings of the National Academy of Sciences* 106 (27) (2009): 10981–86.

59. B. Alberts, M. W. Kirschner, S. Tilghman, and H. Varmus, "Rescuing U.S. Biomedical Research from Its Systemic Flaws," *Proceedings of the National Academy of Sciences* 111 (16) (2014): 5773–77.

60. "OER and You: An Introduction to Extramural Research at NIH," *National Institutes of Health*, 24 September 2015, http://grants.nih.gov/grants/intro2oer.htm; "NIH Budget," 15 May 2015, 2http://www.nih.gov/about/budget.htm.

61. J. Merl, "Stanford President, Beset by Controversies, Will Quit: Education: Donald Kennedy to Step Down Next Year. Research Scandal, Harassment Charge Plagued University," *Los Angeles Times*, 30 July 1991, http://articles.latimes.com/1991-07-30/news/mn-131_1_donald-kennedy.

62. D. Folkenflik, "What Happened to Stanford's Expense Scandal?," *Baltimore Sun*, 20 November 1994, http://articles.baltimoresun.com/1994-11-20/news/1994324051_1_stanford-incidental-expenses-auditors.

63. H. Ledford, *Keeping the Lights On* (London: Nature Publishing Group, 2014).

64. Ibid.

65. M. Mazzucato, *The Entrepreneurial State* (London: Anthem Press, 2013).

66. Department of Health and Human Services: Million Hearts, "About Heart Disease & Stroke," *Million Hearts*, 2014, http://millionhearts.hhs.gov/abouthds/cost-consequences.html, accessed on 1 April 2016.

67. NIH, "National Heart, Lung, and Blood Institute," *National Institutes of Health*, 2014, http://www.nih.gov/about/almanac/organization/NHLBI.htm.

68. G. Kersaint, "Antoine-François de Fourcroy (1755–1809), Sa Vie et son œuvre," *Revue 'Histoire de la Pharmacie* 55 (195) (1967): 589–96.

69. M. S. Bell, *Lavoisier in the Year One: The Birth of a New Science in an Age of Revolution (Great Discoveries)* (New York: W. W. Norton & Company, 2010).

70. É. Grimaux, *Lavoisier, 1743–1794, d'après sa Correspondance, Ses Manuscrits, Ses Papiers de Famille et D'autres Documents Inédits* (Paris, Fr.: Alcan, 1896).

71. G. Cuvier, "Éloge Historique de M. le Comte Fourcroy," *Memoires de l'Instit* 11 (1801): 61.

72. A. Endo, "A Historical Perspective on the Discovery of Statins," *Proceedings of the Japan Academy Series B, Physical and Biological Sciences* 86 (5) (2010): 484.

73. R. Virchow, *Thrombosis and Emboli (1846–1856)* (Sagamore Beach, Mass.: Science History Publications, 1998).

74. I. E. Konstantinov, N. Mejevoi, and N. M. Anchikov, "Nikolai N. Anichkov and His Theory of Atherosclerosis," *Texas Heart Institute Journal* 33 (4) (2006): 417.

75. T. Tucker, *The Great Starvation Experiment: The Heroic Men Who Starved So that Millions Could Live* (New York: Simon and Schuster, 2006).

76. M. Leslie, "The Vexing Legacy of Lewis Terman," 2000, *Stanford*, retrieved 2 February 2007, http://alumni.stanford.edu/get/page/magazine/article/?article_id =40678.

77. A. B. Keys, "Chloride and Water Secretion and Absorption by the Gills of the Eel," *Zeitschrift für Vergleichende Physiologie* 15 (2) (1931): 364–88.

78. E. R. Buskirk, "1: From Harvard to Minnesota: Keys to Our History," *Exercise and Sport Sciences Reviews* 20 (1) (1992): 1–26.

79. Tucker, *Great Starvation Experiment*.

80. K. Bloch, "The Biological Synthesis of Cholesterol," *Nobelprize.org*, 1965, http://www.nobelprize.org/nobel_prizes/medicine/laureates/1964/bloch-lecture.pdf.

81. F. H. Westheimer and W. Lipscomb, "Konrad Bloch. 21 January 1912–5 October 2000," *Biographical Memoirs of Fellows of the Royal Society* 48 (2002): 43–49.

82. L. Oro, A. G. Olsson, S. Rossner, and L. A. Carlson, "Cholestyramine, Clofibrate and Nicotinic Acid as Single or Combined Treatment of Type IIa and IIb Hyperlipoproteinaemia," *Postgraduate Medical Journal* 51 (8), Suppl (1975): 76–81.

83. Bloch, "Biological Synthesis of Cholesterol."

84. J. L. Goldstein, "Joseph L. Goldstein: Biography," *Nobelprize.org*, 1985, http://www.nobelprize.org/nobel_prizes/medicine/laureates/1985/goldstein -bio.html.

85. M. S. Brown and J. L. Goldstein, "A Receptor-Mediated Pathway for Cholesterol Homeostasis," *Science* 232 (4746) (1986): 34–47.

86. P. Landers, "How One Scientist Intrigued by Molds Found First Statin," *Wall Street Journal* (2006).

87. P. R. Vagelos and L. Galambos, *Medicine, Science, and Merck* (New York: Cambridge University Press, 2004).

88. A. W. Alberts, "Discovery, Biochemistry and Biology of Lovastatin," *American Journal of Cardiology* 62 (15) (1988): J10–J15.

89. Vagelos and Galambos, *Medicine, Science, and Merck*.

Chapter Six

1. F. Griffith, "The Serological Classification of Streptococcus Pyogenes," *Journal of Hygiene* 34 (04) (1934): 542–84.

2. O. T. Avery, C. M. Macleod, and M. McCarty, "Studies on the Chemical Nature of the Substance Inducing Transformation of Pneumococcal Types: Indication of Transformation by a Desoxyribonucleic Acid Fraction Isolated from Pneumococcus Type III," *Journal of Experimental Medicine* 79 (2) (1944): 137–58.

3. J. Lederberg and E. L. Tatum, "Gene Recombination in *Escherichia Coli*," *Nature* 158 (1946): 558.

4. J. Lederberg, "Cell Genetics and Hereditary Symbiosis," *Physiological Review* 32 (4) (1952): 403–30.

5. J. Lederberg and E. M. Lederberg, "Replica Plating and Indirect Selection of Bacterial Mutants," *Journal of Bacteriology* 63 (3) (1952): 399.

6. J. D. Watson and F. H. C. Crick, "Molecular Structure of Nucleic Acids," *Nature* 171 (4356) (1953): 737–38.

7. A. Kornberg, I. R. Lehman, M. J. Bessman, and E. S. Simms, "Enzymic Synthesis of Deoxyribonucleic Acid," *Biochimica et Biophysica Acta* 21 (1) (1956): 197–98.

8. P. Berg, "Dissections and Reconstructions of Genes and Chromosomes," Nobel Lecture, *Nobelprize.org*, 8 December 1980, http://www.nobelprize.org/nobel_prizes/chemistry/laureates/1980/berg-lecture.html.

9. C. S. Gillmor, *Fred Terman at Stanford: Building a Discipline, a University, and Silicon Valley* (Palo Alto, Calif.: Stanford University Press, 2004).

10. Ibid.

11. C. Lécuyer, *Making Silicon Valley: Innovation and the Growth of High Tech, 1930–1970* (Cambridge, Mass.: MIT Press, 2006).

12. J. R. Cole, *The Great American University: Its Rise to Preeminence, Its Indispensable National Role, Why It Must Be Protected* (New York: PublicAffairs, 2012); J. C. Williams, "Frederick E. Terman and the Rise of Silicon Valley," *International Journal of Technology Management* 16 (8) (1998): 751–60.

13. R. L. Baldwin, "Recollections of Arthur Kornberg (1918–2007) and the Beginning of the Stanford Biochemistry Department," *Protein Science* 17 (3) (2008): 385–88.

14. P. Berg and S. S. Hughes, *A Stanford Professor's Career in Biochemistry, Science Politics, and the Biotechnology Industry* (Berkeley, Calif.: Program in the History of the Biosciences and Biotechnology, Regional Oral History Office, Bancroft Library, University of California, 2000).

15. I. M. Verma, "Renato Dulbecco (1914–2012)," *Nature* 483 (7390) (2012): 408–08; D. Baltimore, "Renato Dulbecco (1914–2012)," *Science* 335 (6076) (2012): 1587–87.

16. Verma, "Renato Dulbecco"; Baltimore, "Renato Dulbecco."

17. Berg and Hughes, *Stanford Professor's Career.*

18. R. Yoshimori, D. Roulland-Dussoix, and H. W. Boyer, "R Factor-Controlled Restriction and Modification of Deoxyribonucleic Acid: Restriction Mutants," *Journal of Bacteriology* 112 (3) (1972): 1275–79.

19. T. Takano, T. Watanabe, and T. Fukasawa, "Specific Inactivation of Infectious λ DNA by Sonicates of Restrictive Bacteria with R Factors," *Biochemical and Biophysical Research Communications* 25 (2) (1966): 192–98.

20. J. Gitschier, "A Half-Century of Inspiration: An Interview with Hamilton Smith," *PLoS Genetics* 8 (1) (2012): e1002466.

21. S. N. Cohen, "DNA Cloning: A Personal View after 40 Years," *Proceedings of the National Academy of Sciences* 110 (39) (2013): 15521–29.

22. S. N. Cohen and A. C. Y. Chang, "Recircularization and Autonomous Replication of a Sheared R-Factor DNA Segment in *Escherichia Coli* Transformants," *Proceedings of the National Academy of Sciences* 70 (5) (1973): 1293–97.

23. A. C. Clarke, *2001: A Space Odyssey* (New York: RosettaBooks, 2012).

24. A. Toffler, *Future Shock* (New York: Amereon Ltd., 1970).

25. M. Crichton, *The Andromeda Strain* (New York: Random House, 1995).

26. J. Lederberg, "Exobiology: Approaches to Life Beyond the Earth," *Science* 132 (3424) (1960): 393–400.

27. W. J. Broad, "Joshua Lederberg, 82, a Nobel Winner, Dies," *New York Times*, 5 February 2008, B6, http://www.nytimes.com/2008/02/05/us/05lederberg.html?_r=0.

28. M. Crichton, *Jurassic Park: A Novel* (New York: Ballantine Books, 2012).

29. P. Berg and M. F. Singer, "The Recombinant DNA Controversy: Twenty Years Later," *Proceedings of the National Academy of Sciences of the United States of America* 92 (20) (1995): 9011.

30. P. Berg and J. E. Mertz, "Personal Reflections on the Origins and Emergence of Recombinant DNA Technology," *Genetics* 184 (1) (2010): 9–17.

31. R. Pollack, *Signs of Life* (New York: Penguin, 1995).

32. Ibid.

33. Berg and Singer, "Recombinant DNA Controversy."

34. P. Berg, D. Baltimore, S. Brenner, R. O. Roblin, and M. F. Singer, "Summary Statement of the Asilomar Conference on Recombinant DNA Molecules," *Proceedings of the National Academy of Sciences* 72 (6) (1975): 1981.

35. S. N. Cohen, A .C. Y. Chang, H. W. Boyer, and R. B. Helling, "Construction of Biologically Functional Bacterial Plasmids in Vitro," *Proceedings of the National Academy of Sciences* 70 (11) (1973): 3240–44.

36. Berg and Singer, "Recombinant DNA Controversy."

37. G. R. Evans, *Bernard of Clairvaux: Selected Works* (Mahwah, N.J.: Paulist Press, 1987).

38. Berg and Mertz, "Personal Reflections."

39. S. N. Cohen and H. W. Boyer, *Process for Producing Biologically Functional Molecular Chimeras* (U.S. Patent 4,237,224, 1980).

40. M. P. Feldman, A. Colaianni, L. Kang, A. Krattiger, R. T. Mahoney, L. Nelsen, J. A. Thomson, A. B. Bennett, K. Satyanarayana, and G. D. Graff, "Lessons from the Commercialization of the Cohen–Boyer Patents: The Stanford University Licensing Program," *Intellectual Property Management in Health and Agricultural Innovation: A Handbook of Best Practices* 1 and 2 (2007): 1797–1807.

41. R. A. Swanson, "Entrepreneurship and Innovation: Biotechnology, The Positive Sum Strategy," chap. 26 in *Harnessing Technology for Economic Growth* (Washington, D.C.: National Academy Press, 1986), 429–35.

42. K. Itakura, T. Hirose, R. Crea, A. D. Riggs, H. L. Heyneker, F. Bolivar, and H. W. Boyer, "Expression in *Escherichia Coli* of a Chemically Synthesized Gene for the Hormone Somatostatin," *Science* 198 (4321) (1977): 1056–63.

43. I. S. Johnson, "Human Insulin from Recombinant DNA Technology," *Science* 219 (4585) (1983): 632–37.

44. S. S. Hughes, *Genentech: The Beginnings of Biotech* (Chicago: University of Chicago Press, 2011).

45. Ibid.

46. G. B. Kolata, "The 1980 Nobel Prize in Chemistry," *Science* 210 (4472) (1980): 887–89.

47. K. Strebhardt and A Ullrich, "Paul Ehrlich's Magic Bullet Concept: 100 Years of Progress," *Nature Reviews Cancer* 8 (6) (2008): 473–80.

48. M. S. Neuberger and B. A. Askonas, "César Milstein CH. 8 October 1927– 24 March 2002," *Biographical Memoirs of Fellows of the Royal Society* 51 (2005): 267–89.

49. H. Kobayashi, M. Potter, and T. B. Dunn, "Bone Lesions Produced by Transplanted Plasma-Cell Tumors in BALB/c Mice," *Journal of the National Cancer Institute* 28 (3) (1962): 649–77.

50. F. Fenner, "Frank Macfarlane Burnet 1899–1985," *Historical Records of Australian Science* 7 (1) (1987): 39–77.

51. F. Macfarlane Burnet, *The Clonal Selection Theory of Acquired Immunity* (New York: Cambridge University Press, 1959).

52. A. R. Williamson, "Extent and Control of Antibody Diversity," *Biochemical Journal* 130 (2) (1972): 325.

53. F. Melchers, "Georges Köhler (1946–95)," *Nature* 374 (1995): 498.

54. G. Köhler and C. Milstein, "Continuous Cultures of Fused Cells Secreting Antibody of Predefined Specificity," *Nature* 256 (5517) (1975): 495–97.

55. Ibid.

56. Q. F. Ahkong, D. Fisher, W. Tampion, and J. A. Lucy, "Mechanisms of Cell Fusion," *Nature* 253 (1975): 194–95.

57. Köhler and Milstein, "Continuous Cultures of Fused Cells."

58. Ibid.

59. S. De Chadarevian, "The Making of an Entrepreneurial Science: Biotechnology in Britain, 1975–1995," *Isis* 102 (4) (2011): 601–33.

60. E. M. Tansey, D. A. Christie, L. A. Reynolds, P. P. Catterall, and S. V. Willhoft, *Wellcome Witnesses to Twentieth Century Medicine: Volume 1* (London: Wellcome Trust, 1997).

61. K. J. Jones, M. E. Whitham, P. S. Handler, A. Krattiger, R. T. Mahoney, L. Nelsen, J. A. Thomson, A. B. Bennett, K. Satyanarayana, and G. D. Graff, "Problems with Royalty Rates, Royalty Stacking, and Royalty Packing Issues," *Intellectual Property Management in Health and Agricultural Innovation: A Handbook of Best Practices* 1 and 2 (2007): 1121–26.

62. F. E. Russell, "Muscle Relaxants in Black Widow Spider (*Lactrodectus mactans*) Poisoning," *American Journal of the Medical Sciences* 243 (2) (1962): 81–83.

63. P. A. Todd and R. N. Brogden, "Muromonab CD3," *Drugs* 37 (6) (1989): 871–99.

64. S. L. Morrison, "Transfectomas Provide Novel Chimeric Antibodies," *Science* 229 (4719) (1985): 1202–7.

65. G. M. Edelman, "Antibody Structure and Molecular Immunology," *Science* 180 (88) (1973): 830–40.

66. C. Queen, W. P. Schneider, H. E. Selick, P. W. Payne, N. F. Landolfi, J. F. Duncan, N. M. Avdalovic, M. Levitt, R. P. Junghans, and T. A. Waldmann, "A Humanized Antibody that Binds to the Interleukin 2 Receptor," *Proceedings of the National Academy of Sciences* 86 (24) (1989): 10029–33.

67. T. Nicolai, "Risk of Asthma in Children with a History of Croup," *Acta Paediatrica* 85 (11) (1996): 1295–99.

68. J. A. Morris, R. E. Blount, and R. E. Savage, "Recovery of Cytopathogenic Agent from Chimpanzees with Goryza," *Experimental Biology and Medicine* 92 (3) (1956): 544–49.

69. R. M. Chanock, "Association of a New Type of Cytopathogenic Myxovirus with Infantile Croup," *Journal of Experimental Medicine* 104 (4) (1956): 555–76.

70. L. K. Altman, "Dr. Robert M. Chanock, Prominent Virologist, Dies at 86," *New York Times*, 5 August 2010, www.nytimes.com/2010/08/05/health/05chanock.html ?_r=0, 2010.

71. E. Brown, "Robert M. Chanock, Virologist who Studied Children's Diseases, dies at 86," *Washington Post*, 3 August 2010, http://www.washingtonpost.com /wp-dyn/content/article/2010/08/03/AR2010080306484.html; R. M. Chanock and A. B. Sabin, "The Hemagglutinin of St. Louis Encephalitis Virus I. Recovery of Stable Hemagglutinin from the Brains of Infected Mice," *Journal of Immunology* 70 (3) (1953): 271–85; R. M. Chanock and A. B. Sabin, "The Hemagglutinin of Western Equine Encephalitis Virus: Recovery, Properties, and Use for Diagnosis," *Journal of Immunology* 73 (5) (1954): 337–51; C. B. Smith, W. T. Friedewald, and R. M. Chanock, "Shedding of Mycoplasma Pneumoniae after Tetracycline and Erythromycin Therapy," *New England Journal of Medicine* 276 (21) (1967): 1172–75; R. G. Wyatt, H. B. Greenberg, D. W. Dalgard, W. P. Allen, D. L. Sly, T. S. Thornhill, R. M. Chanock, and A. Z. Kapikian, "Experimental Infection of Chimpanzees with the Norwalk Agent of Epidemic Viral Gastroenteritis," *Journal of Medical Virology* 2 (2) (1978): 89–96.

72. K. H. Wilan, "Biotech's Billion Dollar Officer," *Nature*, 2005, http://www .nature.com/bioent/view/022005/full/bioent846.html.

73. K. J. Shay, "MedImmune CEO Speaks Finance and Science," *Washington Post*, 27 September 2004, http://www.washingtonpost.com/wp-dyn/articles/A52787 -2004Sep26.html.

74. J. L. Fox, "FDA Panel Nixes MedImmune's Respigam," *Nature Biotechnology* 12 (1) (1994): 14–15.

75. INN Prop, "MEDI-493 Synagis™," *Drugs of the Future* 23 (9) (1998): 970–76.

76. GAO, "Agencies' Rights to Federally Sponsored Biomedical Inventions," 2002, http://www.gao.gov/products/GAO-03-536.

77. D. Rovell, *First in Thirst: How Gatorade Turned the Science of Sweat into a Cultural Phenomenon* (New York: AMACOM, 2006).

78. J. Kays and A. Phillips-Han, "Gatorade: The Idea that Launched an Industry," *Explore: Research at the University of Florida* 8 (1) (2003).

79. Rovell, *First in Thirst.*

80. A. J. Stevens, "The Enactment of Bayh-Dole," *Journal of Technology Transfer* 29 (1) (2004): 93–99.

81. A. J. Stevens, J. J. Jensen, K. Wyller, P. C. Kilgore, S. Chatterjee, and M. L. Rohrbaugh, "The Role of Public-Sector Research in the Discovery of Drugs and Vaccines," *New England Journal of Medicine* 364 (6) (2011): 535–41.

82. H. Markel, "Patents, Profits, and the American People—The Bayh-Dole Act of 1980," *New England Journal of Medicine* 369 (9) (2013): 794–96.

83. B. Bayh, "Senator Birch Bayh on the Bayh-Dole Act, 2010," *Indiana University Bloomington,* 2010, https://libraries.iub.edu/senator-birch-bayh-bayh-dole-act-2010.

84. Ibid.

85. M. Eberle, "March-In Rights Under the Bayh-Dole Act: Public Access to Federally Funded Research," *Marquette Intellectual Property Law Review* 3 (1999): 155.

86. K. W. McCabe, "Implications of the 'CellPro' Determination on Inventions Made with Federal Assistance: Will the Government Ever Exercise Its March-In Right?," *Public Contract Law Journal,* 1998, 645–68.

87. Bayh, "Senator Birch Bayh on the Bayh-Dole Act"; J. Allen, "The Enactment of Bayh-Dole, An Inside Perspective," *IP Watchdog,* 28 November 2010, http://www.ipwatchdog.com/2010/11/28/the-enactment-of-bayh-dole-an-inside-perspective/id=13442.

88. M. S. Kinch, "The Rise (and Decline?) of Biotechnology," *Drug Discovery Today* 19 (11) (2014): 1686–90.

89. M. S. Kinch and J. Raffo, "Sources of Innovation: An Assessment of Intellectual Property," *Drug Discovery Today* 20 (5) (2015): 500–504.

Chapter Seven

1. International Federation of Pharmaceutical Manufacturers & Associations, "The Pharmaceutical Industry and Global Health: Facts and Figures 2012," *Irish Pharmaceutical Healthcare Association,* 2 February 2013, http://www.ipha.ie/alist/healthcare-facts-and-figures.aspx?article=dc6d83aa-9f1a-4f01-aaa1-6b4429c189b0.

2. A. W. Jones, "Early Drug Discovery and the Rise of Pharmaceutical Chemistry," *Drug Testing and Analysis* 3 (6) (2011): 337–44; E. Patridge, P. Gareiss, M. S. Kinch, and D. Hoyer, "An Analysis of FDA-Approved Drugs: Natural Products and their Derivatives," *Drug Discovery Today* 21 (2) (2015): 204–7.

3. Jones, "Early Drug Discovery"; Patridge et al., "An Analysis of FDA-Approved Drugs."

4. V. T. DeVita and E. Chu, "A History of Cancer Chemotherapy," *Cancer Research* 68 (21) (2008): 8643–53.

5. Ibid.; J. L. Cruikshank and A. W. Schultz, *The Man Who Sold America: The Amazing (but True!) Story of Albert D. Lasker and the Creation of the Advertising Century* (Cambridge, Mass.: Harvard Business Press, 2010); W. B. Morrison, "Cancer Chemotherapy: An Annotated History," *Journal of Veterinary Internal Medicine* 24 (6) (2010): 1249–62.

6. Cruikshank and Schultz, *Man Who Sold America*.

7. National Library of Medicine, "The Mary Lasker Papers," *National Library of Medicine*, http://profiles.nlm.nih.gov/ps/retrieve/Narrative/TL/p-nid/199, accessed on 1 April 2016.

8. Lasker Foundation, "The Lasker Legacy," *The Lasker Foundation*, http://www.laskerfoundation.org/about/legacy.htm, accessed on 1 April 2016; C. G. Zubrod, S. A. Schepartz, and S. K. Carter, "Historical Background of the National Cancer Institute's Drug Development Thrust," *National Cancer Institute Monograph* (45) (1977): 7–11.

9. J. Goodman and V. Walsh, *The Story of Taxol: Nature and Politics in the Pursuit of an Anti-Cancer Drug* (New York: Cambridge University Press, 2001).

10. M. C. Wani, H. L. Taylor, M. E. Wall, P. Coggon, and A. T. McPhail, "Plant Antitumor Agents. VI. Isolation and Structure of Taxol, a Novel Antileukemic and Antitumor Agent from *Taxus Brevifolia*," *Journal of the American Chemical Society* 93 (9) (1971): 2325–27.

11. Goodman and Walsh, *Story of Taxol*; J. D. Adams, K. P. Flora, B. R. Goldspiel, J. W. Wilson, S. G. Arbuck, and R. Finley, "Taxol: A History of Pharmaceutical Development and Current Pharmaceutical Concerns," *Journal of the National Cancer Institute, Monographs* (15) (1992): 141–47.

12. V. Walsh and J. Goodman, "Cancer Chemotherapy, Biodiversity, Public and Private Property: The Case of the Anti-Cancer Drug Taxol," *Social Science & Medicine* 49 (9) (1999): 1215–25; T. A. Hemphill, "Economic Considerations in Cooperative Research and Development Agreements (CRADA): The Case of Taxol, NIH, and Technology Transfer," *Technology in Society* 28 (3) (2006): 321–31.

13. Goodman and Walsh, *Story of Taxol*; Adams et al., "Taxol."

14. Adams et al., "Taxol."

15. Ibid.

16. GAO, "NIH–Private Sector Partnership in the Development of Taxol," *Government Accountability Office*, 2003, http://www.gao.gov/assets/240/238441.pdf, accessed on 1 April 2016.

17. K. C. Nicolau, Z. Yang, J. J. Liu, H. Ueno, P. G. Nantermet, R. K. Guy, C. F. Claiborne, et al., "Total Synthesis of Taxol," *Nature* 367 (17 February 1994): 630–34.

18. J. Guerra-Bubb, R. Croteau, and R. M. Williams, "The Early Stages of Taxol Biosynthesis: An Interim Report on the Synthesis and Identification of Early Pathway Metabolites," *Natural Product Reports* 29 (6) (2012): 683–96.

19. H. Tabata, "Paclitaxel Production by Plant-Cell-Culture Technology," *Biomanufacturing* 87 (2004): 1–23.

20. Goodman and Walsh, *Story of Taxol.*

21. GAO, "NIH–Private Sector Partnership."

22. G. J. Mossinghoff, "Overview of the Hatch-Waxman Act and Its Impact on the Drug Development Process," *Food and Drug Law Journal* 54 (2) (1999): 187–94.

23. W. W. Goodrich, "FDA's Regulation under the Kefauver-Harris Drug Amendments of 1962," *Food Drug Cosmetic Law Journal* 18 (1963): 561.

24. Mossinghoff, "Overview of the Hatch-Waxman Act."

25. Ibid.

26. Goodrich, "FDA's Regulation under Kefauver-Harris."

27. Mossinghoff, "Overview of the Hatch-Waxman Act."

28. M. S. Kinch, A. Haynesworth, S. L. Kinch, and D. Hoyer, "An Overview of FDA-Approved New Molecular Entities: 1827–2013," *Drug Discovery Today* 19 (8) (2014): 1033–39.

29. G. J. Mossinghoff, "Research-Based Pharmaceutical Companies: The Need for Improved Patent Protection Worldwide," *Journal of Law and Technology* 2 (1987): 307.

30. S. D. Danzis, "The Hatch-Waxman Act: History, Structure, and Legacy," *Antitrust Law Journal* (2003): 585–608; Mossinghoff, "Overview of the Hatch-Waxman Act."

31. Mossinghoff, "Overview of the Hatch-Waxman Act."

32. J. J. Wheaton, "Generic Competition and Pharmaceutical Innovation: The Drug Price Competition and Patent Term Restoration Act of 1984," *Catholic University Law Review* 35 (1985): 433; H. Grabowski and J. Vernon, "Longer Patents for Lower Imitation Barriers: The 1984 Drug Act," *American Economic Review*, 1986), 195–98.

33. Mossinghoff, "Overview of the Hatch-Waxman Act."

34. Ibid.

35. D. Reiffen and M. R. Ward, "Generic Drug Industry Dynamics," *Review of Economics and Statistics* 87 (1) (2005): 37–49.

36. A. Rescigno, "Bioequivalence," *Pharmaceutical Research* 9 (7) (1992): 925–28.

37. A. W. Boddy, F. C. Snikeris, R. O. Kringle, G. C. G. Wei, J. A. Oppermann, and K. K. Midha, "An Approach for Widening the Bioequivalence Acceptance Limits in the Case of Highly Variable Drugs," *Pharmaceutical Research* 12 (12) (1995): 1865–68.

38. R. Schall and R. L. Williams, Food, and Drug Administration Individual Bioequivalence Working Group, "Toward a Practical Strategy for Assessing Individual Bioequivalence," *Journal of Pharmacokinetics and Biopharmaceutics* 24 (1) (1996): 133–49; D. C. Heaney and J. W. Sander, "Antiepileptic Drugs: Generic versus Branded Treatments," *Lancet Neurology* 6 (5) (2007): 465–68.

39. M. Webster, "Fact or Fiction: Generic Drugs are Bad for You," *Scientific American*, 12 November 2009, http://www.scientificamerican.com/article/are-generic-drugs-bad-for-you.

40. Reiffen and Ward, "Generic Drug Industry Dynamics."

41. H. G. Grabowski and J. M. Vernon, "Brand Loyalty, Entry, and Price Competition in Pharmaceuticals after the 1984 Drug Act," *Journal of Law and Economics* (1992): 331–50.

42. M. Mitka, "Pay for Delay of Generics," *JAMA* 303 (10) (2010): 929–929.

43. Mossinghoff, "Overview of the Hatch-Waxman Act."

44. A. S. Kesselheim, L. Murtagh, and M. M. Mello, "'Pay for Delay' Settlements of Disputes over Pharmaceutical Patents," *New England Journal of Medicine* 365 (15) (2011): 1439–45.

45. R. H. Ziedonis, "Don't Fence Me In: Fragmented Markets for Technology and the Patent Acquisition Strategies of Firms," *Management Science* 50 (6) (2004): 804–20; D. L. Burk and M. A. Lemley, "Fence Posts or Sign Posts? Rethinking Patent Claim Construction," *University of Pennsylvania Law Review* (2009): 1743–99.

46. Sanofi-Aventis Product Lines, "Drug Patent Expirations and the 'Patent Cliff,'" *U.S. Pharmacist* 37 (6) (2012): 12–20; A. Sheppard, "Generic Medicines: Essential Contributors to the Long Term Health of Society," *Sandoz*, 1 April 2010, http://www.sandoz.com/cs/www.sandoz.com-v4/assets/media/shared/documents/press_releases/100401_Generic_Medicines_GA.pdf.

47. F. M. Ilgenfritz, "Peptic Ulcer Disease Affects Nearly 500,000 Yearly," *Ravalli Republic*, 25 January 2011, http://ravallirepublic.com/lifestyles/health-med-fit/article_172fc38e-28f8-11e0-a107-001cc4c03286.html; T. R. Koch and J. B. Kirsner, "Chronic Gastrointestinal Symptoms of Thomas 'Stonewall' Jackson following Mexican–American War Exposure: A Medical Hypothesis," *Military Medicine* 172 (1) (2007): 6–8.

48. A. Lugli, I. Zlobec, G. Singer, A. K. Lugli, L. M. Terracciano, and R. M. Genta. "Napoleon Bonaparte's Gastric Cancer: A Clinicopathologic Approach to Staging, Pathogenesis, and Etiology," *Nature Clinical Practice Gastroenterology & Hepatology* 4 (1) (2007): 52–57.

49. Ibid.

50. M. Beck, "Solving Darwin's Medical Mystery," *Wall Street Journal*, 10 May 2011, http://www.wsj.com/articles/SB10001424052748704681904576313043723708936.

51. K. Ramakrishnan and R. C. Salinas, "Peptic Ulcer Disease," *American Family Physician* 76 (7) (2007): 1005–12.

52. H. H. Dale and P. P. Laidlaw, "Histamine Shock," *Journal of Physiology* 52 (5) (1919): 355–90.

53. W. I. Card and I. N. Marks, "The Relationship between the Acid Output of the Stomach Following 'Maximal' Histamine Stimulation and the Parietal Cell Mass," *Clinical Science* 19 (1960): 147.

54. S. J. Hill, "Distribution, Properties, and Functional Characteristics of Three Classes of Histamine Receptor," *Pharmacological Reviews* 42 (1) (1990): 45–83.

55. L. K. Altman, "Dr. James Black, Pharmacologist Who Discovered Beta Blockers, Dies at 85," *New York Times*, 23 March 2010, www.nytimes.com/2010/03/23/health/23black.html?_r=0.

56. M. P. Stapleton, "Sir James Black and Propranolol: The Role of the Basic Sciences in the History of Cardiovascular Pharmacology," *Texas Heart Institute Journal* 24 (4) (1997): 336.

57. V. Quirke, "Putting Theory into Practice: James Black, Receptor Theory, and the Development of the Beta-Blockers at ICI, 1958–1978," *Medical History* 50 (01) (2006): 69–92.

58. J. W. Black, W. A. M. Duncan, C. Ji Durant, C. R. Ganellin, and E. M. Parsons, "Definition and Antagonism of Histamine H2-Receptors," *Nature* 236 (1972): 385–90.

59. R. W. Brimblecombe, W. A. Duncan, G. J. Durant, C. R. Ganellin, M. E. Parsons, and J. W. Black, "Proceedings: The Pharmacology of Cimetidine, a New Histamine H2-Receptor Antagonist," *British Journal of Pharmacology* 53 (3) (1975): 435.

60. V. B. Clayman, "Evaluation of Cimetidine (Tagamet): An Antagonist of Hydrochloric Acid Secretion," *JAMA* 238 (12) (1977): 1289–90.

61. M. Agrawal and N. Thakkar, "Surviving Patent Expiration: Strategies for Marketing Pharmaceutical Products," *Journal of Product & Brand Management* 6 (5) (1997): 305–14.

62. D. M. McCarthy, "Ranitidine or Cimetidine," *Annals of Internal Medicine* 99 (4) (1983): 551–53.

63. J. Whitney, *Pharmaceutical Sales 101: Me-Too Drugs* (Toronto, Ontario: Guernica Editions, 2008).

64. S. Pincock, "Nobel Prize Winners Robin Warren and Barry Marshall," *Lancet* 366 (9495) (2005): 1429.

65. B. J. Marshall, J. R. Warren, E. D. Blincow, M. Phillips, C. S. Goodwin, R. Murray, S. J. Blackbourn, T. E. Waters, and C. R. Sanderson, "Prospective Double-Blind Trial of Duodenal Ulcer Relapse after Eradication of *Campylobacter Pylori*," *Lancet* 332 (8626) (1988): 1437–42.

66. B. J. Marshall and J. R. Warren, "Barry J Marshall—Biographical," *Nobelprize.org*, 2005, http://www.nobelprize.org/nobel_prizes/medicine/laureates/2005/marshall -bio.html.

67. B. J. Marshall, "The Pathogenesis of Non-Ulcer Dyspepsia," *Medical Journal of Australia* 143 (7) (1985): 319.

68. J. A. DiMasi and C. Paquette, "The Economics of Follow-On Drug Research and Development: Trends in Entry Rates and the Timing of Development," *PharmacoEconomics* 22 (2 Suppl 2) (2004): 1–14.

69. J. J. Gagne and N. K. Choudhry, "How Many 'Me-Too' Drugs is too Many?," *JAMA* 305 (7) (2011): 711–12.

70. J. A. DiMasi and L. B. Faden, "Competitiveness in Follow-On Drug R&D: A Race or Imitation?," *Nature Reviews Drug Discovery* 10 (1) (2011): 23–27; R. Frothingham, "'Me-Too' Products—Friend or Foe?," *New England Journal of Medicine* 350 (20) (2004): 2100–2101.

71. Frothingham, "'Me-Too' Products—Friend or Foe?"; S. Garattini, "Are Me-Too Drugs Justified?," *Journal of Nephrology* 10 (6) (1997): 283–94; B. Pekarsky, "Should Financial Incentives be Used to Differentially Reward 'Me-Too' and Innovative Drugs?," *PharmacoEconomics* 28 (1) (2010): 1–17.

72. C. Christensen, *The Innovator's Dilemma* (Cambridge, Mass.: Harvard Business Review Press, 1997).

73. K. I. Kaitin and C. P. Milne, "A Dearth of New Meds," *Scientific American* 305 (2) (2011): 16.

74. Tufts Center for the Study of Drug Development, "Cost to Develop and Win Marketing Approval for a New Drug Is $2.6 Billion," *Tufts Center for the Study of Drug Development*, 18 November 2014, http://csdd.tufts.edu/news/complete_story/pr _tufts_csdd_2014_cost_study.

75. A. Jack, "The Fall of the World's Best-Selling Drug," *Financial Times Magazine*, 29 November 2009, https://next.ft.com/content/d0f7af5c-d7e6-11de-b578-00144fe-abdco.

76. A. Smith, "Zocor Losing Patent Protection," *Money*, 23 June 2006, http://money .cnn.com/2006/06/23/news/companies/zoloft_zocor/index.htm?postversion =2006062315.

77. S. King, "The Best Selling Drugs of All Time; Humira Joins the Elite," *Forbes*, 28 January 2013, http://www.forbes.com/sites/simonking/2013/01/28/the-best -selling-drugs-of-all-time-humira-joins-the-elite.

78. F. Alnouri, D. Wood, K. Kotseva, and M. E. Ibrahim, "Which Statin Worked Best to Achieve Lipid Level Targets in a European Registry? A Post-Hoc Analysis of the EUROASPIRE III for Coronary Heart Disease Patients," *Journal of the Saudi Heart Association* 26 (4) (2014): 183–91.

79. J. Cohen and K. Kaitin, "Follow-On Drugs and Indications: The Importance of Incremental Innovation to Medical Practice," *American Journal of Therapeutics* 15 (1) (2008): 89–91.

80. M. S. Kinch and E. Patridge, "An Analysis of FDA-Approved Drugs for Infectious Disease: HIV/AIDS Drugs," *Drug Discovery Today* 19 (10) (2014): 1510–13.

81. P. Vitello, "Jerome Horwitz, AZT Creator, Dies at 93," *New York Times*, 21 September 2012, www.nytimes.com/2012/09/21/health/jerome-p-horwitz-creator-of -azt-dies-at-93.html; Emily Langer, "Researcher Jerome P. Horwitz, 93, Created AZT, the First Approved Treatment for HIV/AIDS," *Washington Post*, 19 September 2012, http://www.washingtonpost.com/national/health-science/researcher-jerome-p-hor witz-93-created-azt-the-first-approved-treatment-for-hivaids/2012/09/19/0c08c38a -0280-11e2-9b24-ff730c7f6312_story.html.

82. Kinch and Patridge, "An Analysis of FDA-Approved Drugs."

83. H. Hatano and S. G. Deeks, "Drug Resistant HIV," *British Medical Journal* 334 (7604) (2007): 1124; K. Paydary, P. Khaghani, S. Emamzadeh-Fard, S. A. Alinaghi, and K. Baesi, "The Emergence of Drug Resistant HIV Variants and Novel Anti-Retroviral Therapy," *Asian Pacific Journal of Tropical Biomedicine* 3 (7) (2013): 515–22.

84. K. Das and E. Arnold, "HIV-1 Reverse Transcriptase and Antiviral Drug Resistance. Part 2," *Current Opinion in Virology* 3 (2) (2013): 119–28.

85. S. C. Matheny and J. E. Kingery, "Hepatitis A," *American Family Physician* 86 (11) (2012): 1027–34, quiz 1010–22.

86. B. Yoffe and C. A. Noonan, "Hepatitis B Virus," *Digestive Diseases and Sciences* 37 (1) (1992): 1–9; A. S. F. Lok and B. J. McMahon, "Chronic Hepatitis B: Update 2009," *Hepatology* 50 (3) (2009): 661–62.

87. S. T. Goldstein, F. Zhou, S. C. Hadler, B. P. Bell, E. E. Mast, and H. S. Margolis, "A Mathematical Model to Estimate Global Hepatitis B Disease Burden and Vaccination Impact," *International Journal of Epidemiology* 34 (6) (2005): 1329–39.

88. A. A. McLean and R. Shaw, "Hepatitis B Virus Vaccine," *Annals of Internal Medicine* 97 (3) (1982): 451–51.

89. M. Houghton, "Discovery of the Hepatitis C Virus," *Liver International: Official Journal of the International Association for the Study of the Liver* 29 Suppl 1 (2009): 82–88; C. W. Shepard, L. Finelli, and M. J. Alter, "Global Epidemiology of Hepatitis C Virus Infection," *Lancet Infectious Diseases* 5 (9) (2005): 558–67.

90. Houghton, "Discovery of the Hepatitis C Virus."

91. S. L. Chen and T. R. Morgan, "The Natural History of Hepatitis C Virus (HCV) Infection," *International Journal of Medical Sciences* 3 (2) (2006): 47.

92. CDC, "Hepatitis C FAQs for Health Professionals," *Centers for Disease Control*, 2015, http://www.cdc.gov/hepatitis/HCV/HCVfaq.htm.

93. J. T. Blackard, M. T. Shata, N. J. Shire, and K. E. Sherman, "Acute Hepatitis C Virus Infection: A Chronic Problem," *Hepatology* 47 (1) (2008): 321–31.

94. J. J. Feld and J. H. Hoofnagle, "Mechanism of Action of Interferon and Ribavirin in Treatment of Hepatitis C," *Nature* 436 (7053) (2005): 967–72.

95. Y. Nagano and Y. Kojima, "Inhibition of Vaccinia Infection by a Liquid Factor in Tissues Infected by Homologous Virus," *Comptes Rendus des Séances de la Société de Biologie et de Ses Filiales* 152 (11) (1958): 1627.

96. A. Isaacs and J. Lindenmann, "Virus Interference. I. The Interferon," *Proceedings of the Royal Society of London. Series B, Containing Papers of a Biological Character* 147 (927) (1957): 258–67.

97. Z. Senyak, "From Isaacs to Silver: Interferons and the MPNs," *MNPforum Magazine*, http://mpnforum.com/interferon-and-mpns.

98. S. J. Hadziyannis, J. Sette, T. R. Morgan, V. Balan, M. Diago, P. Marcellin, G. Ramadori, H. Bodenheimer, D. Bernstein, and M. Rizzetto, "Peginterferon-α2a and Ribavirin Combination Therapy in Chronic Hepatitis C: A Randomized Study of Treatment Duration and Ribavirin Dose," *Annals of Internal Medicine* 140 (5) (2004): 346–55.

99. M. Sanger-Katz, "Why the Price of Sovaldi Is a Shock to the System," *New York Times*, 7 August 2014, http://www.nytimes.com/2014/08/07/upshot/why-the-price-of-sovaldi-is-a-shock-to-the-system.html?_r=0&abt=0002&abg=0.

100. M J. De La Merced, "Bristol-Myers to Acquire Inhibitex for $2.5 Billion," *New York Times*, 7 January 2012, http://dealbook.nytimes.com/2012/01/07/bristol-myers-to-buy-inhibitex-for-2-5-billion.

101. M. Tirrell and R. Flinn, "Gilead to Buy Pharmasset for $11 Billion to Win in Hepatitis," *Bloomberg*, 21 November 2011, http://www.bloomberg.com/news/articles/2011-11-21/gilead-to-acquire-pharmasset-for-11-billion-to-add-hepatitis-c-medicines.

102. A. Pollack, "Bristol-Myers Ends a Hepatitis C Project," *New York Times*, 24 August 2012, http://www.nytimes.com/2012/08/24/business/bristol-myers-ends-work-on-hepatitis-c-drug.html.

103. A. Roy, "How the FDA Stifles New Cures, Part I: The Rising Cost of Clinical Trials," *Forbes*, 24 April 2012, http://www.forbes.com/sites/aroy/2012/04/24/how-the-fda-stifles-new-cures-part-i-the-rising-cost-of-clinical-trials/#3aad32a15bc6.

104. M. I. Zia, L. L. Siu, G. R. Pond, and E. X. Chen, "Comparison of Outcomes of Phase II Studies and Subsequent Randomized Control Studies using Identical Chemotherapeutic Regimens," *Journal of Clinical Oncology* 23 (28) (2005): 6982–91.

105. Tufts Center for the Study of Drug Design, "Cost to Develop and Win Marketing Approval."

Chapter Eight

1. A. L. Demain and N. J. Madison, "Genentech Not First Biotech," *American Chemical Society* 85 (2007): 2–2.

2. T. Poggio, "Donald Arthur Glaser (1926–2013)," *Nature* 496 (7443) (2013): 32–32.

3. R. D. Merrill, "First-Hand: Starting Up Cetus, the First Biotechnology Company; 1973 to 1982," *Engineering and Technology History Wiki*, 4 March 2014, http://www.ieeeghn.org/wiki6/index.php/First-Hand:Starting_Up_Cetus,_the_First_Biotechnology_Company_-_1973_to_1982.

4. Ibid.

5. Ibid.

6. P. Rabinow, *Making PCR: A Story of Biotechnology* (Chicago: University of Chicago Press, 1996).

7. Merrill, "First-Hand."

8. Ibid.

9. M. Freudenheim, "F.D.A. Approves a Multiple Sclerosis Drug," *New York Times*, 24 July 1993, http://www.nytimes.com/1993/07/24/business/company-news-fda-approves-a-multiple-sclerosis-drug.html.

10. Merrill, "First-Hand"; Cape, "Biotech Pioneer and Co-Founder of Cetus."

11. Merrill, "First-Hand."

12. FundingUniverse, "Chiron Corporation History," *FundingUniverse*, 2001, http://www.fundinguniverse.com/company-histories/chiron-corporation-history.

13. M. Malloy, "Merger and Acquisitions in Biotechnology," *Nature Biotechnology* 17 (1999): 11–12.

14. K. B. Mullis, "Kary B. Mullis—Biographical," *Nobelprize.org*, 1993, http://www.nobelprize.org/nobel_prizes/chemistry/laureates/1993/mullis-bio.html, accessed on 1 April 2016; N. Wade, "Scientist at Work / Kary Mullis; After the 'Eureka,' a Nobelist Drops Out," *New York Times*, 15 September 1998, http://www.nytimes.com/1998/09/15/science/scientist-at-work-kary-mullis-after-the-eureka-a-nobelist-drops-out.html.

15. Merrill, "First-Hand."

16. Rabinow, *Making PCR*.

17. Merrill, "First-Hand."

18. Ibid.

19. K. B. Mullis, F. Ferré, and R. A. Gibbs, *The Polymerase Chain Reaction* (Boston: Birkhauser Boston Inc., 1994).

20. Ibid.

21. R. Weiss, "A Hunk of Burnin' Love on a Chain: Weird Science; Nobel Laureate Kary Mullis has a New 'Discovery' for Us—Jewelry that Preserves the DNA of Elvis . . . and Lots of Other Dead Folks," *L.A. Times*, 19 October 1995, http://articles .latimes.com/1995-10-19/news/ls-58742_1_laureate-kary-mullis.

22. V. Bauman, "Looking Back at Immunex and Ahead to Seattle's Biotech Future," *The Business Journals*, 2011, http://www.bizjournals.com/seattle/blog/2011/11/looking -back-at-immunex-and-forward-to.html?page=all; S. Gillis, "25+Years in Biotechnology: Lessons Learned," *American Association of Pharmaceutical Scientists*, 2009, http:// mediaserver.aaps.org/meetings/09nbc/gillis.pdf.

23. FundingUniverse, "Immunex Corporation History," *FundingUniverse*, 14 June 2003, http://www.fundinguniverse.com/company-histories/immunex-corporation -history.

24. Gillis, "25+Years in Biotechnology."

25. Ibid.

26. FundingUniverse, "Immunex Corporation History."

27. Gillis, "25+Years in Biotechnology."

28. M. J. Shear, F. C. Turner, A. Perrault, and T. Shovelton, "Chemical Treatment of Tumors: V. Isolation of the Hemorrhage-Producing Fraction from *Serratia Marcescens* (*Bacillus Prodigiosus*) Culture Filtrate," *Journal of the National Cancer Institute* 4 (1) (1943): 81–97.

29. W. E. O'Malley, B. Achinstein, and M. J. Shear, "Action of Bacterial Polysaccharide on Tumors. II. Damage of Sarcoma 37 by Serum of Mice Treated with *Serratia Marcescens* Polysaccharide, and Induced Tolerance," *Journal of the National Cancer Institute* 29 (6) (1962): 1169–75.

30. A. Gillen and R. Gibbs, "*Serratia Marcescens*: The Miracle Bacillus," *Answers in Genesis*, 20 July 2011, https://answersingenesis.org/biology/microbiology/serratia -marcescens-the-miracle-bacillus.

31. E. A. Carswell, L. Jâ Old, RiL Kassel, S. Green, N. Fiore, and B. Williamson, "An Endotoxin-Induced Serum Factor that Causes Necrosis of Tumors," *Proceedings of the National Academy of Sciences* 72 (9) (1975): 3666–70.

32. L. J. Old, "Tumor Necrosis Factor," *Scientific American* 258 (5) (1988): 59–60, 69–75.

33. B. B. Aggarwal, S. C. Gupta, and J. H. Kim, "Historical Perspectives on Tumor Necrosis Factor and Its Superfamily: 25 Years Later, a Golden Journey," *Blood* 119 (3) (2012): 651–65.

34. B. J. Sugarman, B. B. Aggarwal, P. E. Hass, I. S. Figari, M. A. Palladino, and H. M. Shepard, "Recombinant Human Tumor Necrosis Factor-Alpha: Effects on Proliferation of Normal and Transformed Cells in Vitro," *Science* 230 (4728) (1985): 943–45.

35. Aggarwal, Gupta, and Kim, "Historical Perspectives on Tumor Necrosis Factor."

36. K. Peppel, D. Crawford, and B. Beutler, "A Tumor Necrosis Factor (TNF) Receptor-IgG Heavy Chain Chimeric Protein as a Bivalent Antagonist of TNF Activity," *Journal of Experimental Medicine* 174 (6) (1991): 1483–89.

37. A. F. Suffredini, D. Reda, S. M. Banks, M. Tropea, J. M. Agosti, and R. Miller, "Effects of Recombinant Dimeric TNF Receptor on Human Inflammatory Responses Following Intravenous Endotoxin Administration," *Journal of Immunology* 155 (10) (1995): 5038–45.

38. Gillis, "25+Years in Biotechnology."

39. L. M. Fisher, "Immunex, Cyanamid Unit to Merge," *New York Times*, 16 December 1992, http://www.nytimes.com/1992/12/16/business/company-news-immunex -cyanamid-unit-to-merge.html.

40. Gillis, "25+Years in Biotechnology."

41. A. Pollack, "FDA Approves a New Drug to Relieve Arthritis," *New York Times*, 3 November 1998, http://www.nytimes.com/1998/11/03/us/fda-approves-a-new -drug-to-relieve-arthritis.html.

42. Gillis, "25+Years in Biotechnology."

43. R. Sharpe, "Biotech and the Spoils of Success," *Bloomberg*, 12 August 2001, http://www.bloomberg.com/bw/stories/2001-08-12/biotech-and-the-spoils-of -success.

44. R. Grunbaum, "Immunex a Healthy No. 2," *Business Journals*, 13 March 2000, http://www.bizjournals.com/seattle/stories/2000/03/13/story3.html?page=all.

45. L. Timmerman, "Enbrel is Miracle Drug, Until Supplies Run Dry," *Seattle Times*, 30 April 2002, http://community.seattletimes.nwsource.com/archive/?date =20020430&slug=enbrel300.

46. Gillis, "25+Years in Biotechnology."

47. "Amgen to Buy Immunex," *CNN Money*, 17 December 2001, http://money.cnn .com/2001/12/17/deals/amgen_immunex.

48. A. Gonzalez, "Amgen's Exit a New Blow for Seattle Biotech Industry," *Seattle Times*, 29 July 2014, http://seattletimes.com/html/businesstechnology/2024192920 _amgenseattlexml.html.

49. Gillis, "25+Years in Biotechnology."

50. A. Pollack, "Genentech–Roche Deal May Spur Similar Ties," *New York Times*, 5 February 1990, http://www.nytimes.com/1990/02/05/business/genentech-roche -deal-may-spur-similar-ties.html.

51. L. M. Fisher, "Ciba–Geigy Deal with Chiron Set," *New York Times*, 22 November 1994, http://www.nytimes.com/1994/11/22/business/ciba-geigy-deal-with-chiron-set .html.

52. Gillis, "25+Years in Biotechnology."

53. L. Fletcher, "Corixa Buys Coulter," *Nature Biotechnology* 18 (12) (2000): 1230–30.

54. J. M. Vose, "Bexxar®: Novel Radioimmunotherapy for the Treatment of Low-Grade and Transformed Low-Grade Non-Hodgkin's Lymphoma," *Oncologist* 9 (2) (2004): 160–72.

55. G. J. Silverman and S. Weisman, "Rituximab Therapy and Autoimmune Disorders: Prospects for Anti–B Cell Therapy," *Arthritis & Rheumatism* 48 (6) (2003): 1484–92; P. McLaughlin, A. J. Grillo-López, B. K. Link, R. Levy, M. S. Czuczman, M. E. Williams, M. R. Heyman, I. Bence-Bruckler, C. A. White, and F. Cabanillas, "Rituximab Chimeric Anti-CD20 Monoclonal Antibody Therapy for Relapsed Indolent Lymphoma: Half of Patients Respond to a Four-Dose Treatment Program," *Journal of Clinical Oncology* 16 (8) (1998): 2825–33.

56. S. J. Goldsmith, "Radioimmunotherapy of Lymphoma: Bexxar and Zevalin," *Seminars in Nuclear Medicine* 40 (2) (2010): 122–135.

57. S. J. Horning, A. Younes, V. Jain, S. Kroll, J. Lucas, D. Podoloff, and M. Goris, "Efficacy and Safety of Tositumomab and Iodine-131 Cositumomab (Bexxar) in B-cell Lymphoma, Progressive after Rituximab," *Journal of Clinical Oncology* 23 (4) (2005): 712–19.

58. Gillis, "25+ Years in Biotechnology."

59. J. W. Friedberg and R. I. Fisher, "Iodine-131 Tositumomab (Bexxar®): Radioimmunoconjugate Therapy for Indolent and Transformed B-Cell Non-Hodgkin's Lymphoma," *Expert Reviews in Anticancer Therapy* 4 (1) (2004): 18–26.

60. S. Aggarwal, "What's Fueling the Biotech Engine?," *Nature Biotechnology* 25 (10) (2007): 1097–1104.

61. Gillis, "25+ Years in Biotechnology."

62. B. Cheson, "Bexxar (Corixa/GlaxoSmithKline)," *Current Opinion in Investigational Drugs* 3 (1) (2002): 165–70.

63. V. Prasad, "The Withdrawal of Drugs for Commercial Reasons: The Incomplete Story of Tositumomab," *JAMA Internal Medicine* 174 (12) (2014): 1887–88.

64. Ibid.; Gillis, "25+ Years in Biotechnology."

65. W. Bowes, "William K. Bowes Jr., Bay Area Venture Capitalists: Shaping the Economic and Business Landscape," *Berkeley Library*, 2008, http://digitalassets.lib.berkeley.edu/roho/ucb/text/bowes_william.pdf.

66. Ibid.

67. S. Miller, "Remberances: George Rathmann, 1927–2012," *Wall Street Journal*, 23 April 2012, http://www.wsj.com/articles/SB10001424052702303978104577362390794740510.

68. Academy of Achievement, "George Rathmann Interview," *Academy of Achievement*, 2000, http://www.achievement.org/autodoc/page/rat1int-1.

69. "George Rathmann 1927–2012"; Academy of Achievement, "George Rathmann Interview."

70. V. Oladapo and G. Onyeaso, "Tracing the Trajectory of Industry Leader's Drug Innovation Capability: The Amgen Corporation Case," *Review of Business and Finance Studies* 4 (2) (2013): 69–77.

71. K. Jacobs, C. Shoemaker, R. Rudersdorf, S. D. Neill, R. J. Kaufman, A. Mufson, J. Seehra, S. S. Jones, R. Hewick, and E. F. Fritsch, "Isolation and Characterization of Genomic and cDNA Clones of Human Erythropoietin" *Nature* 313 (6005) (1985): 806–10.

72. A. Anderson, "Growing Pains for Amgen as Epoetin Wins U.S. Approval," *Nature* 339 (6225) (1989): 493.

73. FundingUniverse, "Amgen, Inc. History," *FundingUniverse*, 2000, http://www.fundinguniverse.com/company-histories/amgen-inc-history.

74. A. C. Herman, T. C. Boone, and H. S. Lu, "Characterization, Formulation, and Stability of Neupogen® (Filgrastim), a Recombinant Human Granulocyte-Colony Stimulating Factor," chap. 7 in *Formulation, Characterization, and Stability of Protein Drugs: Case Histories* (New York: Springer, 2002): 303–28.

75. L. Timmerman, "Leukine: Moving in a New Direction," *Seattle Times*, 15 January 2003, http://community.seattletimes.nwsource.com/archive/?date=20030115&slug=berlex15.

76. Bloomberg, "Gordon M. Binder," *Bloomberg*, http://www.bloomberg.com/research/stocks/private/person.asp?personId=169422&privcapId=2755591&previousCapId=129158437&previousTitle=STORECapital, accessed on 1 April 2016.

77. Bloomberg, "Kevin Sharer," *Bloomberg*, http://www.bloomberg.com/research/stocks/people/person.asp?personId=169424&ticker=AMGN, accessed on 1 April 2016.

78. Bloomberg, "Robert Bradway," *Bloomberg*, http://www.bloomberg.com/research/stocks/people/person.asp?personId=33775218&ticker=AMGN, accessed on 1 April 2016.

79. J. T. Sobota and T. L. Copmann, "Orphan Drug Act," *Science* 249 (1990): 346–47.

80. National Organization for Rare Disorders, *NORD Guide to Rare Disorders* (Philadelphia: Lippincott Williams & Wilkins, 2003).

81. R. A. Bohrer and J. T. Prince, "Tale of Two Proteins: The FDA's Uncertain Interpretation of the Orphan Drug Act," *Harvard Journal of Law & Technology* 12 (1998): 365.

82. D. D. Rohde, "The Orphan Drug Act: An Engine of Innovation; At What Cost, " *Food and Drug Law Journal* 55 (2000): 125; M. Wastfelt, B. Fadeel, and J. I. Henter, "A Journey of Hope: Lessons Learned from Studies on Rare Diseases and Orphan Drugs," *Journal of Internal Medicine* 260 (1) (2006): 1–10; O. Wellman-Labadie and Y. Zhou, "The U.S. Orphan Drug Act: Rare Disease Research Stimulator or Commercial Opportunity?," *Health Policy* 95 (2) (2010): 216–28; S. R. Shulman, B. Bienz-Tadmor, P. Son Seo, and J. A. DiMasi, "Implementation of the Orphan Drug Act: 1983–1991," *Food and Drug Law Journal* 47 (1992): 363.

83. S. L. Nightingale, "Orphan Drugs," *American Family Physician* 33 (6) (1986): 235–36.

84. A. G. Engel and C. Angelini, "Carnitine Deficiency of Human Skeletal Muscle with Associated Lipid Storage Myopathy: A New Syndrome," *Science* 179 (4076) (1973): 899–902.

85. M. C. Dalakas, M. E. Leon-Monzon, I. Bernardini, W. A. Gahl, and C. A. Jay, "Zidovudine-Induced Mitochondrial Myopathy Is Associated with Muscle Carnitine Deficiency and Lipid Storage," *Annals of Neurology* 35 (4) (1994): 482–87.

86. Shulman et al., "Implementation of the Orphan Drug Act: 1983–1991."

87. M. S. Kinch, J. Merkel, and S. Umlauf, "Trends in Pharmaceutical Targeting of Clinical Indications: 1930–2013," *Drug Discovery Today* 19 (11) (2014): 1682–85.

88. FundingUniverse, "Genzyme Corporation History," *FundingUniverse,* 2001, http://www.fundinguniverse.com/company-histories/genzyme-corporation -history.

89. R. O. Brady, J. N. Kanfer, and D. Shapiro, "Metabolism of Glucocerebrosides II. Evidence of an Enzymatic Deficiency in Gaucher's Disease," *Biochemical and Biophysical Research Communications* 18 (2) (1965): 221–25.

90. E. B. Roberts and C. E. Eesley, *Entrepreneurial Impact: The Role of MIT* (Delft, The Netherlands: Now Publishers, 2009).

91. FundingUniverse, "Genzyme Corporation History."

92. Ibid.

93. T. Edmunds, "β-Glucocerebrosidase Ceredase® and Cerezyme®," *Directory of Therapeutic Enzymes* 117 (2005).

94. N. Sovich and N. Mennella, "Sanofi to Buy Genzyme for More than $20 Billion," *Reuters,* 16 February 2011, http://www.reuters.com/article/2011/02/16/us-genzyme -sanofi-idUSTRE71E4XI20110216.

95. BankBoston, "MIT: The Impact of Innovation," Economics Department Special Report, *Save Our Heritage,* March 1997, http://www.saveourheritage.com/Library _Docs/Bank%20Boston%20Impact%20of%20Innovation.pdf.

96. Andrew Pollack, "Genzyme Drug Shortage Leaves Users Feeling Betrayed," *New York Times,* 16 April 2010, http://www.nytimes.com/2010/04/16/business /16genzyme.html?pagewanted=all&_r=0.

97. A. P. Abernethy, G. Raman, E. M. Balk, J. M. Hammond, L. A. Orlando, J. L. Wheeler, J. Lau, and D. C. McCrory, "Systematic Review: Reliability of Compendia Methods for Off-Label Oncology Indications," *Annals of Internal Medicine* 150 (5) (2009): 336–43.

98. M. Soares, " 'Off-Label' Indications for Oncology Drug Use and Drug Compendia: History and Current Status," *Journal of Oncology Practice* 1 (3) (2005): 102; K. Tillman, B. Burton, L. B. Jacques, and S. E. Phurrough, "Compendia and Anticancer Therapy under Medicare," *Annals of Internal Medicine* 150 (5) (2009): 348–50; K Traynor, "Oncologists Wary of Manufacturer-Provided Drug Information," *ASHP,* 3 June 2008, http://www.ashp.org/menu/News/PharmacyNews/NewsArticle.aspx ?id=2856.

99. C. Downs, "The Medicare Prescription Drug Improvement and Modernization Act and the Delivery of Cancer Chemotherapy," *American Journal of Health-System Pharmacy* 64 (15 Suppl 10) (2007): S13–15; quiz S21–S23.

100. American Society of Clinical Oncology, "Reimbursement for Cancer Treatment: Coverage of Off-Label Drug Indications," *Journal of Clinical Oncology* 24 (19) (2006): 3206–8; R. M. Conti, A. C. Bernstein, V. M. Villaflor, R. L. Schilsky, M. B. Rosenthal, and P. B. Bach, "Prevalence of Off-Label Use and Spending in 2010 among Patent-Protected Chemotherapies in a Population-Based Cohort of Medical Oncologists," *Journal of Clinical Oncology* 31 (9) (2013): 1134–39.

101. M. J. Berens and K. Armstrong, "Pharma's Windfall: The Mining of Rare Diseases," *Seattle Times*, 9 November 2014, http://apps.seattletimes.com/reports/pharma-windfall/2013/nov/9/mining-rare-diseases.

102. Ibid.

103. A. Côté and B. Keating, "What Is Wrong with Orphan Drug Policies?," *Value in Health* 15 (8) (2012): 1185–91; Kinch, "Trends in Pharmaceutical Targeting of Clinical Indications: 1930–2013."

104. Côté and Keating, "What Is Wrong with Orphan Drug Policies?"

Chapter Nine

1. Maryland Regional Services Center, Montgomery County, "Bethesda Chevy Chase Regional Services Center," *Bethesda Service*, 22 January 2015, http://bethesdaservice.blogspot.com/2015/01/history-of-pike-district.html.

2. R. Orme, *The History of an Expedition Against Fort Du Quesne, in 1755 Under Major-General Edward Braddock* (Philadelphia: Lippincott, Grambo & Co., 1856).

3. R. L. Sinsheimer, "The Santa Cruz Workshop—May 1985," *Genomics* 5 (4) (1989): 954–56.

4. C. DeLisi, "Meetings that Changed the World: Santa Fe 1986; Human Genome Baby-Steps," *Nature* 455 (7215) (2008): 876–77.

5. J. D. Watson, "The Human Genome Project: Past, Present, and Future," *Science* 248 (4951) (1990): 44–49.

6. A. E. Guttmacher, F. S. Collins, and E. W. Clayton, "Ethical, Legal, and Social Implications of Genomic Medicine," *New England Journal of Medicine* 349 (6) (2003): 562–69; E. M. Meslin, E. J. Thomson, and J. T. Boyer, "The Ethical, Legal, and Social Implications Research Program at the National Human Genome Research Institute," *Kennedy Institute of Ethics Journal* 7 (3) (1997): 291–98.

7. G. Ferry and J. Sulston, *The Common Thread: A Story of Science, Politics, Ethics, and the Human Genome* (Washington, D.C.: Joseph Henry Press, 2002).

8. G. J. Annas and S. Elias, *Gene Mapping: Using Law and Ethics as Guides* (New York: Oxford University Press, 1992).

9. G. D. Schuler, M. S. Boguski, E. A. Stewart, L. D. Stein, G. Gyapay, K. Rice, R. E. White, P. Rodriguez-Tome, A. Aggarwal, and E. Bajorek, "A Gene Map of the Human Genome," *Science* 274 (5287) (1996): 540–46; F. S. Collins, A. Patrinos, E. Jordan, A. Chakravarti, R. Gesteland, and L. Walters, "New Goals for the U.S. Human Genome Project: 1998–2003," *Science* 282 (5389) (1998): 682–89.

10. J. Shreeve, *The Genome War: How Craig Venter Tried to Capture the Code of Life and Save the World* (New York: Ballantine Books, 2007).

11. L. Roberts, "Genome Patent Fight Erupts," *Science* 254 (5029) (1991): 184–86.

12. Shreeve, *Genome War: How Craig Venter Tried to Capture the Code of Life and Save the World*.

13. R. Preston, "The Genome Warrior," *New Yorker* 66 (2000): 66–77; J. C. Venter, M. D. Adams, E. W. Myers, P. W. Li, R. J. Mural, G. G. Sutton, H. O. Smith,

M. Yandell, C. A. Evans, and R. A. Holt, "The Sequence of the Human Genome," *Science* 291 (5507) (2001): 1304–51.

14. S. Okie, "Is Craig Venter Going to Save the Planet? Or Is This More Hype from One of America's Most Controversial Scientists?," *Washington Post*, 7 June 2011, http://www.washingtonpost.com/lifestyle/magazine/is-craig-venter-going-to-save -the-planet-or-is-this-more-hype-from-one-of-americas-most-controversial -scientists/2011/06/07/gIQAfr2c8I_story.html; N. Wade, "Craig Venter: A Maverick Making Waves," *New York Times*, 27 June 2000, http://partners.nytimes.com /library/national/science/062700sci-genome-venter.html.

15. J. C. Venter, M. D. Adams, G. G. Sutton, A. R. Kerlavage, H. O. Smith, and M. Hunkapiller, "Shotgun Sequencing of the Human Genome," *Science*, 1998, 1540–41.

16. K. Davies, *Cracking the Genome: Inside the Race to Unlock Human DNA* (Baltimore, Md.: Johns Hopkins University Press, 2002).

17. BioIT World, "Horizons: Craig Venter," *Bio-IT World*, 12 February 2002, http://www.bio-itworld.com/archive/111202/horizons_venter.html.

18. F. Collins, "Francis Collins on Craig Venter and Celera Genomics," *Cold Spring Harbor Laboratory*, 31 May 2003, http://library.cshl.edu/oralhistory/interview/genome -research/gene-patenting/craig-venter-and-celera-genomics/.

19. F. S. Collins, *The Language of God: A Scientist Presents Evidence for Belief* (New York: Simon and Schuster, 2006).

20. B. Nerlich, R. Dingwall, and D. D. Clarke, "The Book of Life: How the Completion of the Human Genome Project Was Revealed to the Public," *Health* 6 (4) (2002): 445–69; Davies, *Cracking the Genome*.

21. R. S. Eisenberg and R. R. Nelson, "Public vs. Proprietary Science: A Fruitful Tension?," *Academic Medicine* 77 (12, Part 2) (2002): 1392–99.

22. Davies, *Cracking the Genome*; Der Spiegel, "SPIEGEL Interview with Craig Venter: 'We Have Learned Nothing from the Genome,'" *Spiegel*, 29 July 2010, http:// www.spiegel.de/international/world/spiegel-interview-with-craig-venter-we-have -learned-nothing-from-the-genome-a-709174.html.

23. Davies, *Cracking the Genome*; Wade, "Craig Venter."

24. Wade, "Craig Venter."

25. Forbes, "Gene Machine," *Forbes*, 21 February 2000, http://www.forbes.com /global/2000/0221/0304070a.html; L. M. McNamee and F. D. Ledley, "Assessing the History and Value of Human Genome Sciences," *Journal of Commercial Biotechnology* 19 (4) (2013): 3–10.

26. M. Robins, "Back to the Lab," *Forbes*, 5 February 2001, http://www.forbes.com /global/2001/0205/081.html.

27. C. Macilwain, "World Leaders Heap Praise on Human Genome Landmark," *Nature* 405 (6790) (2000): 983–84.

28. A. Berenson and N. Wade, "The Markets: Stocks & Bonds; A Call for Sharing of Research Causes Gene Stocks to Plunge," *New York Times*, 15 March 2000, http:// www.nytimes.com/2000/03/15/business/markets-stocks-bonds-call-for-sharing -research-causes-gene-stocks-plunge.html.

29. S. Hensley, "Craig Venter Leaves Celera as Firm Seeks New Direction," *Wall Street Journal*, 23 January 2002, http://www.wsj.com/articles/SB1011714052194210440; N. Adler, "Human Genome Sciences Announces Job Cuts, Haseltine Retirement," *Business Journals*, 22 March 2004, http://www.bizjournals.com/baltimore/stories/2004/03/22/daily24.html.

30. J. Whitfield, "Dog Genome Unveiled," *Nature*, 26 September 2003, http://www.nature.com/news/2003/030926/full/news030922-17.html.

31. Okie, "Is Craig Venter Going to Save the Planet?"; P. McKenna, "Round-the-World Trip to Catalog Genes / Yachting Scientists on Voyage of Discovery," *San Francisco Gate*, 6 June 2005, http://www.sfgate.com/science/article/Round-the-world-trip-to-catalog-genes-Yachting-2665036.php.

32. McKenna, "Round-the-World Trip."

33. T. J. Mullaney, "FDA OKs Preemie Vaccine MedImmune Cleared to Market Respi-Fam," *Baltimore Sun*, 20 January 1996, http://articles.baltimoresun.com/1996-01-20/business/1996020090_1_medimmune-respigam-rsv; MedImmune, "MedImmune's Synagis™ (Palivizumab) Approved for Marketing by FDA," *MedImmune*, 1998, http://phx.corporate-ir.net/phoenix.zhtml?c=83037&p=irol-investornewsArticle&ID=366312.

34. Charly Travers, "Synagis Has Some Legs Left," *Motley Fool*, 21 April 2005, http://www.fool.com/investing/high-growth/2005/04/21/synagis-has-some-legs-left.aspx.

35. K. Bloom-Feshbach, W. J. Alonso, V. Charu, J. Tamerius, L. Simonsen, M. A. Miller, and C. Viboud, "Latitudinal Variations in Seasonal Activity of Influenza and Respiratory Syncytial Virus (RSV): A Global Comparative Review," *PLoS One* 8 (2) (2013): e54445.

36. X. Saez-Llorens, E. Castano, D. Null, J. Steichen, P. J. Sanchez, O. Ramilo, F. H. Top Jr., E. Connor, and MEDI-493 Study Group, "Safety and Pharmacokinetics of an Intramuscular Humanized Monoclonal Antibody to Respiratory Syncytial Virus in Premature Infants and Infants with Bronchopulmonary Dysplasia," *Pediatric Infectious Disease Journal* 17 (9) (1998): 787–91.

37. S. S. Farid, "Process Economics of Industrial Monoclonal Antibody Manufacture," *Journal of Chromatography* B 848 (1) (2007): 8–18.

38. M. A. Schenerman, J. N. Hope, C. Kletke, J. K. Singh, R. Kimura, E. I. Tsao, and G. Folena-Wasserman, "Comparability Testing of a Humanized Monoclonal Antibody (Synagis®) to Support Cell Line Stability, Process Validation, and Scale-Up for Manufacturing," *Biologicals* 27 (3) (1999): 203–15.

39. D. Null Jr., B. Pollara, P. H. Dennehy, J. Steichen, P. J. Sánchez, L. B. Givner, D. Carlin, B. Landry, F. H. Top Jr., and E. Connor, "Safety and Immunogenicity of Palivizumab (Synagis) Administered for Two Seasons," *Pediatric Infectious Disease Journal* 24 (11) (2005): 1021–23.

40. W. Wang, E. Q. Wang, and J. P. Balthasar, "Monoclonal Antibody Pharmacokinetics and Pharmacodynamics," *Clinical Pharmacology & Therapeutics* 84 (5) (2008): 548–58.

41. S. Padmanabhan, T. Amin, B. Sampat, R. Cook-Deegan, and S. Chandrasekharan, "Intellectual Property, Technology Transfer, and Manufacture of Low-Cost HPV Vaccines in India," *Nature Biotechnology* 28 (7) (2010): 671–78.

42. D. R. Lowy and J. T. Schiller, "Papillomavirus-Like Particle Based Vaccines: Cervical Cancer and Beyond," *Expert Opinion on Biological Therapy* 1 (4) (2001): 571–81; S. Inglis, A. Shaw, and S. Koenig, "HPV Vaccines: Commercial Research & Development," *Vaccine* 24 (2006): S99–S105.

43. H. Weinstock, S. Berman, and W. Cates, "Sexually Transmitted Diseases among American Youth: Incidence and Prevalence Estimates, 2000," *Perspectives on Sexual and Reproductive Health* 36 (1) (2004): 6–10.

44. CDC, "Human Papillomavirus (HPV)," *Centers for Disease Control*, 30 September 2015, http://www.cdc.gov/std/hpv.

45. L. Gissmann and H. Zur Hausen, "Partial Characterization of Viral DNA from Human Genital Warts (*Condylomata acuminata*)," *International Journal of Cancer* 25 (5) (1980): 605–9.

46. S. Bulk, J. Berkhof, N. W. J. Bulkmans, G. D. Zielinski, L. Rozendaal, F. J. Van Kemenade, P. J. F. Snijders, and C. J. L. M. Meijer, "Preferential Risk of HPV16 for Squamous Cell Carcinoma and of HPV18 for Adenocarcinoma of the Cervix Compared to Women with Normal Cytology in The Netherlands," *British Journal of Cancer* 94 (1) (2006): 171–75.

47. Lowy and Schiller, "Papillomavirus-Like Particle Based Vaccines."

48. L. L. Villa, R. L. R. Costa, C. A. Petta, R. P. Andrade, K. A. Ault, A. R. Giuliano, C. M. Wheeler, L. A. Koutsky, C. Malm, and M. Lehtinen, "Prophylactic Quadrivalent Human Papillomavirus (Types 6, 11, 16, and 18) L1 Virus-Like Particle Vaccine in Young Women: A Randomized Double-Blind Placebo-Controlled Multicentre Phase II Efficacy Trial," *Lancet Oncology* 6 (5) (2005): 271–78.

49. D. M. Harper, E. L. Franco, C. Wheeler, D. G. Ferris, D. Jenkins, A. Schuind, T. Zahaf, B. Innis, P. Naud, and N. S. De Carvalho, "Efficacy of a Bivalent L1 Virus-Like Particle Vaccine in Prevention of Infection with Human Papillomavirus Types 16 and 18 in Young Women: A Randomized Controlled Trial," *Lancet* 364 (9447) (2004): 1757–65.

50. M. R. McLemore, "Gardasil®: Introducing the New Human Papillomavirus Vaccine," *Clinical Journal of Oncology Nursing* 10 (5) (2006): 559–60.

51. S. Lawrence, "Billion Dollar Babies—Biotech Drugs as Blockbusters," *Nature Biotechnology* 25 (4) (2007): 380–86; J. L. Grimes, "HPV Vaccine Development: A Case Study of Prevention and Politics," *Biochemistry and Molecular Biology Education* 34 (2) (2006): 148–54.

52. M. Guidera, "MedImmune Finishes Buying U.S. Bioscience," *Baltimore Sun*, 25 November 1999, http://articles.baltimoresun.com/1999-11-25/business/9911250254_1_medimmune-bioscience-new-cancer-treatments.

53. U.S. Bioscience, "U.S. Bioscience and ALZA Corporation Announce FDA Approval of ETHYOL™ to Reduce Radiation-Induced Xerostomia (Dry Mouth)," *Evaluate*, 1999, http://www.evaluategroup.com/Universal/View.aspx?type=Story&id=107989.

54. D. M. Brizel, T. H. Wasserman, M. Henke, V. Strnad, V. Rudat, A. Monnier, F. Eschwege, J. Zhang, L. Russell, and W. Oster, "Phase III Randomized Trial of Amifostine as a Radioprotector in Head and Neck Cancer," *Journal of Clinical Oncology* 18 (19) (2000): 3339–45.

55. Guidera, "MedImmune Finishes Buying U.S. Bioscience."

56. A. Pollack, "Agreements on 2 Mergers in Biotechnology Industry," *New York Times*, 4 December 2001, http://www.nytimes.com/2001/12/04/business/04BIOT.html.

57. Aviron, "Aviron Adds Fenton and Hockmeyer to Board of Directors," *PR Newswire*, 15 April 2001, http://www.prnewswire.com/news-releases/aviron-adds-fenton -and-hockmeyer-to-board-of-directors-72975547.html.

58. R. B. Belshe, W. C. Gruber, P. M. Mendelman, H. B. Mehta, K. Mahmood, K. Reisinger, J. Treanor, K. Zangwill, F. G. Hayden, and D. I. Bernstein, "Correlates of Immune Protection Induced by Live, Attenuated, Cold-Adapted, Trivalent, Intranasal Influenza Virus Vaccine," *Journal of Infectious Diseases* 181 (3) (2000): 1133–37.

59. S. Riedel, "Edward Jenner and the History of Smallpox and Vaccination," *Proceedings* (Baylor University, Medical Center) 18 (1) (2005): 21.

60. J. S. Smith, *Patenting the Sun: Polio and the Salk Vaccine* (New York: William Morrow and Company, 1990).

61. S. Robertson, *Module 6: Poliomyelitis: The Immunological Basis for Immunization Series* (Geneva, Switzerland: WHO, 1993).

62. D. J. Wilson, "A Crippling Fear: Experiencing Polio in the Era of FDR," *Bulletin of the History of Medicine* 72 (3) (1998): 464–95; D. M. Oshinsky, *Polio: An American Story* (New York: Oxford University Press, 2005).

63. Oshinsky, *Polio*.

64. R. Keyes, "Jonas Salk Unfolding," *Ralph Keyes*, 1 June 1973, http://www .ralphkeyes.com/wp-content/uploads/2011/08/Human-Behavior-Jonas-Salk -Unfolding.pdf; P. A. Offit, "The Cutter Incident, 50 Years Later," *New England Journal of Medicine* 352 (14) (2005): 1411–12.

65. Keyes, "Jonas Salk Unfolding."

66. J. Pearce, "Salk and Sabin: Poliomyelitis Immunization," *Journal of Neurology, Neurosurgery, and Psychiatry* 75 (11) (2004): 1552; H. Markel, "April 12, 1955: Tommy Francis and the Salk Vaccine," *New England Journal of Medicine* 352 (14) (2005): 1408–10.

67. Keyes, "Jonas Salk Unfolding."

68. Offit, "The Cutter Incident, 50 Years Later."

69. P. A. Offit, *The Cutter Incident: How America's First Polio Vaccine Led to the Growing Vaccine Crisis* (New Haven, Conn.: Yale University Press, 2005).

70. N. Nathanson and A. D. Langmuir, "The Cutter Incident: Poliomyelitis Following Formaldehyde-Inactivated Poliovirus Vaccination in the United States during the Spring of 1955," *American Journal of Epidemiology* 78 (1) (1963): 29–60.

71. Offit, "The Cutter Incident, 50 Years Later."

72. Ibid.

73. Pearce, "Salk and Sabin: Poliomyelitis Immunization."

74. G. Raine, "Nasal Flu Vaccine Passes Test," *San Francisco Gate*, 7 May 1997, http://www.sfgate.com/news/article/Nasal-flu-vaccine-passes-test-3119983.php.

75. T. Mellow, "Hunein F. 'John' Maassab, Developer of Influenza Nasal-Spray Vaccine Known as FluMist, Dies at 87," *School of Public Health, University of Michigan*, 21 March 2014, https://sph.umich.edu/news/releases/031414Maassab.html.

76. H. F. Maassab and D. C. DeBorde, "Development and Characterization of Cold-Adapted Viruses for Use as Live Virus Vaccines," *Vaccine* 3 (5) (1985): 355–69.

77. H. F. Maassab and M. L. Bryant, "The Development of Live Attenuated Cold-Adapted Influenza Virus Vaccine for Humans," *Reviews in Medical Virology* 9 (4) (1999) 237–44.

78. University of Michigan, "A Symposium in Honor of Hunein 'John' F. Maassab," *School of Public Health, University of Michigan*, 2009, https://sph.umich.edu /symposium/2000/john_maassab.html, accessed on 1 April 2016.

79. H. Jin, B. Lu, H. Zhou, C. Ma, J. Zhao, C. Yang, G. Kemble, and H. Greenberg, "Multiple Amino Acid Residues Confer Temperature Sensitivity to Human Influenza Virus Vaccine Strains (FluMist) Derived from Cold-Adapted A/Ann Arbor/6/60," *Virology* 306 (1) (2003): 18–24.

80. Maassab and Bryant, "Development of Live Attenuated Cold-Adapted Influenza Virus Vaccine for Humans."

81. P. Elias, "MedImmune to Buy Aviron for More than $1 Billion," *Berkeley Daily Planet*, 4 December 2001, http://www.berkeleydailyplanet.com/issue/2001-12-04 /article/8718?headline=MedImmune-to-buy-Aviron-for-more-than-1-billion—By-P aul-Elias-The-Associated-Press.

82. M. Petersen, "Doctors Caught in the Middle; Ad Campaign Has Parents Asking for a Costly Drug," *New York Times*, 31 January 2001, http://www.nytimes.com /2001/01/31/business/doctors-caught-in-the-middle-ad-campaign-has-parents -asking-for-a-costly-drug.html.

83. D. Gellene, "Approval Delayed on Inhaled Vaccine," *L.A. Times*, 12 July 2002, http://articles.latimes.com/2002/jul/12/business/fi-flumist12.

84. MedImmune, "FDA Approves Needle-Free FluMist: First Flu Vaccine Delivery Innovation in over 50 Years," *Drugs.com*, 2004, http://www.drugs.com/news/fda -approves-needle-free-flumist-first-flu-vaccine-delivery-innovation-over-50-years -3314.html.

85. W. Patalon, "FluMist's Maker Warns of Shortfall," *Baltimore Sun*, 2 March 2004, http://articles.baltimoresun.com/2004-03-02/business/0403020163_1_medi mmune-flu-vaccine-cents.

86. W. Patalon, "Flu Vaccine Shortage Could Give Needed Boost to MedImmune," *Baltimore Sun*, 6 December 2003, http://articles.baltimoresun.com/2003-12-06/news /0312060077_1_flumist-medimmune-flu-vaccines.

87. A. Pollack, "Anatomy of a Failed Product Introduction: How a Nasal Spray Flu Vaccine Flopped in the Marketplace," *New York Times*, 19 November 2003, www .nytimes.com/2003/11/19/business/media-business-advertising-anatomy-failed -product-introduction-nasal-spray-flu.html.

88. J. Herbst, "Wal-Mart Nixes FluMist Sales Amid State Scrutiny," *Business Journals*, 13 October 2003, www.bizjournals.com/washington/stories/2003/10/13/daily35 .html.

89. A. Wlazelek, "Nasal Spray Flu Vaccine Comes with Risk," *Morning Call*, 21 October 2003, http://articles.mcall.com/2003-10-21/news/3510374_1_nasal-spray-flu-vaccine-flumist-medimmune-vaccines.

90. Patalon, "Flu Vaccine Shortage."

91. Herbst, "Wal-Mart Nixes FluMist."

92. Patalon, "Flu Vaccine Shortage."

93. Pollack, "Anatomy of a Failed Product Introduction."

94. Patalon, "Flu Vaccine Shortage."

95. Pollack, "Anatomy of a Failed Product Introduction."

96. M. S. Rosenwald, "FluMist Sales Falling Short, Survey Finds," *Washington Post*, 2005, http://www.washingtonpost.com/wp-dyn/articles/A51955-2005Jan5.html.

97. S. Berberich, "Food and Drug Administration Panel OKs FluMist for Children under 5," *Gazette.Net*, 18 May 2007, http://ww2.gazette.net/stories/051807/businew204125_32336.shtml.

98. J. Bell, "MedImmune Stock Droops at Deal News," *Baltimore Sun*, 4 December 2001, http://articles.baltimoresun.com/2001-12-04/business/0112040012_1_medimmune-vaccine-generat.

99. M. Robins, "Back to the Lab," *Forbes*, 5 February 2001, http://www.forbes.com/global/2001/0205/081.html.

100. M. S. Rosenwald, "Icahn Pressured MedImmune Board to Sell," *Washington Post*, 16 April 2007, www.washingtonpost.com/wp-dyn/content/article/2007/04/16/AR2007041601608.html.

101. A. Pollack, "AstraZeneca Buys MedImmune for $15.6 Billion," *New York Times*, 24 April 2007, http://www.nytimes.com/2007/04/24/business/24drug-web.html?_r=1&.

102. T Stynes, "Quest Diagnostics to Acquire Celera," *Wall Street Journal*, 17 May 2011, http://www.wsj.com/articles/SB10001424052748704608504576208231120012522.

Chapter Ten

1. C. de Duve and R Wattiaux, "Functions of Lysosomes," *Annual Review of Physiology* 28 (1) (1966): 435–92.

2. A. L. Cowan, "Lilly Selling Its Cosmetics Unit," *New York Times*, 3 April 1987, http://www.nytimes.com/1987/04/03/business/lilly-selling-its-cosmetic-unit.html; FundingUniverse, "Eli Lilly and Company History," *FundingUniverse*, 15 June 2002, http://www.fundinguniverse.com/company-histories/eli-lilly-and-company-history.

3. A. D. Chandler, *Shaping the Industrial Century: The Remarkable Story of the Evolution of the Modern Chemical and Pharmaceutical Industries* (Cambridge, Mass.: Harvard University Press, 2009).

4. B. Ross and J. Rood, "Senior Official Linked to Escort Service Resigns," *ABC News*, 2 May 2007, http://blogs.abcnews.com/theblotter/2007/04/senior_official.html.

5. D. T. Karamitsos, "The Story of Insulin Discovery," *Diabetes Research and Clinical Practice* 93 (2011): S2–S8; I. S. Johnson, "Human Insulin from Recombinant DNA Technology," *Science* 219 (4585) (1983): 632–37.

6. FundingUniverse, "Eli Lilly and Company History."

7. K. Ervin, "Deep Pockets + Intense Research + Total Control = The Formula: Bothell Biotech ICOS Keeps the Pipeline Full of Promise," *Seattle Times*, 12 June 1998, http://community.seattletimes.nwsource.com/archive/?date=19980621&slug =2757327.

8. D. J. Webb, G. J. Muirhead, M. Wulff, J. A. Sutton, R. Levi, and W. W. Dinsmore, "Sildenafil Citrate Potentiates the Hypotensive Effects of Nitric Oxide Donor Drugs in Male Patients with Stable Angina," *Journal of the American College of Cardiology* 36 (1) (2000): 25–31.

9. M. Boolell, M. J. Allen, S. A. Ballard, S. Gepi-Attee, G. J. Muirhead, A. M. Naylor, I. H. Osterloh, and C. Gingell, "Sildenafil: An Orally Active Type 5 Cyclic GMP-Specific Phosphodiesterase Inhibitor for the Treatment of Penile Erectile Dysfunction," *International Journal of Impotence Research* 8 (2) (1996): 47–52.

10. S. A. Ballard, C. J. Gingell, K. Tang, L. A. Turner, M. E. Price, and A. M. Naylor, "Effects of Sildenafil on the Relaxation of Human Corpus Cavernosum Tissue in Vitro and on the Activities of Cyclic Nucleotide Phosphodiesterase Isozymes," *Journal of Urology* 159 (6) (1998): 2164–71.

11. J. Wilson, "Viagra: The Little Blue Pill that Could," *CNN*, 27 March 2013, http:// www.cnn.com/2013/03/27/health/viagra-anniversary-timeline/index.html.

12. D. P. Rotella, "Tadalafil Lilly ICOS," *Current Opinion in Investigational Drugs* 4 (1) (2003): 60–65.

13. K. Neumeyer and P. Kirkpatrick, "Tadalafil and Vardenafil," *Nature Reviews Drug Discovery* 3 (4) (2004): 295–96.

14. Strategic Transactions, "Glaxo, ICOS Develop Anti-Inflammatory, CV Drugs; Ended," *Pharma Intelligence*, 1997, https://www.pharmamedtechbi.com/deals/1991 20395.

15. *MarketWatch.com*, "Eli Lilly, ICOS Team Up for Impotency Drug 10-1-98," *MarketWatch*, 1 October 1998, http://www.marketwatch.com/story/eli-lilly-icos-team -up-for-impotency-drug-10-1-98.

16. K. K. Gaines, "Tadalafil (Cialis®) and Vard Enafil (Levitra®) Recently Approved Drugs for Erectile Dysfunction," *Urologic Nursing* 24 (1) (2004).

17. Associated Press, "Eli Lilly to Acquire ICOS for $2.1 Billion," *NBC News*, 2006, http://www.nbcnews.com/id/15300673/ns/business-us_business/t/eli-lilly -acquire-icos-billion/-.VOXmmlPF96g.

18. A. Pollack, "Eli Lilly Agrees to Buy ImClone Systems for $6.5 Billion," *New York Times*, 7 October 2008, http://www.nytimes.com/2008/10/07/business/07imclone .html?_r=0.

19. G. Anand, "Four Prestigious Labs Ousted Waksal for Questionable Work," *Wall Street Journal*, 2002, http://www.wsj.com/articles/SB1033076483640238993.

20. R. Kolker, "Sam Waksal Was Right All Along," *New York Magazine*, 15 March 2009, http://nymag.com/search/search.cgi?fd=All&Ns=Relevance%7C0&search_type=sw &N=0&textquery=waksal.

21. Anand, "Four Prestigious Labs."

22. Ibid.

23. Ibid.

24. A. Pollack, "For ImClone Drug Entrepreneur, a Past of Celebrity and Notoriety," *New York Times*, 24 January 2002, http://www.nytimes.com/2002/01/24 /business/for-imclone-drug-entrepreneur-a-past-of-celebrity-and-notoriety.html ?pagewanted=1.

25. Ibid.; Anand, "Four Prestigious Labs"; Kolker, "Sam Waksal Was Right."

26. M. Herper, "Bristol Pays Pretty Penny for ImClone Drug," *Forbes*, 19 September 2001, www.forbes.com/2001/09/19/0919bristol.html.

27. L. Thomas and B. L. Keil, "Who Knew?," *New York Magazine*, 8 July 2002, http://nymag.com/news/articles/02/marthastewart; G. Anand, J. Markon, and C. Adams, "Ex-ImClone CEO Waksal Faces Securities Charges," *Wall Street Journal*, 13 June 2002, http://www.wsj.com/articles/SB1023886203386917600.

28. Thomas and Keil, "Who Knew?"; Anand, Markon, and Adams, "Ex-ImClone CEO."

29. C. Adams, "House Panel Turns Up the Heat on Waksal in ImClone Probe," *Wall Street Journal*, 20 August 2002, http://www.wsj.com/articles/SB1029800017815080795.

30. Anand, Markon, and Adams, "Ex-ImClone CEO."

31. Kolker, "Sam Waksal Was Right."

32. FDA, "FDA Approves Erbitux for Colorectal Cancer," *U.S. Food and Drug Administration*, 12 February 2004, http://www.fda.gov/NewsEvents/Newsroom/Press Announcements/2004/ucm108244.htm.

33. A. Pollack, "Harlan Waksal Resigns From ImClone Posts," *New York Times*, 22 July 2003, www.nytimes.com/2003/07/22/business/harlan-waksal-resigns-from -imclone-posts.html.

34. Pollack, "Eli Lilly Agrees."

35. M. S. Kinch, A. Haynesworth, S. L. Kinch, and D. Hoyer, "An Overview of FDA-Approved New Molecular Entities: 1827–2013," *Drug Discovery Today* 19 (8) (2014): 1033–39.

36. Pfizer, "Pfizer Inc: Exploring Our History: 1849–1899," *Pfizer*, http://www .pfizer.com/about/history/1849–1899, accessed on 1 April 2016.

37. Kinch et al., "An Overview of FDA-Approved New Molecular Entities."

38. Bristol-Myers Squibb, "History," *Bristol-Myers Squibb*, http://www.bms.com /ourcompany/Pages/history.aspx, accessed on 1 April 2016.

39. FundingUniverse, "Bristol-Myers Squibb Company History," *FundingUniverse*, 16 June 2001, http://www.fundinguniverse.com/company-histories/bristol-myers -squibb-company-history.

40. Kinch et al., "An Overview of FDA-Approved New Molecular Entities."

41. G. E. Ullyot, B. H. Ullyot, and L. B. Slater, "The Metamorphosis of Smith-Kline & French Laboratories to Smith Kline Beecham: 1925–1998," *Bulletin for the History of Chemistry* 25 (1) (2000): 16.

42. A. Hammer, "Smithline, Beckman Plan Merger," *New York Times*, 26 November 1981, www.nytimes.com/1981/11/26/business/smithkline-beckman-plan-merger .html.

43. M. S. Lesney, "The Ghosts of Pharma Past," *ACS Publications*, January 2004, http://pubs.acs.org/subscribe/archive/mdd/v07/i01/pdf/104timeline.pdf.

44. Novartis, "Company History," *Novartis*, 2015, http://www.novartis.com/about -novartis/company-history.

45. L'Oreal, "L'Oreal: Sanofi and Synthelabo to Merge," *L'Oreal*, 3 December 1998, http://www.loreal.com/press-releases/loreal-sanofi-and-synthelabo-to-merge-elf -aquitaine-and-loreal-to-hold-35-1-and-19-4-shareholdings-respectively-in-the-new -group.aspx?mediatype=cp.

46. Reuters, "FTC OKs Hoechst, Rhone-Poulenc Merger," *L.A. Times*, 8 December 1999, http://articles.latimes.com/1999/dec/08/business/fi-41792.

47. Federal Trade Commission, "Hoechst AG and Rhone-Poulenc S.A., to Be Re-named Aventis S.A," *Federal Trade Commission*, 19 April 2005, http://www.ftc.gov /enforcement/cases-proceedings/9910071/hoechst-ag-rhone-poulenc-sa-be -renamed-aventis-sa.

48. P. Bailey, "The Birth and Growth of Burroughs Wellcome & Co.," *Wellcome Trust*, 4 November 2008, http://www.wellcome.ac.uk/About-us/History/WTX0 51562.htm; Chemical Heritage Foundation, "George Hitchings and Gertrude Elion," *Chemical Heritage Foundation*, http://www.chemheritage.org/discover /online-resources/chemistry-in-history/themes/pharmaceuticals/restoring-and -regulating-the-bodys-biochemistry/hitchings—elion.aspx, accessed on 1 April 2016.

49. Pfizer, "Company History," *Pfizer*, http://www.pfizer.com/about/history/all, accessed on 1 April 2016.

50. Kinch et al., "An Overview of FDA-Approved New Molecular Entities."

51. R. Langreth, "Warner-Lambert Agrees to Deal with Pfizer Worth $90 Billion," *Wall Street Journal*, 2000, http://www.wsj.com/articles/SB949880425106587767.

52. Pfizer, "2000: Pfizer Joins Forces with Warner-Lambert," *Pfizer*, http://www .pfizer.com/about/history/pfizer_warner_lambert, accessed on 1 April 2016; H. N. Moore, "Pfizer's $166.6 Billion Troubled Merger History," (blog), *Wall Street Journal*, 23 January 2009, http://blogs.wsj.com/deals/2009/01/23/pfizers-1666-billion-troubled -merger-history.

53. Pfizer, "2003: Pfizer and Pharmacia Merger," *Pfizer*, http://www.pfizer.com /about/history/pfizer_pharmacia, accessed on 1 April 2016.

54. Ibid.

55. L. Zamosky, "Lipitor Patent Ends: Generic Available; What Now?," *L.A. Times*, 16 January 2012, http://articles.latimes.com/2012/jan/16/health/la-he-lipitor-generic -20120116.

56. Reuters, "Pfizer to Buy Wyeth for $68 Billion," *Reuters*, 26 January 2009, http://www.reuters.com/article/2009/01/26/us-wyeth-pfizer-idUSTRE50M1AQ20090126.

57. R. Lenzner and M. Maiello, "The $22 Billion Gold Rush," *Forbes*, 10 April 2006, www.forbes.com/forbes/2006/0410/086.html.

58. J. Carroll, "Pfizer, J&J Alzheimer's Drug Bapineuzumab Flunks Out in Big PhIII," *FierceBiotech*, 23 July 2012, http://www.fiercebiotech.com/story/jj-pfizer-report-ominous-phiii-failure-bapineuzumab-alzheimers-study/2012-07-23; K. Fiore, "Pfizer's Remoxy Fails to Win FDA Approval," *MedPage Today*, 2014, http://www.medpagetoday.com/PainManagement/PainManagement/27252.

59. NBC News, "Roche to Take Over Genentech for $47 Billion," *NBC News*, 12 March 2009, http://www.nbcnews.com/id/29650518/ns/business-world_business/t/roche-take-over-genentech-billion/-.VOYxB1PF96g.

60. S. S. Hughes, *Genentech: The Beginnings of Biotech* (Chicago: University of Chicago Press, 2011).

61. J. Rockoff, "Merck to Buy Rival for $41 Billion," *Wall Street Journal*, 10 March 2009, http://www.wsj.com/articles/SB123659326420569463.

62. P. Loftus, "Merck Agrees to Buy Idenix for $3.85 Billion," *Wall Street Journal*, 2014, http://www.wsj.com/articles/merck-to-buy-idenix-for-3-85-billion-1402314298; V. L. Nathan and B. Hirschler, "Merck to Take On Superbugs with Cubist Pharma Buy," *Reuters*, 9 December 2014, http://www.reuters.com/article/2014/12/09/us-cubist-pharma-m-a-merck-idUSKBN0JM19X20141209.

63. In the time since the final version of the book was completed, action by the U.S. Department of Treasury resulted in a scrapping of the intended $160 billion Pfizer-Allergan merger. J. LaMattina, "Allergan's Saunders to Be Pfizer CEO: Say It Isn't So!," *Forbes*, 11 November 2015, http://www.forbes.com/sites/johnlamattina/2015/11/11/allergans-saunders-to-be-pfizer-ceo-say-it-isnt-so.

64. FundingUniverse, "Biovail Corporation History," *FundingUniverse*, 15 June 2002, http://www.fundinguniverse.com/company-histories/biovail-corporation-history.

65. E. L. Kinney, R. M. Moskowitz, and R. Zelis, "The Pharmacokinetics and Pharmacology of Oral Diltiazem in Normal Volunteers," *Journal of Clinical Pharmacology* 21 (8–9) (1981): 337–42.

66. S. Sista, J. C-K. Lai, O. Eradiri, and K. S. Albert, "Pharmacokinetics of a Novel Diltiazem HCl Extended-Release Tablet Formulation for Evening Administration," *Journal of Clinical Pharmacology* 43 (10) (2003): 1149–57.

67. Biovail, "Biovail Reports Tiazac Sales Ahead of Target; Modification of Forest Distribution Practices to Have no Impact on Biovail's Tiazac Revenues," *Free Library*, 4 December 1996, http://www.thefreelibrary.com/Biovail+reports+Tiazac+sales+ahead+of+target%3B+modification+of+Forest . . . -a018908950.

68. V. B. Kennedy, "Biovail Soars on Drug Approval," *MarketWatch*, 9 September 2005, http://www.marketwatch.com/story/biovail-soars-on-drug-approval.

69. Valeant, "Key Facts & History," *Valeant*, http://www.valeant.com/about/key-facts, accessed on 1 April 2016.

70. Ibid.; E. Melnyk, "Melnyk Says He Is Pleased Biovail Shareholders Could Be Re-Thinking Their Support of Management," *PR Newswire*, 25 June 2008, http://www.prnewswire.com/news-releases/melnyk-says-he-is-pleased-biovail-shareholders-could-be-re-thinking-their-support-of-management-57544422.html.

71. M. Huckman, "Biovail's Travails and the 'Haunting' Truck Accident," *CNBC*, 24 March 2008, http://www.cnbc.com/id/23782262; A. Feuerstein, "Weighing Biovail's Claims," *The Street*, 14 January 2004, http://www.thestreet.com/story/10136612/1/weighing-biovails-claims.html.

72. D. Brady, "What's Really Banging Up Biovail?," *Bloomberg*, 8 October 2003, http://www.bloomberg.com/bw/stories/2003-10-08/whats-really-banging-up-biovail.

73. D. Paddon, "Melnyk Acted Contrary to Public Interest: OSC," *The Star*, 1 October 2010, http://www.thestar.com/business/2010/10/01/melnyk_acted_contrary_to_public_interest_osc.html; B. Shecter, "Melnyk Banned from the Boardroom for 5 Years," *National Post*, 5 May 2011, http://www.nationalpost.com/related/topics/Melnyk+banned+from+boardroom+years/4734185/story.html.

74. D. Schorn, "Betting on a Fall," *CBS News*, 24 March 2006, http://www.cbsnews.com/news/betting-on-a-fall.

75. I. Austen, "US and Canada Accuse Drug Maker of Fraud," *New York Times*, 25 March 2008, http://www.nytimes.com/2008/03/25/business/25biovail.html?_r=0&gwh=937DFDCC730F51C17874CFE8E020AD41&gwt=pay; D. Starkman, "*60 Minutes's* Biovail Trainwreck (cont.)," *Columbia Journalism Review*, 22 March 2008, http://www.cjr.org/the_audit/60_minutess_biovail_trainwreck.php.

76. FundingUniverse, "ICN Pharmaceuticals, Inc. History," *FundingUniverse*, 2003, http://www.fundinguniverse.com/company-histories/icn-pharmaceuticals-inc-history; C. J. Williams and J. M. Gomes, "Southland Businessman Picked as Yugoslav Premier: Balkans; Milan Panic, an Emigre and Founder of ICN Pharmaceuticals, is to Announce His Decision Today," *L.A. Times*, 2 July 1992, http://articles.latimes.com/1992-07-02/news/mn-1900_1_milan-panic.

77. G. Crouch, "Can-Do Entrepreneur Will Tackle Balkan War: Belgrade; Southland's Milan Panic May Have Taken on His Toughest Task in Agreeing to be Yugoslav Premier," *L.A. Times*, 3 July 1992, http://articles.latimes.com/1992-07-03/news/mn-1518_1_milan-panic.

78. R. D. White, "ICN Chief Milan Panic Resigns," *L.A. Times*, 13 June 2002, http://articles.latimes.com/2002/jun/13/business/fi-icn13.

79. *Businessweek*, "No Peace for Milan Panic," *Bloomberg*, 5 July 1992, www.bloomberg.com/bw/stories/1992-07-05/no-peace-for-milan-panic.

80. M. Jorg, P. J. Scammells, and B. Capuano, "The Dopamine D2 and Adenosine A2A Receptors: Past, Present and Future Trends for the Treatment of Parkinson's Disease," *Current Medicinal Chemistry* 21 (27) (2014): 3188–210.

81. O. Sacks, *Awakenings* (London: Picador, 1991).

82. H. D. Foster and A. Hoffer, "The Two Faces of L-DOPA: Benefits and Adverse Side Effects in the Treatment of Encephalitis Lethargica, Parkinson's Disease, Multiple Sclerosis, and Amyotrophic Lateral Sclerosis," *Medical Hypotheses* 62 (2) (2004): 177–81.

83. Sacks, *Awakenings*.

84. *Businessweek*, "No Peace for Milan Panic."

85. White, "ICN Chief Milan Panic Resigns."

86. Williams and Gomes, "Southland Businessman Picked as Yugoslav Premier."

87. White, "ICN Chief Milan Panic Resigns."

88. J. Reed and J. R. Emshwiller, "ICN's Yugoslav Subsidiary Is Seized by Serbian Police," *Wall Street Journal*, 8 February 1999, http://www.wsj.com/articles/SB9184 20679679118500.

89. G. Johnson and A. Cekola, "ICN Chief Accused of Harassment: Lawsuit: Ex-Employee Says Milan Panic Demanded Sexual Favors, Fathered Her Son. Company Spokesman Denies the Allegations," *L.A. Times*, 1 February 1995, http://articles.latimes .com/1995-02-01/local/me-26741_1_milan-panic.

90. G. Hernandez, "ICN Settles Panic Harassment Suits," *L.A. Times*, 28 October 1998, http://articles.latimes.com/1998/oct/28/news/mn-36897.

91. White, "ICN Chief Milan Panic Resigns."

92. Valeant, "Key Facts & History."

93. Kinch et al., "An Overview of FDA-Approved New Molecular Entities."

94. P. Jordan and E. Dey, "Drugmaker Biovail to Buy Valeant in $3.3 Billion Deal," *Reuters*, 21 June 2010, http://www.reuters.com/article/2010/06/21/us-biovail-valeant -idUSTRE65K1LA20100621.

95. Valeant, "*Key* Facts & History."

96. Kinch et al., "An Overview of FDA-Approved New Molecular Entities."

97. Ibid.

98. Ibid.; M. S. Kinch, "The Rise (and Decline?) of Technology," *Drug Discovery Today* 19 (11) (2014): 1686–90; M. S. Kinch, "Post-Approval Fate of Pharmaceutical Companies," *Drug Discovery Today* 20 (2) (2015): 170–74.

99. Kinch, "The Rise (and Decline?) of Biotechnology."

100. Ibid.

101. Ibid.

102. Ibid.

103. T. Staton, "AstraZeneca Steps Up Its Global Restructuring with 550 New Job Cuts," *FiercePharma*, 6 February 2014, http://www.fiercepharma.com/story/astrazeneca -steps-its-global-restructuring-550-new-job-cuts/2014-02-06.

104. P. Loftus, M. Falconi, and H. Plumridge, "In Drug Mergers, There's One Sure Bet: The Layoffs," *Wall Street Journal*, 29 April 2014, http://www.wsj.com/articles/S B10001424052702304393704579532141039817448.

Chapter Eleven

1. M. S. Kinch, A. Haynesworth, S. L. Kinch, and D. Hoyer, "An Overview of FDA-Approved New Molecular Entities: 1827–2013," *Drug Discovery Today* 19 (80) (2014): 1033–39.

2. Centers for Disease Control and Prevention, "Ten Great Public Health Achievements: United States, 1900–1999," *Morbidity and Mortality Weekly Report* 48 (12) (1999): 241.

3. "Achievements in Public Health, 1900–1999: Control of Infectious Diseases," *Centers for Disease Control and Prevention*, 30 July 1999, http://www.cdc.gov/mmwr /preview/mmwrhtml/mm4829a1.htm.

4. "Achievements in Public Health, 1900–1999: Decline in Deaths from Heart Disease and Stroke; United States, 1900–1999," *Centers for Disease Control and Prevention*, 6 August 1999, http://www.cdc.gov/mmwr/preview/mmwrhtml/mm4830a1.htm.

5. Ibid.

6. Centers for Disease Control and Prevention, "Ten Great Public Health Achievements."

7. J. W. Scannell, A. Blanckley, H. Boldon, and B. Warrington, "Diagnosing the Decline in Pharmaceutical R&D Efficiency," *National Reviews Drug Discovery* 11 (3) (2012): 191–200.

8. Tufts Center for the Study of Drug Discovery, "Cost to Develop and Win Marketing Approval for a New Drug Is $2.6 Billion," *Tufts Center for the Study of Drug Development*, 18 November 2014, http://csdd.tufts.edu/news/complete_story/pr _tufts_csdd_2014_cost_study.

9. Scannell et al., "Diagnosing the Decline."

10. G. E. Moore, "Cramming More Components onto Integrated Circuits, 1965," *Electronics Magazine*, 4 (1965): 82–85.

11. Scannell et al., "Diagnosing the Decline."

12. Ibid.

13. T. E. Bonsall, *Disaster in Dearborn: The Story of the Edsel* (Palo Alto, Calif.: Stanford University Press, 2002).

14. M. S. Kinch, J. Merkel, and S. Umlauf, "Trends in Pharmaceutical Targeting of Clinical Indications: 1930–2013," *Drug Discovery Today* 19 (11) (2014): 1682–85.

15. A. J. Alanis, "Resistance to Antibiotics: Are We in the Post-Antibiotic Era?," *Archives of Medical Research* 36 (6) (2005): 697–705.

16. R. Fox, "The Post-Antibiotic Era Beckons," *Journal of the Royal Society of Medicine* 89 (11) (1996): 602.

17. Alzheimer's Association, "Alzheimer's Disease Growth: U.S. Will See Average 44 Percent Increase in Alzheimer's Disease by 2025," *Alzheimer's Association*, 7 June 2004, http://www.alz.org/alzwa/documents/alzwa_resource_ad_fs_ad_state_growth _stats.pdf.

18. J. LaMattina, "Will Pharma Companies Get Out of Alzheimer's Disease R&D?," *Forbes*, 29 August 2012, http://www.forbes.com/sites/johnlamattina/2012/08/29 /will-pharma-companies-get-out-of-alzheimers-disease-rd; "Drug Companies 'Giving Up' on Alzheimer's Treatment after Series of Expensive Failed Trials," *DailyMail .com*, 18 September 2012, http://www.dailymail.co.uk/news/article-2205339/Leading -pharmaceutical-firms-giving-Alzheimers-treatment-series-expensive-failed-trials .html.

19. M. S. Kinch and E. Patridge, "An Analysis of FDA-Approved Drugs for Psychiatric Disorders," *Drug Discovery Today* 20 (3) (2014): 292–95; M. S. Kinch, "An Analysis of FDA-Approved Drugs for Neurological Disorders," *Drug Discovery Today* 20 (9) (2015): 1040–43; M. S. Kinch, "An Analysis of FDA-Approved Drugs for Pain and Anesthesia," *Drug Discovery Today* 20 (1) (2015): 3–6.

20. R. Naqvi, D. Liberman, J. Rosenberg, J. Alston, and S. Straus, "Preventing Cognitive Decline in Healthy Older Adults," *Canadian Medical Association Journal* 185 (10) (2013): 881–85.

21. M. Ringel, P. Tollman, G. Hersch, and U. Schulze, "Does Size Matter in R&D Productivity? If Not, What Does?," *National Reviews Drug Discovery* 12 (12) (2013): 901–2.

22. J. L. Cummings, T. Morstorf, and K. Zhong, "Alzheimer's Disease Drug-Development Pipeline: Few Candidates, Frequent Failures," *Alzheimer's Research & Therapy* 6 (4) (2014): 37–44.

23. *Reuters*, "Roche Shares Tumble after Alzheimer's Drug Failure," *Reuters*, 19 December 2014, http://fortune.com/2014/12/19/roche-shares-tumble-after-alzheimers-drug-failure.

24. G. Giovannetti, "Insights from 30 Years of Biotech IPOs," *Life Science* (blog), 10 January 2014, http://lifesciencesblog.ey.com/2014/01/10/insights-from-30-years-of-biotech-ipos.

25. B. Booth, "Early Stage Biotech Venture Scarcity: Fitness, Fear, And Greed," *Forbes*, 22 September 2014, http://www.forbes.com/sites/brucebooth/2014/09/22/early-stage-biotech-venture-scarcity-fitness-fear-and-greed.

26. B. Booth, "Venture-Backed Biotech Today: Reflections on Exits, Funding, and Startup Formation," *Forbes*, 22 January 2015, http://www.forbes.com/sites/brucebooth/2015/01/22/venture-backed-biotech-today-reflections-on-exits-funding-and-startup-formation.

27. R. Alexander, "Which Is the World's Biggest Employer?," *BBC*, 20 March 2012, http://www.bbc.com/news/magazine-17429786; *Economist*, "Defending Jobs," *Economist*, 12 September 2011, http://www.economist.com/blogs/dailychart/2011/09/employment.

28. J. J. Dilulio, "Want Better, Smaller Government? Hire Another Million Federal Bureaucrats," *Washington Post*, 29 August 2014, www.washingtonpost.com/opinions/want-better-smaller-governmenthire-1-million-more-federal-bureaucrats/2014/08/29/c0bc1480-2c72-11e4-994d-202962a9150c_story.html.

29. S. Heffler, S. Smith, S. Keehan, M. K. Clemens, M. Zezza, and C. Truffer, "Health Spending Projections through 2013," *Health Care* 24 (2004): 4.79–4.80.

30. J. Cubanski, J. Huang, A. Damico, C. Jacobson, and T. Neuman, *Medicare Chartbook* (Menlo Park, Calif.: Henry J. Kaiser Family Foundation, 2005).

31. A. N. Hofer, J. Abraham, and I. Moscovice, "Expansion of Coverage under the Patient Protection and Affordable Care Act and Primary Care Utilization," *Milbank Quarterly* 89 (1) (2011): 69–89.

32. P. Neuman and J. Cubanski, "Medicare Part D Update: Lessons Learned and Unfinished Business," *New England Journal of Medicine* 361 (4) (2009): 406–14.

33. Ibid.

34. R. M. Walmsley and N. Billinton, "How Accurate Is In Vitro Prediction of Carcinogenicity?," *British Journal of Pharmacology* 162 (6) (2011): 1250–58.

35. InVivo, "The REMS Pioneers: Amgen's Nplate Sets Another New Standard," (blog), *InVivo Blog*, 2008, http://invivoblog.blogspot.com/2008/09/rems-pioneers -amgens-nplate-sets.html.

36. M. Mazzucato, *The Entrepreneurial State* (London: Anthem Press, 2013).

37. Ibid.

38. FASEB, "Sustaining Discovery in Biological and Medical Sciences," *Federation of American Societies for Experimental Biology*, 2015, http://www.faseb.org/Sustaining Discovery/Home.aspx.

39. Ibid.

40. K. Boadi, "Erosion of Funding for the National Institutes of Health Threatens U.S. Leadership in Biomedical Research," *Center for American Progress*, 25 March 2014, http://www.americanprogress.org/issues/economy/report/2014/03 /25/86369/erosion-of-funding-for-the-national-institutes-of-health-threatens-u-s -leadership-in-biomedical-research.

41. Associated Press, "Japan is Racing to Catch Up, Pass the U.S. in Field of Biotechnology," *L.A. Times*, 30 April 1985, http://articles.latimes.com/1985-04-30 /business/fi-20052_1_biotechnology.

42. R. Pear, "Government Ready to Boost Spending for Biomedicine," *New York Times*, 1998, http://partners.nytimes.com/library/politics/010398clinton-budget.html.

43. J. A. Johnson, "Brief History of NIH Funding: Fact Sheet," *Federation of American Scientists*, 23 December 2013, https://www.fas.org/sgp/crs/misc/R43341 .pdf.

44. *Nature*, "Postdoc Pay Rise," *Nature*, 24 April 2013, www.nature.com/naturejobs /science/articles/10.1038/nj7446-539b.

45. J. Van Rheenen and R. B. Freeman, "Perspectives: Be Careful What You Wish For: A Cautionary Tale about Budget Doubling," *Issues in Science and Technology*, 22 September 2008, http://issues.org/25-1/p_freeman; J. Mervis "Dog Bites Man? Researchers Say U.S. Government Should Fund More Science," *Science*, 30 August 2013, http://news.sciencemag.org/funding/2013/08/dog-bites-man-researchers-say -u.s.-government-should-fund-more-science.

46. J. M. Gitlin, "Calculating the Economic Impact of the Human Genome Project," *Human Genome Research Institute*, 12 June 2013, http://www.genome.gov /27544383; C. Y. Johnson, "Did the Human Genome Project Really Have a Trillion Dollar Impact?," *Boston.com*, 12 June 2013, http://www.boston.com/news/science /blogs/science-in-mind/2013/06/12/did-the-human-genome-project-really-have -trillion-dollar-impact/1GaxMUkAc25pxj9oXIORiL/blog.html.

47. A. Chatterjee and R. DeVol, "Estimating Long-Term Economic Returns of NIH Funding on Output in the Biosciences," *Milken Institute*, 31 August 2012, http:// www.milkeninstitute.org/publications/view/535.

48. National Science Foundation, "Research Space at Academic Institutions Increased 3.5 percent Between FY 2009 and FY 2011: Biomedical Fields Account for Most Growth," *National Science Foundation*, 3 January 2013, http://www.nsf.gov/statistics/infbrief/nsf13310.

49. The Scripps Research Institute, "Timeline," *Scripps Research Institute*, 20 March 2015, http://www.scripps.edu/about/history/index.html.

50. The Scripps Research Institute, "Florida Campus," *Scripps Research Institute*, 19 November 2015, http://www.scripps.edu/florida/about.

51. E. C. Hayden, "Scripps Merger Fiasco Highlights US Funding Woes," *Nature* 511 (2014): 274–75.

52. U. Lia, A. Tiv, S. Or, and I. K. Ime, "Scripps and USC Consider Union, for Money and Prestige," *Science*, 344 (2014): 1435–36.

53. Hayden, "Scripps Merger Fiasco Highlights US Funding Woes."

54. H. Thorp and B. Goldstein, *Engines of Innovation: The Entrepreneurial University in the Twenty-First Century* (Chapel Hill: University of North Carolina Press, 2013).

55. FASEB, "Sustaining Discovery."

56. Ibid.

57. National Institutes of Health, "Funding, Award, and Success Rates* for R01-Equivalents," *National Institutes of Health*, 5 March 2014, http://nexus.od.nih.gov/all/2014/03/05/comparing-success-award-funding-rates/fundingawardsuccess-rates_ro1e.

58. FASEB, "Sustaining Discovery."

59. Ibid.; J. Kaiser, "NIH Report Warns of Looming Shortage of Physician-Scientists," *Science*, 10 June 2014, http://news.sciencemag.org/biology/2014/06/nih-report-warns-looming-shortage-physician-scientists.

60. A. McCarthy, "The NIH Molecular Libraries Program: Identifying Chemical Probes for New Medicines," *Chemistry & Biology* 17 (6) (2010): 549–50; C. P. Austin, S. Brady, T. R. Insel, and F. S. Collins, "NIH Molecular Libraries Initiative," *Science* 306 (5699) (2004): 1138–39.

61. Austin et al., "NIH Molecular Libraries Initiative."

62. A. McCarthy, "New NIH Center to Streamline Translational Science," *Chemistry & Biology* 19 (2) (2012): 165–66.

63. M. Wadman, "NIH Director Grilled over Translational Research Centre," *Nature*, 20 March 2012, http://blogs.nature.com/news/2012/03/nih-director-grilled-over-translational-research-center.html.

Chapter Twelve

1. Aristotle, *Physike Akroasis* (Oxford, UK: Clarendon, 1936).

2. H. Thorp and B. Goldstein, *Engines of Innovation: The Entrepreneurial University in the Twenty-First Century* (Chapel Hill: University of North Carolina Press, 2013).

3. M. Wortman, "The Long War," *Yale Medicine*, 41 (1) (Autumn 2006), http://yalemedicine.yale.edu/autumn2006/features/feature/51987.

4. S. Shukla, R. W. Robey, S. E. Bates, and S. V. Ambudkar, "Sunitinib (Sutent, SU11248), a Small-Molecule Receptor Tyrosine Kinase Inhibitor, Blocks Function of the ATP-Binding Cassette (ABC) Transporters P-glycoprotein (ABCB1) and ABCG2," *Drug Metabolism and Disposition* 37 (2) (2009): 359–65.

5. G. Bollag, J. Tsai, J. Zhang, C. Zhang, P. Ibrahim, K. Nolop, and P. Hirth, "Vemurafenib: The First Drug Approved for BRAF-Mutant Cancer," *Nature Reviews Drug Discovery* 11 (11) (2012): 873–86.

6. K. Matsuyama, "Daiichi Sankyo to Buy Plexxikon for Up To $935 Million," *Bloomberg*, 28 February 2011, www.bloomberg.com/news/articles/2011-02-28/daiichi -sankyo-agrees-to-buy-plexxikon-935-million-adding-cancer-drugs.

7. J. Carroll, "Cancer R&D Stars Pitch an $86M Biotech IPO for Kolltan Pharma," *FierceBiotech*, 15 September 2014, http://www.fiercebiotech.com/story/cancer-rd -stars-pitch-86m-biotech-ipo-kolltan-pharma/2014-09-15.

8. R H. Brown, "Yale Partners with Gilead Sciences in Potential $100M Cancer Deal," *Business Journals*, 30 March 2011, http://www.bizjournals.com/boston/blog /mass-high-tech/2011/03/yale-partners-with-gilead-sciences.html.

9. B. Hathaway, "Yale and Gilead Sciences Extend Cancer Research Collaboration," *Yale News*, 23 October 2014, http://news.yale.edu/2014/10/23/yale-and-gilead -sciences-extend-cancer-research-collaboration.

10. R. Keyes, "Present at the Demise: Antioch College, 1852–2008," *Chronicle of Higher Education* 53 (46) (2007): B8.

11. P. Wolfe, *In the Zone: The Twilight World of Rod Serling* (Madison, Wisc.: Popular Press, 1997); Roger G. Baldwin and V. Baker, "The Case of the Disappearing Liberal Arts College," *Inside Higher Education* (2009): 9.

12. Federation of American Societies for Experimental Biology, "Sustaining Discovery in Biological and Medical Sciences," *American Psychological Association*, 2 January 2015, http://www.the-aps.org/mm/Publications/Journals/Physiologist/Archive/2015 -Issues/March-2015-Vol-58No-2/Science-Policy/FASEB-Releases-Sustaining -Discovery-in-Biological-and-Medical-Science.

13. H. Etzkowitz, A. Webster, C. Gebhardt, and B. R. Cantisano Terra, "The Future of the University and the University of the Future: Evolution of Ivory Tower to Entrepreneurial Paradigm," *Research Policy* 29 (2) (2000): 313–30; Thorp, *Engines of Innovation*.

14. Thorp and Goldstein, *Engines of Innovation*.

15. H. Kissinger, "Transcript of Remarks at the 14th Annual John M. Ashbrook Memorial Dinner," *Ashbrook*, 11 September 1997, http://ashbrook.org/events/kissinger -transcript.

16. National Science Foundation, "Research Space at Academic Institutions Increased 3.5% Between FY 2009 and FY 2011: Biomedical Fields Account for Most Growth," January 2013, *National Science Foundation*, www.nsf.gov/statistics/infbrief/nsf13310.

17. Purdue University, "Trask Innovation Fund," *Purdue Office of Technology Commercialization*, 2014, http://otc-prf.org/trask-innovation-fund, accessed on 1 April 2016.

18. B. S. McKeever and S. L. Pettijohn, "The Nonprofit Sector in Brief 2014: Public Charities, Giving, and Volunteering," *Urban Institute,* October 2014, http://www .urban.org/sites/default/files/alfresco/publication-pdfs/413277-The-Nonprofit-Sec tor-in-Brief—.PDF.

19. J. LaMattina, "Will Pharma Companies Get Out of Alzheimer's Disease R&D?," *Forbes,* 29 August 2012, http://www.forbes.com/sites/johnlamattina/2012/08/29/will -pharma-companies-get-out-of-alzheimers-disease-rd; *DailyMail.com,* "Drug Companies 'Giving Up' on Alzheimer's Treatment after Series of Expensive Failed Trials," 18 September 2012, www.dailymail.co.uk/news/article-2205339/Leading-pharmaceu tical-firms-giving-Alzheimers-treatment-series-expensive-failed-trials.html; J. L. Cummings, T. Morstorf, and K. Zhong, "Alzheimer's Disease Drug-Development Pipeline: Few Candidates, Frequent Failures," *Alzheimer's Research & Therapy* 6 (4) (2014): 37–44.

20. Alzheimer's Association, "Alzheimer's Disease Growth: U.S. Will See Average 44 Percent Increase in Alzheimer's Disease by 2025," *Alzheimer's Association,* 2004, http://www.alz.org/alzwa/documents/alzwa_resource_ad_fs_ad_state_growth _stats.pdf.

21. C. A. Lindbergh, "Charles Lindbergh," *Time* 153 (1999): 74–79.

22. M. Senior, "Foundation Receives 3.3 Billion Windfall for Kalydeco," *Nature Biotechnology* 33 (1) (2015): 8–9.

23. S. Salzberg, "Congress Is Killing Medical Research," *Forbes,* 14 January 2013, www .forbes.com/sites/stevensalzberg/2013/01/14/congress-is-killing-medical-research; National Institutes of Health, "OER and You: An Introduction to Extramural Research at NIH," *National Institutes of Health,* 2014, https://grants.nih.gov/grants/intro2oer .htm; "NIH Budget," 17 February 2016, http://www.nih.gov/about/budget.htm; A. Chatterjee and R. DeVol, *Estimating Long-Term Economic Returns of NIH Funding on Output in the Biosciences* (Santa Monica, Calif.: The Milken Institute, 2012); Research-America, "Medical Research: Saving Lives, Reducing the Cost of Health Care, Powering the Economy," *Research America,* 2014, http://www.researchamerica.org/sites/default /files/uploads/EconomicImpactofResearch.pdf.

24. National Science Foundation, "Research Space at Academic Institutions."

25. K. W. Arenson, "At Yale, a New Campus Just for Research," *New York Times,* 4 July 2007, www.nytimes.com/2007/07/04/education/04yale.html?_r=0.

26. M. Wadman, "NIH Director Grilled over Translational Research Centre," *Nature News* (blog), 20 March 2012, http://blogs.nature.com/news/2012/03/nih-director -grilled-over-translational-research-center.html.

27. M. Mazzucato, *The Entrepreneurial State* (London: Anthem Press, 2013).

28. Wadman, "NIH Director Grilled."

29. D. Armstrong, "Overseas Tax Savings for U.S. Drugmakers Under Threat," *Bloomberg,* 11 March 2013, http://www.bloomberg.com/news/articles/2013-03-11/overseas -tax-savings-for-u-s-drugmakers-under-threat.

30. J. D. Rockoff, "Why Pharma Is Flocking to Inversions," *Wall Street Journal,* 14 July 2014, www.wsj.com/articles/why-pharma-is-flocking-to-inversions-1405360384.

31. Armstrong, "Overseas Tax Savings"; S. Thurm and K. Linebaugh, "More U.S. Profits Parked Abroad, Saving on Taxes," *Wall Street Journal*, 10 March 2013, http://www.wsj.com/articles/SB10001424127887324034804578348131432634740.

32. A. Swanson, "Big Pharmaceutical Companies Are Spending Far More on Marketing than Research," *Washington Post*, 11 February 2015, http://www.washingtonpost.com/blogs/wonkblog/wp/2015/02/11/big-pharmaceutical-companies-are-spending-far-more-on-marketing-than-research.

Index